Victims of Sexual Assault
and Abuse

Victims of Sexual Assault and Abuse

Resources and Responses for Individuals and Families

Volume I

Incidence and Psychological Dimensions

Michele A. Paludi and Florence L. Denmark

Women's Psychology
Michele A. Paludi, Series Editor

PRAEGER

AN IMPRINT OF ABC-CLIO, LLC
Santa Barbara, California • Denver, Colorado • Oxford, England

Library of Congress Cataloging-in-Publication Data

Victims of sexual assault and abuse : resources and responses for individuals and families / [edited by] Michele A. Paludi and Florence L. Denmark.
      p. cm. — (Women's psychology)
   Includes bibliographical references and index.
   ISBN 978–0–313–37970–3 (hbk. : alk. paper) — ISBN 978–0–313–37971–0 (ebook)
1. Sex crimes. 2. Sexual abuse victims—Services for. 3. Rape victims—Services for. I. Paludi, Michele Antoinette. II. Denmark, Florence.
HV6556.V53   2010
362.883—dc22   2010014580

ISBN: 978–0–313–37970–3
EISBN: 978–0–313–37971–0

14 13 12 11 10   1 2 3 4 5

This book is also available on the World Wide Web as an eBook.
Visit www.abc-clio.com for details.

Praeger
An Imprint of ABC-CLIO, LLC

ABC-CLIO, LLC
130 Cremona Drive, P.O. Box 1911
Santa Barbara, California 93116-1911

This book is printed on acid-free paper ∞

Manufactured in the United States of America

We dedicate these volumes to survivors of sexual assault and abuse and their loved ones.

Contents

Acknowledgments

I wish to thank Florence L. Denmark for collaborating with me on this two-volume book set on sexual assault and abuse. Being friends with and working with Florence have been gifts to cherish. She has made me feel like part of her family.

I also wish to acknowledge my sisters, Rosalie Paludi and Lucille Paludi, for their encouragement during the writing and editing of this book set. Carmen Paludi, Jr., deserves my recognition for his sage advice, comforting words, and encouragement of my feminist values and work.

Friends brought me great joy during the writing and editing of this book set: Paula Lundberg Love, Darlene DeFour, Tony Deliberti, and Susan Strauss.

Debbie Carvalko continues to inspire me to be a better writer. I thank her for this opportunity.

I also am grateful for participating in the United States Army's Sexual Harassment/Assault Prevention Summit in April 2009. The goals of this two volume book set reflect the goals of the U.S. Army's *I.A.M. Strong* Campaign identified at this Summit: "intervene, act, and motivate."

—*Michele A. Paludi*

It is always a pleasure to work with Michele A. Paludi, and I thank her for inviting me to co-edit two volumes on sexual assault and abuse. I only regret that there are more than 150 miles keeping us from spending more time together, though we maintain a closeness despite the distance between us. I feel privileged to have Michele as a dear friend as well as a colleague.

I was especially fortunate to have my two graduate assistants, Jessica Brodsky and Shanna German, at Pace University, who provided me with valuable research assistance. They were helpful with tracking down references and doing library research. Their ideas, work habits, and warm and ready sense of humor cannot be overstated. I am grateful for their invaluable contribution to *Early Prevention Programs for Child Sexual Abuse*.

Last, but not least, I thank my husband, Robert Wesner, for his commitment to the importance of this work, and his pride in my accomplishments.

—*Florence L. Denmark*

Introduction

Michele A. Paludi and Florence L. Denmark

> One in three women may suffer from abuse and violence in her lifetime. This is an appalling human rights violation, yet it remains one of the invisible and under-recognized pandemics of our time.
>
> —Nicole Kidman

As we were completing this two-volume book set, we were once again reminded in the national media of the tragedy of sexual victimization throughout the world. Secretary of State Hillary Rodham Clinton visited the Congo during August 2009 to bring attention to what she referred to as "one of mankind's greatest atrocities." Clinton noted that Congolese women endure repeated rapes and physical brutality as well as are forced to watch the slaughter of their newborn infants. She stated, "We believe there should be no impunity for the sexual and gender-based violence committed by so many ... that there must be arrests and prosecutions and punishment." Clinton also noted that "The entire society needs to be speaking out against this. ... It should be a mark of shame that this happens anywhere in any country ... We have to speak out against the impunity of those in positions of authority who either commit these crimes or condone them."

INCIDENCE RATES

The global statistics related to sexual violence are alarming (e.g., Marmion, 2006; Rahman & Toubia, 2000; Sigal & Annan, 2008). The United Nations recorded approximately 200,000 cases of sexual violence against girls and women in the Congo region of Goma since 1996. In addition:

- Four million girls and women are trafficked annually.
- "Honor killings" take the lives of thousands of women each year, especially in North Africa, Western Asia, and parts of South Asia.
- Intimate-partner violence against women accounts for more than 60 percent of all murder cases in Zimbabwe.
- Approximately 90 million African girls and women are victims of genital mutilation.
- One million children, most of whom are girls, are forced into the sex trade annually.

The statistics related to sexual violence in the United States are equally disturbing (e.g., Ahrens, Dean, Rozee, & McKenzie, 2008; Denmark, Krauss, Halpern, & Sechzer, 2006; Gerber & Cherneski, 2006; Lundberg-Love & Marmion, 2006; McHugh, Livingston, & Frieze, 2008; Tan & Gregor, 2006). During the course of editing this two-volume set, the following events happened in the United States:

- One in every 20 women college students was raped, with acquaintance rape accounting for more of the rapes than those committed by strangers.
- Approximately 50 percent of women and 15 percent of men college students and employees experienced sexual harassment, including unwanted sexual attention and sexual coercion.
- Approximately 2.6 million women were victims of intimate-partner violence, including being slapped, having objects thrown at them, being pushed, and being grabbed and shoved by their mate or spouse.
- Twenty-one percent of these women were pregnant at the time of the abuse.
- More than 150,000 children were abducted by strangers or non-custodial parents.
- Thirteen percent of women college students were stalked by current or ex-boyfriends for an average of two months, including being spied on; receiving incessant phone calls, emails, or gifts; being followed; having their mail stolen; and being threatened with death.

- Twenty-one percent of women experienced intrafamilial abuse—for example, fondling, intercourse, oral sex, and noncontact abuse.
- Fifty-five percent of college students involved in clubs, teams, and organizations experienced hazing, including being branded, being made to ingest vile substances, having their skin burned, being paddled, and being coerced into drinking large quantities of alcohol.

IMPACT OF SEXUAL ASSAULT AND ABUSE ON VICTIMS

Several reports have documented the high cost of the various forms of sexual abuse and assault on individuals within three major perspectives: (1) psychological or emotional health, (2) physiological or health related, and (3) education/work related (e.g., Ahrens et al., 2008; McHugh et al., 2008; Munson, Hulin, & Drasgow, 2000; Waits & Lundberg-Love, 2008). For example, the following emotional/psychological symptoms have been identified: depression, anxiety, guilt, fear, decreased self-esteem, withdrawal from social situations, and powerlessness. Physiological outcomes include headaches, sleep disturbances, disordered eating, gastrointestinal disorders, nausea, and crying spells. Victims of rape and sexual harassment often exhibit a "post-abuse" syndrome characterized by shock, emotional numbing, constriction of affect, flashbacks, and other signs of anxiety and depression. Victims of intimate-partner violence may experience bruises, cuts, concussions, black eyes, broken bones, scars from burns, knife wounds, loss of hearing and/or vision, and joint damage. Education/work-related outcomes include changing career goals, absenteeism, decreased morale, decreased job satisfaction, performance decrements, and damage to interpersonal relationships at school or work.

Koss (1988) reported that 30 percent of the women identified as rape victims in her research considered suicide after the rape, 31 percent sought psychotherapy, 22 percent took self-defense courses, and 82 percent said the rape had permanently changed them. In addition, Ward and Lundberg-Love (2006) noted that child sexual abuse is a risk factor for sleep disturbances, alcohol and other drug abuse, self-mutilation, and eating disorders. Finally, Lundberg-Love and Wilkerson (2006) reported that women who are victims of intimate-partner violence fear retaliation from the abusive mate/spouse, have few economic resources available to them to take care of themselves and children, have problem-solving deficits, and often engage in substance abuse.

LABELING SEXUAL ASSAULT AND ABUSE

Despite the prevalence of sexual assault and abuse and the major effects of sexual victimization on victims, many individuals do not label their experiences or the experiences of family members and friends as abuse.

Especially when you are young!

Paludi (2002, 2008) has frequently used the following scenario in her teaching and training programs:

> For the next few minutes jot down the behaviors in which you engage as you leave college/work at night to go to your dorm/house/apartment.

This exercise has generated the following responses from women:

- "Take out my can of mace."
- "Look behind me and across the street as I walk home."
- "Look in the backseat of my car before I get into it."
- "Call my roommate to tell her I'm on my way back to the dorm."
- "Call for a campus escort to help get me home."
- "Be sure the lock on my door hasn't been tampered with."
- "Check under my bed and behind the shower curtain."

Men typically do not generate a list of similar behaviors.

When Paludi asks individuals to attach a label to these behaviors, the following responses are generated from both women and men: "phobias" and "real life." Of course, these behaviors are actually rape-avoidance strategies. When confronted with this label, individuals become silent. For some people, it is difficult to use this term to describe their behavior; they do not like putting themselves in the position of being potential victims.

Some people do not label their negative experiences as sexual assault or abuse because they knew their attacker and/or had consented to sexual intercourse with the same individual previously (Koss, 1988; Paludi, 2008). One woman victim of rape had the following response to her attack:

> I didn't tell anyone. In fact, I wouldn't even admit to it myself until about four months later when the guilt and fear that had been eating at me became too much to hide and I came very close to a complete nervous breakdown. I tried to kill myself, but fortunately I chickened out at the last minute. (Warshaw, 1988, p. 67)

In addition, victims of incest typically do not disclose information about the abuse because of shame, guilt, and fear of not being cared for (Lundberg-Love & Marmion, 2006).

Other individuals accept myths about sexual violence, including rape myths—that is, false beliefs and attitudes that deny as well as justify sexual assault and abuse (Lonsway & Fitzgerald, 1994). Rape myths include the following misconceptions:

- Rape is sex.
- Women often make false reports of rape.
- A man cannot rape his wife.
- Rape occurs only at night and only outside.
- Rape is a crime of passion.
- Women ask for rape by their actions and dress.

Research has found that rape myths are more widely accepted by men than by women (Gerber & Cherneski, 2006). In addition, adherence to rape myths is related to the perpetuation of sexual assault (Lonsway & Fitzgerald, 1994).

Similarly, Paludi (1996) noted that men are significantly more likely than women to agree with the following statements reflecting sexual harassment myths:

- Women often claim sexual harassment to protect their reputations.
- Sexually experienced women are not really damaged by sexual harassment.
- It would do some women good to be sexually harassed.
- Many women claim sexual harassment if they have consented to sexual relations but later changed their minds.
- Women put themselves in situations in which they are likely to be sexually harassed because they have an unconscious wish to be harassed.
- In most cases, when a woman is sexually harassed, she deserved it.

Myths surrounding intimate-partner violence are also common (e.g., Lundberg-Love and Wilkerson, 2006; McHugh et al., 2008), including the following misconceptions:

- Intimate-partner violence is rare.
- Intimate-partner violence occurs only in poor and minority families.
- Drug abuse causes intimate-partner violence.
- Intimate-partner violence is usually a one-time, isolated occurrence.
- Battered women are masochistic; they must like the abuse or else they would leave the relationship.
- Intimate-partner violence is not a crime.

INCIDENCE VERSUS REPORTING

Sexual assault and abuse are underreported crimes (Ahrens et al., 2008). In other words, many individuals refuse to report to law enforcement incidents of sexual assault. Sometimes a sense of shame, guilt, or self-blame about their role in the abuse (stemming from stereotypes about sexuality) prevents victims from pressing charges against their assailants. Those individuals who do report the abuse are often met with degrading questions and humiliating experiences (Ahrens et al., 2008), illustrating the acceptance of sexual assault myths and the just world hypothesis (discussed in the next section).

JUST WORLD HYPOTHESIS

Some individuals deny that sexual assault and abuse ever touch their lives, insisting that victimization happens to other people but never to individuals like themselves. These people believe in the "just world hypothesis" (Sinclair & Bourne, 2006)—namely, that bad things happen only to those people who somehow bring on or deserve the consequences of their acts. Statements such as "That's what you get when you dress that way," "I never walk alone in that part of town at night and that's why I didn't get victimized," and "She was not obeying her husband, so she deserved to be beaten" all illustrate this belief. When they believe in the just world hypothesis, individuals try to find a personal reason for an individual's selection as a victim of sexual assault and abuse. Why? The alternative realization is too frightening to contemplate: "It could happen to me or someone I love."

Many individuals want to shield themselves from the truth that sexual assault and abuse do not distinguish between "good" people and "bad" people. The just world hypothesis is a protective mechanism; it shields us from a range of fears. But it is a myth: we must confront the reality that we are not special, immune from violence, or protected from harm.

GOALS OF THIS BOOK SET

We edited this book set to provide information to assist individuals, campuses, and employers in *intervening* when they recognize a threat of sexual assault and abuse to a friend, family member, employee, or student. For example, Mary Moynihan, Sharyn Potter, Victoria Banyard, Jane Stapleton, and Mary Mayhew discuss strategies to empower a college community of bystanders to intervene in sexual violence. Kevin Nadal, Sahran Hamit, and Marie-Anne Issa provide recommendations for overcoming sexual orientation and gender microaggressions. Liam Marshall provides information on assessment and treatment approaches for sexual offenders.

A second goal of the book set is to encourage individuals to *advocate* for victims of assault and abuse in dealings with rape crisis shelters, hospital emergency rooms, attorneys, human resources department or organizations (e.g., National Center for Missing and Exploited Children, National Resource Center on Domestic Violence, Safety on Campus or the Office on Violence Against Women, U.S. Department of Justice). Several chapters in this two-volume set offer strategies for accomplishing this advocacy. For example, Jennifer Martin offers a prevention guide for students, teachers, and parents with respect to bullying and peer sexual harassment. Florence L. Denmark, Jessica B. Brodsky, and Shanna German provide an overview of early violence prevention programs for children. Amanda Nickerson, Melissa Heath, and Leslie Graves offer recommendations for school-based interventions for children who have been harmed by sexual abuse. Alison Kiss discusses sexual assault prevention on college/university campuses through a review of "Security on Campus," which provides education, statistics, and advocacy tips for college student victims of sexual assault and abuse.

Finally, we have as a goal to *motivate* readers to keep themselves—as well as children and peers—safe and to take action against sexual assault and abuse. For example, Jennifer Piazza and Paula Lundberg-Love provide an overview of the psychological sequelae and treatment of adult survivors of incest. Katie Kelly and Michele Paludi offer recommendations for parents for teaching children about child abductions and missing children. Harmony Sullivan, Tracy Lord, and Maureen McHugh review psychological dimensions of and explanations for street harassment. Margaret Stockdale and Lynda Sagrestano identify resources for victims of sexual harassment in educational and workplace settings. Jacqueline Austin and Margaret Bull Kovera discuss the importance of expert witness testimony in child sex abuse cases. As this preview of these authors' work suggest, these two volumes discuss sexual assault and abuse across the life cycle.

We have also included reviews of empirical research on incest (Jennifer Piazza and Paula Lundberg-Love), bullying (Jennifer Martin; Susan Strauss), sexual harassment of students (Susan Strauss; Eros DeSouza and Brent Showalter), sexual harassment of employees (NiCole Buchanan, Isis Settles, Krystle Woods, and Brian Colar), street harassment (Harmony Sullivan, Tracy Lord, and Maureen McHugh), intimate-partner violence (William Schweinle and Betty Hulse; Emilio Ulloa, Donna Castañeda, and Audrey Hokoda; Maureen McHugh and Catherine Siderski), violence against pregnant women (Josephine Tan), violence in pornographic movies (Chyng Sun, Robert Wosnitzer, Ana Bridges, Erica Scharrer, and Rachael Liberman) and cyberbullying (June Chisholm). The recommendations offered by contributors for meeting the goals of intervention, action, and motivation are based on empirical research summarized by these scholars.

We also address cultural influences on sexual assault and abuse, given that sexual victimization is more common in cultures that are characterized by male dominance and a high degree of violence in general. This two-volume book set brings together scholars, consultants, advocates, and educators from several disciplines, including criminal justice, psychology, nursing, education, and educational leadership. We each have in our own work and interpersonal relationships worked for the goals described by Riane Eisler:

> For most of recorded history, parental violence against children and men's violence against wives was explicitly or implicitly condoned. Those who had the power to prevent and/or punish this violence through religion, law, or custom, openly or tacitly approved it. . . . The reason violence against women and children is finally out in the open is that activists have brought it to global attention.

It is our hope that the chapters in these volumes continue to bring sexual assault and abuse to international attention, and that they encourage our readers as well as the contributors to be advocates for victims whose voices need to be heard.

REFERENCES

Ahrens, C., Dean, K., Rozee, P., & McKenzie, M. (2008). Understanding and preventing rape. In F. L. Denmark & M. Paludi (Eds.), *Psychology of women: A handbook of issues and theories* (pp. 509–554). Westport, CT: Praeger.

Denmark, F. L., Krauss, H., Halpern, E., & Sechzer, J. (Eds.). (2006). *Violence and exploitation against women and girls*. Boston, MA: Blackwell.

Gerber, G., & Cherneski, L. (2006). Sexual aggression toward women: Reducing the prevalence. In F. L. Denmark, H. Kraus, E. Halpern, & J. Sechzer (Eds.), *Violence and exploitation against women and girls* (pp. 35–46). Boston, MA: Blackwell.

Koss, M. P. (1988). Hidden rape: Sexual aggression and victimization in the national sample of students in higher education. In M. A. Pirog-Good & J. E. Stets (Eds.), *Violence in dating relationships: Emerging social issues* (pp. 145–168). New York, NY: Praeger.

Lonsway, K., & Fitzgerald, L. (1994). Rape myths. *Psychology of Women Quarterly, 18*, 133–164.

Lundberg-Love, P., & Marmion, S. (2006). *Intimate violence against women*. Westport, CT: Praeger.

Lundberg-Love, P., & Wilkerson, D. (2006). Battered women. In P. Lundberg-Love & S. Marmion (Eds.), *Intimate violence against women* (pp. 31–45). Westport, CT: Praeger.

Marmion, S. (2006). Global violence against women. In P. Lundberg-Love & S. Marmion (Eds.), *Intimate violence against women* (pp. 145–154). Westport, CT: Praeger.

McHugh, M., Livingston, N., & Frieze, I. (2008). Intimate partner violence: Perspectives on research and intervention. In F. L. Denmark & M. Paludi (Eds.), *Psychology of women: A handbook of issues and theories* (pp. 555–589). Westport, CT: Praeger.

Munson, L., Hulin, C., & Drasgow, F. (2000). Longitudinal analysis of dispositional influences and sexual harassment: Effects on job and psychological outcomes. *Personnel Psychology, 53*, 21–46.

Paludi, M. (Ed.). (1996). *Sexual harassment on college campuses: Abusing the ivory power.* Albany, NY: State University of New York Press.

Paludi, M. (2002). *The psychology of women.* 2nd ed. Upper Saddle River, NJ: Prentice Hall.

Paludi, M. (Ed.). (2008). *Understanding and preventing campus violence.* Westport, CT: Praeger.

Rahman, A., & Toubia, N. (Eds.). (2000). *Female genital mutilation: A guide to laws and policies worldwide.* London: Zed Press.

Sigal, J., & Annan, V. (2008). Violence against women: International workplace sexual harassment and domestic violence. In F. L. Denmark & M. Paludi (Eds.), *Psychology of women: A handbook of issues and theories* (pp. 590–622). Westport, CT: Praeger.

Sinclair, C., & Bourne, L. (2006). Cycle of blame or just world. *Psychology of Women Quarterly, 22*, 575–588.

Tan, J., & Gregor, K. (2006). Violence against pregnant women in northwestern Ontario. In F. L. Denmark, H. Kraus, E. Halpern, & J. Sechzer (Eds.), *Violence and exploitation against women and girls* (pp. 320–338). Boston, MA: Blackwell.

Waits, B., & Lundberg-Love, P. (2008). The impact of campus violence on college students. In M. Paludi (Ed.), *Understanding and preventing campus violence* (pp. 51–70). Westport, CT: Praeger.

Ward, C., & Lundberg-Love, P. (2006). Sexual abuse of women. In P. Lundberg-Love & S. Marmion (Eds.), *Intimate violence against women* (pp. 47–68). Westport, CT: Praeger.

Warshaw, R. (1988). *I never called it rape.* New York: Harper & Row.

Part I

Children and Adolescent Victims of Sexual Assault and Abuse

Chapter 1

Denial, Blame, Betrayal, and the Conspiracy of Silence: Educator Sexual Harassment of K–12 Students

Susan Strauss

School should be a fun place where students are on a quest to learn and explore new worlds and relationships in a safe and secure milieu. But sometimes the joy of inquiry is sabotaged by the very people whom students and parents believe they can trust to create and support a positive learning environment—educators, administrators, and other school staff. Probably, the most egregious behavior in which these trusted adults can engage in to undermine student safety, success, and health is that of sexual harassment to students. This phenomenon is confounded when school officials do not aggressively act to prevent and stop the misconduct (Fossey & DeMitchell, 1995; Shakeshaft, 2004).

Sexual harassment of students by educators is loathsome and abhorrent, and unfortunately occurs more often than anyone would like to think. According to the U.S. Department of Education, between kindergarten and twelfth grade, more than 4.5 million children are targets of sexual harassment by a school employee (Shakeshaft, 2004). For the purposes of this chapter, the term "educator" encompasses any school employee, such as administrators, counselors, janitors, bus drivers, coaches, aides, secretaries, and teachers.

DEFINING SEXUAL HARASSMENT

Confusion is abundant as to which term should be used to define sexual misconduct by adult educators in relation to students. "Sexual abuse," "rape," "molestation," "sexual exploitation," and "sexual harassment" are frequently the words and phrases used to describe educator sexual misconduct (Shakeshaft & Cohan, 1995). "Sexual harassment" is the term primarily used for this discussion, in part because it is broader in scope than the other terms listed; it includes a continuum of behaviors from the more subtle, such as staring, to the most egregious misconduct, including sexual assault and rape. Sexual harassment can be electronic/digital, physical, verbal, and visual in nature, and it violates the Civil Rights Act Title IX. This term is defined by the U.S. Department of Education, Office of Civil Rights (2000), as follows:

> Unwelcome sexual advances, requests for sexual favors, and other verbal, nonverbal, or physical conduct of a sexual nature by an employee, by another student, or by a third party, which is sufficiently severe, persistent, or pervasive to limit a student's ability to participate in or benefit from an education program or activity, or to create a hostile or abusive educational environment. (p. 264)

Additionally, the National Advisory Council on Women's Educational Programs makes the following assertion:

> Academic sexual harassment is the use of authority to emphasize the sexuality or sexual identity of the student in a manner which prevents or impairs that student's full enjoyment of educational benefits, climate, or opportunities. (Paludi & Barickman, 1991, p. 4)

RESEARCH, PREVALENCE, AND EXAMPLES

Most school educators are trustworthy and committed to teaching their students. Based on the very few studies of sexual harassment and sexual misconduct by educators in relation to students in school, it seems that only a small percentage of educators engage in this repugnant sexual misconduct (Hendrie, 1998g; Shakeshaft & Cohan, 1995). Colleagues and administrators believe the behavior would be overtly obvious to others within the school. Unfortunately, principals and teachers, while knowing that such behavior occurs, just do not believe that it is common or that it would occur in *their* school, so they often overlook the signs and symptoms of its presence. Even after a trial in which a colleague has been found guilty of criminal sexual misconduct or sexual harassment, fellow teachers may deny the outcome.

It is estimated that 0.04 to 5 percent of teachers sexually abuse students and that roughly 25 percent of school districts are challenged with this problem. Unfortunately, the behavior may continue unabated for years despite rumors, a gut sense, or even actual formal allegations. Indeed, offenders sometimes spend decades with students before getting caught, suggesting that "districts are being too lax, too trusting, or too languid about the possibility of employees abusing students" (Graves, 1994, p. 14). The perpetrators often stay one step ahead of being caught by transferring schools.

Research on school sexual abuse is virtually nonexistent (Sorenson, 1991). A four-year analysis (1987–1999) of cases of child sexual abuse in schools, which had reported in *Education Law Reporter* and identified through a West-law computer search, revealed a small but steady increase in the incidence of such abuse. However, this trend does not necessarily reflect an *actual* increase in abuse. It is estimated that at least one eighth of all U.S. children will be sexually abused by someone other than a family member.

The No Child Left Behind Act of 2001 required a national research study on sexual abuse in the schools. To fulfill this requirement, Shakeshaft (2004) created a synthesis of existing literature using the search term "educator sexual misconduct" at the request of the U.S. Department of Education. She found only a few empirical studies; only one study, by the American Association of University Women (AAUW), was based upon a representative national sample (AAUW, 1993, 2001). Although the AAUW's two studies examined the sexual harassment of students with an emphasis on student-to-student harassment, incidents involving sexual harassment by educators were also assessed. Shakeshaft (2003) then reexamined the results from the AAUW's studies concentrating on educator sexual harassment alone.

The 1993 AAUW study surveyed more than 1,600 students in grades 8 through 11 in 79 public schools, and found that 25 percent of females and 10 percent of males (18% of the total number of students) had been sexually harassed by a school employee. Seven years later, the AAUW surveyed a little more than 2,000 students on the same subject (AAUW, 2001). Students responded to questions inquiring about their sexual harassment experiences during their entire time in school; they also identified the harasser—student, teacher, other school staff, or another person.

The AAUW data were subjected to reanalysis by Shakeshaft (2003), who found that a little less than 10 percent of students reported sexual harassment by educators. A little less than 9 percent reported noncontact sexual harassment, approximately 7 percent indicated they had been subjected to contact/physical sexual harassment, and some students experienced both forms of harassment. Shakeshaft's study estimated that 4.5 million students are sexually harassed by an educator sometime between kindergarten and twelfth grade.

In their study of school-based harassment, Corbett, Gentry, and Pearson (1993) found that 48 percent of students experienced harassing verbal comments and looks, 23 percent were subjected to inappropriate touching, and a full 29 percent engaged in affairs or dating relationships with their teachers. Wishnietsky (1991) concluded that 17.5 percent of 148 North Carolina high school graduates experienced physical sexual harassment from educators, while 43 percent of their classmates were exposed to noncontact sexual harassment. Examples of noncontact harassment included insulting comments, looks, and gestures; contact harassment encompassed unwanted sexual touch and intercourse.

Shakeshaft and Cohan (1995) conducted a four-year study of 225 cases of sexual abuse of students by educators, in which data were collected through interviews with school administration, teachers, attorneys, and parents. The majority of cases that superintendents disclosed occurred in elementary schools, at 38 percent, 20 percent happened in middle schools, 36 percent occurred in high schools, and 6 percent were attributed to other categories of schools. Superintendents' views of noncontact harassment, such as educators' exposing themselves and showing students pornographic pictures, indicated that behaviors in this category were not perceived as harmful. If the sexual harassment was verbal in nature, the superintendents were more likely to label it as a "language indiscretion" and not very serious, even when teachers made such comments as "What's the matter? Isn't your boyfriend giving you enough? Can't he get it up?" Superintendents did not label such comments as sexual harassment and typically did not see what kind of harm these kinds of comments did.

Contact abuse complaints were predominantly leveled against male teachers by female students (Shakeshaft & Cohan, 1995). Often the accused educators were popular teachers who were coaches of athletics, drama, art and music. Seventy-six percent of the victims of male harassers were female and 24 percent were male. If the harasser was a female, 86 percent of the victims were female and 14 percent were male. One superintendent described the behavior of a male teacher who touched elementary students' breasts and genitals as "not serious." In another district, a special education student, who was emotionally developmentally disabled, was told by the school district to "stay away from the teacher" in response to the teacher performing fellatio on the student in a shopping center parking lot in the middle of the afternoon.

The Texas Civil Rights Project (Cedello, 1997) found the largest percentage of students sexually harassed by educators. In response to the question "In the most serious incident, who harassed you?" females reported that 42 percent of those incidents were initiated by school administrators, 29 percent by teachers or counselors, and 58 percent by other school staff. In contrast, male students reported 8 percent of incidents to be initiated by school administrators, 26 percent by teachers or counselors, and 15 percent by school staff. These statistics are particularly alarming when one considers that students were reporting only the most serious incidents.

Education Week conducted a six-month study of sex offenses committed against students by school employees using everything from newspapers to computer databases to gather its data set of 244 cases of abuse (Hendrie, 1998g). Perpetrators' ages ranged from 21 to 75, with 28 as the average age. Seven out of 10 offenders were teachers; however, janitors, bus drivers, principals, and librarians were also accused. Student victims were from grades K–12; 66 percent were older than age 14, with 66 percent being female and 33 percent being male. Twenty percent of the accused harassers were women. Only two cases were determined to have involved false accusation. Some 33 percent of allegations were made against coaches, other athletic instructors, or music or drama teachers.

Sexual harassment of students by coaches has sometimes been referred to as the "sporting culture's dirty little secret" (Nack & Yaeger, 1999, p. 43). In their article, Nack and Yaeger quote psychologist Steven Bisbing, an expert on children's sexual abuse by those in position of authority, who concludes that the sexual abuse of coaches "occurs with enough regularity across the country, at all levels, that it should be viewed as a public health problem" (p. 43).

Bithell (1991) found that 1 percent of adults said they were sexually abused by teachers in elementary school, and 3 percent experienced sexual abuse in high school. Bithell estimated that approximately one in 20 teachers has sexually harassed students, with their abusive behaviors ranging from sexually noxious comments to sexual intercourse.

Examples of sexual harassment engaged in by educators include sexually offensive verbal comments such as calling female students "boobies," complimenting a girl on her nice legs, and commenting on the student's sex life (Shakeshaft & Cohan, 1995). Corbett et al. (1993) found that students were the targets of comments such as "nice ass," "great boobs," and "you could make me want to cheat on my wife," with one coach telling female athletes that they "opened their legs wider than that for their boyfriends" (p. 98). Flattery, consoling, and writing love letters were other examples of abusive behaviors identified by Hendrie (1998c). In their litany of sexual harassment against students, Shakeshaft and Cohan (1995) included exhibitionism, showing students sexually explicit pictures, and various obscene gestures as examples of noncontact sexual harassment, which they labeled Level I. Physical examples, referred to as Level II contact sexual abuse, include touching a female's breasts and legs, requesting hugs, kissing, and sexual intercourse (Corbett et al., 1993; Shakeshaft & Cohan, 1995); touching genitals, fondling, tickling (Shakeshaft & Cohan, 1995); and pinning students against walls and lockers (Hendrie, 1998c).

Male victims' complaints of sexual harassment were taken more seriously by school officials than were female victims' complaints. The female accuser's honesty was sometimes questioned, whereas there were rarely any misgivings about a male student's accusations (Hendrie, 1998d; Snyder, 2001). This discounting or minimizing of female students' experiences further victimizes them because of their gender.

An emerging trend for educator harassers is the use of text messaging, Twitter, e-mail, Facebook, MySpace, and other electronic means to groom and harass their student victim (Maxwell, 2007). Text messaging has become the new primary means of engaging in "digital come-ons" (p. 1). Such electronic tools allow the harasser to extend his or her luring tentacles beyond the school to the point of stalking the student victim. If there is anything positive about the digital come-ons, it is that it leaves evidence of the wrongdoing that school officials can use to support students' allegations.

Sexual abuse by teachers and other school employees is challenging to study because students generally do not report it to their parents (AAUW, 1993) or to school officials (Shakeshaft & Cohan, 1995). When schools are made aware of allegations, they are often hesitant to share the data with researchers (Shakeshaft & Cohan, 1995). Although newspaper articles provide evidence of sexual harassment (and criminal abuse), they are not written in a scholarly mode, and generally no follow-up information is provided.

CHARACTERISTICS OF THE HARASSER

Those educators who are most likely to sexually harass students are often well respected by their colleagues, administrators, students, and parents (Shakeshaft & Cohan, 1995; Snyder, 2001). They are more likely to be male (Bagley & King, 1990) and to be actively involved in coaching students enrolled in extracurricular activities such as music, athletics, and debate (Shakeshaft & Cohan, 1994). Between 1995 and 2003, Jennings and Tharp (2003) discovered that 25 percent of Texas educators who sexually harassed students were either music teachers or coaches. According to Shakeshaft (2004), 18 percent of students are harassed by teachers, 15 percent by coaches, 13 percent by substitute teachers, 12 percent by bus drivers, 6 percent by principals, and 5 percent by counselors.

To research the gender of the perpetrator for the Department of Education's national report on sexual misconduct in U.S. schools, Shakeshaft (2004) analyzed data from her newspaper analysis, states' education disciplinary records, interviews with adults, and surveys of both adults and students. Her search for data found the following study results:

- Jennings and Tharp (2003) found approximately 13 percent of female teachers and 87 percent of male teachers were disciplined for sexual misconduct.

- Hendrie (1998d) concluded that 20 percent of harassers were female and 80 percent were male.

- Shakeshaft and Cohan (1994) discovered that males accounted for 96 percent of sexual offenders, and females 4 percent of sexual offenders.

- The AAUW (1993) study results showed that a little more than 57 percent of harassers were male and a bit more than 42 percent were female.

- A review of the child abuse literature demonstrated that males are much more likely to be sexual offenders than are females, although the number of female perpetrators may be underreported due to the belief that males should be flattered by a female's sexual "interest" (Shakeshaft, 2004).

The female harasser/offender is often researched separately from the male harasser (Hendrie, 1998a; Shoop, 2004). Years ago, a complaint by a male of being sexually harassed, including sexual assault, would have been unheard of; if it did occur, it would have been discounted, largely because of stereotypes claiming that any male would enjoy the behavior (Sutton, 2004). Today, it is acknowledged that even consensual sex between an adult and a student younger than the age of 18 (or younger, depending on state law) is a crime. According to Sutton (2004), almost 43 percent of educator sexual offenders are women, although this estimate may be low.

Female harassers are typically considered socially immature rather than sexually perverse, based on psychological analysis (Driedger, 2003). Women tend to form romantic, love attachments with their victims, which stands in contrast to the behavior of male offenders, who often abuse a series of students over time; the latter behavior is rare in women (Hendrie, 1998a). Reports indicate that women rarely use force or threats to keep their victims silent. They are more likely to acknowledge their misconduct and usually engage in the behavior later in life. Women offenders who target teens for abuse are also not particularly disturbed, in contrast to male offenders, who are generally more disturbed and difficult to treat. Corbett et al. (1993) found that female teachers sexually harassed their male students by exposing themselves, infringing on the student's body space, and, according to one boy, having sex with his friend every other weekend.

Two of the most well-known cases in recent years involved Julie Anne Fell and Mark Kay LeTourneau. LeTourneau, who was married with children, began a sexual relationship with one of her sixth-grade students, became pregnant as a result of their relationship, was caught, and spent seven years in prison. The two are now married with two children. Fell, a 31-year-old married speech coach, English teacher, and mother, had a sexual relationship with one of her tenth-grade students, who still played with action figures at the time. The Fell case ended differently than the LeTourneau case, however: Fell's victim informed the judge that he believes his former teacher to have manipulated him for her own sexual pleasure, and that he believes her to be a monster. Like LeTourneau, Fell served seven years in prison for her offense.

The study conducted by *Education Week* found 250 cases of educator sexual harassment, of which 43 involved female harassers (Hendrie, 1998a). In the offenses committed by those 43 women, five of the victims were female and the remainder were male. It has been suggested that more women may be offending, but are simply not reported due to stereotypes and machismo. If boys were to claim they were having sex with a female teacher, the response from their friends may very well be, "Wow, you are one lucky dude!" according to Shakeshaft (2003).

Same-sex sexual harassment or abuse does not denote homosexual abuse. Shakeshaft and Cohan (1994) discovered that 24 percent of men who harassed males identified themselves as heterosexuals. Shakeshaft's (2003) reanalysis of the AAUW's 2001 study suggested that a little more than 15 percent of cases involved male-to-male harassment, and 13 percent involved female-to-female sexual harassment. There appear to be fewer women who target other females, a finding that was also demonstrated in Shakeshaft and Cohan's study, which found 3 percent of cases involved this type of abuse. The percentages of same-sex harassment found by Shakeshaft and Cohan (1994) and in Shakeshaft's (2003) AAUW reanalysis were 27 percent and 28.3 percent, respectively.

CHARACTERISTICS OF THE TARGET

Students who are vulnerable or excluded from many friendships with other students are frequent targets of educator harassers because they are often grateful for adult attention (Shakeshaft & Cohan, 1994; Snyder, 2001). Snyder's study found that the victims shared the attributes of being shy, average or above-average students, attractive, having dysfunctional backgrounds, and defining themselves as outcasts. Children who struggle with low self-esteem, who are less likely to have close relationships with their parents, and who participate in precarious behaviors or whose parents partake in the same behaviors are often the desired prey (Hendrie, 1998c; Shakeshaft & Cohan, 1994). They are easy marks because they often crave attention and are more likely to not report the harasser. In addition, these students are less likely to be perceived as credible if they lodge a complaint against a well-liked teacher (Hendrie, 1998c; Shakeshaft & Cohan, 1994).

Females, rather than males, are more likely targets of educator sexual harassment (Bagley & King, 1990; Hendrie, 1998c; Shakeshaft, 2003; Shakeshaft & Cohan, 1994; Snyder, 2001), however, it may be that females are more likely to report their victimization than are males (Shakeshaft, 2003). Shakeshaft (2003) concluded that Latino, African American, and American Indian students were the most likely targets of educator sexual harassment, compared to Caucasian and Asian students.

In Sorenson's study (1991), 22 cases involved male harassers and female victims, 11 cases involved male-to-male abuse, two involved a male harasser of both genders, one instance involved a female harasser and a male victim, and one case involve female-to-female abuse. Twenty of the cases included multiple actual and alleged victims; 30 cases involved accusations of multiple incidents against the same victim, which suggests that many more victims may be involved than the count of reported cases indicates. In 18 cases, abusers targeted elementary students; three other victims were in middle school, 18 in high school, one was a preschool student, and three victims were disabled students from various grades. Seventeen of the cases were identified ambiguously as sexual molestation. Five cases included complaints of fondling and/or exposure, 11 victims were raped or experienced "deviate sexual intercourse" (p. 464), and four victims experienced actual or alleged intercourse. These cases encompassed oral, anal, and digital penetration, resulting in severe emotional sequelae for the children.

Students with disabilities are more likely to experience sexual abuse (Sobsey, Randall, & Parilla, 1997; Sullivan & Knutson, 2000). Nevertheless, there are no data available describing the sexual harassment of students with disabilities in schools.

PATTERNS OF EDUCATOR SEXUAL HARASSMENT

The teacher who sexually harasses his or her students behaves like any other sexual predator—namely, by using manipulative techniques such as isolation, blame, and lying (Shakeshaft & Cohan, 1994). These individuals are experts at taking advantage of a student's immaturity (Hendrie, 1998c). Those who target elementary school children (younger than seventh grade) are typically well liked, recognized as master teachers, and often lauded by students, parents, administrators, and other teachers (Shakeshaft, 2003). These teachers may have received a "Teacher of the Year" award or been recognized for their excellence in teaching (Shakeshaft & Cohan, 1994). The harasser's reputation of excellence, coupled with his or her popularity, creates a dilemma for the school administrator who receives a complaint of sexual harassment from a marginalized child. In fact, the recognition of excellence is one of the avenues the harasser uses to abuse his or her victims because it adds to the educator's professional credibility when a complaint is charged.

The harasser of middle and high school students differs from the harasser of elementary students (Shakeshaft & Cohan, 1994). The former educators may or may not be recognized for their excellence and mastery of teaching. According to Shakeshaft and Cohan (1994), when such an individual targets the older child, the behavior is more likely to occur when the harasser seizes an opportunity or demonstrates poor judgment rather than as a premeditated event.

"Pedophile" is the label often used to describe an individual who abuses children (13 and younger), but this label does not apply in most cases of educator harassment (Hendrie, 1998d). Hebophillia refers to the underlying motivations of those persons who target adolescents; hence this classification is sometimes used to define educators who sexually abuse teens. However, educators who harass students typically do not fall into any one category used to label those persons who commit sexual offenses. Some experts believe that educators who harass students may behave this way because of other factors, such as immaturity, stress, or lack of a clear sense of professional boundaries. Others may be considered narcissists, concerned only with their own sexual gratification at the expense of the target's pain. Still others may be considered romantic bad-judgment abusers who target teens. The various labels used tend to stem from various fields of study such as psychology or law. For the purposes of behavior in the schools, however, the choice of a label does not really matter, because the behavior and consequences are the same according to Shakeshaft.

"Grooming" is the term Robins (2000, cited in Shakeshaft, 2004), Shoop (2004), and Patterson and Austin (2008) use to describe the process instigated by a harasser to gain access to the target. This planned progression includes six steps:

1. Initiation of the selection process of the victim
2. Assessment of the student's ability to not tell
3. Determination of the child's compliance
4. Desensitization of the child through increased sexual touch
5. Proffering of experiences the child enjoys and wants to continue
6. Manipulation of the child into believing that he or she is responsible for the abuse because the child did not tell the harasser to stop

According to Shoop, grooming can run the gamut from questionable boundary crossing to obvious inappropriate behavior.

The process of grooming often begins with the educator giving preferential attention to the target, sometimes inquiring about the student's personal life, her boyfriend, and their dating relationship while demonstrating sincere interest and understanding and touching the student (Robins, 2000, cited in Shakeshaft, 2004; Shoop, 2004). Sometimes additional help is given in school subjects, music, or athletics, with the partnership creating a closer relationship with the child (Shoop, 2004). The harassing educator may next engage in sexual conversations with the student, including discussions about the educator's sex life. The student may then feel special that this teacher, whom the student admires and may feel love, is treating her or him as an adult. The relationship may eventually progress to sexual intercourse, with the teacher indicating a love relationship exists, and the teacher telling the student that when the student graduates, the teacher will leave his or her spouse and they will be together. Because children believe in this loving relationship, they often do not define their experience as abuse (Robbins, 2000, cited in Shakeshaft, 2004).

Some of the sexual harassment occurs in the educator's home, in his or her car, or some other location outside the school (Shakeshaft, 2004). Most sexual harassment occurs in the school hallways and offices, as well as in classrooms that are sometimes filled with students during class time. In one example, sexual intercourse occurred during class, in the storage room attached to the classroom (Shakeshaft, 2003; Shakeshaft & Cohan, 1994). In another case, a teacher would call specific boys up to his desk allegedly to discuss their homework (Shakeshaft & Cohan, 1994). As each boy stood at the desk, the teacher caressed and groped the student's penis, while every other child in the room was cognizant of what was occurring. For 15 years this teacher abused boys in his classroom until one student told a school official.

ALLEGATIONS AND SCHOOL RESPONSE

In Shakeshaft's (2003) reanalysis of the AAUW data, 71 percent of students indicated they would inform a school official if they were sexually harassed by a school employee. What happens in reality appears quite different, however. Of those students who were sexually harassed by a school employee, 11.6 percent told a teacher, and 10.6 percent reported the misconduct to another school employee. Wishnietsy (1991) found that only 7 students out of 300 reported the harassment, and 6 of those 7 said nothing was done as a result of the student reporting. Students are not likely to report milder forms of sexual harassment, such as verbal or visual abuse; they are much more likely to report physical forms of abuse, including hugging, kissing, sexual assault, and rape. According to Shakeshaft and Cohan (1994), approximately 90 percent of complaints to superintendents involve physical sexual harassment. Unfortunately, the majority of those complaints are mistrusted or ignored. Victims, as well as other students who know of the harassment, soon learn they cannot trust school officials, teachers, coaches, and other authorities to protect them, resulting in a sense of increased vulnerability, betrayal, and helplessness. According to students, they do not tell school officials about educator-initiated abuse out of a fear that they will not be believed (Robbins, 2000, cited in Shakeshaft, 2004; Snyder, 2001). For example, the female victims of teacher Kenneth DeLuca, who sexually abused 13 students between the ages of 10 to 18 over the course of 21 years, were not believed and were told to transfer to other schools, and their parents were threatened with lawsuits.

The study by *Education Week* cited numerous failings by school officials in relation to sexual harassment by educators, including the following (Hendrie, 1998b, 1998e):

- Failure to believe students and thereby failure to respond to a complaint
- Failure to report suspected abuse to agencies such as law enforcement and child protection
- Failure to conduct, or incompetently conduct, investigations
- Failure to document incidents, complaints, and investigations
- Failure to investigate after a student recanted his or her complaint, not recognizing that the recant might be in response to threats or manipulation to protect the abuser
- Failure to fire the harasser despite numerous complaints
- Failure of the teaching profession to police itself at the state level
- Failure of school districts to implement quality recruitment and hiring practices by not asking the right questions, seeking references, fingerprinting, and other actions
- Providing positive—even glowing—references for the harasser when he or she moves on to the next school district to teach
- Failure to revoke the educator's licenses for sex crimes
- Cutting deals with the offender, such that the district agrees to remain silent about a student's allegations if the educator quietly resigns

The child victim is often blamed for his or her own victimization (Hendrie, 1998b; Snyder, 2001). For example, when one vice principal caught a teacher kissing one of his students in his classroom, the vice principal rebuked the student (Hendrie, 1998b). Another incident involved a school official bringing the victim and the alleged harasser together, allowing the teacher to manipulate the student into recanting her complaint.

Yet another principal, after a nine-year-old third grader cried to her that her teacher had fondled her genitals, told the girl she was wrong, called the teacher to her office, and instructed the student to hug her teacher and make up. The same principal expressed doubt when the parents of a fifth-grade girl exposed their daughter's teacher for touching her breast and running his hands up to her underwear. As a result of the principal's lack of response, the parents went to law enforcement and child protection services with their complaint. Although no criminal charges were filed, the social services agency determined the teacher should be on the child abuse registry. The teacher continued to teach, however, and school officials claimed they were unaware his name was listed on the registry.

Unfortunately, school districts, parents, and students all too often fail to report incidents of educator misconduct to law enforcement or social services agencies (Shakeshaft & Cohan, 1994). When the police are notified, it is most often by parents. Because law enforcement is not informed of physical harassment that may constitute a crime, the abusers are not subjected to criminal sanctions and public knowledge, but rather may receive only school sanctions, which are frequently both private and meager.

The school sanctions may very well be nothing more than a reprimand. Alternatively, the teacher may be allowed to resign quietly, or be fired and go to another school district to repeat the sexual harassment. This phenomenon is sometimes called "passing the trash," where "the trash" means "a mobile molester" (Hendrie, 1998e). Sometimes the harasser/molester leaves when allegations come forward but cannot be substantiated, or before accusations surface. This practice allows the individual to stay one step ahead of the law, and to continue his or her egregious sexual misconduct unabated. When and if the harasser is finally exposed, questions typically arise as to how this mobile molester's behavior could be stifled and neglected.

The issue of false accusations is a concern of school officials and educators that contributes to the likelihood of students not being believed when they make complaints of sexual harassment (Shakeshaft, 2004). Although no studies have examined the frequency of false accusations, child sexual abuse research suggest that these incidents are infrequent. In the study conducted by Shakeshaft and Cohan (1994), all of the 225 complaints of educator sexual misconduct were shown to have occurred. Of these incidents, however, there were several in which the superintendent did not label the behavior as sexual misconduct but rather as touching with no sexual intent. Many school districts are more concerned about being sued by the adult harasser for defamation of character, violation of due process rights, or even being suspended while the school authorities conduct an investigation, than they are about victimized students filing lawsuits (Hendrie, 1998b).

School administrators sometimes feel as though they are restricted in how aggressively they can investigate allegations of sexual abuse, owing to stipulations mandated by union contracts, laws, and privacy rights after a person is informed that he or she has been accused of sexual harassment (Hendrie, 1998b). Also, because hindsight is often 20/20, sexual harassment is often subtle or imperceptible and, therefore, difficult to prove. Victims and their families, however, often provide jarring testimony demonstrating the failure of school officials to respond to complaints of educator sexual harassment and to keep students safe. Throughout the United States, courts have responded in kind by awarding victims sometimes millions of dollars in damages.

One mistake that school administrators make is to think that because law enforcement is conducting an investigation of a student's complaint, the school district can breathe a sigh of relief and think it is off the hook in conducting its own investigation (Hendrie, 1998f). On the flip side, administrators sometimes believe—falsely, as they may discover to their dismay—that if they conduct the investigation and determine the validity of the accusation, they do not need to contact law enforcement. Whenever there is a rumor or allegation of sexual misconduct including physical contact, law enforcement must be contacted to conduct an investigation. School administrators are usually not trained to conduct any type of investigation, let alone a criminal investigation. Consequently, law enforcement personnel suggest, when administrators attempt this type of investigation, they often do more harm than good, and may be accused of obstructing justice. If law enforcement officials conclude that no crime was committed, the school district must conduct its own investigation to determine if the student's civil rights were jeopardized by the form of sexual harassment, or if inappropriate behavior did occur that did not rise to the level of sexual harassment.

Because of the potential for a conflict of interest, and because the superintendent knows the educator, it is highly recommended that an outside investigator—a trained and competent expert in investigating allegations involving children as victims—be called in as the investigator. This tactic also helps minimize allegations of a cover-up because the outside investigator is viewed as impartial. A conspiracy of silence (Corbett et al., 1993; Winks, 1982; Wishnietsky, 1991) is said to exist when administrators, teachers, and students keep silent, and thereby cover up an educator's sexual harassment of a student. The conspiracy adds to the detrimental consequences to both the victim and the district.

Shakeshaft and Cohan (1995) found that most districts were lacking in reporting procedures as well as policies for dealing with allegations against educators. In most cases, the superintendent was the individual charged with questioning the student victim—sometimes with the parents present, and sometimes without the parents having any knowledge of the student's complaint. This questioning was usually incomplete and done in such a way that students were fearful. If the superintendent perceived the allegation to be serious, the school's attorney, board president, and teachers union president were contacted. Questioning the alleged harasser also fell to the superintendent, most often with another person present, such as the school district's attorney, a union representative, or another administrator. Rarely were the police, district attorney's office, or child protection/social services agency contacted. Put simply, investigations were either nonexistent or inadequate. If the accused teacher stated the allegation was a lie, it generally ended the investigation.

In Shakeshaft and Cohan's (1995) study, school superintendents often engaged in discriminatory handling of complaints against male teachers compared to complaints against female teachers. Allegations against women were viewed through a more critical lens, resulting in women frequently being terminated from employment, whereas accused men might receive nothing more than a reprimand. In addition, male targets' experiences were perceived as more serious in nature than the experiences of female victims. While female victims were suspected of lying, male victims' honesty was rarely questioned. Same-sex/homosexual allegations were taken more seriously, and believed to have caused more harm than opposite-sex/heterosexual complaints.

Often superintendents were confused about the dilemma in which they found themselves—protect the educator/abuser or protect the student (Shakeshaft & Cohan, 1995)? Superintendents were mixed on where to devote their support—to the victim or the teacher. They tended to empathize with male abusers, recognizing that what the educator did was wrong, but at the same time rationalizing the behavior ("Gee, the way these girls dress"). That dilemma was confounded when the abuser was an outstanding teacher, and sometimes a friend, and the student victim was a "bad girl" with few friends.

The superintendent's sense of a dilemma was the antithesis of the reactions of the harasser's peers, who strongly supported their accused colleague to the point of interfering with any attempted investigation and intimidating the victim (McGrath, 1994; Shakeshaft & Cohan, 1995). Fellow teachers tended to overreact to the accusation, often accused the superintendent of "going on a witch hunt" (McGrath, 1994) by accusing a wonderful teacher of abhorrent behavior, and perceived the superintendent as not supporting the teaching staff. As a result, Shakeshaft and Cohan discovered that educators switched from discussing the safety and well-being of their students to focusing on the safety and well-being of the accused.

Several disciplinary actions are open to the school district, and ultimately the school board, in handling complaints of sexual harassment that are found to be true. In Shakeshaft and Cohan's (1995) study, the consequences to the perpetrator included the following:

- Resigned, left the district, or retired—38.7 percent
- Terminated or not rehired—15 percent

- Suspended, then resumed teaching—8.1 percent
- Verbal or written reprimand—11.3 percent
- Informal "speaking" to—17.5 percent
- Allegations proven false—7.5 percent
- Veracity of allegations unresolved—1.9 percent

Schools continued to minimize the seriousness of the perpetrator's behavior by encouraging the harasser to retire or resign—even offering retirement benefits, and agreeing not to inform a potential future school employer of why the teacher was leaving the district (Shakeshaft & Cohan, 1995). Superintendents rationalized their actions by stating that terminating the perpetrator might end up costing the district more time and money if the terminated educator decided to sue the district. Some perpetrators taught in other districts that were unaware of the allegations against their new staff member ("passing the trash" [Hendrie, 1998e]). However, 37 percent of accused harassers maintained their teaching contracts in the same district, even when the superintendent acknowledged that the teacher was guilty of sexual abuse.

One superintendent shared his frustration of having to return a teacher to his teaching staff after he was found criminally guilty of sexual abuse when a state hearing panel recommended suspension for two years, counseling, and then reinstatement. Another superintendent allowed the perpetrator to remain in the district teaching because the educator had not *intended* to sexually abuse the child. Another perpetrator was allowed to continue teaching after making an apology to the children's parents (not the children) for sexual touching and sexual comments. One teacher who abused elementary children was transferred to a high school, and another who abused female special education students was allowed to work with male students only.

Sixty percent of the school districts offered no remedial help to the student victims (Shakeshaft & Cohan, 1995). The other victims were offered counseling. Most superintendents assumed that if the abuse no long was occurring, there was no problem for the victims. Nothing was done to prevent or mitigate the tremendous backlash and retaliation suffered by the victim at the hands of other students, school staff, and the community, resulting in many victims leaving the district and sometimes the community (Shakeshaft & Cohan, 1995; Snyder, 2001).

Interestingly, some students in the Corbett et al. (1993) study did not perceive the sexual harassment between students and educators to be particularly serious. One student stated, "I heard about a teacher being sexually active with a student outside of school, but I thought that it was appropriate" (p. 100). Another student indicated that coaches slept with students but because the girls wanted to, it wasn't harassment. Yet another student said, "He had sex with her. She was consenting. She was the school slut" (p. 100). Roughly 36 percent of students said they were aware of students and educators having sex, and 68 percent perceived that the student and the teacher were equally interested in the relationship.

COMMUNITY BACKLASH

The consensus by student victims and their families is that the schools that are more protective of the adult harasser and the school's reputation than they are of the best interests and safety of their students—an attitude that further victimizes the student (Hendrie, 1998f; Snyder, 2001). As a result, students and their families become disillusioned and angry, and feel as though their voices went unheeded by the school district. Many believe schools are more concerned about the school's reputation and liability than they are about the students' well-being. Some school officials become antagonistic and hostile to the families who complain. As a result, families may decide to take the matter to court in hopes of catalyzing the school district to hear their pleas, and to prevent another child's victimization. As news about the student complaint/potential lawsuit trickles into the community, the community often responds by turning on the student and his or her family, sometimes to the point of the family feeling the need to move out of town (Snyder, 2001).

Even if the perpetrator acknowledges his or her guilt, or if the perpetrator is found guilty of criminal sexual conduct or civil sexual harassment in a court of law, the educator's colleagues, students, parents, and the community often continue to support the educator, particularly if he is a favored and successful coach. Examples of this support include letters to the editor in the community paper favoring the abuser, community petitions to the school district in support of the teacher's continued employment as a teacher (and coach), and angry crowds of parents and community citizens who are livid because they believe a teacher is being falsely accused.

Victims may lose their friends when a popular teacher is brandished as an abuser, whereas the victims are labeled as liars by friends, educators, and the community at large (Hendrie, 1998g; Snyder, 2001). This retaliation can be severe and have long-lasting emotional ramifications for the student. The student becomes an outcast at school, and the student and the student's family may be ostracized by members of their church, social networks, and the larger community.

LEGAL ELEMENTS

Numerous state and federal laws outlaw sexual misconduct in U.S. public schools. This type of sexual misconduct may be covered under criminal laws such as child abuse statues, sexual assault and rape laws, and other criminal penalties resulting in imprisonment and/or fines (Shakeshaft & Cohan, 1995). The behavior is also covered under the Civil Rights Act, Title IX (including retaliation), 42 U.S.C. § 1983 (Davis, 2009), and state, county, and municipal laws modeled after Title IX. Potential sanctions described under Title IX and Section 1983, or comparable state laws, include punitive damages, monetary compensation to the victim, lack of federal funding to the district (Title IX only), and other penalties to the school (Shakeshaft & Cohan, 1995). In 2009, the U.S. Supreme Court ruled that students can now sue schools simultaneously with Title IX under the aegis of 42 United States Constitution (U.S.C.) § 1983 (Davis, 2009). Finally, bodies that license teachers and other state regulations can take away the teacher's license, thereby eliminating his or her ability to teach in a public school (Shakeshaft & Cohan, 1995).

Title IX of the Civil Rights Act of 1972 states that for behavior to constitute sexual harassment, it must be unwelcome; sufficiently severe and/or pervasive enough to interfere with a student's ability to get an education, based on the perspective of a reasonable *student*; and sexual and/or gender based (U.S. Department of Education, Office of Civil Rights, 2000). There are two broadly accepted elements of sexual harassment. First, in quid pro quo, sexual activity is demanded from a student in exchange for some benefit, such as a good grade or a recommendation to a college, or, conversely, a threat of punishment is made if the student does not succumb to the demand. Second, sexual harassment may arise in a hostile environment, which generally does not include any threats. This latter type of harassment can be more subtle and nuanced—and more difficult to distinguish—than quid pro quo.

Several U.S. Supreme Court cases have defined how Title IX is enforced under the law in regard to teacher sexual harassment. The first case heard by the Court was *Franklin v. Gwinnett County Public Schools* (503 U.S. 60) in 1992. In this case, the Supreme Court ruled that a student may sue the school district for monetary damages under Title IX. Lacking from the Court's opinion, however, was a definition of the critical elements determining the circumstances under which a school district could be held liable.

The ambiguity of the 1992 Supreme Court decision was eventually addressed in an unpopular 1998 decision. In *Gebser v. Lago Vista Independent School District* (524 U.S. 274), an eighth-grade student who was sexually involved with a teacher for more than a year sued the school district, claiming it had violated her rights under Title IX. The Court opined that the student would not receive monetary compensation for damages unless a school official who had the authority to take corrective action had *actual knowledge* of the misconduct and was *deliberately indifferent* to it. While the Court ruled against Gebser, the justices left the door open for students to sue, albeit under a very strict standard. This decision raised further questions: Which position within the school district constituted "authority"? Which behavior—or lack of behavior—constituted deliberate indifference?

In the *Gebser* case, the district was not held liable because when the school discovered the teacher's sexual harassment, it fired him, thereby avoiding the "deliberate indifference" standard.

Given that the Supreme Court's *Gebser* decision established new roadblocks for plaintiff students wishing to file suits based on educator-to-student sexual harassment (Beck, 2006), some plaintiffs may fare better going through state law to seek redress for their grievances. According to McGrath (1994), state courts may award monetary damages for a school administrator's failure to supervise, investigate, train, hire carefully, warn others, and report child sexual abuse.

After the 1998 *Gebser* decision, a coalition of 17 civil liberties and women's groups immediately wrote key officials in Congress and the Clinton administration requesting that they counter the effects of the ruling by passing federal legislation (Hendrie, 1998h). The coalition's fear was that the ruling would be a successful catalyst allowing school officials "to insulate themselves from being informed about sexual harassment to avoid financial liability" (p. 18). In essence, *Gebser* rewards a district for ensuring ignorance of sexual harassment, thereby allowing the perpetrator to continue to harass children.

In 2005, the Supreme Court ruled that retaliation claims can be brought under Title IX (Davis, 2008). According to Brett Sokolow, president of the National Center for Higher Education Risk Management (NCHERM), "The money behind retaliation cases is bigger than money victims get under Title IX sexual assault cases" (p. 6).

Until a 2009 U.S. Supreme Court's decision, the circuit courts had long disagreed on whether a claim under § 1983 could be brought forward if Title IX was also being used to sue a school district (Davis, 2009). The Court's ruling in *Fitzgerald v. Barnstable School Committee* (2009; 128 S. Ct. 788, U.S.), however, cleared the way for simultaneous lawsuits to proceed under both Title IX and § 1983. Section 1983 allows students to seek redress for sexual harassment claims for equal protection violations, which prohibits anyone acting "under color of state law"—for example, police, school board, or other government employees or organizations (Katz, 2008)—from denying an individual his or her constitutional rights. Under § 1983, a student plaintiff does not have to prove deliberate indifference, as is required by Title IX; thus the former regulation employs a less strict standard. Section 1983 holds that schools have a duty to students to prevent sexual abuse by educators (McGrath, 1994). In *Doe v. Taylor Independent School District* (15F.3d 443, 1993), the court opined that a principal could be held *personally* liable for failing to ensure a student's right to bodily integrity in sexual abuse by an employee.

Under § 1983, two constitutional amendments are most likely to be cited as the basis for sexual harassment complaints brought by students and their families (Back to Basics, 2008, p. 10):

- Fourteenth Amendment (the equal protection clause), which guarantees citizens freedom from government discrimination on any basis, including race, color, sex, religion, national origin, age, or disability.
- Eighth Amendment, which forbids cruel or unusual punishment by government officials (including school officials).

In *Doe v. Dickenson*, the student plaintiff filed a claim under the equal protection clause of the Fourteenth Amendment, claiming that the customs, practices, and policies of the police department of the City of Phoenix resulted in Dickenson, the school resource officer who allegedly sexually abused a 14-year-old boy, not receiving adequate training and supervision. As a result of the city's negligence, the boy suffered egregious emotional trauma, which in turn caused his parents to suffer, and continue to suffer, emotional anguish, medical costs, and other damages. The plaintiffs won their case under the constitutional right of familial association. As a result of the Supreme Court's recent § 1983 decision, school districts must acclimate themselves to the broad range of constitutional claims that may now be brought forward in sexual harassment liability.

Three criteria are required to establish liability under Section 1983: (1) If school officials create and maintain a practice, custom, or policy that condones the abuse of or injury to students, then (2) school officials are liable for injuries to people with whom they have a "special relationship" and (3) officials face potential liability when they create a danger that causes student injury (Lane, 1995, p. 13).

In 2001, the Eighth Circuit Court of Appeals, in the case of *P.H. v. School District of Kansas City, Missouri* (265F.3d 653), held that a teacher's sexual harassment of a student would violate § 1983 if the school district (1) failed to receive, investigate, and act upon complaints of sexual abuse; (2) failed to act when provided notice of alleged inadequacy of its employee training procedures (a provision required to support a § 1983 claim for failure to train employees to protect students from sexual abuse); and (3) failed to act when provided actual notice of sexual abuse (a provision required to support Title IX liability). In this suit, the justices ruled, there had to be proof that the district's failure to train demonstrated deliberate indifference, and that the district had notice that its procedures were inadequate and likely to cause a due process violation of the Fourteenth Amendment. If the need for training is obvious because there is a clear and present pattern of misconduct within the district, then the failure to train demonstrates a violation of § 1983.

Some offenses perpetrated by teachers against students do not rise to the level of a crime, or even to the level of the civil offense of sexual harassment, yet the educators' behavior requires aggressive action by school officials. School officials could, in fact, be sued for not responding to teacher sexual harassment (Graves, 1994). School administrators have been assigned culpability in civil lawsuits, and sometimes criminal complaints, for their failure to act to rectify teacher sexual harassment.

The U.S. Department of Education, Office for Civil Rights (OCR), is the regulatory agency whose task it is to ensure school districts adhere to Title IX or else risk losing federal money (Sutton, 2004). This agency has published guidelines for schools that require prompt and equitable resolution of sex discrimination complaints, including those related to sexual harassment. The Title IX amendment of 1972 does not directly deal with educator sexual harassment, but has a broader scope covering *any* sex-based discrimination, whether that behavior comes from another student or school personnel.

A school district may be out of compliance with Title IX if its policies and procedures have been executed but staff do not understand the policy's complexity and depth (Davis, 2008). This point emphasizes the importance of conducting yearly training of all school employees ensuring, among other aspects, that they are competent in understanding and using the district's policy.

In *Gebser*, the Supreme Court held that a school can be held liable for monetary damages to a student victim when a teacher sexually harasses the student if two criteria are met:

1. The supervisory school official who has authority to institute corrective measures to end the harassment has actual knowledge of the behavior.
2. That official demonstrates deliberate indifference in his or her failure to adequately respond to the behavior.

These criteria stand in contrast to those laid down by the OCR, which exists to enforce Title IX's mandate of nondiscrimination, even if a claim of nondiscrimination does not give rise to monetary damages. In other words, a school district may not be in compliance with the OCR's guidelines because it did not conduct training, publicize the anti-discrimination policy, identify a Title IX Coordinator, and fulfill other obligations, yet not be in violation of Title IX law, because criteria 1 and 2 were met.

There probably are few people who support educators and students having sex, yet 20 states have no criminal laws against this behavior if students are 16, 17, or 18 years old, depending on the state (Hendrie, 1998i). Some states see some gray areas in this seemingly black-and-white issue—consensual sex between a educator and an older teenager, especially if the particular state's laws set the age of consent as young as 16, 17, or 18. In fact, the National School Board Association (NSBA), the American Federation of Teachers (AFT), and the National Education Association (NEA) do not have a policy absolutely outlawing the behavior.

RECOMMENDATIONS

Sexual harassment by educators directed at students is a problem that crushes students, parents, teachers, school districts, and the entire community. It is critical that districts acknowledge the problem, educate all parties about it, and implement steps for the prevention and intervention of the misconduct. The following are recommendations for school officials related to this topic:

1. Develop and widely disseminate and publicize an educator sexual harassment/misconduct policy and reporting procedure to students, parents, teachers, and school staff, and ensure that all parties adhere to the policy.
2. Establish a zero-tolerance policy statement banning retaliation by students, teachers, and staff, as well as prohibiting the use of educator–student electronic communication (e.g., by e-mail, Facebook, or other social networking media).
3. Take all complaints seriously, and follow up with an investigation even if the complaint is not formal, is a rumor, or is based on a gut feeling.
4. In addition to overall sexual harassment training, include training on educator sexual harassment and boundaries for students and staff on a yearly basis, informing all staff of their responsibility to report questionable behavior to social services/child protection agencies and school administers; make it clear that failure to report may result in liability.
5. Implement effective hiring practices, including conducting background checks and fingerprinting of all potential teachers and school staff.
6. Ensure that investigations of any allegations and rumors are conducted by highly trained individuals and/or law enforcement.
7. When an allegation or confirmed sexual harassment has occurred, assign only one or two spokespersons from the district to deal with the media to ensure accurate information is disseminated and to minimize gossip and innuendo.
8. Warn other districts where the alleged harasser is seeking employment—some state laws require this notification.
9. Report the misconduct to the state licensing agency.
10. Monitor the district's environment—listen for rumors, do not ignore warning signs, and trust your professional instincts about questionable employee conduct such as prolonged hugging of students, spending time with students outside of school, and sexual comments.
11. Document all allegations, investigations, and outcomes—do not expunge the findings.
12. Contact the parents of the victim prior to interviewing the student.

13. Do not make "deals" with the perpetrator by agreeing to expunge his or her records if the educator leaves quietly, or by letting the educator retire with full retirement benefits.
14. Only 7 percent of students report their victimization—make your school district one in which students trust that they will be believed and will not be subjected to retaliation if they come forward to complain.
15. Provide a support mechanism for victims.
16. Designate one or two Title IX coordinators to be responsible for receiving all sexual harassment and sexual abuse complaints.

Schools have a long way to go in taking the necessary steps to combat sexual harassment by educators (and students). In addition to the suggestions given here, state licensing boards and state legislatures need to implement stricter rules and laws to effectively prevent and intervene in instances of educator sexual misconduct. Only then can children have more assurance of attending school in an environment that respects them and guards their safety.

REFERENCES

American Association of University Women Educational Foundation (AAUW). (1993). *Hostile hallways: AAUW survey on sexual harassment in American schools*. Washington, DC: Author.

American Association of University Women Educational Foundation (AAUW). (2001). *Hostile hallways: Bullying, teasing and sexual harassment in school*. Washington, DC: Author.

Back to Basics. (2008). Section 1983 and additional avenues for students, employees to pursue claims for sexual harassment. *Educator's Guide to Controlling Sexual Harassment, 16*(1), 9–11.

Bagley, C., & King, K. (1990). *Child sexual abuse: The search for healing*. London: Tavistock/Routledge.

Beck, J. (2006). Entity liability for teacher-on-student sexual harassment: Could state law offer greater protection than federal statues? *Journal of Law and Education, 35*(1), 141–151. Retrieved from ProQuest database.

Birhell, S. B. (1991). *Educator sexual abuse: A guide for prevention in the schools*. Boise, ID: Tudor House.

Cedello, S. (1997). *Peer sexual harassment: A Texas-size problem*. Austin, TX: Texas Civil Rights Project.

Corbett, K., Gentry, C., & Pearson, W. Jr. (1993). Sexual harassment in high school. *Youth and Society. 25*(1), 93–103. Retrieved from EBSCO database.

Davis, M. R. (2008). Educator misconduct: Schools can face lawsuits in sexual assault cases for damages to the parent–child relationship. *Educator's Guide to Controlling Sexual Harassment, 16*(11), 3, 9.

Davis, M. R. (2009). High court broadens school liability, allows pursuit of Title IX, § 1983 Claims. *Educator's Guide to Controlling Sexual Harassment, 16*(6), 1–2, 5–6.

Driedger, S. (2003). The teacher lesson. *Maclean's, 116*(20), 56. Retrieved from EBSCO database.

Fossey, R., & DeMitchell, T. (1995, April). "Let the master respond": Should schools be strictly liable when employees sexually abuse children? Paper presented at the annual meeting of the American Educational Research Association, San Francisco, CA.

Graves, B. (1994). When the abuser is an educator. *School Administrator, 51*(9), 8–14, 16–18. Retrieved from EBSCO database.

Hendrie, C. (1998a). Abuse by women raises its own set of problems. *Education Week, 18*(4), 1, 14–15, 17. Retrieved from EBSCO database.

Hendrie, C. (1998b). Cost is high when schools ignore abuse. *Education Week, 8*(15), 1, 14–16. Retrieved from EBSCO database.

Hendrie, C. (1998c). In youth's tender emotions, abusers find easy pickups. *Education Week, 18*(14), 17. Retrieved from EBSCO database.

Hendrie, C. (1998d). Labels like "pedophile" don't explain the many faces of child sexual abuse. *Education Week, 18*(14), 16. Retrieved from EBSCO database.

Hendrie, C. (1998e). "Passing the trash" by school district frees sexual predators to hunt again. *Education Week, 18*(15), 16–17. Retrieved from EBSCO database.

Hendrie, C. (1998f). Principals face a delicate balancing act in handling allegations of misconduct. *Education Week, 18*(16), 14. Retrieved from EBSCO database.

Hendrie, C. (1998g). Sex with students: When employees cross the line. *Education Week, 18*(14), 1, 12–14. Retrieved from EBSCO database.

Hendrie, C. (1998h). Shifting legal ground on harassment has made it harder for victims to win. *Education Week, 18*(15), 18. Retrieved from EBSCO database.

Hendrie, C. (1998i). "Zero tolerance" of sex abuse proves elusive. *Education Week, 18*, 12–15. Retrieved from EBSCO database.

Jennings, D., & Tharp, R. (2003, May 4–6). Betrayal of trust. *The Dallas Morning News*. Retrieved from ProQuest Newspapers database.

Katz, A. (2008, December 2). Commentary: *Fitzgerald v. Barnstable*, annual Supreme Court review. *Legal Momentum*. Retrieved November 1, 2009, from www.legalmomentum.org/news-room/press-releases/commentary-fitzgerald-v.html.

Lane, F. (1995). Sexual misconduct of school employees: Supervisory school officials' liability under Section 1983. *School Law Bulletin, 46*(2), 9–16. Retrieved from Minitex database.

Maxwell, L. A. (2007). Digital age adds new dimension to incidents of staff–student sex. *Education Week, 27*(13), 1. Retrieved from Galegroup database.

McGrath, M. J. (1994). The psychodynamics of school sexual abuse investigations. *School Administrator, 51*(9), 28–30, 32–35. Retrieved from EBSCO database.

Nack, W., & Yaeger, D. (1999, September 13). Every parent's nightmare. *Sports Illustrated*, p. 40.

Paludi, M. A., & Barickman, R. B. (1991). *Academic and workplace sexual harassment: A resource manual.* Albany, NY: SUNY Press.

Patterson, M. A., & Austin, D. F. (2008, December). Stop the grooming. *American School Board Journal*, 18–20.

Shakeshaft, C. (2003, Spring). Educator sexual abuse. *Hofstra Horizons*, 10–13.

Shakeshaft, C. (2004). *Educator sexual misconduct: A synthesis of existing literature.* U.S. Department of Education Office of Under Secretary, DOC 2004–09, Washington, DC. Retrieved November 4, 2009, from http://www.specialeducationmuckraker.com/Shakeshaft_SchoolSexualAbuse.pdf.

Shakeshaft, C., & Cohan, A. (1994, January). In loco parentis: Sexual abuse of students in schools: What administrators should know. *Administration and Policy Studies Hofstra University.*

Shakeshaft, C., & Cohan, A. (1995). Sexual abuse of students by school personnel. *Phi Delta Kappan, 76*(7), 513–520. Retrieved from EBSCO database.

Shoop, R. J. (2004). *Sexual exploitation in schools: How to spot it and stop it.* Thousand Oaks, CA: Corwin Press.

Sobsey, D., Randall, W., & Parila, R. K. (1997). Gender differences in abused children with and without disabilities. *Child Abuse and Neglect, 21*(8). 707–720. Retrieved from ScienceDirect database.

Sorenson, G. P. (1991). Sexual abuse in schools: Reported court cases. *Educational Administration Quarterly, 27*(4), 460–480. Retrieved from Sage database.

Sullivan, P. M., & Knutson, J. F. (2000). The prevalence of disabilities and maltreatment among runaway children. *Child Abuse and Neglect, 24*(10), 1275–1288. Retrieved from ScienceDirect database.

Sutton, L. C. (2004, December). Educator sexual misconduct: New trends and liability. *School Business Affairs*, 6–8.

U.S. Department of Education, Office of Civil Rights. (2000). Revised sexual harassment guidance: Harassment of students by school employees, other students, or third parties (Federal Document No. FR Doc. 01-1606). *Federal Register, 66*(13), 5512. Retrieved October 30, 2009, from http://www.ed.gov/offices/OCR/archieves/pdf/shguide.pdf.

Winks, P. (1982). Legal implications of sexual contact between teacher and student. *Journal of Law and Education, 11*(4), 433–477.

Wishnietsky, D. (1991). Reported and unreported teacher–student sexual harassment. *Journal of Education Research, 3*, 164–169.

Chapter 2

Missing Children: Abducted and Runaway Youth

Michele A. Paludi and Katie L. Kelly

> There is no trust more sacred than the one the world holds with children. There is no duty more important than ensuring that their rights are respected, that their welfare is protected, that their lives are free from fear and want and that they can grow up in peace.
> —Kofi Annan

INTRODUCTION

The topic of missing children and child abduction often receives national media attention. News programs (e.g., *Nancy Grace* and *America's Most Wanted*) feature photos and descriptions of missing children on each show, asking viewers to assist law enforcement in locating the missing children and adolescents. As we were writing this chapter, the following incidents were prominent in the media.

Christopher Savoie was arrested in September 2009 in Japan for taking his children from their mother on their way to school. His ex-wife, Noriko Savoie, had taken their two children to Japan following receipt of divorce papers from her husband. Noriko has been quoted as saying she felt emotionally abused by Christopher and mistreated by the legal system. Christopher responded that he didn't do anything wrong.

In October 2009, for the first time since her abduction in 2002, Elizabeth Smart testified about the abduction and subsequent physical and sexual abuse she suffered for nine months at the hands of Brian Mitchell and Wanda Barzee.

In September 2009, Jaycee Dugard, who was abducted in 1991 and subsequently imprisoned and abused by Phillip Garrido and Nancy Garrido, was found. Jaycee, now 29, bore two children from the rapes committed by Phillip Garrido.

In June 2009, Lindsey J. Baum was reported missing in Washington. She was last seen leaving the home of a friend.

In February 2009, a 20-year-old missing children's case was solved. Marvin Maple had abducted his granddaughter and grandson from Tennessee. The children, now 28- and 27-year-old adults, were found in California. Maple had abducted the grandchildren on the day he and his wife were ordered by a court to return them to their parents. The Maples had been granted temporary custody after they accused the parents of sexually and physically abusing their children. An investigation into these allegations found no evidence to support the claims.

In May 2009, Karla Victoria Yrigoyen-Rivas, 12 years old, went missing from her home in Texas. The National Center for Missing and Exploited Children believes that that she was abducted by Herman Hernandez Canales, a man to whom Karla's mother was renting a room.

In September 2009, John Couey died in prison while awaiting execution. Couey had abducted nine-year-old Jessica Marie Lunsford from her home in Florida in 2005. He held Jessica captive, raped her, and subsequently murdered the child. Couey was a convicted sex offender. Because of Lunsford's abduction, tougher penalties for sex offenders were implemented in many states, including in Florida, which now bans sex offenders from school grounds.

In October 2009, a woman posing as an immigration agent entered a home in Tennessee, stabbed the mother, and abducted her four-day-old infant. This abductor had followed the mother and infant from a Wal-Mart store to their home.

In September 2009, Congressional Representative Christopher Smith introduced the International Child Abduction Prevention Act, which ensures U.S. compliance with the Hague Convention and which establishes procedures to promptly return to the United States children who were abducted and taken to other countries.

These cases do not come close to presenting the full scope of the pandemic of child abductions in the United States as well as in other countries. According to the National Center for Missing and Exploited Children (2009), each day an average of 2,185 children are missing. Child Find of America (2009) and Boudreaux, Lord, and Etter (2000) report that approximately 203,900 children each year are abducted by a parent or family member in violation of a court decree, custody order or other custodial rights.

Ernie Allen, President of the National Center for Missing and Exploited Children, noted the following statistics in his address to the U.S. Department of Justice in 2009:

> In the United States, Justice Department research found that approximately 800,000 children are reporting missing each year, the largest number of whom are runaways, about 200,000 children are the victims of family abduction, about 58,000 children are the victims of nonfamily abduction, and about 115 children are taken by strangers and either murdered, ransomed, or taken with the intent to keep. (p. 1)

Girls are more likely to be abducted by strangers as well as by family members; boys are more likely to be abducted by family members. In addition, older children are more likely to be victimized than younger children because they are more independent of the supervision of parents and other adults (Finkelhor, 1995).

Allen (2009) noted that in Europe, the following statistics describe the high incidence of missing children each year:

- 105,000 missing children in the United Kingdom
- 50,000 missing children in Germany
- 39,000 missing children in France
- 8,400 missing children in Spain
- 1,100 missing children in Italy
- 500 missing children in Greece

Missing Children Europe (2009) notes that data collection in European countries as well as definitions of "missing" differ among countries, making incidence rates of child abductions and missing children difficult to obtain. According to this organization:

> The absence of reliable data at the European level must on no account allow for the problem to be underestimated. Rough figures, as reported by the Missing Children Europe members and other sources, clearly show that the disappearance and sexual exploitation of children affect a very large number of children. (p. 2)

Furthermore, the incidence of international child abduction is increasing each year due to the greater ease of undertaking international travel and an increase in bicultural relationships (Moskowitz, 2005).

This chapter discusses various types of abductions and missing children, including runaways, throwaways, noncustodial parental abductions, and stranger abductions. In addition, it provides an overview of the empirical research on the effects of abductions on children and adolescents. Furthermore, it reviews the psychological research on perpetrators of abductions, including repeat offenses; the impact of power, not sex, on these crimes; the offenders' modus operandi; and their manipulation process. We begin by discussing legislation dealing with child abductions, including legislation concerning international child abductions.

LEGISLATION DEALING WITH MISSING CHILDREN AND CHILD ABDUCTIONS

> [I]n serving the best interests of children, we serve the best interests of all humanity.
>
> —Carol Bellamy

This section presents an overview of some of the federal statutes and international legislation dealing with child abductions and missing children. For a thorough discussion, we refer the reader to the National Center for Missing and Exploited Children's resources.

Hague Convention on the Civil Aspects of International Child Abduction

The Hague Convention on the Civil Aspects of International Child Abduction is a treaty developed by the Hague Conference on Private International Law in 1980. This treaty aims to provide a quick method to return a child younger than 16 years of age who is taken from one member nation to another. The Hague Convention's mission is explained in its preamble: "to ensure the prompt return of children who have been abducted from their country of habitual residence or wrongfully retained in a contracting state not their country of habitual residence."

The Hague Convention defines "wrongful" removal or retention of a child under the following conditions:

a. It is in breach of rights of custody attributed to a person, an institution or any other body, either jointly or alone, under the law of the State in which the child was habitually resident immediately before the removal or retention; and
b. At the time of removal or retention those rights were actually exercised, either jointly or alone, or would have been so exercised but for the removal or retention. These rights of custody may arise by operation of law or by reason of a judicial or administrative decision,

or by reason of an agreement having legal effect under the law of the country of habitual residence.

The Hague Convention thus seeks to return abducted children to the country where they normally live so that courts of that country may decide on issues of custody and visitation rights (Reynolds, 2006). The treaty does not intervene in deciding custody rights; it simply focuses on the return of the child to the jurisdiction that will hear the custody matter.

The Hague Convention applies only between countries that are both parties to the Convention.[1] The Report on Compliance with the Hague Convention (2008) indicated that in fiscal year 2007, the United States Central Authority assisted "left-behind" parents in the United States in responding to 575 cases of international parental child abductions involving 821 children. In 2007, the Department of State assisted in the return to the United States of 341 children abducted to or wrongfully retained in other countries.

Of these 341 children, 217 returned from countries that are Hague Convention partners with the United States. Moreover, 262 children who were abducted to or wrongfully retained in the United States were returned to their country of origin in 2007. Convention countries with the highest incidence of reported abductions to the United States in 2007 were Mexico, the United Kingdom, Germany, Canada, and Australia. Recovery rates for Hague Convention countries vary based on how well the courts implement the treaty (Report on Compliance with the Hague Convention, 2008). Rates of recovery for abducted children in countries that are not part of the Hague Convention are extremely low.

Missing Children's Act

In 1982, Florida Senator Paula Hawkins and Illinois Representative Paul Simon sponsored the Missing Children's Act. This legislation authorizes the U.S. Attorney General to collect and disseminate information to assist in the identification of and location of missing children. The Missing Children's Act makes it possible to enter this information into the National Crime Information Center. The U.S. Senate declared May 25 to be National Missing Children's Day.

Missing Children's Assistance Act

In 1984, the U.S. Congress passed the Missing Children's Assistance Act, which has since been reauthorized. This legislation requires the Office of Juvenile Justice and Delinquency Prevention in the U.S. Department of Justice to do the following:

1. Create a national, toll-free hotline to receive reports of sightings of missing children and to help in reuniting children with their families.

2. Create a national resource center and clearinghouse to offer technical assistance to individuals trying to locate and recover missing children.
3. Monitor grants and contracts to public agencies and private nonprofit agencies for activities in prevention of abductions, location and recovery of missing children, and research into the psychological dimensions and consequences of missing children.

The National Center for Missing and Exploited Children serves as the national resource center and operates the hotline.

National Child Search Assistance Act

The National Child Search Assistance Act was passed by the U.S. Congress in 1990. This legislation requires each federal, state, and local law enforcement agency to report each case of a missing child to the National Center for Missing and Exploited Children. In addition, law enforcement agencies are required to maintain close contact with the National Center for Missing and Exploited Children for the purposes of exchanging information regarding missing children.

International Parental Kidnapping Crime Act

Passed in 1993, the International Parental Kidnapping Crime Act makes it a federal crime to remove a child from the United States or retain a child who has been in the United States outside of this country with the intent to interfere with parental rights.

Missing Children Europe

Missing Children Europe (2009), a European federation that was established in 2001, represents 23 nongovernmental organizations that assist in locating missing and sexually exploited children. Sixteen member states of the European Union are part of Missing Children Europe.[2] European countries have established a variety of child alert systems, such as the French Alerte Enlèvement and Greek Amber Alert Hellas systems. The goal of these alert systems, similar to the AMBER Alert (discussed in the next subsection), is to involve the public in helping to search for missing children through reports in the media and on road traffic signs.

The Protect Act of 2003: AMBER Alert

Established in 2003 as a voluntary partnership between law enforcement agencies, media broadcasters, and transportation agencies, the Protect Act of 2003—more commonly referred to as the AMBER (America's Missing: Broadcast Emergency Response) Alert program—activates an urgent bulletin in child abduction cases. The goal of the AMBER Alert is to immediately bring together an entire community to assist in the search for and recovery of a missing child (Griffin & Miller, 2008; Zgoba, 2004). AMBER Alerts are issued when the following conditions are met (Miller & Clinkinbeard, 2006; Zgoba, 2004):

1. Confirmation by law enforcement that the child has been abducted
2. Belief by law enforcement that the child faces imminent danger
3. Substantial information regarding the victim, the offender, and the offender's vehicle
4. An abduction involving a child 17 years or younger
5. Entry of the child's name and other critical identification information into the National Crime Information Center computer

AMBERT Alert information is also assembled for public dissemination. This information includes photos of the missing child, the suspected abductor, and the suspected vehicle. These data are faxed to radio stations designated as primary stations under the Federal Communications Commission's Emergency Alert System.

In addition, the National Center for Missing and Exploited Children is notified by law enforcement when an AMBER Alert is issued. This center transmits the relevant information to authorized secondary distributors—that is, companies, businesses, and other organizations that can deliver geographically targeted messages to customers. Some states use electronic highway billboards in their AMBER Alert systems. In addition, wireless AMBER Alerts are available for users who wish to receive such notifications. States have also developed clearinghouses to provide resources to law enforcement, parents, teachers, attorneys, and legislators in recovering missing and abducted children.[3]

Statistics for 2009 indicate that there were 443 successful recoveries of missing children in the United States during that year.

Adam Walsh Child Protection and Safety Act

The Adam Walsh Child Protection and Safety Act, which was passed by the U.S. Congress in 2006, amended a portion of the National Child Search Assistance Act to mandate law enforcement entry of information concerning missing and abducted children into the National Crime Information Center database within two hours of being notified of the abducted or missing child.

The Children's Passport Issuance Alert Program

In 2007, the United States Central Authority began the Children's Passport Issuance Alert Program, which gives parents the opportunity to request that their U.S. citizen children be registered in the U.S. State

Department's Passport Lookout System. For children who are registered in this program, the State Department will alert the child's parent(s) when a passport application is received for the child. Thus parents will be notified in advance of a potential abduction should a passport be requested for a child registered in this program.

CATEGORIES OF MISSING CHILDREN AND CHILD ABDUCTIONS

> When the lives and the rights of children are at stake, there must be no silent witnesses.
>
> —Carol Bellamy

According to Allen's (2009) review, children who are abducted are most commonly:

- Held for ransom
- Kidnapped as retaliation to engender fear or because of some grievance
- Used for extortion
- Sexually victimized
- Used as decoys to obtain information about border security

Both the National Center for Missing and Exploited Children and Child Find of America classify missing children into three major categories: runaways and throwaways, noncustodial parental abduction, and stranger abduction. Each of these categories is summarized in the following subsections (also see Paludi & Kelly, in press).

Runaways and Throwaways

Definitions and Incidence

Runaways are defined as children of 14 years or younger who leave home without permission from a parent or guardian for at least one night or two nights, or more if the child is older than 13 years of age.

"Situational runaways" include youths who leave home for a day or two following a disagreement with their parent(s) or guardians. "Chronic runaways" do not return home but rather live in transitory housing, shelters, or abandoned buildings, or underneath high bridges (Giffords, Alonso, & Bell, 2007; Sanchez, Waller, & Greene, 2006). "Terrified runners" are adolescents who run away because of sexually abusive parents (Finkelhor & Dziuba-Leatherman, 1974; Greene & Esselstyn, 1972; Quina & Carlson, 1989).

"Throwaways" or "thrownaways" are defined as youths who leave home because their parent(s) abandoned them, told them to leave, or subjected them to extreme neglect or physical and sexual abuse. Throwaways are linked with runaways; for example, it is common for youths to run away after parents threaten them with throwing them out of their homes (Sanchez, Waller & Greene, 2005).

Runaway and throwaway adolescents represent the largest category of missing children (Allen, 2009; Hammer, Finkelhor, & Sedlak, 2002), accounting for approximately 45 percent of all children reported missing during each year. Approximately 1.6 million and 2.8 million children and adolescents run away or are thrown out from their homes, respectively each year (Hammer et al., 2002; National Runaway Switchboard, 2009; Sanchez et al., 2006).

Situational runaways represent the largest group of runaways (Denoff, 1991; Pennbridge, Yates, David, & Mackenzie, 1990; Sanchez et al., 2006). Child Find of America (2009) and Kempf-Leonard and Johansson (2007) have reported that the majority of youth who run away or are thrown away are between 15 and 17 years old, with the gender ratio being approximately equal.

The incidence of international runaways has been increasing (Lugalla & Mbwambo, 1999). According to the U.S. Department of State, Foreign Affairs (2005), international runaway adolescents are traveling farther away from their families of origin for the following reasons (pp. 4–5):

1. The increasing number of international marriages, particularly those ending in divorce or separation
2. Availability of inexpensive commercial air transportation
3. The growing number of children with overseas travel experience and passports
4. The increasing availability of funds to minors, particularly the growing practice of issuing credit and debit cards to teenagers
5. The use of the Internet by sexual predators

Psychological Dimensions

Children and adolescents may run away for a variety of reasons: family problems, physical abuse, peer pressure, alcohol and other drug abuse, and sexual abuse (Child Find of America, 2009; Khong, 2008; Peled & Muzicant, 2008; Thompson & Pillai, 2006). Palenski and Launer (1987) identified a process of running away that involves five stages: (1) family disengagement, (2) effects of friends as role models, (3) recognizing the "right" situation, (4) shrinking alternatives, and (5) managing the residuals. According to these authors, in their research youths often did not perceive running away as a feasible solution until they saw peers with similar family problems leave home.

Palenski and Launer (1987) also found that youths frequently had misgivings about running away (managing the residuals). Youth must consider the realities of street life, including their needs for food, shelter, and school. Some runaway programs are available that can assist youth with these realities (Thompson & Pillai, 2006; also see the Appendix at the end of this chapter). However, most youths receive assistance from abductors and abusers they encounter on the street. Huttinger (1984) noted that "local and national call services and 'buy-a-kid' rings sell runaway children for a night or permanently" (p. 112). Runaway youths are the most vulnerable people to further abuse (Molino, 2007; Terrell, 1997). As Tedisco and Paludi (1996) stated:

> Runaway teens are not prepared for the callousness and indifference of individuals they encounter on the street, let alone the cruelty of some individuals who are waiting for the opportunity to abuse them even more. . . . These adolescents as well as those who appear alone and frightened are easily spotted and are quickly identifiable as "the new kids." (Huttinger, 1984)

Child Find of America (2009) reports that approximately 5,000 runaways die on the streets in the United States each year.

Runaway and thrownaway youths do not have health insurance or access to medical care. Consequently, they are prone to diseases. Runaway adolescents are among the groups with the highest rates of contracting HIV infection (Millstein, 1989) and often engage in prostitution to obtain money for their food, shelter, and drugs (Flowers, 2001). Furthermore, abductors use runaways as accomplices to their own crimes (Tedisco & Paludi, 1996).

Noncustodial Parental Abduction

Definition and Incidence

A noncustodial parental abduction is defined as one parent or other relative taking and keeping a child in violation of the custodial parent's rights. The U.S. Department of Justice has reported that approximately 203,900 children are victims of a family abduction, as indicated in the national NISMART study (2002). According to Child Find of America (2009), 35 percent of children abducted by a noncustodial parent are between 6 and 11 years of age. Furthermore, approximately 24 percent of the abductions last between one week and one month. Child Find of America (2009) reports that 21 percent of noncustodial abductions are committed by relatives.

Allen (2009) recently reported that the National Center for Missing and Exploited Children is involved in 558 cases in which children in the United States were abducted by a noncustodial parent to Mexico. He noted that

Mexico is the country to which most noncustodial abductors flee from the United States.

Psychological Dimensions

Noncustodial parents may abduct their children for a variety of reasons, including dissatisfaction with a court's custody decision, denial of visitation for not paying child support, anger against the former spouse or mate for ending the relationship and/or beginning a new relationship, and using the children as pawns in divorce and custody battles (Allender, 2007; Donner, 2006). The typical noncustodial parental abductor is male, less educated, and not born in the United States; has a psychiatric history; has previously faced criminal charges; and is not likely to be employed (Cole & Bradford, 1992; Hegar & Greif, 1991).

It is common practice for noncustodial parental abductors to tell the children that the custodial parent is unfit, ill, or dead; will kill them if they return; or is in a new relationship with a partner who does not want the children. Many of these children are also physically or sexually abused by the abducting parent (Johnston, Girdner, & Sagatun-Edwards, 1999). Consequently, noncustodial parental abductors move frequently and change their names and the names of their children. Children subjected to this experience, therefore, have little opportunity to develop a sense of trust, which is an important part of developing an identity (Donner, 2006).

The National Center for Missing and Exploited Children (2009) has identified conditions under which the likelihood of an international noncustodial parental abduction of a child is great: previous abduction, friends or family living in another country, financial independence (e.g., ability to work anywhere, recent sale of a home, bank account closures, liquidation of assets), no strong ties to the child's home state, instability in relationships, and a prior criminal record.

When abducting parents return to their country of birth, the physical distance makes locating, recovering, and returning children who were internationally abducted difficult (Girdner, 1994). Contributing to this complexity are a lack of sufficient funds to help locate such abducted children and differences in foreign countries' legislation related to child abductions compared to U.S. laws.

Hegar and Greif (1991) found that mothers whose children were abducted by their fathers reported more intimate-partner violence in their marriage, more fault-related reasons for divorce, and more force used in abducting the children than did fathers whose children were kidnapped by their mothers. Walker (1999) found that each year, at least 3.3 million children in the United States between the ages of 3 and 17 years are at risk of exposure to their mothers being battered by their fathers. Children may also be abused by the violent parent. Weiner (2000) noted that seven of nine Hague Convention cases that reached an appeals court in late 2000 involved a mother who abducted her child to escape a battering mate. Furthermore, research by Johnston, Sagatun-Edwards, Bloomquist, and Girdner (2000) concerning 634 abductions in California found that "mothers who abducted were more likely to take the children when they or the children were victims of abuse, and fathers who abducted were more likely to take the children when they were the abusers" (pp. 2–3).

With respect to international abductions, Shetty and Edleson (2005) noted that having children of battered women return to their country of habitual residence will expose them to the batterer while custody decisions take place:

> Mothers who abduct their children and flee to find a safe haven are not perpetrators, as the Hague Convention implies, but are victims of their partner's violence. They are also victims of an international treaty, written with good intentions, but, when implemented, [that] has unintended negative consequences for their safety and that of their children. (p. 135)

Paludi and Kelly (in press) have called for a redefinition of "habitual residence" to include a residence in which the child's well-being is secured and not prone to violence.

Stranger Abduction

Definitions, Incidence, and Psychological Dimensions

A stranger abduction (also referred to as a nonfamily abduction) is defined as an incident in which a stranger takes or detains a child without lawful authority or permission from the child's parents or legal guardians primarily for the purposes of ransom, sadistic or sexual assault, or murder (Finkelhor, Hammer, & Sedlak, 2002; Gallagher, Bradford, & Pease, 2002). Results from the National Incidence Studies of Missing, Abducted, Runaway and Thrownaway Children (NISMAET) estimated that stranger abductions account for approximately 2 percent of all abductions (Sedlak, Finkelhor, Hammer, & Schultz, 2002).

One in four abducted is are murdered by his or her abductor (Boudreaux, Lord, & Jarvis, 2001; Brown & Keppel, 2006). The murder of children by abductors may be classified into three categories (Lanning, 1994): (1) inadvertent, where the abductor may not have intended to murder the child; (2) indiscriminate, where the abductor may or may not have chosen the victim; and (3) most commonly, murder to avoid detection. Research indicates that the majority of victims of stranger abductions are likely to be murdered immediately or within 24 hours following the abduction (Boudreaux, Lord, & Dutra, 1999; Brown & Keppel, 2006; Hanfland,

Keppel, & Weis, 1997). Sex-related murders of abducted children are especially common (Heide, Beauregard, & Myers, 2009). Finkelhor, Hammer, and Sedlak (2002) reported that in 40 percent of stranger kidnappings, the child is murdered. Furthermore, children younger than 4 years and adolescents between 13 and 17 years are at highest risk for murder by a stranger abductor (Dalley, 2000).

Children who are vulnerable to stranger abductions include those who walk alone to or from school, wait for a school bus by themselves, ride a bicycle alone or at night, wait for rides in parking lots after dark, or wear articles of clothing that prominently display their names (thus permitting abductors to portray familiarity with the child).

Four subcategories of stranger abductors have been identified in the literature: pedophiles, profiteers, childless psychotics, and serial killers. The first three of these categories are summarized in the following subsections. We also refer the reader to Paludi and Kelly (in press) for more information.

Pedophiles

The American Psychiatric Association (2000) defines pedophilia as follows:

> [R]ecurrent, intense, sexual urges and sexually arousing fantasies, of at least six month's duration, involving sexual activity with a prepubescent child. The age of the child is generally 13 or younger. The age of the person is arbitrarily set at age 16 years or older and at least five years older than the child.

Thus a pedophile is a significantly older individual who prefers to have sex with persons legally considered children. The sexual fantasies and erotic imagery of the pedophile also focus on children (Stevens, 2001). Of course, not all pedophiles abduct children. Common characteristics of pedophiles include having been sexually molested at a younger age and having had ineffectual parenting and disciplining compared with individuals who were not sexually molested and are not pedophiles (Stevens, 2001).

As a result of their background, pedophiles typically identify with children better than with adults (Bahroo, 2005; Levant & Bass, 1991; Salter, 2004; Spilman, 2006). This identification with children allows them to seduce children; they utilize their understanding of difficulties with school and parents/step-parents to gain access to the targeted children (Tedisco & Paludi, 1996). Furthermore, the majority of pedophiles use child pornography for sexual arousal and gratification. This pornography is a prelude to sexual activity with children (Salter, 2004). The use of pornography in this setting is intended to lower children's inhibitions (Lanning, 1994; Stevens, 2001).

Profiteers

Profiteers are defined as individuals who criminally exploit children by selling them to traffickers, adoptive parents, or pornographers (Chase & Statham, 2005; Rafferty, 2008; Simkhada, 2008). Trafficking is characterized by physical and emotional trauma, humiliation, degradation, and violence associated with treatment of children as a commodity (Ireland, 2006; Rafferty, 2008).

Childless Psychotics

Childless psychotics are those individuals who abduct children—usually infants—because they have not been able to give birth to children of their own or have recently miscarried a child or had a child who was stillborn (Shogan, 2006; Strohman, 2005).

Characteristics of Stranger Abductors

Most stranger abductors share the following characteristics (Hanfland et al., 1997):

- Are male
- Are motivated by power, dominance, and control (not sex)
- Fuse aggression with sexuality
- Target victims within their own race
- Are 27 years old, on average
- Are unmarried
- Live alone or with their parents
- Are mostly unemployed
- Have a history of sexual, alcohol, drug, and mental problems
- Have been arrested for violent crimes
- Select victims from areas where they feel safe and their efforts to abduct children are minimized
- Express little or no concern, trust, or empathy for others, especially their victims
- Believe that the abduction does not have serious consequences for their victims

Types of Stranger Abduction

Burgess and Holmstrom (1974) have identified two kinds of modus operandi that apply to child abductors: "blitz attack" and "confidence assault." In the blitz attack, a stranger appears suddenly and shocks the child, thereby interfering with the child's defensive action and memory of the events. In contrast, the confidence assault is an elaborate scheme set up by the abductor, which entails several different stages:

1. Gaining the confidence or trust of the targeted victim
2. Manipulating the child into physical and psychological vulnerability
3. Convincing the child that he or she is a participant in the crime or caused the crime

Lanning (1994) refers to this kind of confidence assault as a psychological assault rather than a physical one.

Lures Used by Stranger Abductors

Stranger abductors commonly use lures (Boudreaux et al., 2000; Burgess & Holmstrom, 1974; Tedisco & Paludi, 1996), such as asking children for directions, asking children to help locate a missing pet, informing the child that his or her parent has been injured in an accident and is hurt, and offering to give children a ride home. Vulnerable children are more susceptible to these lures—for example, children who are quiet, who appear to have an intense need for adult affection and approval, are withdrawn, have poor social skills with children their own age, and come from divorced homes.

PSYCHOLOGICAL AND PHYSICAL IMPACT OF ABDUCTIONS ON CHILDREN

> There can be no better measure of our governance than the way we treat our children, and no greater failing on our part than to allow them to be subjected to violence, abuse or exploitation.
>
> —Jessica Lange

Research in domestic and international child abductions has documented the effects of such experiences on children's emotional/psychological functioning. These effects include, but are not limited to, guilt, denial, withdrawal from social settings, shame, depression, fear, anger, anxiety, phobias, isolation, fear of crime, helplessness, frustration, shock, and decreased self-esteem (Hatcher, Barton, & Brooks, 1992; Terr, 1983).

Psychological problems stemming from abductions are subtle and may not surface for several years. In addition, young children who have been abducted and abused may not be able to verbalize the effects of this victimization until they are older (Tedisco & Paludi, 1996).

Research has also documented that abducted children may develop post-traumatic stress disorder (PTSD) as a result of the abduction and subsequent physical or sexual abuse. Symptoms of PTSD include emotional numbness, sleep disturbances, irritability, difficulty in concentrating, and flashbacks that induce fearful feelings of reexperiencing the trauma (Lundberg-Love & Marmion, 2006).

In addition, the U.S. Department of Justice (as cited in Report on Compliance with the Hague Convention, 2008) noted that children who are victims of international abductions experience greater difficulty associated with adapting to new cultural norms and values. Furthermore, they may miss months or years of education. Their names are frequently changed, as are their birthdates and physical appearance so as to conceal their identity. According to the Report on Compliance with the Hague Convention (2008):

> If and when the child is reunited with the left-behind parent, they may find that they no longer have a relationship with that parent or even a language in common. They may be distrustful of the left-behind parent and question why that parent did not try harder to get them back. They may find that the left-behind parent has remarried and that they have a new, unfamiliar step-parent and siblings. Children who were abducted while very young may not even remember life with the left-behind parent. (p. 48)

The following are reported physical/health-related effects of abductions: headaches, tiredness, respiratory problems, substance abuse, sleep disturbances, eating disorders, lethargy, gastrointestinal disorders, and inability to concentrate (Finkelhor, Hotaling, & Sedlak, 1990).

Social Impact of Child Abductions

The effects abductions have on social and interpersonal relationships have included the following: withdrawal, fear of new people, lack of trust, changes in social network patterns, and relationship difficulties (Forehand, Long, Zogg, & Parrish, 1989; Schetky & Haller, 1983). Children victims of international abductions have difficulty making friends and, therefore, in forming this aspect of their identity (Report on Compliance with the Hague Convention, 2008). Lundberg-Love and Marmion (2006) note that adult women who were victims of child sexual abuse had emotional problems when compared with nonvictims, including clinical depression, drug abuse, panic, obsessive-compulsive symptoms, suicidal ideation, and deliberate attempts at self-harm. Furthermore, children may experience secondary victimization—that is, boys are likely to be physically assaulted and girls are likely to be sexually assaulted—as a consequence of the abduction (Plass, 2007).

Children and adolescents who try to escape the abductor frequently experience increased violence and the threat of death, blame for the abduction and abuse, and/or death of their family members. In addition, they respond to the victimization by developing a dissociative disorder as a psychological protection. Walker (1999) noted that in children younger than five years, multiple personalities may develop from the dissociation. Bryant (1992) found that children may become preverbal and may continue in a state of chronic shock if not permitted to express feelings related to the trauma.

Radiating Impact of Child Abductions and Missing Children

Parents experience trauma vicariously with their abducted children (Spilman, 2006; Janvier, McCormick, & Donaldson, 1990). Greif and Hegar (1991) also report that parents of abducted children experience feelings of rage, loss, loss of appetite, impaired sleep, and depression. The trauma for parents does not end when the child is recovered, however (Forehand et al., 1989; Hatcher et al., 1992): Many parents have concerns about their child being re-abducted. When an international child abduction occurs, left-behind parents may also have to deal with unfamiliar cultural, legal, and linguistic barriers while searching for their child (Report on Compliance with the Hague Convention, 2008).

Certainly financial pressures of dealing with child abductions, both domestic and international, make parents' emotional symptoms more pronounced. Left-behind parents of children who have been internationally abducted may have insufficient funds to travel to another country and often have an attorney who is unfamiliar with legal issues of abduction in that country. According to Fravel and Boss (1992), siblings of abducted children frequently develop symptoms of developmental regression and phobias. It is also common for parents to "overprotect" the remaining children following the abduction of a child (Forehand et al., 1989).

MAKING USE OF SOCIAL SCIENCE RESEARCH ON CHILD ABDUCTIONS AND MISSING CHILDREN: IMPLEMENTING TRAINING PROGRAMS FOR CHILDREN AND ADOLESCENTS

Bromberg (1997) recommended that training programs incorporate empirically validated principles of learning: modeling new behaviors, drill and reinforcement, maintenance of behaviors, training in neutral environments to promote generalization across settings, and teaching novel problems to ensure transfer of training to new situations. According to Bromberg (1997):

> Presenting children with an abduction prevention program is insufficient; children must receive the right kind of program. Such

programming includes frequent opportunities for rehearsal of
skills and receiving corrective feedback to shape appropriate
responses to potential abductors. (p. 8)

We refer the reader to a more detailed discussion of effective training programs by Paludi and Kelly (in press) that deals with needs assessments
and post-training evaluations.

Despite media attention and scholarly research paid to the issue of
missing children and child abductions, this topic is still not well understood (e.g., Bromberg, 1997; Finkelhor & Dziuba-Leatherman, 1995;
Newman, 1985). Common myths related to child abductions or abductions include the following misconceptions:

- An abductor is a psychotic human being, easily identifiable by chil-
  dren and adults.
- There are no long-term effects of abductions for those who are found.
- It is only young, helpless children who are the prey of abductors.
- Runaway children and adolescents are not targeted for abductions.
- Parental abduction is not a serious matter and is not a form of child
  abuse.
- Abductions do not happen here to the people I know—they happen
  somewhere else (Tedisco & Paludi, 1996).

Goals for training programs on child abductions and missing children
include to the following points:

1. Define "missing," to include nonparental abductions, runaways,
   throwaways, and stranger abductions.
2. Educate students about the legal definitions and behavioral examples of abductions.
3. Define "stranger" for children and adolescents, to include family
   acquaintances, neighbors, and individuals with whom families have
   brief contact (e.g., letter carriers, television repairperson).
4. Discuss "unsafe" places.
5. Discuss the impact of being abducted on children's and adolescents'
   emotional and physical well-being.
6. Discuss the effects of abductions on parents, siblings, friends, and
   schoolmates.
7. Tell children and adolescents what their rights and responsibilities
   are with respect to abductions.
8. Empower children and adolescents to take control of their bodies.
9. Discuss children's and adolescents' fears and anxieties about
   abductions.

10. Discuss lures commonly used by potential abductors.
11. Assist in making the child and adolescent knowledgeable about safety strategies to make the abductor's job of luring them more difficult.
12. Create an environment that is free of the fear of retaliation for speaking out about child abductions (Paludi & Kelly, in press).

Furthermore, training programs require dealing with children's and adolescents' assumptions and misconceptions as well as the anxieties brought about by the training itself. Thus training sessions must devote ample time to dealing with the children's and adolescents' feelings, misconceptions, and questions. Children and adolescents may want to discuss topics related to abductions and abuse following the training program in private with the trainer, without hearing any comments from peers. Because child abduction and abuse are intimate and frightening topics for children and adolescents, they are unlikely to ask questions in public (Paludi & Kelly, in press).

Effective curriculum projects take into account the cognitive stage of development in which children and adolescents currently reside (Tedisco & Paludi, 1996). Children and young adolescents must be provided with concrete examples, not hypothetical situations, so that they can fully understand definitions of missing children. Behavioral rehearsal or behavioral skills training (Poche, Brouwer, & Swearingen, 1981) would be recommended for children—for example, having them role-play positive solutions to conflict situations that are presented to them.

Older adolescents may be taught about abductions using case studies and scenarios about children who are confronted with a potential abduction and strategies for reporting an abduction to school officials, parents, law enforcement, and other authority figures. Examples of these case studies may be found in Tedisco and Paludi (1996). To be successful, such training programs must take into account children's and adolescents' egocentrism and help them to understand their own vulnerability to abductions.

Paludi and Kelly (in press) recommend that training programs focusing on "stranger danger" not be used when discussing noncustodial parental abductions (because the abductor in these cases is often a relative whom the child trusts). Furthermore, programs that encourage children to "Run, Yell, and Tell" may not be reasonable if the potential abduction occurs in a remote area or involves a noncustodial parent or relative. As Bromberg (1997) notes, "[I]t is likely that screaming will infuriate the would-be captor and that the adult is likely to attempt to render the child unconscious to prevent him or her from drawing the attention of individuals who might eventually pass within earshot of the screaming child victim" (p. 5). This strategy is also ineffective with international child abductions (Paludi & Kelly, in press).

In recent years, the National Center for Missing and Exploited Children and the Boys and Girls Clubs of America have recommended NetSmartz as an effective training program on missing children. NetSmartz is an Internet-based safety resource that makes use of educational activities to teach children and adolescents about child abductions. Its main goal is to empower children to make effective decisions in real life. According to the National Center for Missing and Exploited Children (2009), this goal is met through the following actions:

1. Enhancing the ability of children to recognize dangers on the Internet
2. Encouraging children to report victimization to a trusted adult
3. Supporting and enhancing community education efforts
4. Increasing communication between adults and children about online safety
5. Enhancing the ability of children to understand that people they first "meet" on the Internet should never be considered their friend (p. 1)

CONCLUSION

If we don't stand up for children, then we don't stand for much.
　　　　　　　　　　　　　　　　—Marian Wright Edelman

Media attention given to missing children helps break the silence surrounding child abductions and runaway children and adolescents. Recent magazine articles in *People* and programs on the *Oprah Winfrey* show, for example, should prove beneficial in helping the public replace myths with facts about missing children. As Tedisco and Paludi (1996) note, "Silence enhances our illusion of the invulnerability for non victims. It is because none of our children and adolescents are safe that the silence must be broken" (p. 20).

Unfortunately, despite the media attention and scholarly publications devoted to this topic, many individuals simply do not believe their lives can be affected by missing children. All too many parents engage in counterproductive behavior with respect to keeping their children safe. Consider the mother who goes into a store to buy a diet soda for herself and leaves toddlers and infants alone in an unlocked car with the front door open, the parents who dress their young children in clothing and backpacks that prominently display their first names, and the parents who allow toddlers and young children to run around a park unattended. What is equally upsetting is that most individuals witness these occurrences yet do not intervene (Banyard, Plante, & Moynihan, 2003; Berkowitz, 2009).

Lerner's (1980) "just world hypothesis" can help to explain why individuals are reluctant to accept the reality of child abductions and fail to intervene on behalf of children. Most people believe that bad things occur only to those people who bring on or deserve the consequences of their actions. These individuals tend to find a personal reason to explain the abduction: something the child said, poor parenting skills, and so on. According to Paludi and Kelly (in press), this perspective serves as a coping mechanism because the alternative realization for people is frightening— that an abduction could happen to their children or to the children of those people who are close to them.

Furthermore, programs offering to fingerprint children may mislead parents about their children's safety. These programs claim to protect children from being abducted, and parents may believe that they are doing all they can do if they have their child fingerprinted. In reality, fingerprinting does not prevent abductions; it is used to identify a child or a corpse.

To decrease the number of missing children, accurate information must be provided to assist parents and guardians in their roles as child protectors. The National Center for Missing and Exploited Children and Child Find of America both provide recommendations for parents/guardians, teachers, and childcare workers (see the Appendix at the end of this chapter) for prevention, including making the following points (also see Tedisco & Paludi, 1996):

1. Maintain a complete description of the child (e.g., height, weight, hair and eye color, distinguishing features, impairments, scars, birthmarks, broken bones, date of birth).
2. Take head and shoulder photographs of children at least twice a year.
3. Have dental charts prepared by the child's dentist/oral surgeon.
4. Know how to access medical records immediately.

A sample Child Identification Sheet may be found in Tedisco and Paludi (1996).

In addition, we recommend the following parenting strategies:

1. Parents must teach their children their full name, address, and telephone number as soon as possible.
2. Parents must teach children how to dial 911 for emergency assistance.
3. Parents and children must select a "code word" or "code phrase." If the parent is unable to pick up the child at school, the person who claims to be at the school on behalf of the parent must use the code word or phrase before school personnel will allow the child to accompany this individual. Once the code word is used, a new code word must be taught to the child.
4. Parents must teach children the difference between "good touch" and "bad touch."
5. Children must not be taught by parents to give unconditional affection.

6. Parents need to identify uniformed individuals to whom their children can go for assistance.
7. Children must be taught never to answer the door or phone when they are home alone.
8. Children must be taught to never tell anyone they are home alone.
9. Parents must inform babysitters to never release children under any circumstances to anyone unless so designated by the parents.

Behavioral examples of these recommendations may be found in Tedisco and Paludi (1996). In addition, sample curricula for teachers to use in discussing missing children may be found in the same source.

Recommendations for parents and guardians when children are missing include notifying the police ("Please send an officer. I am reporting a missing child.") and providing the following information (Tedisco & Paludi, 1996):

1. Child's name
2. Date of birth of child
3. Weight, height, distinguishing features, scars, and other identifying personal information
4. Unique identifiers(e.g., eyeglasses, pierced ears, braces)
5. Clothing the child was wearing
6. Time the child was last seen

In addition, parents must demand that their child be immediately entered into the National Crime Information Center's Missing Persons File.

A key aspect of protecting children is to provide training programs on child abductions and missing children for parents, childcare workers, and teachers. The main goal of such training programs is for adults themselves to become "street-wise" about this issue. Parents and teachers must make children comfortable about reporting situations when an individual has approached them or touched them inappropriately. Children's ability to disclose this information will, in turn, help law enforcement personnel in their investigations.

Unfortunately, most parenting and child and adolescent development books do not address missing children and child abductions. Instead, these books focus on teaching children to become independent and autonomous, to respect authority and behave according to social rules. This advice very often runs counter to the way parents should be raising "street-smart" children. John Walsh, father of Adam Walsh, a young boy who was abducted and murdered, once noted that he wished he and his wife had spent more time encouraging Adam to respect his safety instead of respecting adults' authority: "If I had taught him to scream, he might be alive now" (quoted in Gelman, 1984, p. 86).

Children and adolescents who survived an abduction and accompanying abuse can teach us what we as parents, educators, and concerned citizens need to know about missing children. Their stories are important for those who develop curricula and policies on missing children, for those who counsel victims and their families and friends, and for those who represent children and adolescents in court. We conclude this chapter with words from survivors of abductions and their families:

Jimmy

> The court decided that I should live permanently with my Dad but keep on seeing my mother on weekends. Well, that made my mother so mad that she decided to steal me. One weekend when I was visiting her, she and Don packed up their car with a lot of stuff and we all piled in. I kept asking her, "Where are we going?" And finally she said, "Take a wild guess." I guessed a couple of places and finally I said Florida because that was the one place she had talked about a lot—she had some relatives who lived there ... I remember asking her, "What about Daddy?" And she just said, "Don't worry about it." (Krementz, 1984, pp. 30–31)

Elizabeth Smart

> after that, he proceeded to rape me.... He said that he would kill anybody that would come into the camp, or kill me if I ever tried to escape or yell out. ("Elizabeth Smart Says She Was Raped Repeatedly," 2009, p. 2)

Terry Probyn (the mother of an abducted and recently found young woman, Jaycee Dugard)

> All of us are doing very well under the circumstances.... We especially appreciate everyone recognizing that what we need most right now is to be allowed to become a family again within a zone of privacy and security. We hope that our story focuses attention on all of the children still missing, and on their need to be found. We must keep looking for them. As Jaycee shows, miracles can happen. ("Jaycee Dugard's Mom," 2009)

Stan Patz (the father of Etan Patz, who went missing in 1979 and who has never been found)

> I have photos of him in my place. He's with us all the time.... In our minds there were only two possibilities ... either Etan was taken by a stranger and killed or he was taken by a ... woman desperate for

a child of her own, and we hoped that such a woman would at least take care of him and keep him safe. ("Etan Patz," 2009, p. 1)

Convinced his son's killer is prisoner Jose Antonio Ramos, Patz sends Etan's missing children's poster to Ramos annually and pens on the back of the photo: "What have you done with my son?" (BellaOnline, 2009).

John Walsh (the father of abducted and murdered child Adam Walsh)

In the years since my son, Adam, was abducted and murdered, I have traveled all across this country to advocate for changes in the system. The only way I have found to make meaningful and permanent change is to work through the system. One of the most effective ways is to change laws. The quality of a child's life in the legal, education, criminal justice, and social services systems varies greatly from state to state. Therefore we need to begin our work in each of the state legislatures if we are to make significant change. (National Center for Missing and Exploited Children, 1993, p. xiii)

All too often, those who have lost or are still searching for a missing child wish they had known where to turn and what to do. It is imperative that resources and education are provided to the public at large, especially parents, teachers, childcare workers, and, of course, children. Knowledge is the first defense against the threat of child abductors and spreading the word, even if it saves one child, is worth all of the effort.

APPENDIX: RESOURCES ON CHILD ABDUCTIONS AND MISSING CHILDREN

AMBER Alert: www.amberalert.gov
Child Abduction Resource Center: www.globalmissing.com
Child Find of America: www.childfindofamerica.org
Childfind Canada (Canada): http://www.childfind.ca/
Child Focus (Belgium): http://www.childfocus.org
Committee for Missing Children, Inc.: www.findthekids.org
Find the Children: www.findthechildren.com
Hague Conference Permanent Bureau-Child Abduction Section: hcch.e-vision.nl/index_en.php?
Lost Children's Network: www.lostchildren.org
Missing Children Society of Canada: www.mcsc.ca
National Center for Missing and Exploited Children: www .missingkids.com
National Runaway Switchboard: http://www.1800runaway.org/
Polly Klaas Foundation: http://www.pollyklaas.org/

Team HOPE: Support for Families with Missing Children: www
    .teamhope.org
Vanished Children's Alliance: www.vca.org

NOTES

1. Partners of the Hague Convention include Argentina, Australia, Austria, Bahamas, Belgium, Belize, Bosnia and Herzegovina, Brazil, Bulgaria, Burkina Faso, Canada, China (Hong Kong and Macau only), Colombia, Costa Rica, Croatia, Cyprus, Czech Republic, Denmark, Dominican Republic, Ecuador, El Salvador, Estonia, Finland, France, Germany, Honduras, Hungary, Iceland, Ireland, Israel, Italy, Latvia, Lithuania, Luxembourg, Macedonia, Malta, Mauritius, Mexico, Monaco, Montenegro, Netherlands, New Zealand, Norway, Panama, Paraguay, Peru, Poland, Portugal, Romania, Saint Kitts and Nevis, San Marino, Serbia, Slovakia, Slovenia, South Africa, Sweden, Switzerland, Turkey, Ukraine, United Kingdom (Bermuda, Cayman Islands, Falkland Islands, Isle of Man, Montserrat), Uruguay, Venezuela, and Zimbabwe.

2. Member states include Austria, Belgium, Czech Republic, Denmark, France, Germany, Greece, Hungary, Ireland, Italy, Poland, Portugal, Romania, Slovak Republic, Spain, and the United Kingdom.

3. Clearinghouses for missing children and child abductions exist in each of the 50 states, the District of Columbia, Puerto Rico, U.S. Virgin Islands, Canada, and the Netherlands. Clearinghouses have the following functions, as identified by the National Center for Missing and Exploited Children (2009):

1. Collecting and maintaining computerized data and investigative information on missing persons in the states
2. Compiling statistics on the number of missing children's cases handled and the number resolved by the clearinghouse each year
3. Assisting in the training of law enforcement and other professionals on issues relating to missing and unidentified persons
4. Operating a clearinghouse of information regarding methods of locating and recovering missing persons
5. Keeping and distributing information regarding methods of locating and recovering missing persons
6. Assisting in the preparation and dissemination of flyers describing missing persons and their abductors
7. Publishing, on a regular basis, a directory of missing persons for dissemination to state and local public and nonprofit agencies and to the public
8. Establishing and operating a statewide, toll-free telephone line for reports of missing persons and reports of sightings of missing persons

REFERENCES

Allen, E. (2009, August). *Child abductions: Globally, nationally and along the U.S./ Mexican border.* Presentation to the U.S. Department of Justice, Office of Justice Programs, San Diego, CA.

Allender, D. (2007, July). Child abductions: Nightmares in progress. *FBI Law Enforcement Bulletin*. Retrieved April 21, 2010, from http://www.fbi.gov/ publications/leb/2007/july2007/july2007leb.htm

American Psychiatric Association. (2001). *Diagnostic and statistical manual of mental disorders* (DSM-IV-R). Washington, DC: Author.

Bahroo, B. (2005). Pedophilia: Psychiatric insights. *Family Court Review, 41*, 497–507.

Banyard, V., Plante, E., & Moynihan, M. (2003). Bystander education: Bringing a broader community perspective to sexual violence prevention. *Journal of Community Psychology, 32*, 61–79.

BellaOnline. (2009). Missing and exploited children site. Retrieved October 15, 2009, from www.bellaonline.com/articles/art22761.asp.

Berkowitz, A. (2009, April). *Bystander intervention*. Presentation made to the U.S. Army Sexual Harassment/Assault Prevention Summit, Arlington, VA.

Boudreaux, M., Lord, W., & Dutra, R. (1999). Child abduction: Age-based analyses of offender, victim, and offense characteristics in 550 cases of alleged child disappearance. *Journal of Forensic Sciences, 44*, 539–553.

Boudreaux, M., Lord, W., & Etter, S. (2000). Child abduction: An overview of current and historical perspectives. *Child Maltreatment, 5*, 63–71.

Boudreaux, M., Lord, W., & Jarvis, P. (2001). Understanding child homicide: The role of access, vulnerability and routine activities theory. *Trauma, Abuse and Violence, 2*, 56–78.

Bromberg, D. (1997). Behavioral versus traditional approaches to prevention of child abduction. *School Psychology Review, 26*, 622–633.

Brown, K., & Keppel, R. (2006). Child abduction murder: An analysis of the effect of time and distance separation between murder incident sites on solvability. *Journal of Forensic Sciences, 52*, 137–145.

Bryant, C. (1992). The victimology of children: A transpersonal conceptual treatment model. In E. Viano (Ed.), *Critical issues in victimology: International perspectives* (pp. 118–129). New York: Springer.

Burgess, A., & Holmstrom, L. (1974). Rape: Sexual disruption and recovery. *American Journal of Orthopsychiatry, 49*, 648.

Chase, E., & Statham, J. (2005). Commercial and sexual exploitation of children and young people in the UK: A review. *Child Abuse Review, 14*, 3–25.

Child Find of America. (2009). www.childfindofamerica.org.

Cole, W., & Bradford, J. (1992). Abduction during custody and access disputes. *Canadian Journal of Psychiatry, 37*, 264–266.

Dalley, M. (2000). *Stranger abduction*. Canada's Missing Children Annual Report. Missing Children's Registry, Royal Canadian Mounted Police. Ottawa, ON.

Denoff, M. (1991). Irrational beliefs, situational attributions, and the coping responses of adolescent runaways. *Journal of Rational-Emotive and Cognitive-Behavior Therapy, 9*, 113–135.

Donner, M. (2006). Tearing the child apart: The contribution of narcissism, envy, and perverse modes of thought to child custody wars. *Psychoanalytic Psychology, 23*, 542–553.

Elizabeth Smart says she was raped repeatedly. (2009). *Fox News*. Retrieved October 15, 2009, from www.foxnews.com/story/0,2933,558548,00.html.

Etan Patz: The boy on milk carton still missing after 30 years. (2009). *NowPublic*. Retrieved October 15, 2009, from www.nowpublic.com/world/etan-patz -boy-milk-carton-still-missing-after-30-years.

Finkelhor, D. (1995). The victimization of children: A developmental perspective. *American Journal of Orthopsychiatry, 65*, 177–193.

Finkelhor, D., & Dziuba-Leatherman, J. (1994). Victimization of children. *American Psychologist, 49*, 173–183.

Finkelhor, D., Hammer, H., & Sedlak, A. (2002). *Nonfamily abducted children: National estimates and characteristics*. Washington, DC: U.S. Department of Justice.

Finkelhor, D., Hotaling, G., & Sedlak, A. (1990). *Missing, abducted, runaway and thrownaway children in America: First report of national incidence studies*. Washington, DC: U.S. Department of Justice.

Flowers, R. (2001). *Runaway kids and teenage prostitution: America's lost, abandoned and sexually exploited children*. Westport, CT: Praeger.

Forehand, R., Long, N., Zogg, C., & Parrish, E. (1989). Child abduction: Parent and child functioning following return. *Clinical Pediatrics, 28*, 311–316.

Fravel, D., & Boss, P. (1992). An in-depth interview with the parents of missing children. *Quantitative Methods in Family Research*, 126–145.

Gallagher, B., Bradford, M., & Pease, K. (2002). The sexual abuse of children by strangers: Its extent, nature and victims' characteristics. *Children and Society, 16*, 346–359.

Gelman, D. (1984, March 19). *Stolen children*. Newsweek, pp. 87–86.

Giffords, E., Alonso, C., & Bell, R. (2007). A transitional living program for homeless adolescents: A case study. *Child and Youth Care Forum, 36*, 131–151.

Girdner, L. (1994). Introduction. In L. Girdner & P. Holt (Eds.), *Obstacles to the recovery and return of parentally abducted children: Final report* (pp. 1–13). Washington, DC: U.S. Department of Justice.

Greene, N., & Esselstyn, T. (1972). The beyond-control girl. *Juvenile Justice, 23*, 13–19.

Griffin, T., & Miller, M. (2008). Child abduction, AMBER alert and crime control theatre. *Criminal Justice Review, 33*, 159–176.

Hammer, H., Finkelhor, D., & Sedlak, A. (2002). *Children abducted by family members: National estimates and characteristics*. NISMART Bulletin. Washington, DC: U.S. Department of Justice.

Hanfland, K., Keppel, R., & Weis, J. (1997). *Case management for missing children homicide investigation*. Olympia, WA: Attorney General of Washington.

Hatcher, C., Barton, C., & Brooks, L. (1992). *Families of missing children: Final report*. Washington, DC: U.S. Department of Justice.

Hegar, R., & Greif, G. (1991). Abduction of children by their parents: A survey of the problem. *Social Work, 36*, 421–426.

Heide, K., Beauregard, E., & Myers, W. (2009). Sexually motivated child abduction murders: Synthesis of the literature and case illustration. *Victims and Offenders, 4*, 58–75.

Huttinger, B. (1984). *My child is not missing: A parent's guidebook for the prevention and recovery of missing children*. Plantation, FL: Child Safe Products.

Ireland, K. (2006). Sexual exploitation of children and international travel and tourism. *Child Abuse Review, 2*, 263–270.

Janvier, R., McCormick, K., & Donaldson, R. (1990). Parental kidnapping: A survey of left-behind parents. *Juvenile and Family Court Journal, 41*, 1–8.

Jaycee Dugard's mom: "Miracles can happen." (2009). *People*. Retrieved October 15, 2009, from www.people.com/people/article/0,,20307746,00.html.

Johnston, J., Girdner, L., & Sagatun-Edwards, I. (1999). Developing profiles of risk for parental abduction of children from a comparison of families victimized by abduction with families litigating custody. *Behavioral Sciences and the Law,* *17,* 305–322.

Johnston, J., Sagatun-Edwards, I., Blomquist, M., & Girdner, L. (2000). *Prevention of* *family abduction through early identification of risk factors.* Washington, DC: Office of Juvenile Justice and Delinquency Prevention, U.S. Department of Justice.

Kempf-Leonard, K., & Johansson, P. (2007). Gender and runaways: Risk factors, delinquency, and juvenile justice experiences. *Youth Violence and Juvenile* *Justice, 5,* 308–327.

Khong, L. (2008). Runaway youths in Singapore: Exploring demographics, motivations and environments. *Children and Youth Services Review, 31,* 125–139.

Krementz, J. (1984). *How it feels when parents divorce.* New York: Knopf.

Lanning, K. (1994, Spring). Child molesters: A behavioral analysis. *School Safety,* pp. 12–17.

Lerner, M. (1980). *The belief in a just world: A fundamental delusion.* New York: Plenum Press.

Levant, M., & Bass, B. (1991). Parental identification of rapists and pedophiles. *Psychological Reports, 69,* 463–466.

Lugalla, J., & Mbwambo, J. (1999). Street children and street life in urban Tanzania: The culture of surviving and its implications for children's health. *International* *Journal of Urban and Regional Research, 23,* 329–344.

Lundberg-Love, P., & Marmion, S. (2006). *Intimate violence against women.* Westport, CT: Praeger.

Miller, M., & Clinkinbeard, S. (2006). Improving the AMBER alert system: Psychology research and policy recommendations. *Law and Psychology Review, 30,* 1–21.

Millstein, S. (1989). *Behavioral risk factors for AIDS among adolescents.* Paper presented at the annual meeting of the Society for Research in Child Development, Kansas City, MO.

Missing Children Europe. (2009). Retrieved October 8, 2009, from www.missing childreneurope.eu/?q=node/15.

Molino, A. (2007). *Characteristics of help-seeking street youth and non-street youth.* Paper presented at the 2007 National Symposium on Homelessness Research., Washington, DC.

Moskowitz, G. (2005). The Hague Convention on international child abduction and the grave risk of harm exception. *Family Court Review, 41,* 580–596.

National Center for Missing and Exploited Children. (1993). *Selected state* *legislation: A guide for effective state laws to protect children.* Arlington, VA: Author.

National Center for Missing and Exploited Children. (2009). www.missingkids .com.

National Runaway Switchboard. (2009). http://www.1800runaway.org/.

Newman, S. (1985). *Never say yes to a stranger.* New York: Perigee.

Palenski, J., & Launer, H. (1987). The process of running away: A redefinition. *Adolescence, 22,* 347–362.

Paludi, M., & Kelly, K. (in press). Missing children and child abductions: An international human rights issue. In M. Paludi (Ed.), *Feminism and women's* *rights worldwide.* Westport, CT: Praeger.

Peled, E., & Muzicant, A. (2006). The meaning of home for runaway girls. *Journal of* *Community Psychology, 36,* 434–451.

Pennbridge, J., Yates, G., David, T., & Mackenzie, R. (1990). Runaway and homeless youth in Los Angeles County, California. *Journal of Adolescent Health Care, 11,* 159–165.

Plass, P. (2007). Secondary victimizations in missing child events. *American Journal of Criminal Justice, 32,* 30–44.

Poche, C., Brouwer, R., & Swearingen, M. (1981). Teaching self-protection to young children. *Journal of Applied Behavior Analysis, 14,* 169–176.

Quina, K., & Carlson, N. (1989). *Rape, incest, and sexual harassment: A guide for helping survivors.* New York: Praeger.

Rafferty, Y. (2008). The impact of trafficking on children: Psychological and social policy perspectives. *Child Development Perspectives, 2,* 13–18.

Report on Compliance with the Hague Convention. (2008). *Civil aspects of international child abduction.* Washington, DC: U.S. Department of State.

Reynolds, S. (2006). International parental abduction: Why we need to expand custody rights protected under the Child Abduction Convention. *Family Court Review, 44,* 464–483.

Salter, A. (2004). *Predators: Pedophiles, rapists, and other sex offenders.* New York: Basic Books.

Sanchez, R., Waller, M., & Greene, J. (2006). Who runs? A demographic profile of runaway youth in the United States. *Journal of Adolescent Health, 39,* 778–781.

Schetky, D., & Haller, I. (1983). Child psychiatry and law: Parental kidnapping. *Journal of the American Academy of Child Psychiatry, 22,* 279–285.

Sedlak, A., Finkelhor, D, Hammer, H., & Schultz, D. (2002). *National estimates of missing children: An overview.* Washington, DC: U.S. Department of Justice.

Shetty, S., & Edleson, J. (2005). Adult domestic violence in cases of international parental child abduction. *Violence Against Women, 11,* 115–138.

Shogan, M. (2006). Emergency management plan for newborn abduction. *Journal of Obstetric, Gynecologic and Neonatal Nursing, 31,* 340–346.

Simkhada, P. (2008). Life histories and survival strategies amongst sexually trafficked girls in Nepal. *Children and Society, 22,* 235–248.

Spilman, S. (2006). Child abduction, parents' distress, and social support. *Violence and Victims, 21,* 149–165.

Stevens, D. (2001). Inside the mind of sexual offenders: Predatory rapists, pedophiles, and criminal profiles. Bloomington, IA: IUniverse

Strohman, L. (2005). Stranger infant abductions: Offense characteristics, victim selection, and offender motivation of female offenders. Thesis submitted to Drexel University. Retrieved April 21, 2010, from http://idea.library.drexel.edu/bitstream/1860/497/9/Strohman_Lisa_Kathleen.pdf.

Tedisco, J., & Paludi, M. (1996). *Missing children.* Albany, NY: State University of New York Press.

Terr, L. (1983). Child snatching: A new epidemic of an ancient malady. *Journal of Pediatrics, 103,* 151–156.

Terrell, N. (1997). Street life: Aggravated and sexual assaults among homeless and runaway adolescents. *Youth Society, 28,* 267–290.

Thompson, S., & Pillai, V. (2006). Determinants of runaway episodes among adolescents using crisis shelter services. *International Journal of Social Welfare, 15,* 142–149.

U.S. Department of State Foreign Affairs. (2005). Runaways, abandoned children, and other unaccompanied minors. Retrieved October 11, 2009, from http://www.state.gov/documents/organization/86824.pdf.

Walker, L. (1999). Psychology and domestic violence around the world. *American Psychologist, 54*, 21–29.

Weiner, M. (2000). International child abduction and the escape from domestic violence. *Fordham Law Review, 69*, 593.

Zgoba, K. (2004). The Amber Alert: The appropriate solution to preventing child abduction? *Journal of Psychiatry and Law, 32*, 71–88.

Chapter 3

Perils in Cyberspace: Current Trends in Cyberbullying

June F. Chisholm

With the increased use of information communication technologies (ICTs) by children and adolescents, the past few years have witnessed the emergence of cyberbullying, involving a range of activities perpetrated by some youths and adults who misuse and/or abuse these technologies so as to endanger the well-being of children, adolescents, and adults alike. Thus, for some, entering cyberspace is more of a trek through a cyber-wilderness, reminiscent of the Wild West in the United States in the 1800s. In other words, the history of the expansion of the United States into the "new frontier" during this period reveals a time of achievements, rapid growth, and development as well as a sense of lawlessness and danger—all of which can be said of the cyber-frontier as well.

Within the past 15 years, a variety of agencies, organizations, and national and international groups have made a concerted effort to formulate policies to ensure cyberspace safety. Preventive strategies continue to be developed to deal with the psychological problems associated with cyberbullying, which threaten to affect many children and adolescents growing up in this digital age. The complexity of the problem, which involves many different constituencies, each with its own perspective and concerns as well as conflicting values, is presented in the literature, which emphasizes the commonalities as well as the substantive differences between conventional bullying and cyberbullying. This chapter provides an overview of the definitions of cyberbullying, reviews the scope of the problem, and explores the physical and psychological effects of the abuse of these digital technologies on children and youth. Current research and future directions for research are discussed as well. The chapter concludes with a review of recommendations for promoting cybersafety through collaborative efforts, from micro- to macro-level perspectives, to develop policies and better preventive strategies to ensure the psychological well-being of children, adolescents, and young adults.

INTRODUCTION

> Sticks and stones may break your bones, but cyber deeds and words can literally and virtually kill you!
> —J. Chisholm (2009)

The oldest members of the "Net" generation are now in their early thirties. The computer and online activity are for them what the telegraph, telephone, and television were for generations who preceded them. The experiences of these different generations have been profoundly affected by the technologies of their respective eras. The knowledge required to use these technologies encompasses both expertise and skills in the mechanical use of the equipment and knowledge about the purpose for which the technology is to be used. For the baby-boomer generation, introduction of the television and visual media heralded the age of information and presaged the era of globalization. By switching TV channels—first manually for a few years, and then later with a remote device—baby boomers could watch programs for entertainment in their living rooms as well as learn about past, present, and future fictional and real events. They were also informed about regional and international cultural, economic, and sociopolitical matters through these media. By comparison, for the "Net" generation, the use of the computer and other ICTs (cell phones, personal digital assistants [PDAs], palm-top devices) has created a global interactive communication and social networking community that transcends personal, geographical, geopolitical, and socioeconomic boundaries.

The following anecdotal account of a student in the author's course on the Psychology of Women illustrates that this virtual community can provide positive experiences:

> I've been extremely lucky to never have been a victim of online bullying. On the contrary, the most memorable experiences I've had with online technology have been positive. In February of last year, I started a blog dealing with gender relations. I felt (and still feel) that

society discourages women my age from reaching their potential by distracting them with body image issues and pressuring them into a convenient stereotype by convincing them that it is the only way they will find a boyfriend. I felt (and still feel) that women are also discouraged from appreciating their bodies and enjoying their sexuality and that there isn't enough feminine energy in our patriarchal society.

I began my blog in the hopes that a couple of people might get something out of it. Perhaps if I talked about sex candidly and accurately, it could encourage another [woman] to be more honest with herself . . . My ambitions were not high.

So it came as a pretty big shock when I realized there were over a hundred people reading my blog. I walked into my class one morning and everyone had something to say about the post from the night before—including my professor. Suddenly I was being interviewed for women's studies and media classes. I was getting messages from strangers, male and female, thanking me. I even got offered a ticket to an Off-Broadway show because the sound guy read my blog! I never expected this to happen when I began. I am so honored that my opinions have sparked some conversation and I'm grateful for the internet for allowing me to do that. (D.S., 2009)

In recent years, the concerns about the abuse and misuse of ICTs as well as the harmful effects on victims of some online activity have been discussed in the literature. In 2005, a private high school in New Jersey banned blogs and MySpace.com accounts in an effort to protect students from exposure to or engagement in inappropriate and/or illegal activities online (e.g., sexual exploitation by predators, harassment). This action generated controversy: Those opposed to the move questioned the legality of the decision as well as the wisdom in banning the online sites rather than educating students about the inherent dangers in using these sites (Bruno, 2004).

Lauren Newby, a high school sophomore from Dallas, Texas. was victimized by nasty messages posted on a message board (e.g., "Lauren is a fat cow MOO BITCH"; "People don't like you because you are a suicidal cow who can't stop eating"); a bottle of acid was thrown at her front door and her car was vandalized (Benfer, 2001). Megan Meier, a teenager from Missouri, committed suicide after discovering that two former friends and their parents were involved in a hoax, creating an online profile of a fictional boy who became friends with her and via messages suggested a romantic interest in her (Pokin, 2007). In January 2009, three adolescent females allegedly sent nude or semi-nude cell phone pictures of themselves to three male classmates in a western Pennsylvania high school. All of the young women who allegedly sent the photos, as well as the teenage boys who received them, were charged with child pornography

("Sexting, Shockingly Common Among Teens," 2009). Indeed, according to a nationwide survey conducted by the National Campaign to Support Teen and Unplanned Pregnancy (n.d.), roughly 20 percent of teens admit to participating in "sexting."

Many youths today are technologically savvy about how to use these technologies (Yan, 2006). Consequently, their access to computers and some online activities have improved their academic performance and enhanced their cognitive abilities (Jackson, von Eye, Biocca, Barbatsis, Zhao, & Fitzgerald, 2006), visual/spatial skills, and image representation skills associated with playing certain types of computer games (e.g., action games that involve rapid movement, intense interaction, and simultaneously occurring multiple activities) (Subrahmanyam, Greenfield, Kraut, & Gross, 2001).

Despite their understanding of the technical complexity of ICTs, many of these youths remain deficient in comprehending the ramifications of some of the uses to which these technologies are applied, especially the complexities associated with social networking and communication (Yan, 2006). The ability of youth to distinguish between online behaviors that pose little or no risk of harm to self and others is contingent upon an interplay of factors including, but not limited to (1) the amount of time spent online engaged in certain social interactive activities; (2) their cognitive/emotional development and level of functioning; and (3) the extent of parental/adult monitoring/supervision of online activity (Liau, Khoo, & Ang, 2005; Mitchell, Finkelhor, & Wolak, 2001).

The ability of some young adults, who have grown up in this digital age, to distinguish between appropriate or inappropriate online behaviors may also be affected by a change in values about the rules of social discourse influenced by the development and use of the newer technologies. I am reminded of a presentation on cyberbullying I gave to 20 young school psychologists in June 2009, describing what they could expect in their schools and what their role might be in addressing this problem. We were reviewing email "netiquette" (i.e., Internet etiquette) and discussing the importance of obtaining permission from the sender of an email message before forwarding all or part of the email message to others unless otherwise instructed within the email. Not obtaining permission and forwarding all or part of an email communication could be a form of harassment, depending on the circumstances. Approximately one third of this group was shocked to hear this statement and acknowledged that they routinely engaged in this behavior.

Their experience and online behavior reflect another aspect of this problem: The policies and preventive strategies that might otherwise effectively combat cyberbullying among our youth are complicated by a shift in values over a number of years of what is customary, ordinary, and acceptable ways of communicating online. Young adults, having grown up in a digital age, may contribute to our understanding of the complexities inherent in the rules of engagement in online activity of which cyberbullying reflects an extreme, unacceptable deviation.

BULLYING DEFINED

The American Psychiatric Association (APA, 2004) has specified that bullying:

1. Is aggressive behavior, different from other forms of aggression, the intent of which is to harm, humiliate, and/or distress someone.
2. Involves a power differential between the bully and the victim, and occurs repeatedly over time.
3. Takes different forms including, but not limited to, teasing, name calling, social exclusion, and physical or sexual harassment.
4. Differs based on gender, such that male victims report more physical abuse, whereas while females are more likely subjected to rumor spreading. Females are more likely to be bullied by females and males, whereas males are more likely to be bullied by males.
5. Has effects on victims that include anxiety, depression, loneliness, lowered self-esteem, school absenteeism, suicidal ideation, and other negative psychological conditions.
6. Is perpetrated by those who tend to condone violence as a means to manage conflict.
7. Is perpetrated by those who exhibit other problem behaviors including drinking alcohol, truancy, vandalism, and other antisocial behaviors.
8. Tends to target members of "out-groups" (e.g., sexual minorities, ethnic minorities, children and youth with disabilities).

CYBERBULLYING DEFINED

Cyberbullying, in some respects, is similar to traditional bullying in terms of the characteristics outlined by the APA (2004). In fact, some research analyzing the difference between traditional bullying and cyberbullying suggests that cyberbullying is a variant of traditional bullying (e.g., many victims know their online harasser) (APA, 2004; Kowalski & Limber, 2007; Li, 2007; Snider, 2004). Others view cyberbullying as distinct from traditional bullying because of the unique psychological processes involved in cyberbullying and being cyberbullied (Beckerman & Nocero, 2002; Harris, Petrie, & Willoughby, 2002; Van der Wal, de Wit, & Hirasing, 2003; Willard, 2003; Ybarra & Mitchell, 2004). Still others suggest that because of a lack of conceptual clarity between traditional or "schoolyard bullying" and cyberbullying, the term "cyberbullying" should be reserved for only those acts of harassment that are connected to offline bullying, whereas the term "online harassment" should refer to all forms of harassment that take place online, regardless of their origin (Wolak, Mitchell, & Finkelhor, 2007). Despite these conceptual differences, the literature suggests that there is overlap in their occurrence. In other words, bullying does often occur both in the schoolyard and online for some victims; some of those online victims bully others online and in the schoolyard, and vice versa; some who are victims of schoolyard bullying, in turn, cyberbully others (Smith, Mahdavi, Carvalho, Fisher, Russelll, & Tippett, 2008).

Cyberbullies, like their traditional counterparts, thrive on an audience of bystanders. Both the audience witnessing the bullying and the behavior of the victim make the bully feel powerful. Unlike face-to-face bullying, however, cyberbullying may have *many* witnesses: Because of the cyberbully's enhanced capacity to reach targets and bystanders with these technologies, the audience of bystanders to the cyberbully can range from a few to several hundred "friends" on MySpace or Facebook to several million viewers on YouTube. In addition, because the bully in cyberbullying takes his or her actions in cyberspace (i.e., is not physically and/or even temporally present, as is the case in traditional bullying), he or she has more ubiquitous and pernicious ways of reaching and hurting targets, anywhere, anytime, anonymously, and fast. The technology allows for the effects of the bullying to spread quickly throughout the online community, greatly intensifying the pressure and experience of harm, humiliation, and exploitation. As Palfrey and Gasser (2008) state:

> Though there is no fundamental change in what is occurring when the online world is the stage rather than the playground, there are differences in the way the impact is felt by the person attacked and by those who can observe its occurrence . . . a local dispute, carried out in online public spaces, can become an international news story. (p. 92)

The ultimate power cyberbullies have over their victims stems from the extent of their competence to use the technology and their ability to hide their identities online while engaged in this activity (Patchin & Hinduja, 2006).

Cyberbullying differs from what is usually deemed to be bullying behavior in the following ways: (1) the rapid, extensive circulation and proliferation of threatening information or pictures to the targeted individual and simultaneously to a multitude of strangers online; (2) the practice of online "slamming" in which bystanders participate in the online harassment; (3) "flaming" (an antagonistic, "in your face" argumentative style of online communication used primarily, but not exclusively by males); and (4) as seen in online games, cheating, forming roving gangs, and blocking entryways (Beran & Li, 2005; Espelage & Swearer, 2003; Fekkes, Pijpers, & Verloove-Vanhorick, 2005; Herring, 1996).

WHERE AND HOW CYBERSPACE BULLYING OCCURS

Cyberspace (also known as the Internet) is an intangible, nonmaterial location or dimension created by computer systems to which people gain access, allowing them to communicate with one another. In cyberspace, files, mail messages, and graphics are the "objects." Also in this medium, different modes of transportation and delivery move the objects around; the movement involved in this type of activity requires pressing keys on a keyboard, moving a mouse, touching a screen, or giving voice commands. Some computer programs consist of games that are designed to give the user an experience that resembles physical reality. In virtual reality, for instance, the user is presented with feedback affecting the sensory systems such that occurrences in cyberspace feel real.

Cyberbullying occurs in chat rooms, online bulletin boards, email, instant messaging, websites, cell phones, massively multiplayer online games (MMOGs) such as World of Warcraft, and virtual worlds (e.g., Second Life). It entails one or more of the following socially inappropriate online behaviors: harassing, humiliating, intimidating, sending derogatory insults or threats in messages, teasing, using inappropriate language, and cheating. Harassment, for instance, encompasses a range of activities: impersonating others online, posting defamatory or embarrassing personal information about others, physical and emotional abuse, stalking people online, and threatening violence (Mitchell, Becker-Blease, & Finkelhor, 2005).

In cyberspace, the bully is able to hide behind a screen name or an avatar. An avatar is a figure created by a user to represent that person's identity online and whose actions are controlled by the user's computer mouse and keyboard. The avatar enables the user to interact with other avatars and objects within the virtual world. The type of avatar chosen by the user is typically determined by the role one chooses to play in the storylines, which are essentially predetermined by the game (Palfrey & Gasser, 2008). Hence the cyberbully can act anonymously with little to no fear of punishment, before a much larger audience, also anonymous and unimaginably huge, spanning continents, cultures, and nationalities as well as time.

Sometimes the consequences of cyberbullying may shift from the psychological to the physical, from cyberspace to a real physical location. In Japan, an 11-year-old girl fatally stabbed a classmate in the schoolyard as a continuation of an intense online argument that had occurred the previous night (Nakamura, 2004). Nansel et al. (2003) found that those students bullied outside of school were more likely to carry a weapon to school. Slonje and Smith (2008) found that 25 percent of cyberbullies and their victims were identified as being from the same school. According to Hinduja and Patchin (2007, 2009), many youths reporting problem offline behaviors (e.g., alcohol and drug use, cheating, truancy) have also been cyberbullied.

PSYCHOLOGICAL VULNERABILITIES OF ADOLESCENTS AND CYBERSPACE

The needs and motivations of Westernized adolescents have been well researched and presented in the psychological literature. These youths are typically focused on establishing an identity, intimacy, and self-esteem; they want to belong within their own social groups while becoming more autonomous and separating from family. They are striving to develop and maintain a more mature way of managing and regulating emotions, and preparing for a career/occupation. In other words, adolescents are learning who they are, what is important to them, what they value, how to relate to others, how to make friends and maintain friendships, what their goals for the future are, and how to develop the skills and competencies needed to become productive citizens, to name but a few of their concerns.

Greenfield and Yan (2006), when surveying the empirical literature on the impact of virtual reality on psychosocial functioning of children and adolescents, asked the following questions: "How should we think of the Internet from a developmental perspective? What are the uses to which the Internet is put and what do children and adolescents get from it?" (p. 392). They suggest that the Internet, when viewed as a "new object of cognition" (p. 393)—that is, in terms of the interplay of Internet involvement and cognitive/emotional development of children, adolescents, and adults—is unlike other media/electronic devices. This difference arises because, unlike users of other media/electronic devices (e.g., TV), Internet users participate in and co-construct the virtual social and physical world associated with this phenomenon.

Cyberspace offers many opportunities for adolescents to satisfy the need to experiment with their identity and learn about the world. Indeed, this generation of adolescents has been described in the literature as being "always on"—that is, as continually connected to ICTs in this digital age. According to Gross (2004), communication is the most important use of the Internet for today's adolescents. While teens continue to learn critical thinking skills, they are not automatically inclined to apply these skills in their face-to-face social interactions as they strive for healthy emotional adjustment. Nor are they inclined to apply—or, indeed, cognitively and emotionally capable of applying—these skills in their online activities. Moreover, their increasing independence from adult scrutiny and their inclination to solve their problems without parental or other adult assistance complicate efforts to develop effective prevention/intervention programs to minimize online victimization.

AT-RISK ONLINE BEHAVIORS

The apparent ability to communicate online without revealing one's "true" identity—the perceived security of being protected behind the computer screen (e.g., pseudoanonymity)—can predispose children, youth, and some adults to succumb to social pressures and behave online in ways that they "know" are unsafe or inappropriate. At-risk online behaviors include the following: giving out personal information online, agreeing to meet in person with someone who was originally met online, receiving and sending photos, receiving and sending suggestive or threatening email, and participating in chat rooms where the content results in discomfort (Hashima & Finkelhor , 1999; Berson, Berson, & Ferron, 2002). Research suggests that troubled youths and youths who tend to have high rates of Internet use, use chat rooms, talk with strangers online, or use the Internet in households other than their own tend to be at higher risk for online victimization (Mitchell et al., 2001).

Another potential risk factor derives from the ease with which young people can access global information and make use of information obtained through digital technologies. On the one hand, this access has the potential to expand their awareness and exposure to diverse cultural and social worldviews. On the other hand, the material obtained online may be illegal, inappropriate, age restricted, or simply inaccurate or intentionally specious. Exposure to and acting on misinformation and inappropriate material online may prove harmful to the cognitive/emotional or physical well-being of youth.

Use of various digital technologies allows youth many possibilities for recreating themselves and experimenting with different roles and lifestyles across a wide range of virtual platforms (e.g., multiple identities). Because of the nature of the Internet, along with our increased capacity to track and record online activity, information about these identities may paradoxically bind, restrict, or otherwise harm youth by keeping these identities "alive" for perpetuity, long after youths have forgotten, outgrown, and discarded them.

PREVALENCE OF CYBERBULLYING

Determining the prevalence and scope of cyberbullying is difficult not only because conceptual confusion exists about what it is, but also because reporting and comparisons across studies are confounded by differences in age-related findings. Some studies have focused on a narrow range of youths, whereas others have studied large age ranges (e.g., "middle school aged youths," "older adolescents") and grade levels (Palfrey, 2008). In one early study, 1 out of every 17 youth reported being threatened or harassed while using the Internet (Berson et al., 2002). A survey of 1,500 students in the United States, in grades four to eight, found that 42 percent had been victims of online bullying and 21 percent had received mean-spirited or menacing emails or instant messages (IMs) (Mitchell et al., 2001). In another survey of 1,500 children between the ages of 10 and 17, 25 percent reported being exposed to unwanted sexual material while online; approximately 19 percent of these young people were propositioned while online (Mitchell, Finkelhor, & Wolak, 2003).

More recent findings challenge the contention that cyberbullying is increasing. In a study carried out by Lenhart and Madden (2007), 67 percent of teenagers reported that bullying happens more offline than online. Other studies have indicated that 42 percent of cyberbully victims are also school bullying victims (Hinduja & Patchin, 2009), and that 54 percent of seventh-grade students are victims of traditional bullying, with less than half that number (25%) reporting cyberbully victimization (Li, 2007). Victimization rates were found to be generally lower in early adolescence (Hinduja & Patchin, 2007; Lenhart & Madden, 2007; McQuade & Sampat, 2008; Ybarra & Mitchell 2004) and higher in mid-adolescence (Hinduja & Patchin, 2009; Kowalski & Limber, 2007; Lenhart & Madden, 2007; Slonje & Smith, 2008). Some studies suggest that eighth grade or 15 years of age is the peak period for online harassment (Hindjua & Patchin, 2009; Williams & Guerra, 2007; Wolak et al., 2007). The Bureau of Justice Statistics shows a decline in offline bullying from seventh to twelfth grades (Devoe, Peter, Noonan, Snyder, Baum, & Snyder, 2005), while Smith et al. (2008) found that cyberbullying tends to peak later in eighth grade and declines only slightly thereafter. Other findings suggest that cyberbullying remains at a constant level through the end of high school and persists in college (Finn, 2004).

The social problems occurring in cyberspace are not limited to the United States. Indeed, the scope of this phenomenon is international, involving many countries (e.g., Australia, Canada, Japan, United Kingdom, Russia, and New Zealand, to name a few), affecting people all around the world from all walks of life (e.g., adults and children, men and women, rich and poor, privileged and disenfranchised). Liau et al. (2005) explored risky Internet behavior among adolescent Internet users in Singapore and found that those adolescents who were frequent users of the Internet (e.g., daily online activity) participated in chat rooms and online games, disclosed personal information online, and had face-to-face meetings with someone first encountered online. In Scotland and New Zealand, social problems have emerged with the increased use of cell phones, especially text messaging, to such an extent that some schools have banned mobile phones (Smith & Williams, 2004). The text message, "When you are feeling down . . . bash a Christian or Catholic to lift up" was found on the cell phone of one of the perpetrators of a gang rape in Sydney, Australia (Wockner, 2002, p. 3). Aficak et al. (2008) found among secondary school Turkish students that more than one third of the 269 participants were exposed to cyberbullying; approximately one fourth were bullied through their cell phones.

How often children and youth are cyberbullied is difficult to determine, and the rates obtained vary from study to study, from a low of 4 percent (Ybarra & Mitchell, 2004) to a high of 72 percent (Juvonen & Gross, 2008). Ybarra et al. (2006) reported that 3 percent of their U.S. sample of youth aged 10 to 17 was cyberbullied three or more times in the previous year. In the study conducted by Li (2007), 9 percent of middle school students indicated that they had been cyberbullied three or more times. According to Palfrey (2008), few students are cyberbullied daily or weekly. Beran and Li (2007), in a Canadian study, found that 34 percent of students in grades seven to nine were cyberbullied once or twice, 19 percent reported being cyberbullied "a few times," 3 reported having these experiences "many times," and 0.01 percent reported being cyberbullied on a daily basis.

Research has found an overlap in victimization and perpetration; between 3 percent and 12 percent of youth have been both online harassers and victims of online harassment (Beran & Li, 2007; Kowalski & Limber, 2007). Patchin et al. (2009) found that 27 percent of adolescent females retaliate for being bullied online by "cyberbullying back." Research suggests some overlap between online and offline bullying and victimization. Patchin and Hinduja (2006) found that 42 percent of victims of cyberbullying were also victims of offline bullying, and that 52 percent of cyberbullies were also offline bullies. Unfortunately, many young people who have had a negative online experience that caused them discomfort do not report the incident or seek help to cope with their reaction (Beran & Li, 2007; Mitchell et al., 2005).

GENDER DIFFERENCES IN ONLINE BEHAVIOR

Efforts to encourage more computer involvement on the part of girls in schools and the advent of cell phones have increased the number of females using ICTs (American Association of University Women [AAUW], 2000; Smith & Williams, 2004). Berson and Berson (2003) found that 92 percent of 10,800 girls ages 12 to 18 who participated in an online survey use a home computer as their primary access site. When online, 58 percent of the girls spend their time sending instant messages or emails to friends; 20 percent surf for new things on the web; and 16 percent spend most of their time in chat rooms. Only 1 percent indicated that the majority of their time online was spent building a website, reading discussion boards, interacting at game sites, or engaging in homework and research.

As female participation has increased in what had previously been considered a "male domain," sex-related differences in online behavior have emerged. As Herring (1996) notes, certain differences in online communication styles can be discerned based on gender. Females use more supportive

language, express appreciation more directly, and foster community building. By comparison, males use more adversarial language (e.g., sarcasm),
self-promotion more than community building, and "flaming" (antagonistic, confrontational speech).

Inexperienced, immature young men and women seeking companionship may tend to act inappropriately online. Subrahmanyam et al. (2006)
found a variety of gender differences in identity presentation and sexual
exploration in monitored and unmonitored online teen chat rooms. Specifically, youth who self-identified as younger and female were more
likely to participate in a protected environment of monitored chat than
were those youth who self-identified as older and male. The latter were
more likely to participate in unmonitored chat rooms. Also, females were
more likely to produce implicit sexual communication (e.g., "eminem is
hot"), whereas males tended to produce more explicit sexual communication (e.g., "whats up horny guys IM me" [p. 399]). Hence the potential
danger in cyberspace is in part due to the desires and needs of those
who use Internet online services for social communication.

Reports of gender differences in victimization suggest that girls are more
likely to be cyberbullied (Agatston, Kowalski, & Limber, 2007; Chisholm,
2006; DeHue, Bolman, & Völlink, 2008; Kowalski & Limber, 2007; Li, 2007).
Conversely, some studies have found no difference in the percentages of victims of cyberbullying by gender. Nevertheless, clear qualitative differences
across gender in the experience of being cyberbullied and in the emotional
response to victimization have been noted (Chisholm, 2006).

The literature on gender differences in the expression of aggression
finds that girls tend to engage in a passive, relational style of aggression
(e.g., spreading rumors, the threat of withdrawing affection, excluding
someone from a social network and/or important social function), which
in turn extends into their online behavior (Crick, Casa, & Nelson, 2002;
Nansel, Overpeck, Pilla, Ruan, Simons-Morton, & Scheidt, 2001; Nansel
et al., 2003). For example, a teen who has not been "IM'ed" (instant mes-
saged) about the color scheme for the clothes to be worn the next day at
school will be tomorrow's social outcast among her peers; wearing the
wrong colors announces to all that she had been excluded from the previous evening's online discussion (Chisholm, 2006). Research suggests
that individuals who do not receive text messages, when they expect to
do so, feel left out and dejected (Taylor & Harper, 2003). With respect to
online bullying, "mean girls" is one kind of bullying done in a group, for
"fun," at the expense of the feelings of the target (Students Using Technology to Achieve Reading and Writing [STAR-W], 2005). As the term suggests, this type of bullying has distinctive characteristics and is typically
seen among females, reflecting another gender-based difference in online
activity (STAR-W, 2005). Lauren Newby and Megan Meier (mentioned
earlier in this chapter) were victims of this type of bullying.

Some research reports that the number of girls and adolescent females engaged in physical aggression comparable to that typically linked to their male counterparts has increased in recent years (Prothrow-Stith & Spivak, 2005). The use of ICTs in conjunction with this kind of violent behavior compounds this phenomenon. For example, in January 2007, a videotape of a group of girls beating a middle school girl in Long Island, New York, was posted on YouTube; its ferocity stunned not just the local community, but the nation as well ("Teen Fight Caught on Tape," 2007). The impact of violence perpetrated by these "mean girls" harms not only the victim and the perpetrator(s), but also the online and offline social network of the victim/perpetrator and the community at large.

It has been suggested that different types of cyberbullies may be distinguished based on their motivation and their online activities (STAR-W, 2005). The "Vengeful Angel" views himself or herself as defending a friend who is being or has been bullied in school by shifting the bullying online. The "Power-Hungry Cyberbully" more closely resembles the playground bully and uses coercion and intimidation to assert their power and control over others; when this bully has technical knowledge and uses the Internet as a tool for bullying, the term "Revenge of the Nerds" is used to describe him or her. This type of cyberbully may damage someone's computer by intentionally sending virus-infected emails, for example. The "Inadvertent Cyberbully" is one whose online reactions stem from misunderstandings online or misconstruing the meaning of a text message.

THE PSYCHOLOGY OF CYBERBULLYING IN CYBERSPACE

Zizek (2004) argues that the social function of cyberspace in our society today is to bridge the gap between an individual's public symbolic identity and that identity's fantasmatic background. Ideas, fantasies, and beliefs—all part of the inner world—are more readily and immediately projected into the public symbolic space. The technological phenomenon of the "screen," and the mechanics of its functioning, create a logic that influences other spheres of psychological or social functioning of the user, especially for youths (Wallace, 1999).

Anonymity and disinhibition are two notable characteristics that distinguish cyberbullying from traditional bullying. Anonymity typically occurs with the creation of a screen name or an avatar, which enables the user to act out fantasies online without his or her real identity being disclosed. For example, a normally withdrawn person may act out aggressions online that he or she would never express in public. Inexperienced, immature young men and women seeking companionship may be especially prone to acting inappropriately online. According to Berson et al. (2002), this "culture of deception" and the anonymity prevalent in online communication raise serious concerns because they lead to disinhibition.

Online disinhibition refers to the loosening of psychological barriers that serve to block the release of innermost, private thoughts, feelings, and needs. In short, online social interactions can and often do change the way in which an individual generally self-discloses and self-creates. As Parks and Floyd (1996) note, youth tend not to think about the risks involved in disclosing personal information online. The effect of disinhibition may be benign or "toxic," depending on whether the risk to explore aspects of oneself occurs in a safe online environment or on the "dark side" of the Internet in unsafe or inappropriate ways. Adolescent youth who spend the majority of their time online in chat rooms, sending emails and instant messages, blogging, and playing online games (MMOGs) are especially vulnerable to this risk.

In today's world, the most common form of online social interaction is "texting." Texting involves typing one's ideas and thoughts and reading those of others seen in email, chat rooms, instant messaging, Short Message Service (SMS) posts, and blogs; this type of communication has its own unique language, a text-based form of communication that helps to forge an identity of membership in a group and/or community. The following text message illustrates this practice: "lmao ur funny ill c u latr iight." It translates into "Laughing my ass off. You are funny. I'll see you later, alright?" Through their shared experience with this unique form of communication, users gain a sense of belonging—but are highly sensitive to signs of being included or excluded, valued or criticized, and so on.

Twitter, a free micro-blogging and social networking service that enables its users to send and read other users' updates (known as tweets), illustrates another aspect of the psychological and social functions of cyberspace. Twittering has become so popular since it was created in 2006 that outages from traffic overloads have occurred. On August 6, 2009, Twitter suffered a denial-of-service attack, causing the website to be offline for several hours (Claburn, 2009). Advocates of this service—both youths and adults—maintain that tweets allow busy people to keep in touch. Others, who are grappling with the burdens of higher cell phone bills, check-in messages at odd hours, and acquaintances telling them in 140 characters or less about mundane, trivial daily routines, have a less positive view of this phenomenon (Lavallee, 2007). Research examining the impact of Twitter on the psychological functioning of youth who use this technology is needed. In particular, the extent to which this technology is being used by cyberbullies needs to be explored. Researchers using macro perspectives need to explore the ways in which this technology is, in and of itself, a cyberbully, constantly bombarding users with messages—that is, harassing our "collective" consciousness.

Suler's (2005) discussion of nine characteristics of cyberspace that may affect psychological functioning and predispose vulnerable youth to act out online or be targeted for abuse supports Zizek's (2004) perspective.

The characteristics identified by Suler include altered perception, equalized status, identity flexibility, media disruption, reduced sensation, social multiplicity, temporal flexibility, texting, and transcended space.

The following discussion of "identity flexibility," "temporal flexibility," and "texting" elucidates the complexities of the interaction of these characteristics in influencing the online behavior of youth, which, depending upon one's perspective, either promotes healthy development or compromises it. Identity flexibility is a consequence of texting because of the lack of face-to-face cues and the sense of anonymity afforded by use of this technology. Users have options regarding how they present themselves; that is, texting as a written form of communication permits opportunities to experiment with self-expression (e.g., being younger or older, male or female, changing ethnicity) in a variety of cyberspace environments.

Cyberspace also creates a unique temporal space (i.e., temporal flexibility) in which the ongoing, interactive time together stretches out. During chat and IM, a person has anywhere from several seconds to a minute or more to reply to the other person—a significantly longer delay than in face-to-face meetings. In email, blogs, and newsgroups, one has hours, days, or even weeks to respond. This provides a convenient "zone for reflection." Compared to face-to-face encounters, one has significantly more time to mull things over and compose a more polished reply.

ANECDOTAL EXPERIENCES OF CYBERBULLYING

Undergraduate students in the author's course on the Psychology of Women were invited to write about any online experiences that caused discomfort for them or others. The following anecdotal accounts highlight these students' experiences as well as illustrate what has been reported in the literature and discussed thus far in this chapter.

Anecdote I

As of May 2004 I graduated from [name omitted] High School, a small Catholic school in California. When I was in school the Internet was merely a tool used for research for upcoming research papers, but in the 2004–2005 school year this changed drastically. During my spring semester of college ... I became aware of an Internet service called "MySpace." It is a free website in which members join, and then create their own web pages. On their pages people put pictures of themselves, schools they have attended, bulletins, and other voluntary information about themselves. The biggest attraction of MySpace is something called a "wall"; each personal page has one. A person's wall consists of comments about them made by fellow MySpace friends (friends can only become friends by request and acceptance).

By May 2005, I had joined MySpace after a friend told me about all the people from her past that she was able to reconnect with. When I joined MySpace, I was also able to get in touch with people I had not seen in years, I was able to talk to them and see how they were doing, I loved the experience.

As I spent more time on the actual site, I became aware that there were people using the site in a negative manner. While I was surfing pages one day, I came upon many pages from the kids who were in the grade below me in high school. They were now seniors and seemed to be out of control. Most of the pages I came across chronicled tales of people's drug abuse and underage drinking, and many of the girls' pages were laden with personal tales of their own sexual exploits. I was shocked to see these things because in my mind these kids were still the innocent juniors I once knew. When I thought I couldn't be any more shocked, I read a bulletin (a mass message sent to all of one's MySpace friends) calling a girl a "slut" and listing her actual phone number "for a good time."

I went home for the summer and decided to ask one of my friend's younger sisters, who was still at my high school, about the MySpace usage. She told me of even more occurrences like the one above. She even told me about students starting sexual rumors about a teacher. The rumors got back to the school, of course, and the teacher was constantly harassed. After this, the school was forced to step in. The first step the school made was to attempt to ban MySpace usage. This was, of course, impossible because it violated [the] rights of students, so [the school] did the next best thing—[it] held many conferences about it and eventually banned MySpace from all school computers.

Today the exact same things are going on because students can, of course, go online at home and do whatever they want. There are a small but powerful group of people who are using this website negatively and it is impacting the reputation of the school and girls everywhere. (M.H., 2005)

This student's account of her experience illustrates several issues. First, she is an older adolescent who observes that her response and participation in cyberspace differs from that of younger adolescents. This difference reflects not only the maturational processes of adolescence but also the time frame in which digital technology has become a significant influence in our society and in the social functioning of youth. Her initial response mirrors how an entire generation, prior to the explosion of this technology, used computers. It is, therefore, important to include cohort variables when conducting research in this area.

Second, what motivated this student to explore this Internet site has been discussed in the literature on gender—namely, the fact that needs for social affiliation and communication are important for females.

Third, the nature of the abuse she witnessed online has been discussed in the literature on belongingness theory (Baumeister & Leary, 1995). Research on ostracism has demonstrated that simply being ignored and excluded is enough to produce depressive symptoms and lower self-reported satisfaction levels of self-esteem (Smith & Williams, 2004; Williams, 2001).

Lastly, this student's commentary on the harmful effect of the behavior of a minority of users on themselves and the rest of the community of users underscores the need for appropriate intervention by the collaborative efforts of Internet service providers, social network sites, academia, education, child safety and public policy advocacy organizations, the technology industry, and parents to curb "out of control" behavior and promote safe online environments (Aftab, 2000; Chisholm, 2006; Palfrey, 2008).

Anecdote II

> My only experiences with cyberbullying have been instances where I was the bully, which is not something that I am proud of at all. As a person who does not like confrontation or to be confrontational, it was easier for me to express anger or dislike behind the cover of an IM chat or MySpace messaging. As I have gotten older, I have learned that this is not the way to handle situations, and after a few instances where my "bullying" has spilled over into real life, I have stopped using IM as a vehicle for my frustration with people.
>
> There was one experience in particular where my harsh way with words proved more harmful to me than to the other person. Of course, I knew that conversations can be copied and pasted and shared with other people, but I did not think that it would be used against me. However, it was and my friends took the other person's side—so not only was I unnecessarily mean-spirited, but I also lost a lot of friends because of it. This particular instance taught me how detrimental cyberbullying can be for all the parties involved. (M.G., 2009)

This student's experience reveals how her use of ICTs when she was younger served defensive/self-protective purposes that enabled her to create a "psychological space" in cyberspace where she could vent angry feelings and release her frustrations upon those people (or mental representations of those people) whom she perceived to be responsible for her emotional distress. Without the benefit of face-to-face encounters, she experienced delays in developing the social skills that would facilitate her capacity to assert herself in more age-appropriate ways when she felt wronged. Thus she became handicapped by the technology; she failed to appreciate that her "angry" talk went beyond the bounds of an active fantasy life.

For this student, her "angry" IMs represented attempts to compensate for hurts in "real" life by projecting them into the social arena of "virtual" life in cyberspace (e.g., her IMs). The technology shielded her from the much-needed "real" *process* of social interactions from which she would adaptively learn to adjust and modify her verbal and nonverbal communication; instead, she developed a style of engagement with others in virtual reality that constituted harassment. The targeted victim of her wrath shared with others the *product* of her bullying (e.g., copies of the offensive IMs) by circulating her messages among their mutual network of friends. In part, it was the technology and this student's lack of technological sophistication to conceal her "real" identity that led to her undoing and—in an ironic twist—paved the way for more emotionally corrective experiences in reality facilitating her maturation.

Anecdote III

> I went through all of middle school, and even all of high school, never once seeing or experiencing cyberbullying. I would watch Lifetime TV dramas depicting this apparent "epidemic" and think, "Wow, I must be really lucky!" Then, I went to college.
>
> My first experience was relatively harmless. My college roommate chose to air her frustrations with me on her Internet blog. She was kind enough to leave my name out, referring to me as "roommate." At the end of a long letter expressing her frustration that I routinely annoyed her by staying up too late doing homework, she exclaimed, "I am not talking to you at all tomorrow; maybe then you will get the message." I was shocked and upset, because my roommate never said anything to me about how my habits bothered her. I would offer to move to the library at night but she would always tell me to stay, that it was "fine." I wanted to talk to her about the issue, but felt so embarrassed by it. I wrote her a letter, apologizing for keeping her up, but also requesting that any future problems be brought to me in person so we could discuss it as two adults. She never acknowledged either the letter or the blog. She rarely talked to me at all for the remainder of the year.
>
> Fortunately, my experience with all roommates since then has been wonderful. And compared to some of the other roommate stories I have heard, mine seems pretty bearable.
>
> My second experience dwarfs the first, but I guess it would have to because it involves an ex-boyfriend, and romance is nothing if not a catalyst for drama. Before I explain what happened, it needs to be mentioned that the "man" (and I use that term loosely) who did this

was 22 years old. He was college educated and even employed with a major company, earning a decent salary for someone his age. After we broke up, he, for some reason, chose to post a fake sex ad on Craigslist, in which he included my name, school, age, and cell phone number. Fortunately, after I contacted Craigslist, [the service] pulled down the ad and gave me some basic information on the user who posted it (an Optimum Online customer from the Bronx). Apparently, impersonation is a recurring problem for [Craigslist].

I do not see what my ex-boyfriend got out of this prank, since he was nowhere near me on Easter Sunday at 9 P.M. (this was the precise time that my phone started ringing off the hook with countless men looking to answer the ad). He did not get to read the disgusting text messages I received, nor did he listen to the disturbing voicemails that filled my inbox. The only thing he got was a message from me asking if he did it. I did not want to accuse him, but Craigslist would only release his IP address if I had a police warrant, which I could have easily received (I went to the local precinct with a printout of the ad and emails I exchanged with Craigslist and filed a report; I was told this was a case of aggravated assault). I explained to [my ex-boyfriend] that he was the only person I knew from the Bronx and that if he were not the perpetrator, I would have to follow through and press charges to determine exactly who did it. However, I certainly had no desire to have the police trace the IP address to my ex, since I feared such actions would ruin his life by leaving him with a misdemeanor on a once-spotless record. He confessed, completely mortified and seemingly shocked that I took any steps at all to find out who did this to me.

Today, I can laugh about both these stories—though that is not to say that I consider myself completely unscathed. I still find myself paranoid about my roommates, bombarding them with questions that go something like this: "Do you mind if I . . . " and "Are you sure?" Also, I simply don't trust Craigslist, at all. I hear people talk about the apartments and jobs they find there, and every time I look at the site I automatically assume everything posted is illegitimate or based on some kind of sexual exchange. But if cyberbullying has done nothing other than make me annoyingly polite and leery of an already risky website, I have to say things could certainly be worse. (M. S., 2009)

This student's recollections convey several important points. She had reached late adolescence in this digital age without an incident of cyberbullying, but the experiences she had as a young adult were significant and caused her considerable pain and suffering at the time of the occurrences and afterward. Researchers need to look into the complex social interactions in "real" time among children and adolescents complicated by the differences in their use or abuse of ICTs. This student's roommate bullied her in a way similar to the previous student's bullying behavior—specifically, disagreements were not communicated in face-to-face conversations in private, but rather were aired publicly on a blog. This student had to cope with someone close to her using the Internet to vent their frustration in a way that was hurtful and harassing.

This student's second experience with an ex-boyfriend demonstrates, once again, differences in how peers use and abuse ICTs for communication and social networking and how those differences can negatively affect social interactions among them in "real" time. Moreover, inappropriate online activity seems to increase and may be exacerbated when negative emotions are triggered—in this case, when a romantic relationship ended. The young man's behavior represents a particularly insidious type of cyberbullying, which is both extreme and criminal in nature. The student's appropriate response to stop it, as well as her thoughtful and compassionate reaction/stance toward him (i.e., determining that he was responsible for the onslaught of interest in the bogus sex posting, confronting him and getting an admission, and then not pursuing criminal charges to avoid ruining his life), reflect a young woman who is considerate, intelligent, and mature by our societal standards. The young man's behavior, in contrast, characterizes the harmful effects of anonymity and disinhibition experienced by some digital natives who, without attempting insight or reflection, engage in cyberbullying or (in this case) criminal behavior.

Anecdote IV

> The best experience I had with Facebook was when I was entering college as a freshman. [When I was] moving into the dorms and starting a new school, Facebook gave me the opportunity to meet my new roommate before I actually met her. We met on Facebook after we were assigned to be roommates and it was a huge relief. We were able to talk about certain furniture and decorations before the move-in date. Facebook also helped me to meet new people at [my college] ...
>
> My worst experience with Facebook was after a three-year relationship ended. It is hard enough to go through a breakup, but Facebook and MySpace made it a hundred times harder. You have to deal with your ex even when you don't want to. I would have to see my ex hanging out with my friends without me and meeting new girls. Even when I tried to avoid him, he would pop up all over my friends' pages. It made it almost impossible to move on. I had to choose whether to delete my Facebook and MySpace [profiles] altogether or just bite the bullet. The good thing is that Facebook created new privacy settings and blocks, which made it easier. However, Facebook made my breakup much harder than it had to be ... Facebook

has everyone's business posted publicly and, depending on what you want to see or don't want to see, it can affect a person differently. Although I had some bad experiences with Facebook, I think the pros greatly outweigh the cons. (K.D., 2009)

While this student's experience does not involve intentional cyberbullying, her participation in Facebook illustrates the added demands on our youth who must navigate and negotiate the complexities of social life in both the real and virtual worlds.

Anecdote V

I have had very few interactions in cyberspace, and that is because I have made a point not to. I do not participate in MySpace, Facebook, or any of the other social networking websites. It seems like a waste to me to spend so much time and effort typing all your thoughts and "tagging" all your pictures so that everyone can see what you did last weekend and know how you felt about it. The people who need to know were either there or you can call and tell them about it. I even avoided email until I arrived at [my college] and was given an email address and told that I had to check it on a regular basis to stay successful as a student. That is the only email that I use/check. In general, I find that it can be incredibly difficult to convey tone in text, meaning you run a very high risk of not getting your point across or—worse—getting the wrong point across when you write to someone. This can be a problem for me, since I like to use sarcasm in conversation . . . I have definitely considered the value of the social networking websites. However, the drawbacks deter me. (M.B., 2009)

This student is a few years older than her classmates (she is in her mid-twenties); how many others of her age cohort and background share her reluctance to embrace these technologies needs to be explored. She is aware of and comfortable with her style of communicating on a face-to-face basis and chooses not to risk misunderstandings in cyberspace that may result from the absence of the auditory and visual cues that would be present in face-to-face interactions. It is also informative to consider that she reluctantly began to use the technology so that she could successfully complete her college education. She was essentially "coerced" to use ICTs by her institution of higher learning because it has shifted from older technologies (e.g., telephones, faxes, "snail mail," hard copies of data) to ICTs to communicate with, exchange, and store information about its constituencies. In this particular case, the student's determined effort to refrain from becoming digitalized has been thwarted by pressure from an institution. Research into the effects of the social pressure from peers and other segments of society to become "digital" is needed.

Prevention of Cyberbullying

Preventing cyberviolence—and especially cyberbullying—is difficult because so much of this activity takes place between minors who know one another or know of one another through involvement in online and offline social networks. The problem is further complicated by the ways in which bullying moves between online and offline contexts as well as shifts between victims and perpetrators (e.g., reciprocal harassment). Modifying online pseudoanonymity by creating online identity authentication for all online users regardless of age or using filters could lead to more appropriate online behavior, thereby reducing online harassment. With these strategies, individuals could presumably be held accountable for their online behavior; their identities would be known and their access to sites and information could be restricted. However, implementing such technological mechanisms would undoubtedly have to overcome many hurdles, including, but not limited to, legal and privacy concerns.

Many youth are capable of disabling these technological mechanisms by using proxies to circumvent filters or by reformatting their computers to remove parental controls. Also, many handheld devices have WiFi capabilities, and unsecured wireless networks can be accessed anywhere. To date, most filtering technologies have focused on sexual context and inappropriate language. Some have failed to restrict access to violent content, hate content, and self-harm content. Many also fail to address the rise of youth-generated problematic content that is distributed virally.

Cyberbullying prevention requires a holistic approach—a complex endeavor encompassing the commitment of financial resources to fund a variety of interventions. These interventions need to be informed by knowledge in which coordinated efforts across communities and domains including education, health, justice, the Internet community, and the workplace are marshaled to combat the social forces and norms that give rise to this form of online behavior (Palfry, 2008). For example, the Children's Online Privacy Act (COPA) enhances monitoring of the online activities of youngsters. COPA, which went into effect in the United States in 2000, requires that website operators and Internet service providers obtain verifiable parental consent when personal information is collected online from children younger than the age of 13 (COPA, 2006).

Additional preventive activities/strategies include development of awareness programs for teachers, parents and youth; legislation designed to criminalize certain inappropriate online activity (e.g., the Electronic Antistalking Act of 1995); hotlines where people can report illegal content on Internet sites; age-appropriate supervision and monitoring of online activity; discussion with parent(s) about online safety; instruction by teachers about cybersafety; and technological developments that help to limit the amount of unwanted/harmful content.

Several initiatives have launched projects to accomplish these objectives. In the United States, the Multi-State Working Group on Social Networking, comprising 50 State Attorneys General, charged the Internet Safety Technical Task Force with determining the extent to which today's technologies could help to address these online safety risks, with a primary focus on social network sites in the United States. The group's final report makes a series of recommendations for public policy advocacy to promote youth online safety with the input from technology experts (Palfry, 2008).

ECPAT International (End Child Prostitution, Child Pornography and Trafficking of Children for Sexual Purposes) is a network of organizations and individuals working around the world to protect children from all forms of sexual exploitation and violence (www.ecpat.net). As part of the United Nations study in 2005 on violence against children, ECPAT generated a report that contained a section on cyberbullying, which sought to contribute to the international effort to protect youth from violence (Muir, 2005).

I-SAFE America is a nonprofit educational foundation that was established in 1998 and seeks to provide students with the awareness and knowledge they need to recognize and avoid dangerous, harmful online behavior. This objective is accomplished through two major activities: (1) providing the I-SAFE school education curriculum to schools nationwide and (2) engaging in community outreach, which includes events for the community at large and school-based assemblies for the student population at which Internet safety issues are discussed (I-SAFE America, 2003).

The Internet Safety Group (ISG) from New Zealand is an independent organization whose members include educators at all levels of the school system (elementary grades through college), government groups, representatives of law enforcement agencies, the judiciary, community groups, businesses, libraries, and individuals (ISG, 2001). In 2000, the Internet Safety Kit for schools, the NetSafe website, and a toll-free NETSAFE Hotline was launched (www.netsafe.org.nz) as part of ISG's work.

What is stressed in these programs and projects is that education (e.g., curricula) designed for specific groups (e.g., youth, parents, teachers, school administrators, law enforcement, legislators) is crucial to reducing or eliminating at-risk online behavior. For example, from parents' perspective (especially for parents who were born before the rise of the digital age), this technology is a tool to be used for practical and business purposes. In contrast, their children typically view this technology as their way of being connected in their social world. Empowering parents with knowledge about existing unsafe activities and teaching them skills so that they can adequately monitor and supervise online activities are deemed important components of many intervention strategies. It is noteworthy, however, that parental supervision techniques have not been especially effective in lowering adolescents' risky online activity. This shortcoming may partly reflect the attitudes of teens, who do not disclose information about their online activities with their parents. Moreover, studies measuring parental monitoring are, in fact, assessing the level of parental knowledge rather than parents' efforts in tracking and surveillance (Liau et al., 2005; Kerr & Statin, 2000).

For youth and adult users to become "netizens,", the literature encourages "netiquette" and "nethics"—that is, online manners encouraging acceptable conduct when engaged in an interchange with people in cyberspace (Berson, 2000; Cole et al., 2001; Willard, 2002). Clearly articulated rules assist youth in behaving courteously and respectfully to others, facilitating their positive social interactions with others. The application of the rules enables young people to apply critical thinking skills to online activity, thereby promoting healthy, productive social discourse and participation (Kubey, 2002).

While these rules of "netiquette" make sense to the more mature users who will follow them, younger users may not readily adopt sound online strategies, such as not sharing one's password with anyone other than a parent or guardian or refraining from sharing secrets, photos, or anything online that might be embarrassing if someone (or an entire school) found out—precisely because these activities are deemed important to remaining connected to the group. Younger users' inexperience and cognitive, emotional, and social immaturity give rise to a kind of reasoning that makes them vulnerable to abusing others and being abused online. Moreover, many types of bullying involving impersonation, password stealing, and the distribution of embarrassing images and video may confuse and intimidate younger users, who may not feel comfortable disclosing their discomfort with an adult whose knowledge of the technology as a social tool is limited. A colleague and friend of the author, who is a social worker for a public elementary school in a township in New Jersey, shared e her overwhelmingly positive interactions with students who participated in the school implementation of the NetSafe school kit in 2008. Many of the children expressed delight and relief that there were adults with whom they could communicate their online experiences, knowing that these adults would "understand" and "help" them (R. Walker, personal communication, 2008).

HOW TO REPORT CYBERVIOLENCE

Incidents of cyberviolence can be handled in a variety of ways, including reporting the incident to a supportive adult, CyberTipline, the Internet service provider, school official(s), and the local police. Enlisting the aid of an adult may facilitate taking appropriate action to stop the bullying. Unsolicited, obscene materials and threats can be reported online to

CyberTipline at http://www.missingkids.com/cybertip/ or by calling 1-800-843-5678. One can also report the harassment to the offender's Internet service provider and request that the abuser's account be suspended or blocked (it is important to note that some bullies have further harassed a victim by reporting the victim as the bully and having the victim's account blocked). Many schools now include online bullying in their antiharassment policies and code of conduct. Contacting the police may be in order if the bullying behavior threatens violence or violates other laws, as illustrated in Anecdote III.

DIRECTIONS FOR FUTURE RESEARCH AND TRAINING

The discussion of cyberbullying presented in this chapter reflects the need for additional lines of inquiry into the detrimental influences of the misuse of ICTs in the lives of children and adolescents. Psychological theories and research in this area are in the early stages; the studies to date have typically relied on questionnaires or surveys, conducted both online and offline. The focus has mainly been on identifying types of online activities and the frequency of use among young people. Mitchell et al. (2005) suggest that:

> [T]he implementation of population-based studies about Internet use and problematic Internet experiences should help in the development of norms in this area, which, in turn, is an important component in the development of public policy, prevention, and intervention in this field. More research is also needed concerning the mental health impact of various problematic Internet experiences. Internet problems may be adding some unique dynamics to the field of mental health that require special understanding, new responses, and interventions in some cases . . . For example, are persons with impulse control problems drawn to certain aspects of the Internet, such as pornography and gaming, which could further exacerbate their symptoms? Does Internet exposure exacerbate preexisting mental health difficulties?" (p. 507)

Cyberbullying requires much more empirical study to further our understanding of this phenomenon. Results from existing studies need to be replicated and validated. Researchers need to develop additional measures to determine how to reduce the risk of being victimized, how to identify and assist those who have been subjected to cyberbullying, and how to prevent this kind of behavior. Future research may explore developmental trends of bullying across age groups and domains. For example, are the schoolyard bullies of 15 years ago the office online bullies of today in the workplace?

It is important for researchers, clinicians, and other professionals who work with youth to better understand the diversity among the victims of cyberbullying as well as the diversity among cyberbullies. Current research indicates that considering the age, gender, social class, access to ICTs, and individual preferences regarding online activities of children and adolescents is crucial to understanding the interplay of the online activity and the user's experience of being bullied and bullying. The trend for increasingly younger children to have access to this technology as the technology continues to evolve requires that researchers, experts in these technologies, and other professionals collaborate in earnest to promote the safe use of ICTs and facilitate healthy development for children and adolescents.

Existing support services need to become sensitized to the needs of children and adolescents who have suffered abuse or are abusing others in this venue to appropriately address their vulnerability and victimization. As discussed in the literature, many youths never report their experiences of cyberbullying, but instead cope with the negative feelings and experiences on their own. Therefore, additional training at the graduate and postgraduate levels for mental health and other professionals is necessary to enable them to recognize the signs of cyberbullying that contribute to psychological distress, give rise to interpersonal difficulties, and interfere with the normal developmental tasks of childhood and adolescence.

REFERENCES

Aftab, P. (2000). *The parent's guide to protecting your children in cyberspace*. New York: McGraw-Hill.

Agatston, P. W., Kowalski, R., & Limber, S. (2007). Students' perspectives on cyber bullying. *Journal of Adolescent Health, 41*, S59–S60.

American Association of University Women (AAUW). (2000). *Tech savvy: Educating girls in the new computer age*. Washington, DC: AAUW Educational Foundation Research.

American Psychiatric Association (APA). (2004). APA resolution on bullying among children and youth. www.apa.org/pi/cyf/bully_resolution_704.pdf.

Baumeister, R. F., & Leary, M. R. (1995). The need to belong: Desire for interpersonal attachments as a fundamental human motivation. *Psychological Bulletin, 117*, 497–529.

Beckerman, L., & Nocero, J. (2002). You've got hate mail. *Principal Leadership, 3*(4), 38–41.

Benfer, A. (2001, July 3). Cyber slammed. *Salon.com*. Retrieved September 14, 2009.

Beran, T., & Li, Q. (2005). Cyber-harassment: A study of a new method for an old behavior. *Journal of Educational Computing Research, 32*, 265–277.

Beran, T., & Li, Q. (2007). The relationship between cyberbullying and school bullying. *Journal of Student Wellbeing, 1*, 15–33.

Berson, I., & Berson, M. (2003). Digital literacy for effective citizenship. *Social Education. 67*, 164–167.

Berson, I., Berson, M., & Ferron, J. (2002). Emerging risks of violence in the digital age: Lessons for educators from an online study of adolescent girls in the

United States. *Meridian: A Middle School Computer Technologies Journal, 5*(2). Retrieved September 28, 2005, from http://www.ncsu.edu/meridian/ sum2002/cyberviolence/index.html.

Berson, M. J. (2000). Rethinking research and pedagogy in the social studies: The creation of caring connections through technology and advocacy. *Theory & Research in Social Education, 28,* 121–131.

Bruno, L. (2005, October 24). Blogging ban provokes debate over cyberspace. *Daily Record,* pp. 1–6.

Chisholm, J. F. (2006). Cyberspace violence against girls and adolescent females. In F. Denmark, H. Krauss, E. Halpern, & J. Sechzer (Eds.), *Violence and exploitation against women and girls* (pp. 74–89). *Annals of the New York Academy of Sciences, 1087.*

Claburn, T. (2009, August 6). Twitter downed by denial of service attack. *Information-Week.* Retrieved August 6, 2009, from http://www.informationweek.com/ news/security/attacks/showArticle.jhtml?articleID=219100308.

Cole, J. I., et al. (2001). *UCLA Internet report 2001: Surveying the digital future year two.* Los Angeles, CA: UCLA Center for Communication Policy. www.ccp.ucla.edu.

COPA. (2006). Retrieved August 8, 2006, from http://www.ftc.gov/bcp/conline/ pubs/buspubs/coppa.htm.

Crick, N. R., Casa, J. F., & Nelson, D. A. (2002). Toward a more comprehensive understanding of peer maltreatment: studies of relationship victimization. *Current Directions in Psychological Science, 11,* 96–101.

DeHue, F., Bolman, C., & Völlink, T. (2008). Cyberbullying: Youngsters' experiences and parental perception. *CyberPsychology & Behavior. 11*(2), 217–223.

Devoe, J. F., Peter, K., Noonan, M., Snyder, T. D., Baum, K., & Snyder, T. D. (2005, November). *Indicators of school crime and safety: 2005.* U.S. Department of Justice. http://www.ncjrs.gov/App/publications/abstract.aspx ?ID=210697.

Espelage, D. L., & Swearer, S. M. (2003). Research on school bullying and victimization: What have we learned and where do we go from here? *School Psychology Review, 32,* 365–383.

Fekkes, M., Pijpers, F. I. M., & Verloove-Vanhorick, S. P. (2005). Bullying: Who does what, when and where? Involvement of children, teachers and parents in bullying behavior. *Health Education Research, 20,* 81–91.

Finn, J. (2004). A survey of online harassment at a university campus. *Journal of Interpersonal Violence, 19,* 468–483.

Greenfield, P. M., & Yan, Z. (2006). Children, adolescents and the Internet: A new field of inquiry in developmental psychology. *Developmental Psychology, 42,* 391–394.

Gross, E. F. (2004). Adolescent Internet use: What we expect, what teens report. *Journal of Applied Developmental Psychology, 25,* 633–649.

Harris, S., Petrie, G., & Willoughby, W. (2002). Bullying among 9th graders: An exploratory study. *NASSP Bulletin, 86,* 1630.

Hashima, P., & Finkelhor, D. (1999). Violent victimization of youth versus adults in National Crime Victimization Survey. *Journal of Interpersonal Violence, 14,* 799–819.

Herring, S. C. (1994). Bringing familiar baggage to the new frontier: Gender differences in computer-mediated communication. In J. Selzer (Ed.), *Conversations* (pp. 1069–1082). Boston: Allyn & Bacon.

Hinduja, S., & Patchin, J. (2007). Offline consequences of online victimization: School violence and delinquency. *Journal of School Violence, 6,* 89–112.

Hinduja, S., & Patchin, J. (2009). *Bullying beyond the schoolyard: Preventing and responding to cyberbullying.* Thousand Oaks, CA: Sage.

I-SAFE America. (2003). Retrieved August 8, 2006, from http://www.ncjrs.gov/pdffiles1/nij/ISAFE.pdf.

ISG. (2001). Girls on the net: The survey of adolescent girls' use of the Internet in New Zealand. Auckland: New Zealand Internet Safety Group. Retrieved September 19, 2005, from http://www.netsafe.orgnz/research/research_girls.aspx.

Jackson, L. A., von Eye, A., Biocca, F. A., Barbatsis, G., Zhao, Y., & Fitzgerald, H. E. (2006). Does home Internet use influence the academic performance of low-income children? *Developmental Psychology, 42,* 429–435.

Juvonen, J., & Gross, E. F. (2008). Extending the school grounds? Bullying experiences in cyberspace. *Journal of School Health, 78,* 496–506.

Kerr, M., & Statin, H. (2000). What parents know, how they know it, and several forms of adolescent adjustment: Further support for a reinterpretation of monitoring. *Developmental Psychology, 36,* 366–380.

Kowalski, R. M., & Limber, S. P. (2007). Electronic bullying among middle school students. *Journal of Adolescent Health, 41,* S22–S30.

Kubey, R. (2002). How media education promotes critical thinking, democracy, health, and aesthetic appreciation. In *Thinking critically about media: Schools and families in partnership* (pp. 1–6). Alexandria, VA: Cable in the Classroom. www.ciconline.org.

Lavallee, A. (2007, March 16). Friends swap twitters, and frustration. *The Wall Street Journal.* Retrieved May 7, 2008, from http://online.wsj.com/public/article/SB117373145818634482-ZwdoPQ0PqPrcFMDHDZLz_P6osnI_20080315.html.

Lenhart, A., & Madden, M. (2007, April 18). Teens, privacy, and online social networks. *Pew Internet and American Life Project.* http://www.pewinternet.org/PPF/r/211/report_display.asp.

Li, Q. (2007). New bottle but old wine: A research of cyberbullying in schools. *Computers in Human Behavior, 23,* 1777–1791.

Liau, A. K., Khoo, A., & Ang, P. H. (2005). Factors influencing adolescents engagement in risky Internet behavior. *CyberPsychology & Behavior, 8,* 513–520.

McQuade, S. C., & Sampat, N. M. (2008). Survey of Internet and at-risk behaviors: Undertaken by school districts of Monroe County, New York. Retrieved September 13, 2008, from http://www.rrcsei.org/RIT%20Cyber%20Survey%20Final%20Report.pdf.

Mitchell, K. J., Becker-Blease, K. A., & Finkelhor, D. (2005). Inventory of problematic Internet experiences encountered in clinical practice. *Professional Psychology: Research and Practice, 36,* 498–509.

Mitchell, K., Finkelhor, D., & Wolak, J. (2001). Risk factors for and impact of online sexual solicitation of youth. *Journal of the American Medical Association, 285,* 3011–3014.

Mitchell, K., Finkelhor, D., & Wolak, J. (2003). The exposure of youth to unwanted sexual material on the Internet: A national survey of risk, impact, and prevention. *Youth & Society, 34,* 330–358.

Muir, D. (2005). *Violence against children in cyberspace.* ECPAT International. ECPAT_cyberspace_2005_ENG.

Nakamura, A. (2004, June 5). Killing stokes fears over impact of net. *The Japan News.* http://202.221.217.59/print/news/nn06-2004/mn20040605a5.htm.

Nansel, T. R., Overpeck, M. D., Haynie, D. L., Ruan, J. W., & Scheidt, P. C. (2003). Relationships between bullying and violence among U.S. youth. *Archives of Pediatrics & Adolescent Medicine, 157*, 348–353.

Nansel, T. R., Overpeck, M., Pilla, R. S., Ruan, J. W., Simons-Morton, B., & Scheidt, P. (2001). Bullying behaviors among U.S. youth: Prevalence and association with psychosocial adjustment. *Journal of the American Medical Association, 16*, 2094–2100.

National Campaign to Support Teen and Unplanned Pregnancy. (n.d.). Sex and tech: Results from a survey of teens and young adults. www.TheNationalCompaign.org/sextech.

Palfrey, J. (2008). *Enhancing child safety and online technologies: Final report of the Internet Safety Technical Task Force to the Multi-state Working Group on Social Networking of State Attorneys General of the United States.* Cambridge, MA: Berkman Center for Internet and Society at Harvard University.

Palfrey, J., & Gasser, U. (2008). *Born digital: Understanding the first generation of digital natives.* New York: Basic Books.

Parks, M. R., & Floyd, K. (1996). Making friends in cyberspace. *Journal of Computer-Mediated Communication, 46*, 80–97.

Patchin, J., Burgess-Proctor, A., & Hinduja, S. (2009). Cyberbullying and online harassment: Reconceptualizing the victimization of adolescent girls. In V. Garcia & J. Clifford (Eds.), *Female victims of crime: Reality reconsidered* (pp. 162–176). Upper Saddle River, NJ: Prentice Hall.

Patchin, J., & Hinduja, S. (2006). Bullies move beyond the schoolyard: A preliminary look at cyberbullying. *Youth Violence and Juvenile Justice, 4*, 148–169.

Pokin, S. (2007). Pokin around: A real person, a real death. *St. Charles Journal.* http://stcharlesjournal.stltoday.comarticles2007/11/10/nesj2tn20071110-1111stc_pokin_1.ii1.txt.

Prothrow-Stith, D., & Spivak, H. (2005). *Sugar and spice and no longer nice: How we can stop girls' violence.* San Francisco: Jossey-Bass.

Sexting, shockingly common among teens. (2009, January 15). *CBSNews.com.* http://www.cbsnews.com/stories/2009/01/15/.../main4723161.shtml.

Slonje, R., & Smith, P. K. (2008). Cyberbullying: Another main type of bullying? *Scandinavian Journal of Psychology, 4*, 147–154.

Smith, A., & Williams, K. (2004) R U there? Ostracism by cell phone text messages. *Group Dynamics: Theory, Research and Practice, 8*, 291–301.

Smith, P. K, Mahdavi, J., Carvalho, M., Fisher, S., Russelll, S., & Tippett, N. (2008). Cyberbullying: Its nature and impact in secondary school pupils. *Journal of Child Psychology and Psychiatry, 49*, 376–385.

Snider, M. (2004, May 24). Stalked by a cyberbully. *Macleans, 117*(21/22), 76.

Students Using Technology to Achieve Reading and Writing (STAR-W). (2005). Retrieved September 19, 2005, from http://www.starw.org/b2b/4TypesofCybullies.htm.

Subrahmanyam, K., Greenfield, P., Kraut, R., & Gross, E. (2001). The impact of computer use on children's and adolescents' development. *Applied Developmental Psychology, 22*, 7–30.

Subrahmanyam, K., Greenfield, P., & Smahel, D. (2006). Connecting developmental constructions to the Internet: Identity presentation and sexual exploration in online teen chat rooms. *Developmental Psychology, 42*, 395–406.

Suler, J. (2005). The psychology of cyberspace. http://www.rider.edu/suler/psycyber/psycyber.html.

Taylor, A. S., & Harper, R. (2003). The gift of the gab: A design oriented sociology of young people's use of mobiles. *Journal of Computer Supported Cooperative Work, 12*, 267–296.

Teen fight caught on tape. (2007, January 30). CBSNews.com. http://www.cbsnews .com/video/watch/?id=2368636n&tag=related;photovideo.

Van der Wal, M. F., de Wait, C. A. M., & Hirasing, R. A. (2003). Psychosocial health among young victims and offenders of direct and indirect bullying. *Pediatrics, 111*, 1312–1317.

Wallace, P. (1999). *The psychology of the Internet.* Cambridge, UK: Cambridge University Press.

Willard, N. (2002). *Computer ethics, etiquette and safety for the 21st century student.* Eugene, OR: International Society for Technology in Education.

Willard, N. (2003). Off-campus, harmful online student speech. *Journal of School Violence, 1*(2), 65–93.

Williams, K. A. (2001). *Ostracism: The power of silence.* New York: Guilford Press.

Williams, K. R., & Guerra, N. G. (2007). Prevalence and predictors of Internet bullying. *Journal of Adolescent Health, 41*, S14–S21.

Wocker, C. (2002, July 17). Bash a Christian: Rapists' hi-tech message of hate. *The Daily Telegraph*, p. 3.

Wolak, J., Mitchell, K. J., & Finkelhor, D. (2007). Does online harassment constitute bullying? An exploration of online harassment by known peers and online-only contacts. *Journal of Adolescent Health, 41*, S51–S58.

Yan, Z. (2006). What influences children's and adolescents' understanding of the complexity of the Internet? *Developmental Psychology, 42*, 418–428.

Ybarra, M., & Mitchell, K. (2004). Online aggressor/targets, aggressors, and targets: A comparison of associated youth characteristics. *Journal of Child Psychology and Psychiatry, 45*, 1308–1316.

Ybarra, M., Mitchell, K., Wolak, J., & Finkelhor, D. (2006). Examining characteristics and associated distress related to Internet harassment: Findings from the second youth internet safety survey. *Pediatrics, 118*, e1169–e1177.

Zizek, S. (2004). What can psychoanalysis tell us about cyberspace? *Psychoanalytic Review, 91*, 801–830.

Chapter 4

Bullying and Peer Sexual Harassment: A Prevention Guide for Students, Parents, and Teachers

Jennifer L. Martin

> In nineteen minutes, you can order a pizza and get it delivered. You can read a story to a child or have your oil changed. You can walk a mile. You can sew a hem. In nineteen minutes, you can stop the world, or you can just jump off it. In nineteen minutes, you can get revenge.

Bullying and harassment can have devastating effects on its victims. The above quotation, from Jodi Piccoult's *19 Minutes* (p. 5), illustrates what can happen when a student, subjected to bullying and harassment over a period of years, takes the problem into his own hands and retaliates, and how often these victims, who are systematically brutalized and harassed, view violence as the "normal" response. Bullying is misconceived by many as a normal part of growing up, which we all experience it at some time in their lives—as something that it makes us stronger. Some parents and professionals view all types of harassment as bullying. As discussed in this chapter, all phenomenon dealing with harassment should *not* be conflated under the umbrella of bullying, and harassment does *not* have to be an experience accepted as "normal." There are things that students, parents, and professionals can do to lessen the problem of harassment; this chapter also discusses some potential solutions and proactive responses to the problem of peer harassment.

Bullying is not illegal in most states, and thus "bullying" is typically not a legal term. Given this fact, "harassment" should be used as the umbrella term to describe the varieties of abusive behaviors students may experience in school; bullying is but one form of harassment. Title IX protects students from sexual harassment in federally funded schools; however, many schools have side-stepped the requirements of Title IX through a curricular sleight of hand. Today's elementary, middle, and high schools have been besieged with programs to prevent "bullying." The concepts of cyberbullying and female aggression have proliferated in the popular press, as have ideas to prevent bullying in schools.

Ostensibly, such programs seem like a good move on the part of schools. Yes, bullying is harmful and should be prevented. Yes, teachers should not turn a blind eye to school bullying and pass it off as normal social development preparing students for the pecking order of adulthood. However, a subtle danger arises from this push for censure of bullying. To perceive certain behaviors as bullying can mask the deeper and more criminal nature of certain acts—for example, sexual harassment. Sexual harassment is actionable under federal law. Under Title IX, students can sue for damages if schools do not adequately deal with the harassment. If schools define instances of sexual harassment as bullying, and if students and parents are unaware of their rights, then students are not protected by the law, given that bullying is not illegal in most states. Moreover, no monetary compensation is available for the victims of bullying. Therein lies the danger of the focus on bullying that is occurring in today's schools: sexual harassment is in danger of being eclipsed under the new educational Band-Aid applied to bullying in general. If educators allow this to happen, many victims of sexual harassment will have no legal recourse.

Recently, Title IX provisions have been applied in cases where students have been victimized because of their real or perceived sexual orientation, gender identification, and expression. If students are harassed because their appearance, behavior, or some other characteristic deviates from traditional gender norms, then this harassment constitutes sex discrimination based on sex-role stereotyping. Current case law utilizing Title IX as a right of action is discussed later in this chapter.

School-based harassment is unwanted behavior, which can be verbal or nonverbal, written, or graphic or subtle, sexual, or physical, that is directed at an individual or group. Harassment often is targeted at a perceived defining characteristic, such as race, sex, gender identity or sexual minority status, color, or ethnicity. According to Steineger (2001), harassment is "about intimidation, control, misuse of power, and the attempt to deny the victim equality" (p. 14). Types of harassment include institutionalized racism, quid pro quo and hostile environment sexual harassment, bullying, and cyberbullying, among others. Behaviors that qualify as harassment may include name calling; slurs based on stereotypes; graffiti; the dissemination of offensive materials or drawings (such as racist or sexist literature); vandalism; comments about personal appearance; sexual innuendoes; sexual leering; unwanted touching; inappropriate gestures; unwanted contact via phone, Internet, email, or other means; unwanted gifts and attention; repeated and unwanted requests for dates; pressure for sexual favors; sexual rumors; and sexual assault (actual, attempted, simulated, or threatened) (Steineger, 2001). According to Eckes (2006), as many as 80 percent of U.S. students have experienced some form of harassment in school.

Historically, school based harassment has been difficult to define: what one may perceive as teasing, another may see as abuse. School officials often consider peer harassment in many forms as representing one person's word against another. In reality, this line of thinking merely simplifies the matter and does nothing to resolve the situation. It is not the intent of the harasser that is at issue here. Whether an instance of harassment was intended to be a joke is of no consequence; rather, it is the perception of the victim that determines whether harassment has taken place. For example, an appropriate response to those who claim that they were only kidding or just having fun would be "If it hurts, it isn't funny" (Steineger, 2001, p. 14).

Because harassment is a sensitive issue, with raw feelings at the core, often people are hesitant to talk about it. This failure to address specific incidents of harassment, or to address the issue in general, causes many misconceptions in the minds of children, adolescents, and adults. Many of these misconceptions involve victim blame; for example, some people believe that victims invite harassment by the way they act or dress. The truth is that no one invites harassment.

Other misconceptions about harassment include the following myths: (1) talking about harassment and the right to sue encourage people to file false complaints and lawsuits; (2) harassment is usually a case of one person's word against another's; (3) if teachers witness student-to-student harassment but no one complains, the teachers do not have to do anything about it; (4) harassment is just a normal part of growing up (kids will be kids); (5) someone who complains about a little teasing just cannot take a joke; and (6) cracking down on jokes and teasing will lead to a humorless learning environment or workplace.

BULLYING

Research on child and adolescent bullying began in Scandinavia in the 1970s. Currently, research is being conducted on the subject in Scandinavia, the United Kingdom, and the United States. In these studies, approximately 81 percent of school-aged males and 71 percent of school-aged females report being bullied. Younger children experience even higher levels of victimization (Casey-Cannon, Hayward, & Gowen, 2001). Many early adolescents who are bullied by peers have been found to suffer psychological trauma, including a decrease in self-esteem, depression, loneliness, and anxiety (Olweus, 1993). Bullying has also been associated with absenteeism and decreased academic performance (Casey-Cannon et al., 2001).

Bullying has been defined as behavior that is intended to harm or disturb, that occurs repeatedly over time, and that represents an imbalance of power, with a more powerful person or group attacking a less powerful one (Mayo Clinic, 2001). Children who report being bullied by older children do not feel any less in control than victims who are bullied by others of the same age. This finding suggests that an imbalance of power characterizes the victim/bully dynamic (Hunter & Boyle, 2002). A power dynamic exists within the bully/victim dynamic similar to the one that exists within the dynamic of sexual harassment. This power dynamic implies interpersonal power, as opposed to other types of power based on age or institutional position.

O'Connell, Pepler, and Craig (1999) have examined the role of peers in bullying episodes in preadolescence. Their findings reveal the central role that peers play in bullying behavior on the playground. The overall point that O'Connell et al. make is that bullying does not occur in a vacuum, but rather takes place within a broader social context, involving a delicate balance of power. Peer behavior in support of the victim may do much to shift the balance of power away from the bully, although peer behavior most often reinforces bullying behavior. O'Connell et al. found that peers spend approximately 21 percent of their time actively reinforcing bullying behavior on the playground. These researchers suggest that successful interventions created to combat the problem of bullying should not only mandate clear consequences for bullies, but also focus attention on peers for the following reasons: to reduce the influence of the bully on peers, to increase empathy for the victim, to transcend the dynamics of the peer group, and to instruct peers and bystanders on the inappropriateness of this type of aggression.

The notion of diffusion of responsibility—also known as the bystander effect, in which individuals in a group do not assist in an emergency situation because they believe others will (Darley & Latané, 1968)—has much to do with the bully/victim dynamic. Bullying *may* be reduced by reaching bystanders (Salmivalli, 2001). However, O'Connell et al. (1999) found that 54 percent of the time peers reinforced bullying behavior by passively observing the scenario and not attempting to assist the victim. Many of these same peers will also insist that they are guilty of nothing. Successful interventions should reinforce the notion that inaction can, in fact, imply guilt. They must also target the peer group—the bystanders—to emphasize their alliance with the victim instead of tacitly reinforcing bullying behavior by doing nothing. McMahon (1995), for example, found that reported incidents of bullying among middle school students can be reduced through peer mediation and group exercises.

Salmivalli (1999) examined bullying as a group phenomenon that is enabled by the peer group: different students take on participant roles in the bullying dynamic such as "assistants of the bully," "reinforcers of the bully," or "outsiders" (p. 453). The dynamic of bullying involves more than just victims and bullies; other children and adolescents may be involved in the process as well. For example, some children and adolescents actively assist the bully by joining in the abuse. Other children and adolescents, although they may not overtly attack the victim, may give positive feedback to the victim by providing an audience, laughing, or applauding. These children and adolescents are referred to by Salmivalli as "reinforcers." Outsiders, by comparison, allow bullying to occur or continue by silently acquiescing to it. Defenders are those who emphasize or stand up for the victim.

Salmivalli (1999) found that although the majority of students' attitudes were found to be antibullying, the majority of their behaviors did not correspond to their attitudes (Stevens, Van Oost, and de Bourdeaudhuij [2000] echo this finding). Many non-involved children are motivated by the belief that they either will lose social influence if they challenge the bully or will be bullied themselves (Stevens et al., 2000). Salmivalli (1999) argues that the group dynamic influences behaviors through conformity to pressure students to act in certain ways to reinforce bullying.

Dijkstra, Lindenberg, and Veenstra (2008) argue that added status is often the reward obtained by high-status adolescents through bullying. Thus begins a vicious cycle: when popular students engage in bullying behaviors, such behaviors begin to lose some of their negative connotations; other students then imitate these bullying behaviors (Dijkstra et al., 2008). Although most children and adolescents theoretically and hypothetically disapprove of bullying, many of these same students may play an active role in the bullying process for these very reasons (Salmivalli & Voeten, 2004). Often, the popular students set the behavioral norms within schools and classrooms.

High-status students tend to combine antisocial, bullying behaviors with positive personality or attractiveness features; in other words, it is not just their bullying behaviors that define their popularity. Conversely, when low-status students imitate bullying behaviors engaged in by popular students, many of which they are typically on the receiving end, such action has a counterproductive effect. In short, it does not increase their status among their peers (Dijkstra et al., 2008).

Salmivalli (1999) argues that interventions created to combat bullying should be directed to target the whole group. This author further suggests that successful interventions should include awareness-raising, self-reflection, opportunities to role-play positive peer behavior, and assertiveness training (which includes instruction in how to resist group pressure). As part of these efforts, trained peer supporters may be used to assist in combating bullying behavior and in the creation of a more positive school culture.

Stevens, Van Oost, and de Bourdeaudhuij (2000) evaluated the effect of an antibullying intervention on students' attitudes toward bullying. This program focused on increasing positive attitudes toward children who are bullied and encouraging bystander intervention to reduce bullying. Because most students do not take action against bullying, the program participants were taught strategies to deal with bullies, such as how to support victims, how to seek assistance from teachers, and what the benefits and drawbacks of intervening are.

Interventions created to combat bullying should be research based and involve students in developing the policies intended to alter the school climate with regard to bullying so as to promote positive interaction between students; this kind of collaboration will serve to encourage inclusion and empowerment for students (Casey-Cannon et al., 2001). Interventions should also send a clear message that bullying will not be tolerated. Teachers, administrators, parents, and all school staff should be included in these educational efforts, as well as students. It is only when the entire school community is included that successful change can occur (Olweus, 2003).

SEXUAL HARASSMENT

Brandenburg (1997) found that peer sexual harassment is the most common form of sexual harassment occurring among students in K12 schools and that it affects approximately 60 to 75 percent of students. In their study of junior high school students, Roscoe, Strouse, and Goodwin (1994) found that 50 percent of females and 36.8 percent of males experienced behaviors constituting sexual harassment. These findings are is consistent with those of an American Association of University Women (AAUW Educational Foundation, 2001/1993) study, which revealed that males are consistently the perpetrators of harassing behavior toward female students. Timmerman (2002) found that the most likely form of peer sexual harassment is of a verbal nature (65%). Boys tend to report more verbal experiences than girls (70% and 47%, respectively), whereas girls report more physical forms of sexual harassment than boys (21% and 11%, respectively).

These studies suggest that students in K–12 schools are more likely to experience sexual harassment than individuals in the workplace or in higher education. Peer sexual harassment is a problem for both females and males, but females experience the majority of harassment. Males often experience sexual harassment at the hands of other males, whereas the sexual harassment experienced by females is most often perpetrated by males. Females also experience more instances of physical harassment than do males.

Sexual harassment is a complicated phenomenon involving various interrelated factors, such as gender, patriarchal norms, and issues of power. Because the phenomenon is so complex, researchers and educators often have difficulty agreeing on one precise definition of sexual harassment. Sexual harassment is defined by the AAUW as follows:

> [U]nwanted and unwelcome sexual behavior that interferes with your life. Sexual harassment is not behaviors that you like or want (for example, wanted kissing, touching, or flirting). (2001/1993, p. 2)

This definition of sexual harassment has become widely accepted by educators and researchers working within the K–12 environment.

The AAUW study suggests that individuals do not routinely report incidents of sexual harassment. To compound this problem, schools often do not take action when incidents of sexual harassment are reported (Kopels & Dupper, 1999). This failure on the part of schools causes a cadre of other problems for the victims. Ignoring claims of sexual harassment or viewing them as typical adolescent behavior or as mere bullying will not make the problems go away. In fact, to not deal with the issue of sexual harassment in a proactive manner merely serves to create an environment that is more hostile, where students do not feel safe and protected by the adults around them.

Schools that do not intervene in the issue of sexual harassment may be doing more than reinforcing the traditional hierarchy and devaluing the voices of girls: they may be implicitly encouraging a pattern of male violence. As Stein (1996) states, "If school authorities do not intervene and sanction students who sexually harass, the schools may be encouraging a continued pattern of violence in relationships: schools may be training grounds for the insidious cycle of domestic violence" (p. 22). In essence, a lack of intervention on the part of the school can adversely affect both the victim and the perpetrator. If students who harass do not experience any negative consequences for their actions or receive corrective information on how to interact with others, their problems with harassment and victimization may grow steadily worse (Stein, 1996).

According to the AAUW study (2001/1993), students are six times more likely to report incidents of sexual harassment to a friend than they are to a school official, despite the fact that students also report awareness of sexual harassment policies and procedures. Moreover, although students are aware of sexual harassment policies and procedures in their schools, neither girls nor boys are likely to file formal complaints (AAUW Educational Foundation, 2001/1993). As alluded to previously, one possible reason for the failure of students to report sexual harassment to the adults in their schools is the perception that school officials, whether implicitly or explicitly, condone this behavior; this perception may be a core belief that contributes to the culture of the school and serves to perpetuate a hostile environment. Research suggests that to combat sexual harassment in schools, educators must take a proactive approach (Fineran & Bennett, 1998; Kopels & Dupper, 1999).

According to Steineger (2001), "Targets of harassment may feel confused, guilty, helpless, angry, frightened, hopeless, scared, and alone. They may think: I can't believe this is happening to me. Why me? What did I do? I hate you for doing this. If I say anything, everyone will think I'm crazy" (p. 21). The consequences of harassment include social withdrawal, avoidance, and a lack of participation in school and in after-school activities (Bishop et al., 2004).

Peer sexual harassment has been found to have detrimental academic and social consequences for both girls and boys. According to Fineran and Bennett (1998), peer sexual harassment can cause performance difficulty including absenteeism, decreased quality of schoolwork, skipping or dropping courses, lower grades, loss of friends, tardiness, and truancy in its victims. Kopels and Dupper (1999) suggest that girls suffer a variety of long-term effects as a result of peer sexual harassment, such as feeling embarrassed or self-conscious, not wanting to attend school, not wanting to speak up as much in class, and difficulty staying focused.

HARASSMENT OF SEXUAL MINORITIES

According to the AAUW study of sexual harassment on campuses (Hill & Silva, 2005), lesbian, gay, bisexual, and transgender (LGBT) students are more likely to be victims of harassment than are heterosexual students; males are more likely to be harassers compared to females; the majority of harassers think their actions are humorous; and the majority of victims do not report sexual harassment. Antigay harassment is also a common experience for college students (Hill & Silva, 2005).

In a study conducted by Human Rights Watch (Bochenek & Widney Brown, 2001), 90 percent of LGBT participants reported hearing antigay language in their schools to the point where they felt uncomfortable. Approximately 60 percent reported being victims of verbal harassment in school; half of these students reported being verbally harassed on a daily basis. This type of harassment typically occurs in unstructured areas such as hallways and lunch rooms. Unfortunately, teachers, administrators, and other staff members often fail to respond to or report anti-LGBT language and harassment when they hear it (Sadowski, 2001). Some students even reported hearing school personnel use anti-LGBT and inflammatory language themselves (Sadowski, 2001).

In a survey conducted by the Gay, Lesbian, and Straight Education Network (GLSEN, 2007), 86 percent of sexual minority students reported being harassed verbally because of their sexual orientation, 44 percent had been physically harassed, 22 percent had been physically assaulted, and 75 percent had heard homophobic remarks. Ninety percent of students heard the word "gay" used in a negative manner, such as "That's so gay." Tragically, 60 percent of these students failed to report these incidents to school staff members because they felt that nothing would be done about it. Thirty-one percent of students who did report their incidents of harassment indicated that nothing was done in response. Homophobic and sexist language is common in today's schools—but language is also often where harassment starts. If school officials are expected to intervene when they hear harassing language used, they may prevent more serious offenses from being committed. Teachers must be encouraged to intervene when they hear this type of language and be trained in how to do so effectively.

Students who experience harassment based on their LGBT status may experience severe consequences. Sexual minority youth report having more problems emotionally and behaviorally than do their sexual majority counterparts; they also experience both verbal and physical harassment more frequently. Additionally, these youth report having less access to family and peer support than do their heterosexual peers (Williams, Connolly, Pepler, & Craig, 2005). The effects of harassment on sexual minority youth are great, including avoiding certain parts of the school, having difficulty in paying attention in classes, participating less in classes, and skipping classes altogether (Sadowski, 2001).

According to Williams, Connolly, Pepler, and Craig (2005), between 1 percent and 3 percent of adolescents report being gay or bisexual; another 10 percent are questioning their sexual identity. Sexual harassment has been reported to be a significant problem for sexual minority youth, as is a hostile peer environment (Williams et al., 2005). Sexual minority youth are also three times as likely as their non-minority status peers to skip school because of safety issues, and to report having been injured by or threatened with a weapon. These students are more than twice as likely to report being in a physical fight at school. Finally, sexual minority youth are more than four times as likely to attempt suicide. Suicide is a leading cause of death for these youths, who report feeling greater levels of alienation, helplessness, hopelessness, loneliness, and worthlessness than their heterosexual peers.

According to Rivers and Noret (2008), students who report being harassed because of actual or perceived sexual minority status also report engaging in more heath-risk behaviors such as drug use. Unfortunately, most schools do not specifically include the category of sexual minority status in policies and procedures prohibiting bullying.

Schools with gay–straight alliances (GSAs) have been found to be more welcoming to sexual minority students than schools without such organizations (Sadowski, 2001). Staff training on LGBT issues is also instrumental in creating a safe school climate for all students.

THE LAW

Title IX has been instrumental in sexual harassment case law. Title IX of the Educational Amendments (1972) states, "No person in the United States shall, on the basis of sex, be excluded from participation in, be denied benefits of, or be subjected to discrimination under any educational program or activity receiving federal financial assistance." Further, this legislation requires that federally funded educational institutions establish a complaint procedure for victims of sex discrimination, and that they appoint, train, and make available to the public a Title IX coordinator to oversee complaints. In theory, schools have always had an implicit responsibility to protect their students. In cases of sexual harassment, however, protection of all students does not always occur. There are often different interpretations of what constitutes sexual harassment. Unfortunately, there are also examples of teachers, and schools in general, failing to intervene when cases of sexual harassment do occur. These instances have led to lawsuits that have, in turn, set new precedents within the courts. Specifically, as a result of these rulings, school districts may now be held financially liable for failing to intervene in reported sexual harassment cases. School districts are now obligated to respond to peer sexual harassment under Title IX.

Title IX is enforced by the Office for Civil Rights of the U.S. Department of Education. *Alexander v. Yale University* (1980) was the first sexual harassment case that involved students and faculty; in this case, the courts was found that sexual harassment constituted sex discrimination under Title IX.

For schools to be held liable for harassment of students, they must have actual knowledge of the harassment and act with deliberate indifference to it; the harassing behavior must be severe, pervasive, and offensive; and it must have the impact of negatively affecting the victim's educational process (Eckes, 2006). Notably, the Supreme Court rulings in the *Gebser v. Lago Vista Independent School District* (1998) and *Davis v. Monroe County Board of Education* (1999) cases have created harsh standards for claims of sexual harassment, which rest on the notion of a district's "deliberate indifference." In effect, these decisions have done two things: (1) they have caused the dismissal of many claims of sexual harassment on the part of students, and (2) they have created a culture of fear in school administrators and board members. Tacit policies have been initiated in their wake that promote an agenda of denial in which schools do not educate their children about their rights for fear of incurring liability. It is imperative that both students and parents are aware of their rights, and of the laws that protect students from harassment in school.

As previously stated, Title IX mandates the appointment of a Title IX coordinator in educational institutions receiving federal funds to oversee the schools' compliance with the law, to deal with complaints, and to oversee reporting procedures; schools are also required to make this information public so that students and parents can obtain assistance and support. In reality, schools often do not make public the name and contact information of Title IX coordinators, if they have one at all—which makes it difficult for parents and students to know what to do and where to go if a problem arises. Many schools rely on the public's ignorance of the law to escape their own liability in cases of harassment.

Moreover, if schools have Title IX coordinators, these individuals are often superintendents or other high-level administrators who are far removed from daily contact with students. A Title IX coordinator is an advocacy position, which suggests that this role should not be filled by an individual in an administrative position with a vested interest in taking the expedient route (what is easiest and most cost-effective for the school), as opposed to what is best for the student. This dual role of administrator and advocate may represent a conflict of interest. Ideally, the role of Title IX coordinator should be performed by individuals who are already working in positions of student advocacy, and they should be directly accessible to students and parents—such as teachers or counselors. Additionally, Title IX coordinators should be adequately trained in their responsibilities, in sex discrimination, different forms of harassment, the effect of harassment on victims, and other pertinent concerns. They should also be apprised of new developments in case law.

In the recent past, many conflicts have arisen within the circuit courts regarding sexual harassment in schools and school liability. The U.S. Supreme Court resolved these conflicts in *Gebser v. Lago Vista Independent School District* (1998). In a 5–4 decision, the Court found that a school's "actual knowledge" and "deliberate indifference" were required to impose liability on a school district (Titus, 1999). In other words, plaintiffs must prove what the school knew.

Title IX does not expressly authorize a private right of action. However, in its ruling in *Cannon v. University of Chicago* (1979), the Supreme Court determined that Title IX includes an implicit private right of action, allowing individuals to bring private civil suits for sexual discrimination committed by federally funded institutions. The *Franklin v. Gwinnett*

County Public Schools (1992) case establishes the right to sue school districts for compensatory damages under Title IX.

In May 1999, the Supreme Court first *explicitly* addressed the issue of school liability for *peer* sexual harassment in *Davis v. Monroe County Board of Education*. The two-pronged test, which is used to assess teacher liability for teacher-harassing-student sexual harassment under Title IX in the *Gebser* ruling, provided the foundation for the Court's decision in *Davis*. The Supreme Court found that "recipients of federal funding may be liable for subjecting their students to discrimination where the recipient is deliberately indifferent to known acts of student-on-student sexual harassment, and the harasser is under the school's disciplinary authority" (as cited in Manke, 2000, p. 149). In other words, the *Davis* decision mandated that all recipients of federal education funding are obligated to investigate claims of peer sexual harassment and that a decision to do nothing in the case of peer sexual harassment is a decision that may incur liability under Title IX. The *Davis* ruling placed a higher burden of proof on a victim of peer sexual harassment than on a victim of sexual harassment by a teacher or other adult affiliated with the school. Despite the fact that the burden of proof relies heavily on the victim, the *Davis* decision put more weight behind Title IX. As a result, school districts may now suffer severe financial consequences if they fail to investigate or take action when claims of sexual harassment arise.

As of 2008, seven states (California, Iowa, Maine, Maryland, Minnesota, New Jersey, and Vermont) and the District of Columbia had laws protecting students from harassment based upon sexual orientation and gender expression. California has added the category of gender identity to these protections. However, existing federal laws may cover claims of harassment and discrimination of students based on sexual orientation and gender identity if schools fail to deal effectively with these claims. These federal laws include the First Amendment, the Equal Protection Clause of the Fourteenth Amendment, and Title IX of the Educational Amendments. In 1997, the Office for Civil Rights issued an interpretation of policy that included sexual harassment of gay students to be prohibited by Title IX. *Tinker v. Des Moines Independent Community School District* (1969) is the U.S. Supreme Court's controlling precedent covering harassment based on sexual identity; it relies on the First Amendment's freedom of speech protection.

Many examples can be cited regarding the effectiveness of Title IX in addressing discrimination against sexual minorities, including LGBT students and those individuals who do not conform to traditional gender roles. According to the Women's Sports Foundation (2008), "Though Title IX does not directly address discrimination based on sexual orientation, gender expectations linked with stereotypes of lesbians and gay men often are related. When gender stereotyping occurs in incidents of discrimination and harassment of lesbian, gay, bisexual students or students who are perceived to be lesbian, gay, or bisexual, Title IX may provide legal grounds for challenging this discrimination" (p. 1).

In 1995, Derek Henkle, an openly gay high school student in Nevada, was subject to prolonged and abusive peer sexual harassment. Although he reported a variety of incidents over time, school officials did nothing to assist him, and some even condoned the harassment by laughing or by blaming the victim. Henkle was eventually told that he should hide his sexuality, and then the harassment would perhaps lessen. When the problem did not subside, Henkle sued the school district. Henkle had cause under Title IX: he sued for monetary damages because the district showed "deliberate indifference" in addressing his claims (under the Fourteenth Amendment, for the district's failure to protect Henkle from peer harassment based on sexual orientation, and under the First Amendment, in that he was denied the expression of his sexual identity). According to Sadowski (2001), "The federal statute Title IX . . . can be applied where students are targeted—or their complaints are ignored—because they are perceived as not conforming to gender norms. Moreover, anti-LGBT behavior can be construed as sexual harassment where a perpetrator's actions involve sexual gestures or similar conduct, and school personnel can be held liable if they fail to respond under these circumstances" (p. 3).

Prior to the court's decision on the Title IX issue, the school district agreed to settle Henkle's claims and paid out $451,000, including Henkle's attorneys' fees and court costs. Part of the settlement included stipulations that the district revise its policy on harassment, that it train students and staff on harassment, and that it acknowledge students' freedom to discuss their sexual orientation. The Seventh Circuit Court of Appeals decided in Henkle's favor on the Fourteenth Amendment claim. Prior to the settlement decision, the district offered to pay $900,000 in damages.

In *Ray v. Antioch Unified School District* (2000), the courts found that harassment based on a student's perceived sexual orientation is a form of sexual harassment. Federal district courts (1st, 5th, and 8th) have all "recognized same-same peer harassment as actionable under Title IX" (Eckes, 2006, p. 40). For example, in *Nabozny v. Podlesny* (1996), the U.S. Court of Appeals for the 7th Circuit ruled in favor of a student who was subjected to antigay harassment. In this ruling, the justices found that the school failed to protect the student from such harassment, thereby violating the student's right to equal protection and due process under Title IX. In *Theno v. Tonganoxie Unified School District* (2005), Title IX was cited in support of a male student's claim that harassment on the basis of other students' perceptions of his gender and sexual orientation was not dealt with on behalf of the school, but was met with deliberate indifference.

In *Schroeder v. Maumee Board of Education* (2003), referring to Title IX protections, the court found that a school was liable for showing deliberate indifference to the verbal and physical harassment of a student who demonstrated advocacy for gay students in the school. The justices found that targeting a person for harassment based on perceived sexual orientation and gender stereotyping was a form of sex discrimination.

In *Patterson v. Hudson Area Schools* (2009), the U.S. Court of Appeals for the 6th Circuit ruled that school districts can be held liable for "deliberate indifference" to peer sexual harassment based on sexual orientation, whether real or perceived. In essence, if schools do not take reasonable steps to end patterns of harassment, they can be subject to lawsuits.

In these cases, Title IX was used to successfully address the sexual harassment of students based on other students' perceptions of the victim's sexual orientation, gender identification, or expression stemming from gender stereotyping. Thus the "courts ruled that discrimination or harassment based on gender non-conformity is a form of sex discrimination and, therefore, Title IX applies" (Women's Sports Foundation, 2008, p. 1). Schools must be held accountable to the requirements of Title IX to encourage them to protect students from harassment and to create safe and equitable educational environments for all students. One way to ensure this compliance is for parents to be aware of the law, and the requirements of schools under the law. In short, to create safer schools, parents must become advocates for their children.

SOLUTIONS

> If we don't change the direction we are headed, we will end up where we are going.
>
> —Chinese proverb

Educators, parents, and students must understand that anger and conflict are normal human emotions that arise in many different situations; even so, harassment and bullying must not be seen as normal. Learning how to deal with emotions and stressful situations should be a priority of schools. Avoidance of these issues will simply perpetuate the problems of harassment and bullying. The key to stopping school-based harassment and creating a more positive school culture is normative hegemony: by targeting third parties, or bystanders. If third parties are taught to eschew harassment and bullying, others will follow their lead (Bishop et al., 2004). Ultimately, the goal of schools should be inclusive normative hegemony. If a school is dominated by a popular crowd whose members dictate the behaviors of other cliques, then an intervention should target this group, albeit not to the exclusion of other groups. Interventions intended to curb harassment should begin early, in elementary school, and should be reinforced throughout the secondary years.

Students should be encouraged to stand up for victims of harassment and to report incidents of harassment that they witness; anonymity of these third parties should be protected. Teachers should not only be trained on the harasser/victim dynamic (including what harassment is, which behaviors constitute harassment, and how harassment affects victims), but also should be expected to intervene when they witness harassment in their classrooms or on school grounds, and be trained regarding how to do so.

It is important that interventions to combat school-based harassment as well as antiharassment policies identify clear definitions of harassing behavior in its many forms and specify clear consequences for these behaviors. Policies should be reinforced with students, in student-friendly language, with examples of prohibited behaviors, enumerated categories of groups and identities often used to harass (e.g., sex, race, religion, sexual minority status, appearance, ableism), statements of the effects harassment has on victims, consequences for perpetrators, reporting procedures, a non-retaliation statement for those who report incidents of harassment, and information on where to go for support in dealing with harassment. This information should be posted throughout the school and shared with parents.

School Faculty and Staff

Every student is entitled to equal access to educational opportunity in a safe environment. If teachers and administrators are unaware of harassment, they cannot do anything to stop it. Although education must be part of the solution in reducing harassment in schools, rules alone are not enough. In the past, teachers may have turned their backs on harassment and bullying because they did not know how to deal with it. This is no longer an acceptable response. Schools have an obligation to protect *all* students, including sexual minority students. To fulfill this responsibility, schools must stop perpetuating the notion that bullying is normal. Victims should be provided with support on how to deal appropriately with a bully or harasser. However, such training does not negate the school's responsibility for dealing with the harasser and doling out the necessary consequences to the harasser. It is not the victim's responsibility to stop harassment.

Schools must document and track incidents of harassment occurring within their halls and classrooms. Districts should investigate all claims promptly and thoroughly, and take corrective measures when warranted. Problem areas such as buses, cafeterias, and hallways should be monitored. School harassment typically occurs where adult supervision is absent, whether that is because no adults are present or because the adults who are present fail to intervene when harassment occurs.

Teachers and administrators must keep current on this issue by examining the research on bullying and harassment. Much insight can be gleaned from intervention research on harassment and bullying. Both teachers and administrators should be monitored for their effectiveness in dealing with these issues.

Schools must develop an atmosphere of classroom and curricular equity; they should not wait for a crisis to occur to address harassment-related issues. Districts that take a proactive approach may avoid future lawsuits; some suggestions in this regard are to appoint an equity coordinator as well as a Title IX coordinator, and to support the creation of school GSAs. Districts can create and disseminate a handbook for students and parents that defines harassment and provides examples of prohibited behaviors. This handbook should also outline reporting procedures, provide information about where students can go for help, and include a statement prohibiting retaliation for reporting. The same policies and procedures should be posted throughout the halls, in classrooms, and in the counseling office of the school.

Schools can use surveys to assess their internal climate with regard to harassment students are facing. Often, schools do not want to know the true extent of the harassment that occurs within their hallways. If harassment is known to be a major problem, then schools are obligated to act. If teachers and administrators are aware of what is occurring within their classrooms and hallways with regard to harassment, that recognition can serve as the first step in alleviating the problem. Educators can then identity problem areas, targeted groups, and other areas of concern, and potentially create a research-based intervention that will promote a healthier, more equitable environment for their students. As an aside, such actions might enable the school officials to head off future lawsuits against the school district. In sum, administrators should take a proactive approach when it comes to issues of harassment, because in the long run this stance is the best option for enhancing the culture of the school as well as the health and well-being of the students.

Teachers play a crucial role in alleviating harassment. They must be present and available to students, supervising children vigilantly at recess and during unstructured time. Teachers must be present in the hallways, and must step in when they see harassing or bullying behaviors of any sort—verbal, physical, or otherwise. In previous research, teachers have been found to condone bullying (to validate the antisocial behaviors of popular students so they will not get pulled into the cycle). That is, it is often easier for teachers to either ignore harassment or to go along with it for fear that they will become targets of bullying or retaliatory behaviors on the part of popular students. Teachers should address bullying in the classroom through curriculum and instruction, and behaviorally when "teachable moments" occur.

As part of their vigilance, teachers can look for the following signs of harassment: overt discrimination and harsher sanctions for behavioral misconduct for certain racial, ethnic groups, based on gender, or based on sexual minority status. Teachers should examine whether there is bias toward providing positive feedback for particular student groups (e.g., athletes). In addition, they should look for curricular bias. Teachers should also be aware of the denial of racist, sexist, heterosexist, or ethnocentric actions on the part of school staff or students.

Teachers must speak up when they witness harassing behavior of any kind, and be careful to use affirmative and inclusive language in their interactions with students. They should avoid inappropriate or exclusionary humor, and avoid victim blame. They must educate students to avoid such behavior as well. All educators must confront their own biases and encourage others to do the same, respect others and interact in a positive way, and model this behavior for students.

Teachers should stand up for students who are being bullied, not validate the popular students when they bully others (either overtly or covertly), and stand up when sexual minorities are being harassed, even if their lifestyle choices deviate from the teacher's own beliefs. When they witness harassment, whether in a classroom or elsewhere, teachers are morally required to step in and put an end to it, but not to simply leave it at that. Teachers should report the incident to the administration, no matter how small it might seem. Sometimes the victim simply needs an ally: a teacher making a comment to a bully in defense of a victim can have great impact. It is imperative that teachers do not tacitly condone bullying and harassment by virtue of their silence—because silence implies consent.

The first step in creating a harassment-free school is to provide comprehensive and ongoing training for all staff members, district employees, and students. When providing training for all students and staff, the following points should be included:

- Definitions of harassment, the different forms harassment can take, and discussions of the effects of harassment.
- A discussion of the language of harassment. Everyone should be aware of what constitutes hate speech. Prohibitions against racist, sexist, and homophobic language should be made.
- The creation, discussion, and implementation of an antiharassment policy written in student-friendly language that includes examples of prohibited behaviors, enumerated categories of groups and identities often used to harass (including sexual minority status), the effects harassment has on victims, consequences for perpetrators, reporting procedures, a non-retaliation statement for those who report incidents of

harassment, and information on where to go for support in dealing with harassment.

Additional suggestions for training include the following measures:

- Empower staff and students to become the trainers—then schools will also have a built-in support network of people whom students and parents can access when they or their children experience harassment. Also, if staff and students are included in the planning and implementation of the training, they will have more of a vested interest in the results, and take a more active role in maintaining a more positive school culture.
- Punishment/sanctions for offenders should be applied equitably. Rules and examples of prohibited behaviors should be clearly communicated to all students.

Additional tips for administrators to prevent harassment include the following ideas:

- Set clear expectations for students and staff with regard to harassment.
- A support person should be designated for teachers to consult to gain insight into how to deal with harassment in their classrooms and within the school in general. Open communication with regard to dealing with issues of harassment is key.
- Provide for a diverse staff.
- Expand the library collection to incorporate titles that reflect diversity and ensure that the curriculum reflects multiple perspectives as well.
- Provide assertiveness training for victims.
- Provide support groups for students in which they can share their experiences and gain strength.

Students

If you, as a student, are experiencing harassment, do not blame yourself. Keep a journal of the incidents you experience, with times, dates, witnesses, and other pertinent information. Give as much detail as possible about what happened and what was said. Students also need support to help deal with this situation: tell a parent or school personnel. If you feel safe enough, communicate to the perpetrator that this behavior is not okay with you, that it makes you feel uncomfortable. You may want to define the behavior as harassment.

Read and familiarize yourself with your school's harassment policy. Inquire about the process that will be followed in your case. Follow any directions that specify the victim's role in reporting the claim. If you are unsatisfied with the outcome of your claim, go to a higher school authority. Keep documenting what you experience. Ask for counseling or support if necessary.

Parents

Parents can take many steps to help their children deal with peer harassment. A key point is to start by raising children in a consistent environment where limits are set. When disciplining children, parents should follow these guidelines:

- Set limits for children's behavior.
- Avoid using coercion and control when imposing discipline; such tactics can cause aggressive tendencies in children ("Bullying," 2001).
- Be consistent when using disciplinary measures. Inconsistency and coercion can contribute to the production of a bully. Be firm, consistent, and loving when imposing discipline.

Another way parents can help their children deal with peer harassment or prevent their children from experiencing harassment in school is to become an advocate for the child:

- Become familiar with the school's policies and procedures by reading the student handbook.
- Be aware of the laws that protect children from harassment in schools and schools' obligations under these laws.
- Join (or advocate for) a parents' group to discuss these and other issues relevant to children.
- Inform community members and parents about these expectations (namely, that harassment of any kind will not be tolerated).
- Conduct student, teacher, parent, and community focus groups to address the problems of harassment and bullying in school (Pirozzi, 2001).
- Attend school-based anti-bullying training attended by the child.

REFERENCES

American Association of University Women (AAUW) Educational Foundation. (2001/1993). *Hostile hallways: Bullying, teasing, and sexual harassment in school*. Washington, DC: Author.
Bishop, J., Bishop, M., Bishop, M., Gelbwasser, L., Peterson, E., Rubinsztaj, A., & Zuckerman, A. (2004). Why we harass nerds and freaks: A formal theory of student culture and norms. *Journal of School Health, 74*. 235–251.

Bochenek, M., & Widney Brown, A. (2001). *Hatred in the hallways: Violence and discrimination against lesbian, gay, bisexual, and transgender students in U.S. schools*. New York: Human Rights Watch. Retrieved March 13, 2009, from www.hrw.org/reports/2001/uslgbt/toc.htm.

Brandenburg, J. (1997). *Confronting sexual harassment: What schools and colleges can do*. New York: Teachers College Press.

Bullying. (2001). *ERIC Digest* (ED459405).

Casey-Cannon, S., Hayward, C., & Gowen, K. (2001). Middle-school girls' reports of peer victimization: Concerns, consequences, and implications. *Professional School Counseling, 5*, 138–147.

Darley, J., & Latané, B. (968). Bystander intervention in emergencies: Diffusion of responsibility. *Journal of Personality and Social Psychology, 8*, 377–383.

Dijkstra J., Lindenberg, S., & Veenstra, R. (2008). Beyond the class norm: Bullying behavior of popular adolescents and its relation to peer acceptance and rejection. *Journal of Abnormal Child Psychology, 36*, 1289–1299.

Eckes, S. (2006). Reducing peer sexual harassment in schools. *Principal Leadership, 6*, 58–62.

Fineran, S., & Bennett, L. (1998). Teenage peer sexual harassment: Implications for social work practice in education. *Social Work, 43*, 55–64.

Franklin v. Gwinnett County Public Schools, 503 U.S. 60 (1992) 503 U.S. 60.

Gay, Lesbian, and Straight Education Network (GLSEN). (2007). Executive summary. In *The 2007 National School Climate Survey: Key findings on the experiences of lesbian, gay, bisexual and transgender youth in our nation's schools*. Retrieved March 13, 2009, from http://www.google.com/search?sourceid=navclient&ie=UTF-8&rlz=1T4ADBS_enUS244US259&q=glsen+2007+national+climate+survey+executive+summar.

Hill, C., & Silva, E. (2005). *Drawing the line: Sexual harassment on campus*. Washington, DC: American Association of University Women Educational Foundation.

Hunter, S., & Boyle, J. (2002). Perceptions of control in the victims of school bullying: The importance of early intervention. *Educational Research, 44*, 323–336.

Kopels, S., & Dupper, D. (1999). School-based peer sexual harassment. *Child Welfare, 78*(4), 435–460.

Manke, C. (2000). Student-on-student sexual harassment: A case comment on the Supreme Court's decision in Davis v. Monroe county board of education. "119 S. Ct. 1661 (1999)." *Denver University Law Review, 78*(1): 149–172.

Mayo Clinic. (2001). Headline watch: One-third of U.S. kids affected by bullying. Mayo Foundation for Medical Education and Research (MFMER). http://www.mayoclinic.com/findinformation/conditioncenters/invoke.cfm?objectid=09C423AB-1A81-B9730315E83291E4.

McMahon, P. (1995). *Stemming harassment among middle school students through peer mediation exercises*. Doctoral practicum paper, Nova Southeastern University (ERIC Document Reproduction Service No. ED393027).

O'Connell, P., Pepler, D., & Craig, W. (1999). Peer involvement in bullying: Insights and challenges for intervention. *Journal of Adolescence, 22*, 437–452.

Olweus, D. (1993). *Bullying at school: What we know and what we can do*. Oxford: Blackwell.

Olweus, D. (2003). A profile of bullying. *Educational Leadership, 60*, 12–17.

Piccoult, J. (2007). *Nineteen minutes*. New York: Atria Books.

Pirozzi, K. (2001). We don't allow that here. *Harvard Education Letter, 17*, 4–7.

Rivers, I., & Noret, N. (2008). Well-being among same-sex and opposite-sex attracted youth at school. *School Psychology Review, 37*, 174–187.

Roscoe, B., Strouse, J., & Goodwin, M. (1994). Sexual harassment: Early adolescents' self-reports of experiences and acceptance. *Adolescence, 29*, 515–523.

Sadowski, M. (2001). Sexual minority students benefit from school-based support —where it exists. *Harvard Education Letter, 17*, 1–5.

Salmivalli, C. (1999). Participant role approach to school bullying: Implications for interventions. *Journal of Adolescence, 22*, 453–459.

Salmivalli, C. (2001). Peer-led intervention campaign against school bullying: Who considered it useful, who benefited? *Educational Research, 43*, 263–278.

Salmivalli, C., & Voeten, M. (2004). Connections between attitudes, group norms, and behavior in bullying situations. *International Journal of Behavioral Development, 28*, 246–258.

Stein, N. (1996). From the margins to the mainstream: Sexual harassment in K-12 schools. *Initiatives, 57*, 19–26.

Steineger, M. (2001). *Preventing and countering school-based harassment: A resource guide for K-12 educators*. Portland, OR: Northwest Regional Educational Laboratory.

Stevens, V., Van Oost, P., & De Bourdeaudhuij, I. (2000). The effects of an anti-bullying programme on peers' attitudes and behaviour. *Journal of Adolescence, 23*, 21–34.

Timmerman, G. (2002). A comparison between unwanted sexual behavior by teachers and by peers in secondary schools. *Journal of Youth and Adolescence, 31*, 397–404.

Titus, K. (1999). Students, beware: *Gebser v. Lago Vista Independent School District*. *Louisiana Law Review, 60*, 321–348.

Williams, T., Connolly, J., Pepler, D., & Craig, W. (2005). Peer victimization, social support, and psychosocial adjustment of sexual minority adolescents. *Journal of Youth and Adolescents, 34*, 471–482.

Women's Sports Foundation: Equal Play. (2008). Title IX and discrimination based on sexual orientation. Retrieved March 31, 2009 from http://womanssportsfoundation.org/Content/Articles/Issues/Homophobia/T/Title-IX-and-Discrimination-Based-on-Sexual-Orientation.aspx.

Chapter 5

Teen Relationship Violence

Emilio Ulloa, Donna Castañeda, and Audrey Hokoda

An early exploratory study examining the problem of teen relationship violence found that 61.5 percent of the college population knew someone who had been in a violent dating relationship, and 21.2 percent had "at least one direct personal experience" with dating violence (Makepeace, 1981, p. 98). A few years later, Roscoe and Callahan (1985) found that 35 percent of their high school sample had known someone who experienced relationship violence. Furthermore, out of those high school students in Roscoe and Callahan's study, 9 percent indicated physical violence had occurred at some time during their own relationship. As a result of such findings, O'Keeffe, Brockopp, and Chew stated, in their 1986 article, "In recent years, the occurrence of violence among intimates outside the family has been explored, particularly the idea that intracouple violence is not limited to married adults, as had previously been assumed" (p. 465).

Over the next 25 years, researchers further defined teen relationship violence (TRV), describing its prevalence as well as its health and mental health outcomes. Research has described numerous correlates of TRV, including possible predictors and risk and protective factors across different levels of influences (e.g., family, peers, community, culture). Moreover, educators, law enforcement, and policymakers have developed strategies to educate, prevent, and respond to TRV. This chapter synthesizes the research in this area and reviews developments in the area of TRV in the past few decades.

DEFINITION AND PREVALENCE OF TRV

Teen relationship violence (TRV) has been defined as "any attempt to control or dominate another person physically, sexually, or psychologically, causing some level of harm" (Wekerle & Wolfe, 1999, p. 436). Although dating violence is similar to adult domestic violence in terms of the acts involved, TRV refers to non-cohabitating adolescents, typically those up to age 18 or 19, both in and out of school (e.g., Bergman, 1992). Physical abuse refers to the use of force to harm another person and consists of behaviors such as hitting, throwing of objects, grabbing, and shoving, and any physical force used with the intention to harm, disable, injure, or kill another person (Centers for Disease Control and Prevention [CDC], n.d.). Psychological abuse, which includes emotional abuse, can be verbal or nonverbal in nature; such behaviors are designed to control and subjugate another person through the use of fear, humiliation, guilt, manipulation, or other nonphysical means. Sexual abuse is (1) the use of physical force to compel a person to engage in a sexual act against her or his will, whether or not the act is completed; (2) the attempted or completed sex act involving a person who is unable to understand the nature or condition of the act, to decline participation, or to communicate unwillingness to engage in the sexual act due to illness, disability, or the influence of alcohol or other drugs, or due to intimidation or pressure; or (3) any kind of abusive sexual contact (CDC, n.d.).

Some teen relationships are guided by romanticized perceptions of relationship behavior often associated with acts of devotion, high passion, and emotionality, and are defined by acts of jealousy, possessiveness, and controlling behaviors, toward the partner. At least some teens believe that this type of aggression demonstrates the partner's love and devotion, and that a lack of this type of behavior translates into a lack of love (Johnson, Frattaroli, Campbell, Wright, & Pearson-Fields, 2005). Recent research has expanded the definition of TRV behaviors to include stalking in the context of dating relationships (Coker, Sanderson, Cantu, Huerta, & Fadden, 2008) and romantic relational aggression—behaviors that harm by damaging the romantic relationship (Linder, Crick, & Collins, 2002). Relational aggression can include behaviors such as flirting with another person to make the partner angry or threatening to leave the relationship if a partner does not comply with a request.

The explosion of cell phone technology, social networking sites, and Internet chat has opened up new avenues through which relationships may form and be maintained and, consequently, for TRV to occur. Types of abuse that employ these technologies include sending threatening or insulting messages via email or text messaging; excessive text messaging or phone calls in an attempt to keep tabs on a partner; checking a partner's phone logs, texts, email, and web browsing histories, including logging in to a partner's Facebook or MySpace account; and posting insults or defamatory information on a partner's Facebook or MySpace profile page. In a recent survey report sponsored by apparel manufacturer Liz Claiborne (Picard, 2007), the use of technology in stalking and dating violence was highlighted as a serious problem. According to the report, one in three teens (30%) reported receiving 10 to 30 text messages within an hour by a partner inquiring where they are, what they were doing, or who they were with; one in four teens in a relationship (25%) said they had been called names, harassed, or put down by their partner using cell phones and texting; and one in five teens in a relationship (22%) had been asked to engage in sex acts by cell phone or the Internet when they did not want to.

Examining prevalence rates of TRV is complicated by the nature of dating relationships, particularly during adolescence. Listening to teens describe "dating," it becomes clear they ascribe to a wide variety of definitions of this term. Teen dating can be short term or long term, and is not clearly defined by a formal set of rules or behaviors. Great diversity exists across teen relationships in the level of commitment, intimacy, and exclusiveness of the relationship. As one teen put it:

> Many of us, both guys and girls equally, seem to be avoiding the label of "boyfriend" or "girlfriend." It's about being a teenager and having fun with a guy you like, so I tend to notice that many high school relationships consist of simply "hanging out" and bonding with that person you like. (Discovery Health, 2009)

Some teens initiate and sustain a relationship through the use of Internet chat rooms, social networking sites, email, or text messaging long before they ever meet their date in person, or without meeting in person at all.

Although reported rates of TRV vary widely across studies, the consensus is that relationship violence among adolescents is not uncommon. A recent study of serious dating violence (i.e., sexual and physical assault and/or drug- or alcohol-facilitated rape by a dating partner) in a nationally representative sample of adolescents aged 12 to 17 years found the lifetime prevalence of dating violence to be 1.6 percent (2.7% of girls, 0.6% of boys) (Wolitzky-Taylor et al., 2008). This rate translates into approximately 400,000 adolescents in the United States who experience significant forms of violence in their dating relationships. In another national study conducted by Marquart and colleagues (2007), approximately 16 percent of students in grades 10 through 12 reported ever having a dating partner hit, push, or threaten them.

Whitaker and colleagues (2007) gathered data from the 2001 National Longitudinal Study of Adolescent Health, which contained information about partner violence and injury reported by 11,370 respondents. Results indicated that approximately 24 percent of all relationships included some violence. In yet another study of TRV, which defined psychological abuse as monopolization, degradation, and isolation that has occurred at least once in a relationship, an astonishing 82 percent of girls and 76 percent of boys reported this type of victimization (Jackson, Cram, & Seymour, 2000). O'Keefe and Treister (1998) found that approximately 44 percent of high school students reported physical aggression victimization from their dating partner at least once. Jackson and colleagues (2000) found that 77 percent of female high school students and 67 percent of male high school students experienced some form of sexual coercion, which included unwanted kissing, hugging, genital contact, and sexual intercourse.

In addition to general prevalence estimates of TRV, research indicates that dating violence perpetration and victimization among adolescents often co-occurs; in other words, being a perpetrator of dating violence is associated with being a victim of dating violence (Bennett & Fineran, 1998; Gaertner & Foshee, 1999; Gray & Foshee, 1997; Malik, Sorenson, & Aneshensel, 1997; O'Leary, Slep, Avery-Leaf, & Cascardi, 2008). Furthermore, perpetration of one form of dating violence (physical, psychological, or sexual) is associated with perpetration of other forms of dating violence (Cano, Avery-Leaf, Cascardi, & O'Leary, 1998; O'Leary & Slep, 2003; Ozer, Tschann, Pasch, & Flores, 2004; Silverman, Raj, Mucci, & Hathaway, 2001). Finally, research indicates high stability across time in dating violence perpetration and victimization among both girls and boys in high school dating couples (O'Leary & Slep, 2003).

The wide range in prevalence estimates across studies of TRV listed previously (i.e., 1.6% to 82%) can be attributed to a number of methodological issues, such as use of different measurement tools, differences in types of abuse assessed, lack of clear separation of social class from ethnicity/race in study design, use of population versus convenience samples, lifetime versus time-limited prevalence, sample self-selection bias and social desirability demands, one-sided versus mutual violence profiles, and even the effect of regional variations (Dutton & Hemphill, 1992; Foshee, Matthew, Flannery, Vazsonyi, & Waldman, 2007; Gray & Foshee, 1997; Lewis & Fremouw, 2001; Marquart et al., 2007). These methodological issues notwithstanding, TRV, in the form of physical, psychological, and sexual violence, is clearly present among adolescents in the—United States, though its prevalence varies across gender, ethnic/racial, and sexual orientation groups.

GENDER

The role of gender in TRV is complex. As Hickman, Jaycox, and Aronoff (2004) point out in their review of single studies of TRV, estimates of dating violence among adolescents show two tendencies: (1) they are higher than the rates found in national probability surveys and (2) highly disparate rates are found across studies with respect to gender. For example, in their summary of gender differences in studies of dating violence, Hickman and colleagues found that estimates of physical victimization ranged from 8 percent to 57 percent among girls and from 6 percent to 38 percent among boys. For sexual victimization, estimates range between 14 percent and 43 percent for girls and between 0.3 percent and 36 percent for boys. Estimates of physical perpetration for girls range from 28 percent to 33 percent, compared to 11 percent to 20 percent for boys. For sexual perpetration, estimates for girls range from 2 percent to 24 percent; for boys, they range from 3 percent to 37 percent.

Gender symmetry—that is, similar rates for females and males—in dating violence is more often found in studies of TRV than in studies of adult intimate-partner violence; a number of studies show perpetration of dating violence by girls to actually be higher than the incidence of such acts committed by boys (e.g., Foshee, 1996; Malik et al., 1997; Muñoz-Rivas, Graña, O'Leary, & González, 2007; O'Leary et al., 2008). When looking at specific behaviors, girls more often engage in behaviors such as pushing, slapping, or biting, whereas boys are more likely to act in ways that are seriously harmful, such as punching or using a weapon as a threat (Schwartz, Magee, Griffin, & Dupuis, 2004). In fact, girls are often more likely than boys to experience physical injuries (e.g., cuts, bruises, black eye) and to need medical attention or hospitalization from dating violence than are boys (Foshee, 1996; Muñoz-Rivas et al., 2007). One exception is a study that found the rate of injury from a dating partner's aggression severe enough to require medical attention was the same (3%) for high school girls and boys (O'Leary et al., 2008).

With regard to the most extreme consequence of TRV, girls are more likely to be killed by a dating partner than are boys. Data from the Department of Justice, Bureau of Justice Statistics (n.d), indicate that 5 percent of homicides of girls aged 12 to 17 are perpetrated by an intimate partner, whereas fewer than 0.5 percent of boys in that age group are killed by an intimate partner. The National Crime Victimization Survey (NCVS) conducted by the Department of Justice indicates that, from 2001 to 2005, the average annual nonfatal victimization rate for girls aged 12 to 15 was 1.5 percent, while for boys in the same age group it was 0.2 percent. The rate increased for older adolescents aged 16 to 19, but girls continue to report a higher rate of victimization by an intimate partner (6.3%) compared to boys (0.6%) (Catalano, 2007).

Another national data source, the Youth Risk Behavior Survey (YRBS), is a school-based survey conducted by the CDC every two years among high school students in grades 9 to 12 (CDC, 2008). It covers six categories of health risk behavior, including violence. One question on dating violence is included, which asks if an individual has been "hit, slapped, or physically hurt on purpose by their boyfriend or girlfriend during the 12 months before the survey." Unlike the NCVS, for the period from 1999 to 2005, rates for victimization by a girlfriend or boyfriend among high school girls and boys were quite similar and ranged from 8.8 percent to 9.8 percent for girls and 8.3 percent to 9.1 percent for boys. In 2007, however, the rate of victimization for girls (8.8%) remained stable, while the rate of victimization for boys (11%) increased to the highest level for both genders since 1999 (National Youth Risk Behavior Study, 2007).

The higher rates of dating violence reported in the YRBS compared to the NCVS are partly attributable to differences in questions asked and samples used. Unlike the YRBS, the NCVS includes questions about both physical and sexual victimization in the context of intimate-partner relationships and it includes youths through age 19, whereas the YRBS includes a more limited age range of participants (those in grades 9 through 12) and asks only about physical violence perpetrated by a girl or boyfriend. Certainly, the methodology associated with each survey is different (paper-and-pencil self-report versus telephone interviews) and the purpose of each survey is different (assessment of crime victimization for the NCVS versus health risk behavior for the YRBS).

ETHNICITY/RACE

Compared to studies examining TRV from the perspective of gender, much less research has explored the prevalence of TRV across differing ethnic/racial groups. As with gender-based research, the few available studies that include data on ethnic/racial TRV prevalence present disparate findings, but in general the prevalence of TRV among adolescents from differing ethnic/racial groups is high. In research that investigated the psychosocial factors associated with dating violence victimization in a national sample of adolescent boys in grades 9 through 12, the prevalence of dating violence differed by ethnicity: African American boys (10.67%) and boys whose ethnicity/race was classified as "other" (10.81%) were significantly more likely to report dating violence than Hispanic (7.43%) or White (7.31%) boys (Howard & Qi Wang, 2003a). In a parallel study using the same data set, but this time examining girls in grades 9 through 12, African American girls (14.15%) were significantly more likely than Hispanic (11.31%), White (7.43%), and "other" girls (10.08%) to report dating violence victimization (Howard & Qi Wang, 2003b). Foshee and colleagues (2007) found that minority adolescents—in this case, primarily

African American youths—reported perpetration of moderate and severe physical violence in dating relationships to a significantly greater extent than White adolescents. In a report examining national data from the 2007 YRBS, White students were less likely (8.4%) than Hispanic (11.1%) and Black students (14.2%) to have ever been hit, slapped, or physically hurt on purpose by their girlfriend or boyfriend in the last year (National Youth Risk Behavior Survey, 2007).

By comparison, in a study of multiethnic high school students (White, African American, Latino, mixed ethnic, and other), O'Leary et al. (2008) found no ethnic/racial differences in the rate of physical aggression perpetration by girls and only one significant ethnic/racial difference among boys. In this case, only 3 percent of male Asian students reported engaging in physical aggression against a dating partner, compared to 23 percent of non-Asian male students. Raiford, Wingood, and DiClemente (2007) found the rate of dating violence among African American girls to be high, at 28 percent, but this rate is similar to the rates found in other studies of dating violence involving White samples (see Hickman et al., 2004; Lewis & Fremouw, 2001).

The few studies focused specifically on Latino adolescents have found rates of TRV among Latino adolescents to be at least as high as among non-Latino White adolescents and somewhat lower than among African American adolescents (Howard & Qi Wang, 2003a, 2003b; Malik et al., 1997; O'Keefe & Treister, 1998; Silverman et al., 2001). A longitudinal study that included both Mexican American and White adolescents aged 16 to 20 found no difference in the rate of dating violence perpetration: across both groups, boys' rate of dating violence perpetration was 10 percent and girls' rate was 12.5 percent (Ozer et al., 2004). Another study of dating violence victimization among Latino ninth graders found prevalence rates of 8.7 percent for girls and 6.4 percent for boys (Sanderson, Coker, Roberts, Tortolero, & Reininger, 2004). Finally, an examination of physical dating violence among Latino youth aged 11 to 13 reported a prevalence of 12.9 percent among boys and 14.4 percent among girls (Yan, Howard, Beck, Shattuck, & Hallmark-Kerr, 2009).

Dating violence is markedly understudied among Asian American/ Pacific Islander and American Indian/Alaska Native youth. Nevertheless, available research shows that they, like youths from other ethnic/racial groups, may be at high risk for TRV. For example, one study investigating verbal and psychological abuse victimization among Filipino, Japanese, Native Hawaiian, and Samoan adolescents found that 58.3 percent reported experiencing emotional dating violence, 43.7 percent reported experiencing insulting/verbal abuse, and 43.3 percent reported they were victims of controlling behaviors (Choi-Misailidis, SooJean, Hishinuma, & Chesney-Lind, 2008). Although the number of participants was small, one study of ninth through twelfth graders found that among Native

American adolescents, the proportion who reported experiencing severe dating violence was significantly higher (2.1%) than the percentage who did not report experiencing severe dating violence (0.7%). Conversely, among Asian American adolescents in that same study, the proportion who reported experiencing severe dating violence was significantly smaller (0.5%) than the percentage who did not report experiencing severe dating violence (1.2%) (Coker et al., 2008).

Ethnicity/race is an important factor to examine with respect to prevalence of TRV. Even so, research suggests that when important variables related to the psychological, behavioral, or environmental context are included, the magnitude of ethnic/racial differences is diminished. For example, Wolitzky-Taylor and colleagues (2008) found in a nationally representative sample of adolescents that female gender, older age, experience of traumatic events, and recent stressors were risk factors for having ever experienced severe forms of dating violence; ethnicity/race was *not* a risk factor in this study. In their examination of the prevalence of dating violence (and sexual harassment) in middle and high school students across four categories of bullies and victims (uninvolved, victims, bully-victims, and bullies), Espelage and Holt (2007) did not find a significant difference in the rate of dating-partner violence between African American and White middle and high school students. Instead, these researchers found that students who scored high on both bullying and victimization (bully-victims) reported the highest rate of physical dating violence victimization across all four categories and experienced significantly more emotional abuse in dating relationships than those categorized as uninvolved or victims. In other words, victimization in one domain (such as peer victimization in the school environment) appears to be more strongly related to victimization in another domain (dating relationships), rather than simply to ethnicity/race.

GLBT YOUTH

Dating violence among gay, lesbian, bisexual, and transgender (GLBT) adolescents is sometimes perceived to be less serious than that among heterosexual adolescents due to the idea that the partners are of the same gender and, therefore, equal in physical size and strength. In fact, this perception is incorrect. Research on TRV among GLBT adolescents is only starting to emerge, but it suggests that TRV is a serious problem among this population as well.

For instance, Freedner, Freed, Yang, and Austin (2002) surveyed a sample of gay, lesbian, bisexual, and heterosexual young adults, aged 13 to 22, regarding their lifetime experience of dating violence, including physical, sexual, or emotional abuse, as well as the threat of outing (i.e., publicly revealing an individual's sexual orientation) as a type of abuse. Results indicate that across all of the sexual orientation categories, 41.5 percent of males and 37.1 percent of females had experienced some type of dating violence in their relationships, but some differences exist. For instance, male bisexuals were significantly more likely than male heterosexuals to report the experience of dating violence, and they were significantly more likely than male homosexuals to report being threatened with outing. Female bisexuals were significantly more likely to report the experience of sexual violence from a date or partner; also, compared to lesbians, they were significantly more likely to report being threatened with outing. Finally, compared to female heterosexuals, lesbians were significantly more likely to report that a date or partner had made them scared about their safety.

The study by Freedner and colleagues demonstrates that LGBT youth face additional threats when it comes to TRV, such as the threat of outing. It also indicates that bisexual adolescents, compared to gay, lesbian, or heterosexual youth, may be especially at risk for TRV in their dating relationships.

CONSEQUENCES OF TRV

In addition to its prevalence, dating violence is worthy of attention due to both the immediate and long-term detrimental consequences for those involved. The Supplementary Homicide Reports (as cited in Hickman et al., 2004) found that 10 percent of all murdered teenage girls between the ages of 12 to 15 are killed by an intimate partner. This rate is even higher among girls aged 16 to 19. In this age group, 22 percent of murders are committed by an intimate partner. Some of the negative outcomes of TRV that have been identified in the literature include increases in physical injuries (Simonelli & Ingram, 1998), mental health problems (Ackard, Eisenberg, & Neumark-Sztainer, 2007; Carlson, McNutt, Choi, & Rose, 2002; Simonelli & Ingram, 1998), increased levels of anger (Jackson et al., 2000), and decreases in both self-esteem (Simonelli & Ingram, 1998) and relationship satisfaction (Rusbult, Martz, & Agnew, 1998). Dating violence has been associated with increased depression, poor education outcomes, and physical injury (Banyard & Cross, 2008). In fact, Silverman and colleagues (2001) found that the outcomes of dating violence for females specifically include increased risk of substance use (e.g., cocaine), unhealthy weight control behaviors (e.g., use of laxatives and/or vomiting), sexual risk behaviors (e.g., first intercourse before age 15), pregnancy, and suicidality (e.g., attempted suicide).

Additionally, dating violence victimization itself has been associated specifically with negative sexual health outcomes. A female victim of physical or sexual dating violence is 2.6 times more likely to test positive for a sexually transmitted infection (STI) than women who do not have abusive partners (Decker, Silverman, & Raj, 2005; Raj, Silverman, & Amaro, 2004). Although the reasons for this association are not well understood, research by Buelna, Ulloa, and Ulibarri (2009) suggests that dating abuse may negatively affect relationship power dynamics and the ability to make sexual and relationship decisions, which in turn puts young adults at risk for STIs and other negative sexual health outcomes. In their study, Buelna and colleagues found evidence that sexual relationship power mediates the relationship between dating violence and being tested for an STI.

Finally, teen relationship violence has been linked to longer-term harmful consequences. More specifically, TRV may be the first step in a cycle of violence that proves to be self-perpetuating. Rich and colleagues (2005), in their study of more than 500 college students, found that dating violence significantly predicted violence in subsequent dating relationships, and some research has linked TRV to subsequent marital violence (Perry, 2002).

A MODEL OF TRV

Most empirical studies of dating violence—among adolescents, in particular—have not yet been guided by any underlying theoretical model. Although a few theoretical models exist (Riggs & O'Leary, 1989), Sugarman and Hotaling (1989) have referred to the situation as "a phenomenon that is searching for a theory" (p. 28). The social–ecological (SE) model proposed by Bronfenbrenner (1979) provides a theoretical framework for identifying risk and protective factors across different levels of influence. Such models of behavior are characterized by multiple levels of influence on behavior and an emphasis on environmental and policy influences.

Individual Factors

At the individual level, there may be a set of cognitive factors, such as acceptance of violence beliefs, anger expressive style, and lack of empathy, that accompany TRV. Indeed, research has identified several risk factors at the individual level that are associated with teen dating violence; these factors include attitudes and skills as well as physical characteristics, such as gender.

For example, Gray and Foshee (1997) found that adolescents who perpetrate violence were more accepting of violence, or justified its use more, compared to other adolescents. In another study, Josephson and Proulx (2008) found a direct causal relationship between violence-tolerant attitudes, psychologically aggressive strategies, and physical violence against adolescent dating partners. Studies have also produced evidence suggesting that gender differences exist in terms of how acceptance of violence beliefs are related to perpetration of dating violence (e.g., Cano et al., 1998). For female adolescents, research has inconsistent evidence, with some studies reporting that acceptance of violence beliefs relate to perpetration of violent dating behaviors (e.g., Cate, Henton, Koval, Christopher, & Lloyd, 1982), whereas other studies do not find such a relationship (Bookwala, Frieze, Smith, & Ryan, 1992; Schwartz, O'Leary, & Kendziora, 1997).

Anger expression style refers to how a person typically responds to anger or regulates emotions. Studies have revealed that adult individuals who have a history of fighting with others (i.e., higher general levels of interpersonal aggression) are also more likely to demonstrate aggression against their romantic partner (Riggs & O'Leary, 1996). Wolf and Foshee (2003) examined anger expression styles in adolescents and report that for females, destructive direct anger expression styles mediated the relationship between witnessing family violence and dating violence perpetration. Similarly, Wolfe, Wekerle, Reitzel-Jaffe, and Lefebvre (1998) reported that for adolescent girls, interpersonal hostility mediated the relationship between child maltreatment and dating violence. In contrast, for boys, the presence of interpersonal hostility strengthened the relationship between child maltreatment and dating violence. In a study of Mexican teens, Clarey, Hokoda, and Ulloa (in press) found that both anger control and acceptance of violence were related to dating violence perpetration.

Lack of empathy skills has been proposed as another factor relating to perpetration of aggression. Although the link between a lack of empathy and violence is well documented in other contexts—for example, in research on aggression in school-aged children (Eisenberg, Carlo, & Edwards, 2005), sexual predators of children, and rapists (Ginsburg, Wright, Harrell, & Hill, 1989; Simons, Wurtele, & Heil, 2002)—there is also evidence the link exists in the context of dating relationships. Wolfe, Wekerle, Scott, and Grasley (2004), for example, found that attitudes about dating violence, low self-efficacy, and lack of empathy were all associated with TRV.

Family Factors

Some research has focused on the family environment as a primary influence on the development of aggressive behaviors and attitudes. Research suggests that a number of factors may increase the probability of TRV; these factors include, but are not limited to, exposure to family and community violence, poor parenting practices, poverty, problematic attitudes, and cultural values. For example, research demonstrates that family interactions predict relationship quality in adolescence (Conger, Cui, Bryant, & Elder, 2000). Youths with histories of maltreatment are particularly at risk for experiencing relationship problems. Research shows that child abuse and power-assertive parenting put teens at high risk for TRV. Childhood sexual abuse, in particular, has been identified in the literature as an antecedent of subsequent relationship violence (Briere & Runtz, 1987; Herman & Hirschman, 1981; Mapp, 2006; Whitfield, Anda, Dube, & Felitti, 2003). In a five-year longitudinal study of adolescent boys, corporal punishment predicted dating aggression but not delinquent behaviors (Simons, Lin, & Gordon, 1998). The authors suggest that corporal punishment "teaches that it is both legitimate and effective to hit those you love" (Simons et al., 1998, p. 475).

Similarly, parental conflict has been positively correlated with adolescent dating violence victimization (Stocker & Richmond, 2007). Teens may model relationship violence after family members, as several studies show a link between domestic violence in the family and teen dating violence. Witnessing one parent hit another parent is positively associated with perpetration of violence by both males and females (Foo & Margolin, 1995; O'Keefe, 1997). For girls, witnessing domestic violence is associated with greater acceptance of violence beliefs. Furthermore, O'Keefe (1997) found that the relationship between exposure to interparental violence and dating violence was mediated by acceptance of violence beliefs in boys.

Numerous researchers have discovered that the degree of parental knowledge, supervision, or monitoring of their teens' behaviors plays a significant role in predicting adolescent problem behaviors, including alcohol and drug use (Cookston, 1999). Crouter and McHale (2005) found that lack of parental knowledge about their adolescent children's activities, whereabouts, and companions predicted risky behavior one year later, including alcohol, drug, and tobacco use and skipping school. Parental monitoring may relate to dating violence as well. Straus and Savage (2005) report that neglectful behavior by parents is a consistent predictor of violence against dating partners across 17 nations. One study revealed that the relationship a teen has with her or his parent does, indeed, influence the interpersonal competence of that teen in both same-sex friend and dating-partner relationships (Bartle-Haring, 1997).

The home environment includes the siblings in addition to parents, and research has documented that sibling violence is linked to dating violence. Simonelli, Mullis, Elliott, and Pierce (2002) found that emotional, physical, and sexual sibling violence was associated with later perpetration of and victimization by dating violence. This type of violence often remains unacknowledged because parents view sibling violence as an important way for children to learn to negotiate conflict (Goodwin & Roscoe, 1990). Straus et al. (1980) found that sibling violence peaks as the oldest sibling in the dyad reaches 10 to 14 years of age, probably because the older child begins spending less time with sibling(s) and more time with peers around that age. Once adolescents begin to spend more time with peers, the opportunity for dating violence arises (Noland, Liller, McDermott, Coulter, & Seraphine, 2004). Noland and colleagues (2004) report that perpetrating sibling violence plays a strong role in predicting dating violence perpetration.

Peer Factors

Adolescence is a period when young people begin to shift from parental influence being the most important factor in their lives to placing greater importance on the attitudes and behaviors of their peers. Relationships with peers become a major part of adolescent lives, and a significant amount of youths' energy is spent thinking about and engaging in dating relationships.

Research on social influences on adolescent behavior indicates that with increasing age, a shift in emphasis from familial to peer influence (Ellickson, Tucker, Klein, & Saner, 2004) occurs, and that peers can be a powerful influence for adolescents. Consequently, the way that friends deal with conflict in their relationships may have at least as significant an influence on dating violence as individual- and family-level influences. For example, early involvement with antisocial peers has been shown to be linked to adolescent dating violence perpetration (Schnurr & Lohman, 2008). Arriaga and Foshee (2004) found that (after controlling for other variables) peer involvement in dating violence was associated with perpetration and victimization, and that this factor consistently predicted later dating violence. Similarly, Gwartney-Gibbs, Stockard, and Bohmer (1987) identified a correlation between peer involvement in dating violence and the person's own use of dating violence among college students. In a study of adolescent boys (17 to 18 years old), Capaldi et al. (2001) observed that hostile and derogatory talk about women with their peers was related to boys' aggression toward dating partners at ages 20 to 23. Peers' general level of aggression toward others has also been shown to have an influence on teens' own use of violence in dating relationships (Brendgen, Vitaro, Tremblay, & Wanner, 2002).

Peer pressure may cause shame in females who do not have a boyfriend; consequently, they may not terminate a relationship despite recognizing it as abusive (Roscoe & Callahan, 1985). Furthermore, teens tend to seek help from peers more often than from adults, even though peers' lack of experience with relationships may make their advice less helpful. In fact, some researchers have found that social support from peers can increase the risk of dating aggression among adolescents from violent families compared to those from nonviolent families (Levandosky,

Huth-Bocks, & Semel, 2002). Peer involvement in dating violence may communicate the idea that dating violence is acceptable, potentially increasing the likelihood of adolescents' own participation in dating violence. In addition, adolescents who are involved in an abusive relationship may be more likely to seek out peers who share their own views and who are also tolerant of violence.

Community Factors

At the community level, adolescents who are exposed to high levels of violence in the community are at greater risk for dating violence (O'Keefe et al., 1986; Schubiner, Scott, & Tzelepis, 1993). In fact, Malik et al. (1997) found that exposure to violence in the community is the strongest predictor for later dating violence, and that common demographic factors were not significantly associated with dating violence when controlling for exposure to violence in the community. These researchers reported that community violence, family violence, and dating violence are all associated, and that violence in one situation seems to have carry-over effects in other situations, no matter whether a person is the victim or the perpetrator.

Conversely, a community may also have a positive influence in regard to dating violence. The stronger the ties an adolescent has within his or her community (such as strong identification with a religious group), the lower that individual's risk for dating violence (Gover, 2004). In fact, research has shown that the more an individual attends religious services, the more protection he or she has from dating violence (Howard, Qiu, & Boekeloo, 2003). Given the profound impact of community factors have in regard to dating violence in young people, further research into how the community can help provide protection from dating violence would be a worthy endeavor.

Acculturative Factors

Some researchers have proposed that cultural values may influence the prevalence of partner violence among ethnic groups such as Latinos (Sorenson & Telles, 1991). For example, many Latinos may be taught that males should be dominant, authoritarian figures, whereas females should be caregivers who attend to others' needs before their own (e.g., Perilla, Bakerman, & Norris, 1994). Ingram (2007) compared acceptance of dating violence in Latinos to non-Latinos and found that while the majority of Latinos and non-Latinos did not view dating violence as acceptable, significantly more Latinos believed that it was acceptable to slap their partner on at least some occasions. These traditional gender roles, which are characterized by a disparity of power and control, may contribute intimate-partner violence in some Latino families (Perilla et al., 1994).

Research has demonstrated that acculturation does, in fact, have some relationship to the frequency of dating violence among Latino teens. For example, level of acculturation is associated with how knowledgeable and accepting Latino youth are about violence (Ulloa, Jaycox, Marshall, & Collins, 2004). Generally, the less acculturated (i.e., more traditional) youth are, the less knowledgeable and more accepting they are about dating violence. Moreover, medium-acculturated teens (as measured by language preference), compared to high- and low-acculturated adolescents, have less tolerant attitudes toward dating violence (Hokoda, Galván, Malcarne, Castañeda, & Ulloa, 2007). In addition, acculturative stressors, such as having conflicted ethnic identity and family acculturation conflict, are generally associated with more tolerant attitudes toward, and higher rates of perpetration of, dating violence. The results of this line of research suggest that among Mexican American adolescents, acculturation and acculturative stress are important variables influencing dating violence.

While identifying variables that relate to TRV is critical to understanding the phenomenon of dating violence and informing prevention interventions, as research in TRV becomes more sophisticated researchers are recognizing the importance of identifying how these variables are related to one another. For example, a more recent trend in TRV research has worked toward identifying mediating mechanisms that help explain the relationship between predictors of TRV and the perpetration or victimization of TRV itself. This vein of research focuses, for instance, on uncovering mechanisms that explain how family-level predictors such as exposure to violence or interparental violence are related to TRV. Notable examples from the literature include recent work by Wolf and Foshee (2003), which demonstrates how exposure to interparental violence and dating violence are related. Their study found evidence that anger expression acts as the mediating mechanism between exposure to interparental violence and dating violence. Similarly, Clarey, Hokoda and Ulloa (in press) found that among Mexican teens, both anger control and acceptance of violence were mediating factors that helped explain the relationship between exposure to interparental violence and TRV perpetration. Findings such as these have important implications for prevention interventions, especially when it is difficult or unethical to target the predictors of TRV directly.

INTERVENTIONS

Prevention and intervention strategies (primary, secondary, and tertiary) have the potential to curb rates of TRV. As yet, however, little empirical research on the prevention of TRV has been conducted. In a review of evidence-based prevention/intervention efforts, Hickman and colleagues (2004) called attention to the general lack of theory-based interventions as well as a lack of evaluations for TRV prevention programs. Nonetheless, some evidence suggests that interventions—and particularly early interventions—may yield promising results. What is clear is that the focus, goals, and approaches to TRV prevention are quite varied.

Many programs are designed to increase knowledge or influence attitudes about dating violence. One of the earliest recorded evaluations of a dating violence intervention was conducted by Jones (1991). This program, named the Minnesota School Curriculum Project, was delivered in middle and high school classrooms across the state of Minnesota and was designed to increase knowledge and change attitudes about dating violence. The post-test results indicated that participation in the program did increase knowledge about dating violence, but had relatively little effect on attitudes.

Similar results were found by Macgowan (1997), who evaluated a dating violence intervention in Florida that also focused on increasing knowledge and changing negative attitudes. Macgowan found positive changes, in the pre- to post-test time frame, in scores on a measure of knowledge and attitudes about abuse.

Likewise, after administering a three-session violence prevention program that focused on legal issues, Jaycox and colleagues (2006) found that students showed improved knowledge of dating violence, lower acceptance of female-to-male aggression, and enhanced perception of the helpfulness and likelihood of seeking assistance from sources immediately after the end of the program. Improved knowledge and perceived helpfulness of an attorney were still seen six months later. These results suggest that the interventions improved knowledge and increased tendencies to seek help that may aid in the prevention of dating violence among teens.

Some intervention programs also aim to build skills related to dating violence prevention, such as effective communication, anger management, and prosocial skills. For example, Avery-Leaf and colleagues (1997) administered a program focused not only on changing attitudes that support violence and gender inequality, but also on improving communication skills believed to help prevent violence. Although these authors did not assess changes in teen relationship violence-related behaviors specifically, the results of the evaluation indicated a positive change has occurred in participants' views about violence as a form of conflict resolution.

One of the more well-known interventions combines many of the approaches outlined here. The Safe Dates program is an adolescent dating violence prevention program focused on changing norms associated with partner violence, decreasing gender stereotyping, increasing knowledge about community resources, and improving conflict management skills (Foshee, 1996; Foshee, Bauman, Greene, Koch, Linder, &

MacDougall, 2000). In one study, after receiving the Safe Dates intervention, eighth and ninth graders reported less sexual and physical dating violence perpetration and victimization. This reduction in violence persisted four years after students had completed the Safe Dates program compared to students who did not participate in the intervention (Foshee, Bauman, Ennett, Linder, Benefield, & Suchindran, 2004).

Some prevention programs are targeted toward populations believed to be at higher risk for relationship violence. The framework provided by Gordon (1983) refers to these prevention efforts as "selective" or "indicated"; it characterizes the risk for acquiring a particular disease or outcome for these targeted populations as "above average." In this chapter, we refer to these programs as "targeted programs." Populations can be targeted based on any factor known to be associated with relationship violence, such as history of abuse or maltreatment, ethnicity, or history of other types of aggression.

In a review of dating violence programs, Foshee and colleagues (2007) discovered that most relationship violence prevention programs are universal in nature—that is, they are not specifically targeted toward certain at-risk populations. Instead, these programs cast a wide net across a community or school in an effort to curb the potential for relationship violence. This approach has its advantages, as it can be difficult and expensive to identify individuals at higher risk so as to enroll them in prevention programs. In addition, universal programs may benefit from the interactions between students who are deemed to be at higher risk and those who are not by helping to foster a culture of nonviolence.

One of the disadvantages of universal prevention programs, compared to targeted programs, is that they lack the same degree of efficiency. Because a smaller percentage of students in a particular school are at risk for experiencing and practicing relationship violence, it is reasonable to conclude that some of the prevention programs' efforts are unnecessarily wasted on those adolescents who would not engage in relationship violence anyway. Furthermore, because participants are recruited specifically for their particular risk, curricula in targeted programs can be tailored in a way that can be more relevant for participants based on that risk.

One of the more well-known targeted prevention programs is the Youth Relationships Project, which was designed and evaluated by Wolfe and colleagues (2009). This program, which is delivered in the community, targets at-risk students—specifically, those with a history of maltreatment. Its focus also includes changing attitudes and building skills. An additional goal is to increase the social competence of participants. The Youth Relationships Project is one of the few programs to formally document a reduction in physical dating violence perpetration and victimization in the pre- to post-intervention time frame.

Unfortunately, notable limitations are associated with the existing TRV interventions. For example, many programs are short term in nature and do not follow participants longitudinally. Relatively few longitudinal studies on TRV have been conducted; instead, most studies merely highlight associations with TRV and lack the ability to draw conclusions about causality or long-term predictive validity.

In their review of dating violence prevention measures, Foshee and colleagues (2009) make a few suggestions about effective practices in relationship violence prevention programs. Among them are the suggestions to target mediating variables; make sure that the programs target these mediators for change in their design; measure these variables in their intervention studies; and test for mediation statistically. These authors also suggest that family-based programs (i.e., programs that are implemented in the home or involve parents and/or siblings) have proven their effectiveness in reducing other behaviors and may prove effective in relationship violence programs. Similarly, Foshee and colleagues suggest that based on their success in changing other problem behaviors, programs that target change at higher ecological levels of influence (e.g., school and peer contexts) instead of individual-level variables may fare better.

CONCLUSIONS

While the research associated with teen relationship violence is clearly increasing, the field remains in its infancy. The factors that make teen dating relationships distinct from adult relationships clearly have implications for violence in those relationships, and merit further attention from researchers who might elucidate the various influences on relationship violence in teens.

Some conclusions can be drawn from the literature published to date. Although the prevalence rates of TRV gleaned across studies vary widely, when these data are examined together, researchers are beginning to recognize the wide range of abusive behaviors that teens perpetrate against one another in a dating context. These include forms of stalking behavior and the use of Internet and cell phone technology to control, threaten, or harm dating partners. Moreover, the gender picture in regard to this behavior is complex. Not only are boys and girls both victims and perpetrators of relationship violence, but predictors of violence may also be different for boys than girls.

How gender is played out in TRV is critically important to understand— it has direct implications for TRV policy development and prevention programs. Greater investigation to untangle the role of gender in TRV is needed, particularly the use of innovative research designs and both qualitative and quantitative analyses that can examine a range of individual, partner, and other contextual variables (e.g., Foshee et al., 2007; O'Leary & Slep, 2003), as well as the meanings and themes that adolescents themselves use to guide and explain their behavior (e.g., Foshee et al., 2007; Hettrich & O'Leary, 2007; Muñoz-Rivas et al., 2007).

While some national estimates of TRV among different ethnic groups have been constructed that allow investigators to begin to make comparisons, more research is needed that focuses on different ethnic and cultural groups specifically. Finally, intervention programs vary in their scope, design, and theoretical approaches, but many have yielded promising results in terms of their ability to prevent prevention of relationship violence among teens.

Teen relationship violence is a product of many factors at different levels of influence. The picture of TRV is complex and its mechanisms not yet well understood. Given the crucial social developmental nature of this period a person's life, it is important to further document the extent and distribution of the problem as well as the factors that contribute to dating violence during adolescence. Research and interventions aimed at addressing TRV have come a long way in recent years, but they have also helped highlight gaps in understanding and point to promising future directions for investigators.

REFERENCES

Ackard, D. M., Eisenberg, M. E., & Neumark-Sztainer, D. (2007). Long-term impact of adolescent dating violence on the behavioral and psychological health of male and female youth. *Journal of Pediatrics, 151*(5), 476–481.

Arriaga, X. B., & Foshee, V. A. (2004). Adolescent dating violence: Do adolescents follow in their friends', or their parents' footsteps? *Journal of Interpersonal Violence, 19*(2), 162–184.

Avery-Leaf, S., Cascardi, M., O'Leary, K., & Cano, A. (1997). Efficacy of a dating violence prevention program on attitudes justifying aggression. *Journal of Adolescent Health, 21*, 1–17.

Banyard, V. L., & Cross, C. (2008). Consequences of teen dating violence: Understanding intervening variables in ecological context. *Violence Against Women, 14*(9), 998–1013.

Bartle-Haring, S. (1997). The relationships among parent–adolescent differentiation, sex role orientation and identity development in late adolescence and early adulthood. *Journal of Adolescence, 20*(5), 553–565.

Bennett, L., & Fineran, S. (1998). Sexual and severe physical violence among high school students: Power beliefs, gender, and relationship. *American Journal of Orthopsychiatry, 68*(4), 645–652.

Bergman, L. (1992). Dating violence among high school students. *Social Work, 37*(1), 21–27.

Bookwala, J., Frieze, I. H., Smith, C., & Ryan, K. (1992). Predictors of dating violence: A multivariate analysis. *Violence and Victims, 7*(4), 297–311.

Brendgen, M., Vitaro, F., Tremblay, R. E., & Wanner, B. (2002). Parent and peer effects on delinquency-related violence and dating violence: A test of two mediational models. *Social Development, 11*(2), 225–244.

Briere, J., & Runtz, M. (1987). Post sexual abuse trauma: Data and implications for clinical practice. *Journal of Interpersonal Violence, 2*(4), 367–379.

Bronfenbrenner, U. (1979). Contexts of child rearing: Problems and prospects. *American Psychologist, 34*(10), 844–850.

Buelna, C., Ulloa, E. C., & Ulibarri, M. D. (2009). Sexual relationship power as a mediator between dating violence and sexually transmitted infections among college women. *Journal of Interpersonal Violence, 24*(8), 1338–1357.

Cano, A., Avery-Leaf, S., Cascardi, M., & O'Leary, D. (1998). Dating violence in two high school samples: Discriminating variables. *Journal of Primary Prevention, 18*(4), 431–446.

Capaldi, D. M., Dishion, T. J., Stoolmiller, M., & Yoerger, K. (2001). Aggression toward female partners by at-risk young men: The contribution of male adolescent friendships. *Developmental Psychology, 37*, 61–73.

Carlson, B. E., McNutt, L. A., Choi, D., & Rose, I. M. (2002). Intimate partner abuse and mental health: The role of social support and other protective factors. *Violence Against Women, 8*, 720–745.

Catalano, S. (2007). *Intimate partner violence in the United States.* U.S. Department of Justice, Bureau of Justice Statistics. Retrieved November 16, 2009, from http://www.ojp.usdoj.gov/bjs/intimate/ipv.htm.

Cate, R., Henton, J., Koval, J., Christopher, F., & Lloyd, S. (1982). Premarital abuse: A social psychological perspective. *Journal of Marriage and the Family, 3*(1), 71–90.

Centers for Disease Control and Prevention (CDC). (2008, June 6). *Youth Risk Behavior Surveillance—United States, 2007.* Atlanta, GA: Author, 57, SS-4. www.cdc.gov/mmrw.

Centers for Disease Control and Prevention (CDC). (n.d.). *Violence prevention: Intimate partner violence: Definitions.* Atlanta, GA: National Center for Injury Control and Prevention. http://www.cdc.gov/ViolencePrevention/intimatepartnerviolence/definitions.html.

Choi-Misailidis, S., Hishinuma, E. S., Nishimura, S. T., & Chesney-Lind, M. (2008). Dating violence victimization among Asian American and Pacific Islander youth in Hawaii. *Journal of Emotional Abuse, 8*(4), 403–422.

Clarey, A., Hokoda, A., & Ulloa, E.C. (in press). Anger control and justification of violence as a mediator in the relationship between witnessing interparental violence and perpetration of dating violence in Mexican adolescents. *Journal of Family Violence.*

Coker, A. L., Sanderson, M., Cantu, E., Huerta, D., & Fadden, M. K. (2008). Frequency and types of partner violence among Mexican American college women. *Journal of American College Health, 56*(6), 665–673.

Conger, R. D., Cui, M., Bryant, C., & Elder, G. H. (2000). Competence in early adult romantic relationships: A developmental perspective on family influences. *Journal of Personality and Social Psychology, 79*(2), 224–237.

Cookston, J. T. (1999). Parental supervision and family structure: Effects on adolescent problem behaviors. *Journal of Divorce & Remarriage, 32*(1), 107–122.

Crouter, A. C., & McHale, S. M. (2005). Work, family, and children's time: Implications for youth. In S. Bianchi, L. Casper, & R. B. King (Eds.), *Work, family, health, and well-being* (pp. 49–66). Mahwah, NJ: Lawrence Erlbaum.

Decker, M. R., Silverman, J.G., & Raj, A. (2005). Dating violence and sexually transmitted disease/HIV testing and diagnosis among adolescent females. *Pediatrics, 116*(2), 272–276.

Department of Justice, Bureau of Justice Statistics. (n.d.). Percent of all murders by intimates, 1976–2005. Retrieved October 2009 from http://www.ojp.usdoj.gov/bjs/intimate/table/agea.htm.

Discovery Health, Teen Center. (n.d.). One teen's perspective on dating. Retrieved November 9, 2009, from http://health.discovery.com/centers/teen/relationships/jonna.html.

Dutton, D. G., & Hemphill, K. J. (1992). Patterns of socially desirable responding among perpetrators and victims of wife assault. *Violence and Victims, 7*(1), 29–39.

Eisenberg, N., Carlo, G., & Edwards, C. P. (2005). The development of empathy-related responding. In C. Carlo & C. Edwards (Eds.) *Moral motivation through the life span* (pp. 73–117). Lincoln, NE: University of Nebraska Press.

Ellickson, P. L., Tucker, J. S., Klein, D. J., & Saner, H. (2004). Antecedents and outcomes of marijuana use initiation during adolescence. *Preventive Medicine: An International Journal Devoted to Practice and Theory, 39*(5), 976.

Espelage, D. L., & Holt, M. K. (2007). Dating violence and sexual harassment across the bully–victim continuum among middle and high school students. *Journal of Youth and Adolescence, 36*(6), 799–811.

Foo, L., & Margolin, V. (1995). A multivariate investigation of dating aggression. *Journal of Family Violence, 10*(4), 351–377.

Foshee, V. A. (1996). Gender differences in adolescent dating abuse prevalence, types and injuries. *Health Education Research, 11*(3), 275–286.

Foshee, V. A., Bauman, K. E., Ennett, S. T., Linder, G. F., Benefield, T., & Suchindran, C. (2004). Assessing the long-term effects of the Safe Dates program and a booster in preventing and reducing adolescent dating violence victimization and perpetration. *American Journal of Public Health, 94*(4), 619–624.

Foshee, V. A., Bauman, K. E., Linder, F., Rice, J., & Wilcher, R. (2007). Typologies of adolescent dating violence: Identifying typologies of adolescent dating violence perpetration. *Journal of Interpersonal Violence, 22*(5), 498–519.

Foshee, V. A., Matthew, R. A., Flannery, D. J., Vazsonyi, A. T., & Waldman, I. D. (2007). Adolescent dating abuse perpetration: A review of findings, methodological limitations, and suggestions for future research. In *The Cambridge handbook of violent behavior and aggression* (pp. 431–449). New York: Cambridge University Press.

Freedner, N., Freed, L. H., Yang, Y. W., & Austin, S. B. (2002). Dating violence among gay, lesbian, and bisexual adolescents: Results from a community survey. *Journal of Adolescent Health, 31*(6), 469–474.

Gaertner, L., & Foshee, V. (1999). Commitment and the perpetration of relationship violence. *Personal Relationships, 6*(2), 227–239.

Ginsburg, H., Wright, L. S., Harrell, P. M., & Hill, D. W. (1989). Childhood victimization: Desensitization effects in the later lifespan. *Child Psychiatry & Human Development, 20*(1), 59–71.

Goodwin, M. P., & Roscoe, B. (1990). Sibling violence and agonistic interactions among middle adolescents. *Adolescence, 25*(98), 451–467.

Gordon, R. S. (1983). An operational classification of disease prevention. *Public Health Reports, 98*(2), 107–109.

Gover, A. R. (2004). Risky lifestyles and dating violence: A theoretical test of violent victimization. *Journal of Criminal Justice, 32*(2), 171–180.

Gray, H. M., & Foshee, V. (1997). Adolescent dating violence: Differences between one-sided and mutually violent profiles. *Journal of Interpersonal Violence, 12*(1), 126–141.

Gwartney-Gibbs, P. A., Stockard, J., & Bohmer, S. (1987). Learning courtship aggression: The influence of parents, peers, and personal experiences. *Family Relations, 36*(3), 276–282.

Herman, J., & Hirschman, L. (1981). Families at risk for father–daughter incest. *American Journal of Psychiatry, 138*(7), 967–970.

Hettrich, E. L., & O'Leary, K. D. (2007). Females' reasons for their physical aggression in dating relationships. *Journal of Interpersonal Violence, 22*(9), 1131–1143.

Hickman, L. J., Jaycox, L. H., & Aronoff, J. (2004). Dating violence among adolescents: Prevalence, gender distribution, and prevention program effectiveness. *Trauma, Violence, & Abuse, 5*(2), 123–142.

Hokoda, A., Galván, D. B., Malcarne, V. L., Castañeda, D. M., & Ulloa, E. C. (2007). An exploratory study examining teen dating violence, acculturation and acculturative stress in Mexican-American adolescents. *Journal of Aggression, Maltreatment & Trauma, 14*(3), 33–49.

Howard, D., & Wang, M. (2003a). Psychosocial factors associated with adolescent boys' reports of dating violence. *Adolescence, 38*, 519–533.

Howard, D. E., & Qi Wang, M. (2003b). Risk procedures of adolescent girls who were victims of dating violence. *Adolescence, 38*(149), 1–14.

Howard, D. E., Qiu, Y., & Boekeloo, B. (2003). Personal and social contextual correlates of adolescent dating violence. *Journal of Adolescent Health, 33*(1), 9–17.

Ingram, E. (2007). A comparison of help seeking between Latino and non-Latino victims of intimate partner violence. *Violence Against Women, 13*(2), 159–171.

Jackson, S. M., Cram, F., & Seymour, F. W. (2000). Violence and sexual coercion in high school students' dating relationships. *Journal of Family Violence, 15*(1), 23–36.

Jaycox, L. H., McCaffrey, D., Eiseman, B., Aronoff, J., Shelley, G. A., Collins, R. L., et al. (2006). Impact of a school-based dating violence prevention program among Latino teens: Randomized controlled effectiveness trial. *Journal of Adolescent Health, 39*(5), 694–704.

Johnson, S. B., Frattaroli, S., Campbell, J., Wright, J., & Pearson-Fields, A. S. (2005). "I know what love means": Gender-based violence in the lives of urban adolescents. *Journal of Women's Health, 14*(2), 172–179.

Jones, L. E. (1991). The Minnesota School Curriculum Project: A statewide domestic violence prevention project in secondary schools. In B. Levy (Ed.), *Dating violence: Young women in danger* (pp. 258–266). Seattle: Seal Press.

Josephson, W. L., & Proulx, J. B. (2008). Violence in young adolescents' relationships: A path model. *Journal of Interpersonal Violence, 23*(2), 189–208.

Levandosky, A. A., Huth-Bocks, A. l., & Semel, M. A. (2002). Adolescent peer relationships and mental health functioning in families with domestic violence. *Journal of Clinical Child and Adolescent Psychology, 31*, 206–218.

Lewis, S. F., & Fremouw, W. (2001). Dating violence: A critical review of the literature. *Clinical Psychology Review, 21*(1), 105–127.

Linder, J. R., Crick, N. R., & Collins, W. A. (2002). Relational aggression and victimization in young adults' romantic relationships: Associations with perceptions of parent, peer, and romantic relationship quality. *Social Development, 11*(1), 69–86.

Macgowan, M. J. (1997). An evaluation of a dating violence prevention program for middle school students. *Violence and Victims, 12*(3), 223–235.

Makepeace, J. M. (1981). Courtship violence among college students. *Family Relations, 30,* 97–102.

Malik, S., Sorenson, S. B., & Aneshensel, C. S. (1997). Community and dating violence among adolescents: Perpetration and victimization. *Journal of Adolescent Health, 21*(5), 291–302.

Mapp, S. C. (2006). The effects of sexual abuse as a child on the risk of mothers physically abusing their children: A path analysis using systems theory. *Child Abuse & Neglect, 30*(11), 1293–1310.

Marquart, B. S., Nannini, D. K., Edwards, R. W., Stanley, L. R., & Wayman, J. C. (2007). Prevalence of dating violence and victimization: Regional and gender differences. *Adolescence, 42*(168), 645–657.

Muñoz-Rivas, M. J., Graña, J. L., O'Leary, K. D., & González, M. P. (2007). Aggression in adolescent dating relationships: Prevalence, justification, and health consequences. *Journal of Adolescent Health, 40*(4), 298–304.

National Youth Risk Behavior Survey. (2007). *Percentage of high school youth who experienced dating violence, by sex and race/ethnicity, 2007.* http://www.cdc.gov/healthyyouth/yrbs/slides/yrbs07_injury_violence.ppt#1115,29, Percentage of High School Students Who Experienced Dating Violence, by Sex and Race/Ethnicity, 2007. http://www.cdc.gov/HealthyYouth/yrbs/pdf/yrbs07_us_disparity_sex.pdf.

Noland, V. J., Liller, K. D., McDermott, R. J., Coulter, M. L., & Seraphine, A. E. (2004). Is adolescent sibling violence a precursor to college dating violence? *American Journal of Health and Behavior, 28*(suppl 11), S13–S23.

O'Keefe, M. (1997). Predictors of dating violence among high school students. *Journal of Interpersonal Violence, 12*(4), 546–568.

O'Keefe, M., & Treister, L. (1998). Victims of dating violence among high school students: Are the predictors different for males and females? *Violence Against Women, 4*(2), 195–223.

O'Keeffe, N. K., Brockopp, K., & Chew, E. (1986). Teen dating violence. *Social Work, 31*(6), 465–468.

O'Leary, K. D., & Slep, A. M. S. (2003). A dyadic longitudinal model of adolescent dating aggression. *Journal of Clinical Child and Adolescent Psychology, 32*(3), 314–327.

O'Leary, K. D., Slep, A. M. S., Avery-Leaf, S., & Cascardi, M. (2008). Gender differences in dating aggression among multiethnic high school students. *Journal of Adolescent, 42*(5), 473–479.

Ozer, E. J., Tschann, J. M., Pasch, L. A., & Flores, E. (2004). Violence perpetration across peer and partner relationships: Co-occurrence and longitudinal patterns among adolescents. *Journal of Adolescent Health, 34*(1), 64–71.

Perilla, J. L., Bakerman, R., & Norris, F. H. (1994). Culture and domestic violence: The ecology of abused Latinas. *Violence and Victims, 9*(4), 325–339.

Perry, K. B. (2002). Physical aggression in dating relationships: A typology of male perpetrators. *Dissertation Abstracts International: Section B: The Sciences and Engineering. US, ProQuest Information & Learning, 62,* 3386.

Picard, P. (2007). Abuse in teen relationships study. Retrieved November 9, 2009, from http://www.loveisrespect.org/wp-content/uploads/2009/03/liz-claiborne-2007-tech-relationship-abuse.pdf.

Raiford, J. L., Wingood, G. M., & DiClemente, R. J. (2007). Prevalence, incidence, and predictors of dating violence: A longitudinal study of African American female adolescents. *Journal of Women's Health, 16*(6), 822–832.

Raj, A., Silverman, J., & Amaro, H. (2004). Abused women report greater male partner risk and gender-based risk for HIV: Findings from a community-based study with Hispanic women. *AIDS Care, 16*(4), 519–529.

Rich, C. L., Gidycz, C. A., Warkentin, J. B., Loh, C., & Weiland, P. (2005). Child and adolescent abuse and subsequent victimization: A prospective study. *Child Abuse & Neglect, 29*(12), 1373–1394.

Riggs, D. S., & O'Leary, K. D. (1989). A theoretical model of courtship aggression. In M. A. Pirog-Good & J. E. Stets (Eds.), *Violence in dating relationships: Emerging social issues* (pp. 53–71). New York: Praeger.

Riggs, D. S., & O'Leary, K. D. (1996). Aggression between heterosexual dating partners: An examination of a causal model of courtship aggression. *Journal of Interpersonal Violence, 11*(4), 519–540.

Roscoe, B., & Callahan, J. E. (1985). Adolescents' self-report of violence in families and dating relations. *Adolescence, 20*(79), 545–553.

Rusbult, C. E., Martz, J. M., & Agnew, C. R. (1998). The Investment Model Scale: Measuring commitment level, satisfaction level, quality of alternatives, and investment size. *Personal Relationships, 5*(4), 357–391.

Sanderson, M., Coker, A. L., Roberts, R. E., Tortolero, S. R., & Reininger, B. M. (2004). Acculturation, ethnic identity, and dating violence among Latino ninth-grade students. *Preventive Medicine: An International Journal Devoted to Practice and Theory, 39*(2), 373–383.

Schnurr, M. P., & Lohman, B. J. (2008). How much does school matter? An examination of adolescent dating violence perpetration. *Journal of Youth and Adolescence, 37*(3), 266–283.

Schubiner, H., Scott, R., & Tzelepis, A. (1993). Exposure to violence among inner-city youth. *Journal of Adolescent Health, 14*(3), 214–219.

Schwartz, J. P., Magee, M. M., Griffin, L. D., & Dupuis, C. W. (2004). Effects of a group preventive intervention on risk and protective factors related to dating violence. *Group Dynamics: Theory, Research, and Practice, 8*(3), 221–231.

Schwartz, M., O'Leary, S. G., & Kendziora, K. T. (1997). Dating aggression among high school students. *Violence and Victims, 12*(4), 295–305.

Silverman, J. G., Raj, A., Mucci, L. A., & Hathaway, J. E. (2001). Dating violence against adolescent girls and associated substance use, unhealthy weight control, sexual risk behavior, pregnancy, and suicidality. *Journal of the American Medical Association, 286*(5), 572–579.

Simonelli, C. J., & Ingram, K. M. (1998). Psychological distress among men experiencing physical and emotional abuse in heterosexual dating relationships. *Journal of Interpersonal Violence, 13*(6), 667–681.

Simonelli, C. J., Mullis, T., Elliott, A. N., & Pierce, T. W. (2002). Abuse by siblings and subsequent experiences of violence within the dating relationship. *Journal of Interpersonal Violence, 17*(2), 103–121.

Simons, D., Wurtele, S. K., & Heil, P. (2002). Childhood victimization and lack of empathy as predictors of sexual offending against women and children. *Journal of Interpersonal Violence, 17*(12), 1291–1307.

Simons, R. L., Lin, K.-H., & Gordon, L. C. (1998). Socialization in the family of origin and male dating violence: A prospective study. *Journal of Marriage & the Family, 60*(2), 467–478.

Sorenson, S. B., & Telles, C. A. (1991). Self-reports of spousal violence in a Mexican-American and non-Hispanic White population. *Violence and Victims, 6*(1), 3–15.

Stocker, C. M., & Richmond, M. K. (2007). Longitudinal associations between hostility in adolescents' family relationships and friendships and hostility in their romantic relationships. *Journal of Family Psychology, 21*(3), 490–497.

Straus, M. A., & Savage, S. A. (2005). Neglectful behavior by parents in the life history of university students in 17 countries and its relation to violence against dating partners. *Child Maltreatment, 10*(2), 124–135.

Straus, M., Gelles, R., & Steinmetz, S. (1980). *Behind closed doors: Violence in the American family.* Garden City, NY: Anchor Books.

Sugarman, D. B., & Hotaling, G. T. (1989). Dating violence: Prevalence, context, and risk markers. In M. A. Pirog-Good & J. E. Stets (Eds.), *Violence in dating relationships: Emerging social issues* (pp. 3–30). New York: Praeger.

Ulloa, E. C., Jaycox, L. H., Marshall, G., & Collins, R. (2004). Acculturation, gender stereotypes, and attitudes about dating violence among Latino youth. *Violence and Victims, 19*(3), 273–287.

Wekerle, C., & Wolfe, D. A. (1999). Dating violence in mid-adolescence: Theory, significance, and emerging prevention initiatives. *Clinical Psychology Review, 19*(4), 435–456.

Whitaker, D. J., Haileyesus, T., Swahn, M., & Saltzman, L. S. (2007). Differences in frequency of violence and reported injury between relationships with reciprocal and nonreciprocal intimate partner violence. *American Journal of Public Health, 97*(5), 941–947.

Whitfield, C. L., Anda, R. F., Dube, S. R., & Felitti, V. J. (2003). Violent childhood experiences and the risk of intimate partner violence in adults: Assessment in a large health maintenance organization. *Journal of Interpersonal Violence, 18*(2), 166–185.

Wolf, K. A., & Foshee, V. A. (2003). Family violence, anger expression styles, and adolescent dating violence. *Journal of Family Violence, 18*(6), 309–316.

Wolfe, D. A., Crooks, C. C., Chiodo, D., & Jaffe, P. (2009). Child maltreatment, bullying, gender-based harassment, and adolescent dating violence: Making the connections. *Psychology of Women Quarterly, 33*(1), 21–24.

Wolfe, D. A., Wekerle, C., Reitzel-Jaffe, D., & Lefebvre, L. (1998). Factors associated with abusive relationships among maltreated and nonmaltreated youth. *Development and Psychopathology, 10*(1), 61–85.

Wolfe, D. A., Wekerle, C., Scott, K., & Grasley, C. (2004). Predicting abuse in adolescent dating relationships over 1 year: The role of child maltreatment and trauma. *Journal of Abnormal Psychology, 113*(3), 406–415.

Wolitzky-Taylor, K. B., Ruggiero, K. J., Danielson, C. K., Resnick, H. S., Hanson, R. F., Smith, D. W., et al. (2008). Prevalence and correlates of dating violence in a national sample of adolescents. *Journal of the American Academy of Child & Adolescent Psychiatry, 47*(7), 755–762.

Yan, F. A., Howard, D. E., Beck, K. H., Shattuck, T., & Hallmark-Kerr, M. (2009). Psychosocial correlates of physical violence dating victimization among Latino early adolescents. *Journal of Interpersonal Violence, 20*, 1–24.

Chapter 6

Harassment of Sexual Minority College Students on U.S. Campuses

Eros R. DeSouza and Brent D. Showalter

This chapter reviews relevant literature concerning the harassment of lesbian, gay, bisexual, and transgender (LGBT) individuals, including hate crimes and stigma due to sexual orientation. Anti-LGBT attitudes are frequently manifested through verbal, physical, and psychological harassment. LGBT students at institutions of higher education often face hostile environments, which have been linked to an array of serious consequences that negatively affect their mental and physical health as well as their quality of life, including career development.

This chapter also presents findings from a new study conducted to investigate the role of social disclosure of a person's sexual orientation and perceptions of campus climate in predicting the experience of subtle harassment toward LGBT college students. Academic, psychological, and physical well-being outcomes were also investigated. In the study, 135 LGBT college students (74% reported to be White) completed an online survey. Seventy-five percent of the total sample reported having experienced some form of

Preliminary findings of this research were presented at the 2009 annual meeting of the American Psychological Association and the 2009 annual meeting of the Association for Psychological Science.

subtle sexual orientation harassment at least once within the past 12 months. The findings also revealed that such experiences negatively influenced their perceptions of the campus climate and were associated with intentions to leave their institution and a lower grade-point average (GPA). Those who perceived the campus climate more negatively were more likely to report alcohol or drug use and were more likely to state their intentions to leave the institution as compared to those students with more favorable perceptions. In addition, social disclosure of one's sexual orientation was positively associated with perceptions of campus climate, self-esteem, and life satisfaction and negatively associated with anxiety and depression. These findings highlight the importance of recognizing the problems facing LGBT students and provide a rationale for enacting nondiscriminatory policies at institutions of higher education.

INTRODUCTION

College/university campuses are widely recognized as an important educative setting for traditional students (18 to 22 years of age), regardless of their sexual orientation, who undergo significant personal development and growth during their postsecondary education (Evans, 2001; Hogan & Rentz, 1996). Experiences related to diversity issues are often lacking until a person enrolls in an institution of higher education, where students explore various issues related to their social identities, including race, culture, religious background, political affiliation, gender, and sexual orientation.

The college/university campus should provide an important opportunity for many young lesbian, gay, bisexual, and transgender (henceforth referred to as LGBT or sexual minority) students to explore their sexuality without fear of reprimand and judgment by high school friends and family members. Despite the relative self-awareness of sexual orientation that most LGBT individuals acknowledge having during early adolescence, the majority have not yet "come out" prior to entering an institution of higher education; in other words, most LGBT individuals reveal their sexual orientation sometime during the traditional college years (D'Augelli, 1991; Waldo, 1998). Thus it is often on college/university campuses where LGBT students should have the necessary freedom to fully develop their sexual identity and experience public tolerance and acceptance.

Ideally, every college/university campus should value diversity. Unfortunately, in many cases, LGBT students (and other stigmatized groups, such as women, racial/ethnic minorities, and persons with mental or physical disabilities) face a "chilly" or outright hostile campus climate. This type of climate is reflected in personal victimization and heightened levels of fear, affecting student recruitment, retention, and satisfaction (Cortina, Swan, Fitzgerald, & Waldo, 1998; Rankin, 2003; Waldo, 1998).

Despite enacted state and local laws, as well as institutional initiatives to prohibit sexual orientation discrimination, research indicates that harassment directed at LGBT students, faculty, and staff persists (Bieschke, Eberz, & Wilson, 2000; Rankin, 2003; Ryan & Rivers, 2003; Waldo, 1998). For many LGBT students, college/university campuses become a threat rather than a catalyst for interpersonal development and positive well-being. This threat may be either formal (i.e., institutional policies, discrimination) or informal (interpersonal anti-LGBT harassment) in nature, including harassment that is subtle yet still hurtful. In oppressive environments, negative attitudes toward LGBT individuals may be manifested as verbal abuse and physical violence, including hate crimes motivated by sexual orientation bias.

FREQUENCY RATES, TYPES, AND CONSEQUENCES OF HATE CRIMES AGAINST LGBT INDIVIDUALS

Research indicates that violence against LBGT individuals is widespread. Since the U.S. Congress passed the Hate Crime Statistics Act in 1990, the Federal Bureau of Investigation (FBI) has compiled annual statistics on hate crimes—that is, crimes motivated by a bias against the victim's perceived race, religion, ethnicity, disability, or sexual orientation. Hate crime offenses include intimidation, simple physical assault (i.e., without a weapon), aggravated assault (i.e., with a weapon), rape, and murder. During 2007, 17 percent of all hate crimes were motivated by sexual orientation bias (FBI, 2008). Of these offenses, 60 percent were motivated by an offender's anti-male homosexual bias, 13 percent by anti-female homosexual bias, and 1.5 percent by anti-bisexual bias. Eleven percent of all hate crimes against LBGT individuals occurred in schools or colleges.

These statistics include only those crimes that were reported to police, so they obviously underestimate the true prevalence of hate crimes against LGBT individuals. Because reporting is voluntary, hate crimes due to sexual orientation are less likely to be reported to police than non-bias crimes, for several reasons (Herek, Gillis, & Cogan, 1999). In particular, LGBT victims of hate crimes often do not report such attacks for fear that their sexuality might be disclosed to their family and community or for fear that the police might react with indifference or even hostility (D'Augelli & Grossman, 2001). Hence, it is important to conduct surveys that tap into the true rate of victimization, potentially revealing hate crimes committed against LGBT persons that may otherwise go unreported.

For instance, among young gay and bisexual male adults (18 to 27 years, with an average age of 23 years; 59% of the total sample was White) sampled in three Southwestern U.S. cities, 37 percent reported having experienced anti-gay verbal harassment, 11 percent discrimination, and 5 percent physical violence because of their sexual orientation during the previous 6 months (Huebner, Rebchook, & Kegeles, 2004). In a sample comprising LGB youth (15 to 21 years, with an average age of 19 years; 66% of the total sample was White) recruited from service agencies across the United States, 83 percent of all respondents reported having been victimized at least once due to their sexual orientation: 80 percent experienced verbal insults, 44 percent were threatened with violence, 33 percent had objects thrown at them, 31 percent were chased or followed, 23 percent had their property damaged, 22 percent were sexually assaulted, 18 percent were victims of simple physical assault, 13 percent were spat on, and 9 percent were victims of aggravated assault (Pilkington & D'Augelli, 1995). In a separate study with the same sample, these youth also indicated that their victimization had negative psychological consequences on their mental health, with 42 percent reporting a past suicide attempt (Hershberger & D'Augelli, 1995). There was a significant association between past victimization with suicide ideation and attempt. In this study, family support acted as a buffer against the harmful effects of victimization, but only for low levels of victimization.

Using a representative sample of Massachusetts high school students (average age was 16 years; 79% of the total sample was White), Garofalo, Wolf, Wissow, Woods, and Goodman (1999) found that LGB students and those who were not sure of (questioning) their sexual orientation were 3.4 times more likely than their heterosexual peers to report a suicide attempt in the past year. Significant gender differences were found in this study, however, with sexual orientation being an independent predictor of suicide for boys but not girls.

A more recent study examined childhood gender atypicality (i.e., not behaving according to one's prescribed gender roles), lifetime victimization based on sexual orientation, and mental health, including trauma symptoms and post-traumatic stress disorder (PTSD), among LGB youth (15 to 19 years, with an average age of 17 years; 62% of the total sample was White) recruited from the greater New York City area (D'Augelli, Grossman, & Starks, 2006). The findings revealed that 78 percent of the sample reported verbal victimization, 11 percent physical assault, and 9 percent sexual assault, with men consistently reporting significantly more victimization than women. Sexual minority men reported being victimized almost exclusively by other men (94%), whereas sexual minority women were victimized approximately equally by men (56%) and women (44%). Compared to those who were perceived as gender typical, those who were perceived as gender atypical in childhood (e.g., called "sissy" or "tomboy") reported more victimization and more recent mental health problems, including PTSD.

Herek, Gillis, and Cogan (1999) examined the psychological consequences of hate crime victimization among a large group of LGB adults (18 to 82 years, with a median age of 34 years; 79% of the total sample was White) in the greater Sacramento, California, area. These researchers found that 28 percent of gay men, 19 percent of lesbians, 27 percent of bisexual men, and 15 percent of bisexual women reported having experienced a hate crime, with men being more likely than women to be victimized. The authors also found that victims of recent hate crimes (within the past five years) consistently reported higher levels of psychological distress compared to all other groups, such as victims of recent nonbiased crimes, victims of earlier crimes (more than five years earlier), and nonvictims. In addition, hate crime victims were less likely to believe in the goodness of people, showed more fear of crime, felt more vulnerable, demonstrated lower levels of autonomy, and were more likely to attribute negative life events to sexual prejudice than did nonbias victims, victims of earlier crimes, and nonvictims.

In a recent national probability sample of LGB adults (average age was 39 years; 65% of the total sample was White), 49 percent of all respondents reported having experienced verbal abuse; 25 percent had experienced violence, property crime, or attempted crime; and 23 percent had been threatened with violence at some time in their life (Herek, 2009). Gay men (38%) were significantly more likely than lesbians or bisexuals to be victims of such crimes (11% to 13%).

HETEROSEXISM AND SELF-STIGMA

The previously described studies indicate that hate crimes due to sexual orientation bias are more commonly committed against gay men compared to other sexual minority groups. Moreover, gay men's attackers are generally heterosexual men who hold more negative attitudes toward gay men than they do toward lesbians (Herek, 2002). Overall, heterosexual women have more favorable attitudes toward LGBT individuals than do heterosexual men (Herek, 2007).

Negative attitudes toward LGBT individuals are derived from widespread heterosexism in society. Heterosexism is defined as an "ideological system that denies, denigrates, and stigmatizes any non-heterosexual form of behavior, identity, relationship, or community" (Herek, 1990, p. 316). Under such a lens, LGBT individuals are perceived as inferior or deviant, because, according to this view, every individual should be heterosexual. Thus heterosexism renders LBGT people as invisible citizens or stigmatizes their identity (if they are "out"), behavior, and romantic relationships. That is, LGBT individuals, their behavior and same-sex relationships are assumed to be abnormal and unnatural. Society regards them as inferior, as requiring explanation, and as appropriate targets for hostility, discrimination, and violence, whereas heterosexuals are regarded as the prototype of the category *human*, whose behavior and different-sex relationships are tacitly accepted as normal and natural (Herek, 2007).

Heterosexism becomes internalized by LGBT individuals, a process that Herek (2007) refers to as self-stigma. Under the aegis of self-stigma, LGBT individuals accept society's negative evaluation of their identity, behavior, and romantic relationships, causing confusion, doubt, and mistrust of themselves as worthwhile human beings (Cass, 1984; Fassinger, 1991; Mohr & Fassinger, 2000). Self-stigma is minimized by "coming out" or publicly disclosing one's sexual orientation (Malyon, 1982). Research suggests that levels of psychological adjustment, life satisfaction, and self-esteem are higher among those who are publicly committed to their sexual orientation compared to those who are "closeted" (Bell & Weinberg, 1978; Garnets, Herek, & Levy, 1990; Herek, 2003). In addition, because the need to conceal one's sexual orientation is experienced and opportunities to express concerns are limited, negative attitudes toward homosexuality often become further reinforced internally when self-stigma is present (Rostosky & Riggle, 2002). The implications of denying one's sexual orientation are twofold. On the one hand, censorship of one's sexual minority status may prevent the person from potentially being targeted and victimized. On the other hand, internal psychological functioning is likely to suffer as a result of identity suppression.

Button (2004) has proposed a three-factor model of strategy implementation by gay men and lesbians: counterfeiting, avoidant, and integration. *Counterfeiting* refers to the denial of one's sexual minority status as a LGB person in favor of an artificial identity of heterosexuality (e.g., altering gender-specific pronouns when discussing actual same-sex relationships). The *avoidance* strategy involves a more neutral stance: the person neither publicly denies nor claims an LGB identity—an approach executed by avoiding personal communication (e.g., revealing nothing and appearing asexual). Such silence about one's sexuality is, however, an implicit attempt to pass as heterosexual. The *integration* strategy is the personal and public acceptance of LGB identity; it involves the implicit and explicit acknowledgment and embracement of one's true identity by incorporating one's sexual orientation into private and public life. Thus it serves as a gauge of commitment to the LGB lifestyle and willingness to accept the social consequences of taking such a stance.

HARASSMENT ON CAMPUS AND PERCEPTIONS OF THE CAMPUS CLIMATE

Just on a daily basis we were taunted, called "fags" to the point where ... we didn't even want to go to the cafeteria, we'd just go out to eat. Then nightly we pretty much, we never knew what we were going to wake up to or be awakened by in the night, like someone urinating on the door or sticking stuff, something on the door ...

When people write "fag" on your door and that was one of the main
things . . . Put a gay sticker on the door with one guy bent over and
another behind him with a big line through it . . . It was so awful.
(Herek, Cogan, & Gillis, 2002, p. 327)

Institutions of higher education can help LGBT students to develop a
positive self-concept. However, as the preceding quote suggests, on many
college campuses, LGBT students are often not accepted or respected;
instead, they experience a chillier campus climate than do their heterosexual
counterparts (Cortina et al., 1998; Waldo, 1998). Although not technically a
hate crime, sexual harassment is illegal in work and educational settings.
The Equal Employment Opportunity Commission (EEOC, 2008) defines
sexual harassment as a form of sex discrimination that violates Title VII of
the Civil Rights Act of 1964. The EEOC recognizes two types of sexual
harassment: quid pro quo (e.g., sexual coercion by a superior toward a
subordinate so as to obtain sexual favors) and behavior that creates a hostile
or abusive environment (e.g., unwanted sexual attention and gender
harassment).

In a stratified random sample of college women (34% White) enrolled
in a large Midwestern university, Cortina et al. (1998) found that, compared to 51 percent of heterosexual women, 81 percent of lesbians or
bisexual women reported having been targets of sexual harassment at
least once. Lesbians or bisexual women were especially likely to experience gender harassment (e.g., sexist comments) compared to heterosexual
women (64% versus 36%, respectively). These incidents had a profound
and negative impact on these students' perceptions of the campus climate.

Fiske and Glick (1995) suggest that sexist attitudes toward women
may increase the likelihood of gender and sexual orientation discrimination and harassment. That is, such attitudes reinforce and justify patriarchy, including heterosexual hostility toward women who deviate
from traditional gender roles (e.g., lesbians; Glick & Fiske, 1997). According to Franke (1997), sexual harassment can be seen as a "technology of
sexism": sexist beliefs are widespread in society and sexual harassment
is the tool to punish women and men who deviate from traditional
gender roles. Hence, sexual harassment is sex discrimination not because
the conduct is sexual, but rather because the sexual conduct is used to
perpetuate, enforce, or police traditional gender norms and stereotypes
(i.e., heterosexism).

Waldo (1998) reported findings from a survey of a stratified random
sample of male and female college students (35% White) enrolled in a
large Midwestern university. The data showed that LGB students viewed
the campus climate significantly more negatively (e.g., inhospitable and
less accepting) than did their heterosexual counterparts. Politically
conservative heterosexual students were significantly less supportive of

pro-LGB campus policies and events and were less open to interpersonal contact with LGB students.

Hill and Silva (2005) reported findings from a stratified random sample of college students (18 to 24 years old; 73% of the total sample was White) across the United States who completed an online survey. Although women (62%) and men (61%) were equally likely to report having a sexually harassing experience during college, there were significant differences by sexual orientation. LGBT students (73%) were more likely than their heterosexual counterparts (61%) to be sexually harassed in college and to be sexually harassed often (18% versus 7%, respectively). Their harassers were most likely to be other students (92% versus 78%, respectively), followed by faculty members (13% versus 7%, respectively), and staff (11% versus 5%, respectively). The reactions to these sexually harassing experiences significantly affected more LGBT students than their heterosexual counterparts, including producing anger (67% versus 42%, respectively); feeling self-conscious or embarrassed (61% versus 45%, respectively); feeling less confident or sure of themselves (42% versus 25%, respectively); worrying about whether they could have a happy, romantic relationship (36% versus 16%, respectively); feeling afraid or scared (32% versus 20%, respectively); feeling confused or conflicted about who they were (31% versus 16%, respectively); feeling disappointed with their college experience (25% versus 14%, respectively); worrying about whether they could have a successful career or work life (16% versus 6%, respectively); and worrying about whether they had what it takes to graduate from college (13% versus 4%, respectively).

At the departmental level, Sears (2002) reported research based on a national sample of lesbian, gay, and bisexual education faculty members and researchers (86% of the total sample was White), which showed that 65 percent of respondents described their campus climate as gay affirmative (i.e., campus leaders work in a proactive way to reduce anti-gay attitude and heterosexism) or gay tolerant (i.e., campus leaders are supportive of initiatives undertaken by students and faculty), whereas 22 percent rated it as gay intolerant or gay hostile. These perceptions were mostly positive, possibly due to respondents' high organizational power and their interpersonal relations at the departmental level.

Sexual orientation may no longer be a barrier in hiring LGBT faculty members, especially in large institutions of higher education. Nevertheless, stigma against LGBT faculty members may present in subtle ways, such as by deterring their research productivity, including funding, on LGBT issues; many universities also lack same-sex partner benefits (e.g., health insurance coverage). This stigma is exemplified by the following comment: "It's very difficult putting your heart into working at an institution when you're not being treated the same as [heterosexual] colleagues down the hall" (Bollag, 2007, p. B10).

Rankin (2003) reported findings from a national survey of LGBT faculty, staff, and students (80% of the total sample was White) across 14 universities that showed widespread stigma, violence, and discrimination against sexual minorities. For instance, 43 percent of all respondents and 74 percent of students rated their campus climate as homophobic, 51 percent of all respondents concealed their sexual orientation in an effort to avoid intimidation, and 36 percent of undergraduate students and 29 percent of all respondents reported having been victims of harassment in the past year because of their sexual orientation. Of those who experienced harassment, 89 percent reported that derogatory remarks about homosexuals were the most common form of harassment experienced, especially by students (79 percent). Twenty percent of all respondents feared for their physical safety because of their sexual orientation.

In one Midwestern university, Brown, Clarke, Gortmaker, and Robinson-Keilig (2004) compared perceptions of the campus climate between LGBT students, general students, residence hall assistants (RAs), faculty members, and student affairs staff members. These researchers found that LGBT students perceived their campus climate more negatively, had more knowledge of and interest in LGBT issues (e.g., history and culture), and participated more in LGBT-related activities than did general students, RAs, faculty members, and student affairs staff members. The student affairs staff members had more knowledge of and interest in LGBT issues, more participation and interest in LGBT-related activities, and were more likely to confront a student who was making anti-LGBT remarks compared to faculty members. Within the faculty group, those in the soft sciences (e.g., education and psychology) held more positive attitudes toward LGBT issues and had more interest in LGBT-related activities compared to faculty members in the hard sciences (e.g., chemistry and engineering). After a year in college, RAs reported a more significant change in attitude toward LGBT students and LGBT issues and concerns than did general students. These findings indicate that both faculty members (especially those in the hard sciences) and general students may benefit from sensitivity training and a more inclusive and LGBT affirming curriculum. In addition, RAs may need additional training, as they are often the first resource for LGBT students when they reveal their sexual orientation to other residence hall residents (Evans, 2001).

In another study, Evans (2001) interviewed 20 LGBT college students. These students often reported feeling invisible. Evans identified three factors that summarized LGBT students' coping with harassment experiences in residence halls: (1) minimization of negative experiences, (2) exaggeration of positive experiences, and (3) perception of even neutral incidents as positive. These findings support previous research by Love (1997), who concluded that social ostracism (e.g., feeling invisible) and overt harassment often lead LGBT students to drop out of college.

In a recent study conducted at a Midwestern state university, Gortmaker and Brown (2006) compared perceptions of the campus climate among gay and lesbian college students who were "out" versus those who were "closeted." These researchers found that out students were significantly more likely to report being unfairly treated due to their sexual orientation by academic administrators than were closeted students. In addition, compared to out students, closeted students were significantly more likely to hide their sexual orientation from other students, faculty, and health care providers for fear of unfair treatment. Gortmaker and Brown also reported that out students perceived the campus climate significantly more negatively than did closeted students. Interestingly, out students were most likely to report anti-homosexual incidents to faculty members, whereas closeted students were more likely to report such incidents to diversity program staff, suggesting the importance to train these individuals about LGBT issues and concerns. Out students suggested the development of institution policy statements about LGBT issues as a measure to improve the campus environment for LGBT students, whereas closeted students favored more library books, magazines, and LGBT courses and organizations.

THE CURRENT STUDY

During 2008, the authors of this chapter investigated indirect LGBT harassment, defined as relational aggression (e.g., social exclusion and spreading malicious rumors) toward LGBT students that is subtle, yet detrimental. Specifically, we examined perceptions of the campus climate from the perspective of LGBT college students, and the degree to which these perceptions as well as public disclosure of their sexual identity predicted indirect LGBT harassment. Academic, psychological, and physical outcomes were examined as well. Finally, we investigated associations between disclosure of one's sexual identity and psychological well-being after controlling for negative affectivity.

To conduct the study, we contacted 10 LGBT student advocacy groups (e.g., PRIDE and Colors of Pride) in Illinois. These groups agreed to assist with recruitment of participants by forwarding our email, which contained an embedded electronic link to the online survey, to all their members. A snowball sampling technique was also implemented by asking these members to forward the email to other LGBT students who were not members of their organization. In addition, the 10 LGBT advocacy groups forwarded two reminders, spaced three weeks apart, asking participants to consider participation and thanking them if they had already completed the online survey. The email and reminders informed participants of their rights (e.g., participation was voluntary and participants were free to withdraw at any time without penalty or loss of any kind).

A total of 150 individuals accessed the online survey. In response to a screening question about one's sexual orientation, 3 participants indicated that they were exclusively heterosexual; they were thanked for their participation and the survey was terminated. In addition, 14 surveys were missing significant amounts of data; thus they were removed from future analyses. This left 133 self-identified LGBT students who completed the online survey. The total sample was primarily White (74%) and was evenly split by gender. Most respondents self-identified as exclusively homosexual (44%), followed by mostly homosexual (32%) and bisexual (25%). Participants ranged in age from 18 to 40, with an average age of 22 years. Fifty-seven percent of the sample reported membership in some type of LGBT advocacy group, while 43 percent did not.

Survey respondents completed the following measures:

- *Disclosure*, using a 10-item integration subscale of sexual identity management (Button, 2004), $\alpha = .87$
- *Perceived campus climate*, a 4-item measure adapted from Rankin (2003), $\alpha = .79$
- *Indirect LGBT harassment*, a 19-item measure adapted from Forrest, Eatough, and Shevlin (2005), $\alpha = .93$
- *Intention to leave current academic institution*, a 2-item measure adapted from Porter, Crampon, and Smith (1976), $\alpha = .77$
- *Self-reported GPA; self-reported class attendance; global self-esteem*, using the 10-item Rosenberg Self-esteem Scale (Rosenberg, 1986), $\alpha = .92$
- *Anxiety/depression*, using the 5-item measure developed by Veit and Ware (1983), $\alpha = .86$
- *Global life satisfaction*, using the 5-item Satisfaction with Life Scale developed by Diener, Emmons, Larsen, and Griffin (1985), $\alpha = .90$
- *Physical well-being*, a 3-item measure adapted from Miner-Rubino and Cortina (2007), $\alpha = .79$
- *Substance abuse*, a 2-item measure also adapted from Miner-Rubino and Cortina (2007), $\alpha = .50$
- *Negative affect*, using the 10-item negative affect subscale of the PANAS (Watson, Clark, & Tellegen, 1988), $\alpha = .87$

Preliminary analyses did not show differences by gender, sexual orientation (lesbian, gay man, or bisexual), or race/ethnicity (White, person of color) for these variables. Thus these groups were collapsed together. We found that 75 percent of the total sample reported having experienced some form of indirect sexual orientation harassment at least once during the past 12 months.

We controlled for negative affectivity in all analyses so as to rule out the possibility that these respondents were hypersensitive, reacting negatively in general to social interactions. Contrary to the results from earlier research by Gortmaker and Brown (2006), we found that LGBT students who were open about their sexual orientation rated their campus climate more positively than did closeted LGBT students.

As expected, students who experienced indirect LGBT harassment during the past year perceived their campus climate more negatively than those who did not experience it. In turn, perceptions of a chilly (hostile) campus climate significantly predicted intention to leave the institution. In addition, those with a negative perception of their campus climate were more likely to use alcohol and drugs than those with a positive perception. This last finding is especially alarming, as it suggests a maladaptive way of coping with indirect LGBT harassment.

Indirect LGBT harassment during the past year was also linked to intention to leave the institution and students' GPA. Thus harassed LGBT students were significantly more likely to state their intention to leave their institution and to have a lower GPA than nonharassed students. These findings are worrisome, as indirect LGBT harassment appears to interfere with academic achievement and career development of LGBT students.

Lastly, LGBT students who were more open about their sexual orientation reported higher levels of self-esteem and life satisfaction and lower levels of anxiety and depression than those persons who were less committed to their sexual identity. These findings are in keeping with the results produced by past studies (e.g., Herek, 2003; Jordan & Deluty, 1998; Morris, Waldo, & Rothblum, 2001), suggesting that LGBT individuals with established positive sexual orientation identities enjoy more psychological benefits compared to closeted individuals.

To shed further light on the above findings, we investigated the percentage of the respondents' friends who were LGBT advocates and found a significant link with public disclosure and life satisfaction. That is, individuals with more friends as LGBT advocates were also more likely to be open about their sexual orientation and to exhibit higher levels of life satisfaction compared to those with few or no friends as LBGT advocates. It seems that having friends as LBGT advocates functions as a social support system, possibly buffering against the ill effects of LGBT harassment and discrimination. These findings, then, seem to partly explain the more positive perceptions of the campus climate found among out students compared to closeted students.

CONCLUSION

Our study fills a gap in the LGBT-related literature by focusing on everyday, relational micro-aggressions, which seem to be widespread. Students who experience subtle sexual orientation harassment seem to form negative impressions about the campus climate, leading to a greater desire to leave their university. These findings indicate that both harassment and "chilly" campus climate perceptions come together to promote academic withdrawal and increase the likelihood that students depart from their institution. Furthermore, chilly campus climate perceptions were also linked to substance abuse. As LGBT students felt increasingly disrespected, their tendency to use alcohol and drugs correspondingly increased. This unfortunate consequence arises as students confront an uncivil and sometimes hostile environment. These findings suggest that alcohol and drug use may be an unfortunate method of coping with and escaping from the stress caused by social exclusion, harassment, and discrimination due to sexual orientation. Policymakers and administration officials interested in student retention and health should take special note of these findings and work to create prevention strategies.

This study highlights the importance of coming out for LGBT students, as the findings suggest that being out is related to experiencing a positive campus climate and social support. In addition, as LGBT students become more open about their sexual orientation, their heterosexual friends and acquaintances in turn become aware of the circumstances and challenges faced by the LGBT population. In doing so, enlightened heterosexuals may potentially become allies and even advocates.

As demonstrated by past studies, the strongest predictor for positive attitudes toward the LGBT community is interpersonal experience with gay men and lesbians (Basow & Johnson, 2000; Cotten-Huston & Waite, 2000; DeSouza, Solberg, & Elder, 2007; Herek & Capitanio, 1996). Individuals with LGBT friends are able to dispel social stereotypes first-hand and shift attitudinal perspective. Given this understanding, university officials need to creatively and tactfully bring heterosexual students—especially politically conservative students who have been shown to have limited contact with and strong negative attitudes toward LGBT students (e.g., Waldo, 1998)—into repeated and friendly dialogue with LGBT students.

In addition, past studies have shown that social support has beneficial effects on psychological well-being, especially in times of stress (e.g., Cohen & Wills, 1985). In our study, the out students had a larger number of friends who served as LGBT advocates compared to the closeted students. Clearly, there is an argument to be made for open disclosure and enacting an advocacy network of social support. On the part of campus officials, these findings encourage the formation and support of LGBT organizations.

Providing support for LGBT advocacy organizations seems to be essential to this population's well-being. As students' access to platforms and venues through which to pursue relationships within the sexual minority community expands, their psychological well-being increases. That is, these organizations provide a safe haven for LGBT students to explore aspects of their identity as LGBT individuals in a nonthreatening, supportive environment. Such efforts need to begin before college, given that junior high and high school can be hostile environments for LGBT students as well (American Association of University Women Education Foundation, 2001; D'Augelli, Pilkington, & Hershberger, 2002; Strauss, 2003). As LGBT individuals begin dealing with their sexualities at an earlier age, there is a real and urgent need to implement this type of support as early as possible.

Although attention given to existing LGBT support organizations is crucial, faculty members and administrators can also offer and expand the LGBT-related curriculum, as shedding light on these issues seems to help closeted students (Gortmaker & Brown, 2006). Furthermore, adopting these types of courses and providing LGBT-related books, journals, and magazines in the library send an unambiguous message that LGBT issues, history, and culture are taken seriously by university officials. Sponsoring this type of curriculum is a progressive step currently being undertaken by leading colleges, including Yale University, University of California–Berkeley, University of California–Los Angeles, DePaul University, and many others (Younger, 2008).

Another way in which to bolster this community entails the creation of "safe zones"—that is, designated areas around campus in which university faculty and staff publicly state their support for LGBT students. Some evidence suggests that safe zones have a positive impact on the visibility and support of LGBT individuals and issues (Evans, 2002). When locations and individuals who are inclined to offer assistance are publicly recognized, students are afforded tangible social support linked directly to their institution. Creation of safe zones is a small, but positive and significant step through which campus officials can intervene on behalf of the LGBT community.

University officials can also take note and recognize the achievements of LGBT students. In recognizing students individually, faculty members and administrators show support for the entire LGBT community. Public recognition of the accomplishments of LGBT students has the potential to encourage and inspire other LGBT students to succeed and build bridges among the student body.

Lastly, universities should work to attract and retain more LGBT faculty and staff by extending health benefits to same-sex partners and supporting research on LGBT issues, especially issues related to other areas of oppression (e.g., gender and race/ethnicity). Most of the samples in the studies reviewed in this chapter were overwhelmingly White and potentially overlook the needs of LGBT people of color who are a minority within a minority. For instance, LGBT people of color are often forced to take sides, choosing one community over another (Milville & Ferguson, 2004).

More research is needed to shed light on the intersections of heterosexism, sexism, and racism, as these systems of oppression devalue anyone who is different. Furthermore, addressing only one system of inequality is short-sighted, as the solutions implemented may prove ineffective over the long run. Multiple forms of social inequalities need to be researched and confronted simultaneously and at various levels (e.g., individual, family, institution, community, and society at large) so as to truly create an inclusive and welcoming environment to all.

REFERENCES

American Association of University Women Education Foundation. (2001). *Hostile hallways: Bullying, teasing and sexual harassment in school.* Washington, DC: Author.

Basow, S., & Johnson, K. (2000). Predictors of homophobia in female college students. *Sex Roles, 42*(5/6), 391–404.

Bell, A., & Weinberg, M. (1978). *Homosexualities: A study of diversity among men and women.* New York: Simon & Schuster.

Bieschke, K., Eberz, A., & Wilson, D. (2000). Empirical investigations of the gay, lesbian, and bisexual college student. In V. A. Wall & N. J. Evans (Eds.), *Toward acceptance: Sexual orientation issues on campus* (pp. 31–58). Oxford, UK: University Press of America.

Bollag, B. (2007). Gay professors face less discrimination, but many still fight for benefits. *Chronicle of Higher Education, 54*(5), B10–11.

Brown, R. D., Clarke, B., Gortmaker, V., & Robinson-Keilig, R. (2004). Assessing the campus climate for gay, lesbian, bisexual, and transgender (GLBT) students using a multiple perspectives approach. *Journal of College Student Development, 45*(1), 8–26.

Button, S. (2004). Identity management strategies utilized by lesbian and gay employees: A quantitative investigation. *Group and Organization Management, 29*(4), 470–494.

Cass, V. (1984). Homosexual identity formation: Testing a theoretical model. *Journal of Sex Research, 20*(2), 143–167.

Cohen, S., & Wills, T. A. (1985). Stress, social support, and the buffering hypothesis. *Psychological Bulletin, 98*(2), 310–357.

Cortina, L. M., Swan, S., Fitzgerald, L. F., & Waldo, C. (1998). Sexual harassment and assault: Chilling the climate for women in academia. *Psychology of Women Quarterly, 22*, 419–441.

Cotten-Huston, A. L., & Waite, B. M. (2000). Anti-homosexual attitudes in college students: Predictors and classroom interventions. *Journal of Homosexuality, 38*(3), 117–133.

D'Augelli, A. (1991). Gay men in college: Identity processes and adaptations. *Journal of College Student Development, 32*(2), 140–146.

D'Augelli, A. R., & Grossman, A. H. (2001). Disclosure of sexual orientation, victimization, and mental health among lesbian, gay, and bisexual older adults. *Journal of Interpersonal Violence, 16*(19), 1008–1027.

D'Augelli, A. R., Grossman, A. H., & Starks, M. T. (2006). Childhood gender atypicality, victimization, and PTSD among lesbian, gay, and bisexual youth. *Journal of Interpersonal Violence, 21*(11), 1462–1482.

D'Augelli, A., Pilkington, N., & Hershberger, S. (2002). Incidence and mental health impact of sexual orientation victimization of lesbian, gay, and bisexual youths in high school. *School Psychology Quarterly, 17*(2), 148–167.

DeSouza, E. R., Solberg, J., & Elder, C. (2007). A cross-cultural perspective on judgments of woman-to-woman sexual harassment: Does sexual orientation matter? *Sex Roles, 56,* 457–471.

Diener, E., Emmons, R., Larsen, R., & Griffin, S. (1985). The satisfaction with life scale. *Journal of Personality Assessment, 49*(1), 71–75.

Equal Employment Opportunity Commission (EEOC). (2008, March 4). Sexual harassment. Retrieved January 31, 2009, from http://www.eeoc.gov/types/sexual_harassment.html.

Evans, N. J. (2001). The experiences of lesbian, gay, and bisexual youths in university communities. In A. R. D'Augelli & C. J. Patterson (Eds.), *Lesbian, gay, and bisexual identities and youth* (pp. 181–198). New York: Oxford University Press.

Evans, N. J. (2002). The impact of an LGBT safe zone project on campus climate. *Journal of College Student Development, 43*(4), 522–539.

Fassinger, R. (1991). The hidden minority: Issues and challenges in working with lesbian women and gay men. *Counseling Psychologist, 19*(2), 151–176.

Federal Bureau of Investigation (FBI). (2008, October). Hate crime statistics, 2007. Retrieved December 23, 2008, from http://www.fbi.gov/ucr/hc2007/index.html.

Fiske, S. T., & Glick, P. (1995). Ambivalence and stereotypes cause sexual harassment: A theory with implications for organizational change. *Journal of Social Issues, 51,* 97–115.

Forrest, S., Eatough, V., & Shevlin, M. (2005). Measuring adult indirect aggression: The development and psychometric assessment of the indirect aggression scales. *Aggressive Behavior, 31,* 84–97.

Franke, K. M. (1997). What's wrong with sexual harassment? *Stanford Law Review, 49*(4), 691–772.

Garnets, L., Herek, G., & Levy, B. (1990). Violence and victimization of lesbians and gay men: Mental health consequences. *Journal of Interpersonal Violence, 5*(3), 366–383.

Garofalo, R., Wolf, R. C., Wissow, L. S., Woods, E. R., & Goodman, E. (1999). Sexual orientation and risk of suicide attempts among a representative sample of youth. *Archives of Pediatric Adolescent Medicine, 153,* 487–493.

Glick, P., & Fiske, S. T. (1997). Hostile and benevolent sexism: Measuring ambivalent sexist attitudes toward women. *Psychology of Women Quarterly, 21,* 119–135.

Gortmaker, V., & Brown, R. (2006). Out of the college closet: Differences in perceptions and experiences among out and closeted lesbian and gay students. *College Student Journal, 40*(3), 606–619.

Herek, G. M. (1990). The context of anti-gay violence. *Journal of Interpersonal Violence, 5,* 316–333.

Herek, G. M. (2002). Gender gaps in public opinion about lesbians and gay men. *Public Opinion Quarterly, 66,* 40–66.

Herek, G. M. (2003). Why tell if you're not asked? Self-disclosure, intergroup contact, and heterosexuals' attitudes toward lesbians and gay men. In L. D. Garnets & D. C. Kimmel (Eds.), *Psychological perspectives on lesbian, gay, and bisexual experiences* (pp. 270–298). New York: Columbia University Press.

Herek, G. M. (2007). Confronting sexual stigma and prejudice: Theory and practice. *Journal of Social Issues, 63*(4), 905–925.

Herek, G. M. (2009). Hate crimes and stigma-related experiences among sexual minority adults in the United States. *Journal of Interpersonal Violence, 5*, 316–333.

Herek, G. M., & Capitanio, J. P. (1996). "Some of my best friends": Intergroup contact, concealable stigma, and heterosexuals' attitudes toward gay men and lesbians. *Personality and Social Psychology Bulletin, 22*, 412–424.

Herek, G. M., Cogan, J. C., & Gillis, J. R. (2002). Victim experiences in hate crimes based on sexual orientation. *Journal of Social Issues, 58*(2), 319–339.

Herek, G. M., Gillis, J. R., & Cogan, J. C. (1999). Psychological sequelae of hate-crime victimization among lesbian, gay, and bisexual adults. *Journal of Consulting and Clinical Psychology, 67*(6), 945–951.

Hershberger, S. L., & D'Augelli, A. R. (1995). The impact of victimization on the mental health and suicidality of lesbian, gay, and bisexual youths. *Developmental Psychology, 31*(1), 65–74.

Hill, C., & Silva, E. (2005). *Drawing the line: Sexual harassment on campus.* Washington, DC: American Association of University Women.

Hogan, T., & Rentz, A. (1996). Homophobia in the academy. *Journal of College Student Development, 37*(3), 309–314.

Huebner, D. M., Rebchook, G. M., & Kegeles, S. M. (2004). Experiences of harassment, discrimination, and physical violence among young gay and bisexual men. *American Journal of Public Health, 94*(7), 1200–1203.

Jordan, K., & Deluty, R. (1998). Coming out for lesbian women: Its relation to anxiety, positive affectivity, self-esteem and social support. *Journal of Homosexuality, 35*(2), 41–63.

Love, P. G. (1997). Contradiction and paradox: Attempting to change the culture of sexual orientation at a small Catholic college. *Review of Higher Education, 20*, 381–398.

Malyon, A. (1982). Psychotherapeutic implications of internalized homophobia in gay men. *Journal of Homosexuality, 7*(2/3), 59–69.

Milville, M. L., & Ferguson, A. D. (2004). Impossible "choices": Identity and values at a crossroad. *Counseling Psychologist, 32*, 760–770.

Miner-Rubino, K., & Cortina, L. M. (2007). Beyond targets: Consequences of vicarious exposure to misogyny at work. *Journal of Applied Psychology, 92*(5), 1254–1269.

Mohr, J., & Fassinger, R. (2000). Measuring dimensions of lesbian and gay male experience. *Measurement & Evaluation in Counseling & Development, 33*(2), 66–90.

Morris, J., Waldo, C., & Rothblum, E. (2001). A model of predictors and outcomes of outness among lesbian and bisexual women. *American Journal of Orthopsychiatry, 71*, 61–71.

Pilkington, N. W., & D'Augelli, A. R. (1995). Victimization of lesbian, gay, and bisexual youth in community settings. *Journal of Community Psychology, 23*, 34–56.

Porter, L., Crampon, W., & Smith, F. (1976). Organizational commitment and managerial turnover: A longitudinal study. *Organizational Behavior & Human Decision Processes, 15*, 87–98.

Rankin, S. (2003). *Campus climate for gay, lesbian, bisexual, and transgender people: A national perspective.* New York: National Gay and Lesbian Task Force Policy Institute.

Rosenberg, M. (1986). *Conceiving the self.* Malabar, FL: Krieger.

Rostosky, S., & Riggle, E. (2002). "Out" at work: The relation of actor and partner workplace policy and internalized homophobia to disclosure status. *Journal of Counseling Psychology, 49*(4), 411–419.

Ryan, C., & Rivers, I. (2003). Lesbian, gay, and bisexual and transgender youth: Victimization and its correlates in the USA and UK. *Culture, Health, & Sexuality, 5*(2), 103–119.

Sears, J. T. (2002). The institutional climate for lesbian, gay and bisexual education faculty: What is the pivotal frame of reference? *Journal of Homosexuality, 43,* 11–37.

Strauss, S. (2003). Sexual harassment in K–12. In M. Paludi & C. A. Paludi, Jr. (Eds.), *Academic and workplace sexual harassment: A handbook of cultural, social science, management, and legal perspectives* (pp. 105–145). Westport, CT: Praeger.

Veit, D., & Ware, J. (1983). The structure of psychological distress and well-being in general populations. *Journal of Consulting and Clinical Psychology, 51*(5), 730–742.

Waldo, C. (1998). Out on campus: Sexual orientation and academic climate in a university context. *American Journal of Community Psychology, 26*(5), 745–774.

Watson, D., Clark, L., & Tellegen, A. (1988). Development and validation of brief measures of positive and negative affect: The PANAS scales. *Journal of Personality and Social Psychology, 54*(6), 1063–1070.

Younger, J. (2008). University LGBT/queer programs. Retrieved August 1, 2008, from John G. Younger, University of Kansas Web site, http://www.people.ku.edu/~jyounger/lgbtqprogs.html.

Part II

Adult Victims of Sexual Assault and Abuse

Chapter 7

Adult Survivors of Incest: Psychological Sequelae and Treatment

Jennifer A. Piazza and Paula K. Lundberg-Love

INTRODUCTION

In the recent past, survivors of childhood incest have broken their silence. It is because of their bravery and courage in telling their stories that more is now known about incest than ever before. It was not too long ago that people believed incest was a rare occurrence. As more survivors have spoken out, the public has acknowledged that this terrible act has affected and continues to affect many lives everywhere, regardless of age, gender, ethnicity, socioeconomic status, or education (Klump, 2006; Koss, Bailey, & Yuan, 2003). Incest has a profound impact on the lives of survivors as well as on the lives of the family members and friends with whom they share a relationship. Survivors learn—generally at a young age—that other people's actions can be very harmful. To those who have experienced incest, the world is no longer a safe and trusting place.

This chapter describes the psychological sequelae that are associated with incestuous abuse that can affect the lives of adult survivors, including depression, anxiety, dissociation, substance abuse, and eating disorders. Recent research and treatment options that have been shown to improve·psychological welfare are discussed as well.

PREVALENCE AND INCIDENCE OF INCEST

The definition of incest varies from state to state. However, a general definition of incest is any type of sexual activity between family members. Even though incest is most frequently reported in the father–daughter relationship, it can occur in other relationships, including father–son, mother–daughter, mother–son, sibling, grandparent–grandchild, and stepfather–daughter, among many others. The definition of incest even has been broadened to include anyone responsible for the care of the child including a nonblood relative, step-parents, or anyone who has assumed a family role (Brohl & Potter, 2004). Incest can take the form of contact abuse (fondling, masturbation, intimate kissing, and oral, anal, or vaginal intercourse) or noncontact abuse (sexualized talk, voyeurism, and making pornographic materials available to the child).

To determine the magnitude of the amount of incest that occurs in a particular population, one must consider studies that assess its prevalence and incidence. The *prevalence* of incest is the total number of new and old cases in the population. These numbers are used to show how common incest is in the sample studied; those data are then extrapolated to the general population. The *incidence* of incest is the number of cases reported in a given time period—usually one year, although the span can be any specified amount of time.

These epidemiological rates are partly determined by the legal definition used for incest. As a consequence, rates of incest may vary from state to state. A second factor that affects prevalence and incidence rates is the type of sample studied—specifically, whether it is a community or clinical sample. Community samples are drawn from individuals in the general population, whereas clinical samples consist of those individuals who are in psychotherapy and/or hospital settings. Currently, the best method for collecting prevalence data for incest is use of retrospective surveys in a community sample (Lundberg-Love, 1999). Even so, the results obtained are dependent on the methodology used (i.e., mail or telephone surveys or face-to-face interviews), the sample surveyed, and the type of questions asked (Finkelhor, 1994).

Two well-known epidemiological studies investigating the prevalence of incest were conducted by Gail Wyatt (1985) and Diana Russell (1986). The Wyatt study consisted of 248 women living in the Los Angeles area. Wyatt defined contact child sexual abuse as fondling, intercourse, and oral sex and noncontact abuse as nonbody contact such as solicitations to engage in sexual behavior and exhibitionism prior to the age of 18 with a perpetrator who was at least five years older than the victim. She found that 62 percent of the sample had experienced either contact or noncontact sexual abuse and 45 percent had experienced some form of contact sexual abuse. In Wyatt's study, 21 percent of the women reported intrafamilial abuse.

While the Russell study provided data on all types of sexual assault, it also yielded data on the prevalence of incestuous abuse. Russell interviewed 930 randomly selected women living in the San Francisco area. In her study, incestuous abuse was defined as any form of exploitative sexual contact or attempted sexual contact that occurred before the age of 18 by any relative, no matter how distant the relationship. Russell found that 16 percent of the participants were victims of childhood incestuous abuse. The study also determined the rate of incest as a function of age. When Russell considered women aged 18 to 36 years old, the prevalence of incest was 19 percent. When Russell extrapolated her data to the general population, they suggested that there were at least 160,000 survivors of incestuous abuse per 1 million female children.

Several studies have explored how differences in the definitions of child sexual abuse and incest used in any given study can significantly affect prevalence rates. For example, several studies suggested that when controlling for the definition of abuse, prevalence rates of incest for females range between 10 percent and 13 percent in the community sample and between 13 percent and 70 percent in clinical samples (Everett & Gallop, 2001; Molnar, Buka, & Kessler, 2001). Clinical samples tend to yield higher prevalence rates than community samples because incest often affects the psychological well-being of the victim. Many incest survivors experience various psychological difficulties during adulthood that may benefit from or require psychotherapy. In a national nonclinical sample, the prevalence rate decreased from 21–32 percent to 15–26 percent when a narrower definition of abuse was used (Vogelanz, Wilsnack, Harris, Wilsnack, Wonderlich, & Krisjanson, 1999).

It is important to keep in mind that the actual prevalence rate of incest is unknown (Crowley & Seery, 2001; Lundberg-Love, 2006). In fact, the prevalence rates reported in the literature are most likely underestimates of the extent of the problem. Due to the stigma associated with incest as well as the secrecy of the relationship, victims and their families are often reluctant to report the incidents (Hyde & Kaufman, 1984).

The National Incident-Based Reporting System (NIBRS) has documented several statistics related to the incidence of incest among child sexual abuse survivors (U.S. Department of Justice, 2000). For instance, 67 percent of all sexual assault victims reported to this system were younger than the age of 21, with half of them being younger than the age of 18. Furthermore, 14 percent of sexual assault victims were younger than the age of 6 at the time of the assault. Of all female victims who experienced some type of child sexual abuse, 33.9 percent were abused by a family member. More specifically, 47 percent of them were sexually abused by a family member prior to the age of 13. Male child sexual abuse rates were similar to the rates for females. Approximately 36 percent of males who were sexually abused prior to 18 years of age were abused by a family member. Additionally, 40 percent of male victims were abused prior to age 13 by a family member.

An overwhelming majority of child sexual abuse cases are perpetrated by a family member—particularly a male family member—as opposed to a friend, an acquaintance, or a stranger. Indeed, some individuals are victims of *polyincest*. Polyincestuous abuse is defined as "more than one family member (related by blood, adoption, or marriage) engaged in long-term coercive exploitation of other family members, usually women and children" (Crowley & Seery, 2001). It has been reported that 23 percent of female childhood sexual abuse (CSA) survivors experience polyincestuous abuse by two or more family members. Overall, approximately 41 to 56 percent of reported CSA cases are perpetrated by a family member: 9.2 to 12.8 percent by the father, 5.2 to 5.7 percent by a stepfather or the mother's boyfriend, 6.3 to 8.5 percent by a brother, and 2.6 to 3.6 percent by a female relative (U.S. Department of Justice, 2000). It is important to recognize the magnitude of these numbers as well as the possibility of sexual abuse by multiple family members because incestuous abuse can result in damaging psychological consequences that can emerge during adulthood.

BIOLOGICAL CONSEQUENCES OF ADVERSE CHILDHOOD EXPERIENCES

Incest is a stressor that shapes the child psychologically, socially, behaviorally, and even biologically well into adulthood. The body automatically responds to stress in an attempt to protect the individual from a potentially dangerous situation. First, the body begins to prepare for the potential threat. In the normal stress response, the hypothalamic–pituitary–adrenal (HPA) axis is activated, which results in the release of corticotrophin-releasing factor (CRF), adrenocorticotrophic hormone (ACTH), and glucocorticoids such as cortisol. The body also releases chemical messengers such as epinephrine (adrenaline), norepinephrine (noradrenalin), dopamine, acetylcholine, and opioids. Cortisol increases the amount of energy available to the body by increasing the level of glucose, which in turn sharpens the senses (Mills, Reiss, & Dombeck, 2009). It also suppresses systems such as digestion, reproduction, and growth, which are not important in the stressful moment. Once the stressful event has passed, the body's systems return to normal by the process of feedback. High levels of stress hormones—primarily cortisol—turn off the release of CRF, which decreases the levels of other chemicals in a cascading effect (Harvard Medical School, 2005).

Stress can trigger the alarm reaction, during which the body reacts to a perceived threat by increasing heart rate, blood pressure, respiratory rate, and blood flow to the muscles (Mills et al., 2009). During this response, blood flow increases to the skeletal muscle and brain, and decreases to the stomach, kidney, skin, and liver. The body's natural painkillers, such as endorphins, are released into the bloodstream. Sensory awareness is heightened. Fats and sugars supply the body with energy.

The alarm reaction allows the individual to respond quickly and appropriately to eliminate the stressor or remove the person from the stressful event. Specifically, the body can respond physically through the fight–flight–freeze reactions, where the options are to stay and fight, flee, or freeze, respectively. However, children who experience incest typically are not able to fight off the perpetrator or flee from the situation. Oftentimes, freezing is the only option because the perpetrator is usually stronger and faster than the child victim. When this occurs, the alarm stage lessens and the adaptation stage begins. During this phase, the body's physiological systems work at a more moderate pace and respond to ongoing threats. Although the adaptation stage does not require as much energy as the alarm stage, the body still needs a significant amount of energy to remain in this stage; thus persistence of the adaptation stage can lead to health problems such as ulcers, high blood pressure, atherosclerosis, and arthritis.

Before, during, and after the incestuous act, sensory cues may become associated with the painful experience (e.g., the scent of the father's cologne, the sound of the door opening late at night). These sensory triggers are sent to the brain's limbic system, particularly the amygdala, where the situation and cues are assigned an emotional valence. The amygdala projects to multiple areas in the brain that regulate the stress response, including the hypothalamus, which controls autonomic and HPA axis activity, and the locus coeruleus, which serves as a gauge for emotionality and the initiation of the stress response (Spiegel, 2003). The cortex organizes the multiple cues and responses, and plays a key role in the consolidation of memory for the incestuous event.

This complicated sequence is vulnerable to chronic or severe stressors during critical periods of childhood brain development, which can become permanently altered and engender long-lasting consequences (Heim & Nemeroff, 2001; Teicher, 2000). Indeed, the chronic and severe stress of incest is an adverse experience that can affect one's health and the quality of life throughout adulthood (Anda et al., 2006). During the normal stress response, the provoked circuit in the brain is able to compensate for the effects and, therefore, avoid producing symptoms such as anxiety, depression, and post-traumatic stress disorder (PTSD) (Stahl, 2008). In contrast, when the circuit is chronically activated by overwhelming trauma, such as incest, it can become sensitized to future adult stressors. Thus, when an incest survivor faces adult stressors, it becomes more likely that symptoms such as anxiety, depression, and PTSD will surface. It is also possible for the circuit to be activated without stressful stimuli. Clearly, the incestuous relationship can biologically burden the adult survivor with more obstacles to overcome in handling life's inevitable stressors.

PSYCHOLOGICAL SEQUELAE ASSOCIATED WITH INCEST

The experience of incest is related to many types of symptoms that can manifest themselves during the victim's adulthood. The literature indicates that survivors' personal growth and development is affected by childhood incest in psychological, behavioral, physiological, and cognitive ways (Ward & Lundberg-Love, 2006). Long-term incest is associated with more severe psychological consequences than sexual abuse perpetrated once or by someone outside of the family. While some incest survivors experience few symptoms, others describe an adult life consumed with a myriad of psychological disturbances (Lundberg-Love, 1999). This section discusses the most common psychological disturbances associated with incest, including depression, anxiety, dissociation, substance abuse, and eating disorders.

Depression and Suicide

Depression is the most commonly reported psychological symptom in those who have experienced incest. Instead of being alert and vigilant to stress or strong emotions, a depressed person is often chronically lethargic and apathetic or agitated and anxious (Harvard Medical School, 2005). Feelings associated with depression resulting from incest include, but are not limited to, stigmatization, guilt, alienation, hopelessness, and low self-esteem. Experiencing any type of child abuse is the most common predictor of depression in adulthood. Nevertheless, survivors of sexual abuse are more than four times more likely to experience depressive symptoms later in adulthood as compared to those persons who were not sexually abused (Lundberg-Love, 2006). Researchers have found that 39.3 percent of women with sexual abuse histories develop depression at some point in their lives, compared to 21.3 percent of women without such histories (Molnar et al., 2001). Researchers have also found that delays in disclosure of the incestuous experience are associated with the development of depression (Ruggiero et al., 2004).

Some incest survivors—perhaps not surprisingly—turn to suicide as a way out of an almost unbearable emotional and mood state. According to researchers, 16 percent of female incest survivors attempt suicide, whereas only 6 percent of females who have not been sexually abused attempt suicide (Saunders, Villeponteaux, Lipovsky, & Kilpatrick, 1992). This significant difference in the rate of suicide attempts between those who have incestuous experiences and those who do not places incest survivors at a greater risk of mortality and should be taken seriously.

Depression is also associated with the development of multiple other health concerns, including cardiovascular disease and decreased immune response. High levels of cortisol can reduce the body's white blood cell count, which places the individual at greater risk for contracting an illness or disease (Lundberg-Love, 2006). Other factors connected to the detrimental effects of depression include poor eating habits, use of tobacco, use and misuse of alcohol and other drugs, poor sleep hygiene, and a lack of physical activity; all of these factors also have their own destructive consequences.

Anxiety Disorders

Anxiety is a mood state characterized by worry and fear in anticipation of future stressors. It is a normal response to stress that allows an individual to cope better with life stressors. In fact, anxiety can be a motivating force. For example, the anxiety provoked by an upcoming test may motivate a student to study or the possibility of a job promotion may motivate a worker to demonstrate better performance. Conversely, excessive worry and fear regarding real or imagined stressors can lead to an anxiety disorder.

A variety of anxiety disorders are associated with the internalization of incest trauma (Lundberg-Love, 2006). Sexual abuse survivors are five times more likely to develop anxiety disorders such as panic disorder, obsessive-compulsive disorder, generalized anxiety disorder, and specific phobias. Nevertheless, PTSD is the anxiety disorder most commonly reported by incest survivors. In PTSD, the individual has previously experienced, witnessed, or was confronted by an event that involved actual or threatened death or serious injury (American Psychiatric Association [APA], 1994). A person often responds to events such as incest with intense fear, helplessness, or worry. "Reexperiencing" the event through thoughts, perceptions, dreams, or actually feeling and thinking that the event is recurring are also symptoms of PTSD. The incest survivor typically tries to avoid stimuli associated with the events or triggers that can remind the individual of the incest or the perpetrator. In addition, PTSD is characterized by problems associated with increased autonomic nervous system arousal, such as difficulty sleeping, irritability, difficulty concentrating, hypervigilance, and exaggerated startle response. The diagnosis of PTSD should always be considered when an incest survivor displays any type of emotional and/or cognitive difficulty (Anderson, Rowan, Foy, Rodriguez, & Ryan, 1994).

It is largely accepted that childhood incest increases the likelihood of developing PTSD symptoms. Having a history of sexual abuse also increases symptom severity as compared to the symptoms experienced by those persons who have PTSD but lack such a history (Bolstad & Zinbarg, 1997).

Furthermore, the risk increases when a survivor also has experienced physical abuse during childhood (Schaaf & McCanne, 1998). Approximately one third of sexually abused children in the general population develop PTSD later in life (Ward & Lundberg-Love, 2006). By comparison, 64 to 69 percent of those person in a clinical population with sexual abuse histories were found to develop PTSD symptoms (Anderson et al., 1994). One study even found a gender difference in the development of PTSD symptoms after incest: males who were sexually abused were 5.64 times more likely to develop PTSD than males who were not sexually abused, whereas female survivors were 2.14 times more likely to develop PTSD (Hanson et al., 2008). Girls were more likely to report perceived life threat. Boys were less likely to report the incest—a factor that can increase the risk of poorer mental health outcome because boys are less likely to receive needed treatment.

Complex post-traumatic stress disorder, a concept proposed by Judith Herman (1992), is a diagnosis specific to survivors of prolonged, repeated trauma such as incest. Complex PTSD goes beyond a stressful event to encompass long-term abuse. According to Herman, simple PTSD does not take into account the unique nature that those who experience incestuous relationships endure; thus complex PTSD offers a more complete explanation for the consequences of long-term trauma. Complex PTSD symptomatology includes seven categories (Lundberg-Love, 2006):

1. Difficulty regulating emotions, such as extreme emotional states from which the person is unable to easily recover
2. Changes in consciousness such as dissociation (spacing out) under stress, the reexperiencing of emotionally traumatic events, and the forgetting of or inability to recall emotionally traumatic events
3. Changes in self-perception, including self-blame, sense of helplessness, guilt, and shame
4. Changes in the perception of the perpetrator as powerful and alterations in the perception of the relationship between the victim and the perpetrator
5. Changes in relationships with others, including isolation, distrust, and a search for a rescuer
6. Changes in one's system of meanings, including a sense of hopelessness, despair, and no sustaining meaning of faith
7. Changes in nervous system activity associated with increased arousal (i.e., exaggerated startle response, hypervigilance, and physical symptoms)

Acknowledging the difference in the psychological sequelae between PTSD and complex PTSD that accounts for the prolonged nature of incest may influence the type of treatment that incest survivors receive.

Post-traumatic stress disorder has the capability of changing the normal physiological response to stress, thereby affecting various parts of the brain (Lundberg-Love, 2006). In PTSD, cortisol levels tend to be abnormally low and norepinephrine levels tend to be abnormally high. As discussed earlier in this chapter, cortisol levels are important in regulating the physiological response to stress. Low levels of cortisol can cause overactivity in the nervous system because other stress hormones are not appropriately regulated. In contrast, high levels of norepinephrine have been linked to the intrusive thoughts associated with PTSD as well as the severity of other PTSD symptoms. Given that incest occurs largely throughout childhood and early adolescence—a time when crucial brain development is occurring—PTSD has the potential to alter the development and growth of brain structures.

For example, consider the effects of incest on the hippocampus, a brain structure involved in learning and memory. As compared to adults without a sexual abuse history, survivors show smaller hippocampal volume, which may provide an explanation for the memory problems often experienced by incest survivors. Conversely, studies have shown no difference in volume in the amygdala, caudate nucleus, or the sensory cortex (other areas involved in learning and memory) in incest survivors and persons without a history of sexual abuse. The amygdala—a brain structure that registers fear—includes links to the hypothalamus, hippocampus, and cerebral cortex (Harvard Medical School, 2005). Incest can activate the amygdala, which enhances these connections and makes the strength of emotionally charged memories difficult to modify so that the individual can recognize a similar threat in the future. It is not necessarily the memory to which a survivor reacts, but rather the emotions that various cues and triggers can provoke.

Dissociation and Disengagement

Dissociation is a mental process that helps an individual cope with many types of traumatic events in an effort to avoid overwhelming the person (Lundberg-Love, 2006). Dissociation compartmentalizes traumatic experiences and prevents integration of thoughts, memories, emotions, and behaviors.

Recognized dissociative disorders include dissociative amnesia, dissociative fugue, depersonalization disorder, and dissociative identity disorder (APA, 1994). Dissociative amnesia is characterized by the inability to recall important personal information beyond that of normal forgetting. The most common form of dissociative amnesia, called localized amnesia, is the inability to recall information—usually of a traumatic and stressful nature—for a period of time. Dissociative fugue is a sudden, unexpected travel from home or familiar areas with an inability to recall some or all of the past. This experience may also include confusion about the person's own identity or even the assumption of a new identity. Persons experiencing depersonalization disorder episodes have feelings of detachment and estrangement from the mental processes of their own body. Dissociative identity disorder (DID), formerly called multiple personality disorder, is described as having two or more distinct and separate personalities; persons with DID are also unable to recall personal information beyond that of normal forgetting. Incest survivors who experience abuse or trauma prior to age six are at risk for developing dissociative disorders.

Female survivors of early childhood incest tend to dissociate more than women without such a history (Briere & Conte, 1993)—a finding that has prompted researchers to propose multiple theories to explain it. According to Kluft (1990), the fragmented identity and sense of self arises because dissociative defenses interfere with cognitive processes. In other words, identity remains divided and unable to integrate in a fluid manner. Dissociative strategies may be used to provide the perception of protection and relief in a situation over which the child has little or no control (Classen, Koopman, & Spiegel, 1993). Dissociation also may prevent the processing of external cues associated with incest (Shalev, 1997). As a consequence, experiences are not able to integrate with other past events and the identity of the individual remains fragmented.

One type of dissociation, peritraumatic dissociation, is characterized by the depersonalization/derealization common to dissociation but tends to occur during or immediately after the traumatic event. Not long ago, it was believed that peritraumatic dissociation resolved quickly on its own (Putnam, 1997). More recently, however, researchers have consistently shown a relationship between early dissociation and later PTSD symptoms (Johnson, Pike, & Chard, 2001). While some have found that peritraumatic dissociation occurring during childhood sexual abuse produces higher levels of PTSD symptomatology, others have found that combined sexual and physical abuse must be present during childhood to produce similar levels of PTSD (Hetzel & McCanne, 2005).

Incest victims often employ disengagement methods such as denial, wishful thinking, avoidance, and self-criticism during the incestuous experience (Gibson & Leitenberg, 2001). While these techniques permit the child to handle the situation to the best of his or her ability, they may lead to subsequent psychological and affective problems. In particular, the same disengagement coping techniques tend to be used by the individual through adulthood. Reliance on these coping mechanisms is not conducive to the type of cognitive and emotional processing that is thought to be important in reducing psychological symptomatology. It also has been suggested that incest victims may have more distressing thoughts and feelings to avoid and, therefore, tend to disengage or dissociate more than those who have not experienced incestuous abuse.

Substance Abuse

Numerous studies have identified a link between the trauma of incest and later substance abuse and dependence. The prevalence of a history of incest in participants in substance treatment programs is significantly higher than that of the general population (Edwards, Dunham, Ries, & Barnett, 2006). Estimates of the percentage of persons with such a history range anywhere from 24 percent to 85 percent of individuals with a substance use problem. Researchers have also found that in incest survivors, 55 percent of the variance accounted for regarding alcohol use could be explained by traumatic stress symptoms associated with adverse childhood experiences. One group of researchers found that the use of illicit drugs, alcohol, and nicotine was strongly correlated with adverse experiences such as incest (Anda et al., 2006).

Researchers also have investigated the reasons why incest survivors are at increased risk to misuse drugs and/or alcohol. While it is not surprising that incest survivors may use alcohol and other drugs to modify symptoms of anxiety and depression (Rohsenow, Corbett, & Devine, 1988), some researchers have suggested that the abuse of alcohol and other drugs is often a response to incest (Glover, Janikowski, & Benshoff, 1996). Others have proposed that drug use may initially serve to suppress memories and deny the emotions and thoughts associated with incestuous abuse, but later turn into a serious problem of drug dependency and addiction (Bass & Davis, 1988; Janikowski & Glover-Graf, 2003). Alcohol and drug use can lower inhibitions, boost confidence, and reduce social anxiety (Lundberg-Love, 2006).

The susceptibility to misuse drugs and alcohol by incest survivors may also be explained biologically. A pathway in the brain connects the ventral tegmental area (VTA) and the nucleus accumbens (Stahl, 2008). Incest can result in the activation and sensitization of these brain pathways—a phenomenon also seen in drug abuse—which may then lead to addiction (Lundberg-Love, 2006).

Eating Disorders and Obesity

Some incest survivors also struggle with patterns of disturbed eating. Of course, eating disorders and obesity are problems for many people who lack any history of incest. The National Institute of Mental Health (NIMH) estimates that 0.5 to 3.7 percent of all females will suffer from anorexia in their lifetime, 1.1 to 4.2 percent will suffer from bulimia, and 2 to 5 percent of Americans suffer from binge-eating disorder (National Institute of Health, 2008). Nevertheless, adults who have histories of sexual abuse seem to be at a higher risk for developing disturbed eating patterns than those who have no such history (Lundberg-Love, 2006). Specifically, individuals who experience incest are more likely to develop an eating disorder than those who were victimized by someone outside of the family (Baldo, Wallace, & O'Halloran, 1996). Three of the most common patterns of disturbed eating that incest survivors may experience are anorexia nervosa, bulimia nervosa, and obesity.

Anorexia nervosa is characterized by exceptionally low body weight and a body image distortion, such that the affected individual obsesses over the fear of gaining weight or becoming fat. An overwhelming majority of those persons who suffer from anorexia are females, although males can also develop this pattern of disturbed eating. Anorexia nervosa can lead to osteoporosis, heart problems, infertility, depression, and even death (De Angelis, 2002). Individuals with sexual abuse histories who are diagnosed with anorexia nervosa are more likely to engage in binge–purge behavior rather than have the restricting type of disease (Carter, Bewell, Blackmore, & Woodside, 2006). Individuals with the binge–purge subtype of the disorder are also more likely to be impulsive and terminate treatment early, as opposed to those persons with the restricting type, either with or without histories of incest. Others have found a relationship between partial anorexia nervosa—which is not classified as an eating disorder, but includes people who show tendencies toward anorexia—and a history of sexual abuse (Sanci, Cofy, Olsson, Reid, Carlin, & Patton, 2008). Even so, the link between incest and anorexia nervosa is not as strong as the relationship between incest and both bulimia nervosa and obesity (Wonderlich, Brewerton, Jocic, & Dansky, 1997).

Bulimia nervosa is characterized by binge eating usually followed by purging, such as via self-induced vomiting or the use of laxatives. Many of the problems that stem from bulimia are due to vomiting, including erosion of tooth enamel, the rupture of the esophagus or stomach, and heart and kidney problems stemming from blood chemistry imbalances (Lundberg-Love, 2006). The risk of developing this eating disorder increases when an individual has a history of childhood sexual abuse (Baldo et al., 1996). Young women who have experienced two or more episodes of sexual abuse during childhood are five times more likely to develop bulimic disorders than those who have not experienced sexual abuse (Sanci et al., 2008). An even greater risk for developing a severe form of disturbed eating behaviors is noted in those persons who were incestuously abused as opposed to those who experienced extrafamilial sexual abuse.

One study also found a relationship between sexual trauma, eating disorders, and PTSD (Holzer, Uppala, Wonderlich, Crosby, & Simonich, 2008). The correlation between sexual abuse and the presence of an eating disorder was significantly reduced when statistically controlling for the concomitant presence of PTSD. For example, women who have a history of incest and develop PTSD are more likely to develop an eating disorder as compared to those women who have not developed PTSD as a result of their incestuous abuse. Some researchers have suggested that internalized shame may be a mediating factor between sexual abuse and this eating disorder (Murray & Waller, 2002). Specifically, internalized shame is associated with bulimia nervosa to a greater extent when the abuse came from a family member. The secrecy of the abuse may also influence bulimic attitudes and affect.

Obesity is a medical crisis that is characterized by an excess of body fat that leads to poor health and a reduction in life expectancy. Persons who are severely overweight have a higher risk for developing health problems including heart disease, increased blood pressure, stroke, diabetes, high cholesterol, and cancer (Lundberg-Love, 2006). Researchers have found that women who have experienced any type of sexual or physical abuse during childhood are twice as likely to become obese as adults (Rhode et al., 2008). The percentages of people who suffer from binge eating greatly outnumber those who suffer from other eating disorders. Both this eating disorder and its main consequence, obesity, need to be studied further with respect to their connection to incest.

Consequences of eating disorders and obesity can be severe, serious, and even life threatening. While a history of incest is associated with a greater risk of developing an eating disorder in adolescence and adulthood, it is important to remember that not all incest survivors will battle this problem. For health care practitioners, it is imperative to recognize the link between disturbed eating patterns and emotions when treating incest survivors with eating disorders.

Sexual Self-Schema and Shame

The sexual self-schema is the way a person cognitively views himself or herself as a sexual being. Cognitive views of the self are influenced by the experience a person has internally as well as through self–other interactions (Bowlby, 1969). Sexual self-schemas not only mediate intrapersonal (within the self) feelings and communications, but they also affect interpersonal relationships between two or more people (Andersen & Cyranowski, 1994). Characteristics of these schemas can be attitudinal, behavioral, physiological, emotional, and cognitive.

Researchers have proposed that the makeup of sexual self-schemas includes two positive characteristics—romantic/passionate and open/direct self-schema—and one negative characteristic—embarrassment/conservatism. The first two features facilitate sexual cognitions, behaviors, and emotions, while the last discourages sexual cognitions, behaviors, and emotions. These three self-views can be organized into four main categories: positive schema, negative schema, co-schematic, and aschematic (Cyranowski & Andersen, 1998). A positive sexual self-schema shows high positive schema characteristics and low negative schema characteristics.

A negative sexual self-schema shows high negative schema characteristics and low positive schema characteristics. Co-schematics show high positive and negative characteristics, whereas aschematics show low positive and negative characteristics. Sexual self-schema characteristics can be affected by intrafamilial sexual abuse.

Positive and negative sexual self-schema characteristics are important in understanding the self-image of an incest survivor. Women with negative schemas show higher levels of embarrassment/conservatism and lower levels of the romantic/passionate and open/direct characteristics compared to women with positive schemas (Cyranowski & Andersen, 1998). They also display more anxiety about sexual activity and the fear of being unloved or abandoned than women with positive schemas. Individuals with a history of sexual abuse during childhood often exhibit an inverse relationship between depression and the romantic/passionate sexual self-schema on various measures of a sexual self-schema scale (Meston, Rellini, & Heiman, 2006). In other words, as their level of depression increases, their romantic/passionate view of the self decreases. A possible explanation for why the romantic and passionate view of the sexual self is diminished among incest survivors may be that early sexual experiences have become paired with frightening and negative connotations. Those who have a lower score on this scale also show higher levels of depression, anxiety, and negative sexual affect during sexual activity. Incest may affect the positive self-schema by lowering subjective feelings of passion and romance, yet not affect the negative self-schema by increasing feelings of embarrassment.

Among incest survivors, sexual activity and intimacy often become paired with shame and anxiety (Meston et al., 2006). The experience of shame is a "desire to hide the damaged and degraded self from exposure to the censure of others" (Feiring, Simon, & Cleland, 2009). Shame can produce many problems in the developing self, including fear of disclosure, fear of intimacy, and anxiety about self-value (Tangney & Dearing, 2002). Shame is a part of the emotional damage that is done by incest, and it becomes an element of the person's identity (Hunter, 1990). In effect, the incest survivor integrates the aftermath of the events—something that is not the victim's fault—into his or her self-identity.

One study found that internalized shame associated with sexual abuse during childhood increased the likelihood of verbal conflict in intimate relationships in adulthood (Kim, Talbot, & Cichetti, 2009). In addition, family conflict and physical abuse by an intimate partner were associated with more severe forms of sexual abuse, such as chronic abuse and incest. It has been proposed that the shame that incest survivors may experience can be related to unassertiveness, angry defensiveness, and aggression as well as an increased likelihood of being physically abused in an intimate relationship. The longer internalizing shame remains a problem for incest survivors, the more difficulties they may encounter in later life, including sexual difficulties, aggression, and intimacy problems (Feiring et al., 2009). Moreover, the longer shame persists, the greater the chance that sexual difficulties and dating aggression may surface. It may also lead to intimacy problems, such as fear of intimacy, if shame continues well into adulthood.

Revictimization

Revictimization typically occurs when individuals who have previously experienced childhood sexual abuse are subsequently victimized in adolescence and/or adulthood (Widom, Czaja, & Dutton, 2008). Being aware of the greater risk of revictimization is important because it gives some control back to the victim. When they understand their risk for revictimization, survivors are able to reclaim control in their lives. Specifically, they can learn the appropriate skills and strategies to protect themselves against further attack.

Multiple factors have been proposed to influence the relationship between sexual abuse during childhood and adult revictimization, including dissociation (Kessler & Bieschke, 1999), shame, locus of control (Bolstad & Xinbarg, 1997), coping mechanisms (Gibson & Leitenberg, 2001), and psychological resilience (Walsh, Blaustein, Knight, Spinazola, & van de Kolk, 2007). Dissociation and shame were discussed in previous sections; locus of control, coping mechanisms, and resilience are discussed in more detail here.

Many studies have found significant relationships between incest and revictimization, both physical and sexual, in adulthood in men and women. In fact, sexual abuse survivors are two to three times more likely to be revictimized than persons who have not been sexually abused as children, and the chances increase with the presence of physical contact during the abuse (Arata, 2002). The rates of revictimization that have been proposed most likely underestimate the true magnitude of the problem because of the complicated nature of this issue—namely, the details of both the victimization in adulthood and the prior victimization in childhood need to be revealed to understand this phenomenon.

Numerous studies have investigated the probability of revictimization in adulthood after experiencing various forms of childhood physical, sexual, and incestuous abuse. According to one study, 68.83 percent of women who experienced CSA also experienced sexual assault as adults, compared with 41.62 percent of women without a history of CSA (Kessler & Bieschke, 1999). Shame was an intervening factor in this study, suggesting that greater feelings of shame are associated with a greater risk of victimization. The study also compared women who experienced intrafamilial sexual abuse to those who were sexually abused by someone outside of the family, as well as those who were not sexually abused as children. Women who were incestuously abused were 5.6 times more likely to experience adulthood sexual coercion and 9.35 times more likely to experience attempted rape than their non-CSA counterparts. Women who were incestuously victimized were 5.13 times more likely to experience sexual coercion and 4.85 times more likely to experience rape than those who were abused by perpetrators outside of the family.

Although victimization in adulthood increases with the history of incest, childhood physical abuse is also a factor associated with later revictimization. Approximately 50 percent of women who have experienced CSA also have experienced child physical abuse (Anderson et al., 1994). The highest rate of adult revictimization was found in those persons who had been abused both physically and sexually as children (Schaaf & McCanne, 1998). In one study, victimization rates for women who experienced only sexual abuse as children were similar to rates for women who did not report any type of childhood abuse. The combination of childhood physical and sexual abuse, however, doubles the risk for revictimization when compared to individuals who were sexually abused or those who were not abused during childhood. This point is an important consideration given the high percentage of adults who have experienced both forms of abuse. It is also important to acknowledge both types of abuse during the healing process.

Locus of control (LOC) is a concept that describes a person's beliefs and perceptions about why things happen and what causes those things to happen. An individual who perceives things as happening to him or her because of outside forces and who believes he or she has no way to control those forces is described as having an external locus of control. An individual who believes that things happen because he or she is in control of them has an internal locus of control. Many children who have experienced sexual abuse develop an external locus of control (Simmons & Weinman, 1991). The nature of the abuse takes control away from the child, which can manifest itself as lowered perceptions of control in adulthood (Bolstad & Zinbarg, 1997). These perceptions may render survivors vulnerable to future victimization because they believe they have less control than others over any given situation (Walsh et al., 2007). Therapeutic resolution with respect to perceptions of control may be beneficial, thereby enabling incest survivors to prevent revictimization in adulthood. In other words, reclaiming a sense of control can enhance the future coping skills of incest survivors.

Although revictimization occurs among a substantial proportion of incest survivors, it is important to remember that not all incest survivors are revictimized during adulthood. Certain characteristics and coping styles can render a person either more or less vulnerable to revictimization (Walsh et al., 2007). For instance, positive coping styles such as discussing incestuous experiences, minimization, and positive refra-ming are associated with emotional adjustment that decreases the risk of revictimization (Gibson & Leitenberg, 2001). In contrast, incest survivors who develop maladaptive coping styles, such as inhibited disclosure of incestuous experiences and magnification, are at a greater risk for revictimization.

The ability to cope with stressful situations and adapt to the environ-ment in a positive way—a capacity that has been termed *resilience*—is a concept that combines locus of control, cognitive coping mechanisms, and the perception regarding whether an experience was abusive or non-abusive when it occurred (Davis, 2001). The trauma that is associated with incest does not resolved suddenly (Lundberg-Love, 1999). In fact, for most individuals, treatment is beneficial. Also, the ability to heal from psychological trauma does not depend solely on the individual. Thera-peutic intervention can enable a survivor to resolve most of the psycho-logical issues that are associated with incestuous abuse.

Psychological Sequelae among Men Who Have Experienced Incest in Their Childhoods

Not as much attention and research has been devoted to males who have been incestuously abused as compared to females who have ex-perienced such abuse. Recent research, however, has shown that male victims of incest experience psychological sequelae similar to and differ-ent from female survivors. Incestuous abuse of a young boy is often per-petrated by an older male in a manner that results in prolonged, repetitive victimization (Fields, Malebranche, & Feist-Price, 2008). Similar to female victims, male victims feel powerless during these experiences and are at risk for developing some of the same adulthood psychological disturbances.

As mentioned previously, males who experience sexual abuse are 5.64 times more likely to develop PTSD than those who were not abused, whereas while female survivors are 2.14 times more likely to develop PTSD than those who were not abused (Hanson et al., 2008). Males with a CSA history also are more likely to exhibit problem behaviors such as aggressiveness and drug and alcohol use and abuse than are abused girls (Garnefski & Arends, 1998). These differences among the psychological sequelae experienced by survivors may reflect the fact that males are less likely to disclose the incestuous events and are less likely to be met with positive and helpful responses when they do disclose such information (Ullman & Filipas, 2005). The lack of disclosure may be a function of a fear that they may be perceived as homosexual, the belief that boys are rarely victims, or even a fear of becoming an abuser themselves (Alaggia & Kirshenbaum, 2005). Although disclosure can lead to personal growth and foster the ability to trust others, when males disclose they are less likely than females to divulge details of their abuse (Sorsoli, 2004). Disclosure can aid in the healing process. Young boys who do not disclose the incestuous abuse are not able to receive the therapeutic intervention that has been shown to improve the lives of adult survivors of incest.

TREATMENT

Incestuous abuse may dramatically influence the adult life of the child victim. With appropriate therapeutic intervention, however, it is possible to reduce its impact, so that the victim recovers from the sexual trauma (Lundberg-Love, 2006). Most experts believe that therapy helps incest survivors tell their stories, make sense of their lives, and begin to understand how their experiences influence the way they think and behave. The therapist's role is to be a teacher, a mentor, a collaborator, and a listener—not a friend, a substitute parent, or even a healer. The therapist can not only provide education about incest and its consequences, but also help identify problematic thoughts, behaviors, and emotions. Through appropriate treatment, clients learn how to identify their maladaptive thoughts and behaviors, learn new coping strategies, and focus on their present and future.

Judith Herman has identified a series of 10 steps of recovery to assist incest victims heal from their deep and painful wounds. These steps are used as a general guide as to what to expect from therapy as a road to recovery (Everett & Gallop, 2001):

1. *Readiness.* Not all incest survivors are ready to begin a therapeutic healing process. There are three recognized types of potential clients: visitors, complainants, and customers. *Visitors* are clients who do not believe they have a problem and have been sent to therapy by a spouse, relative, or friend, or even by court order. *Complainants*, who include the majority of incest survivors, realize there is a problem but do not understand that it is *their* problem; rather, they believe that someone else is responsible and the problem is beyond their control. *Customers* are persons who realize that not only is there a problem, but it is their problem and they have a responsibility to act. The therapist should remain open and find common ground with the client, no matter which type he or she represents.
2. *Believe.* The therapist creates an environment conducive to a productive and beneficial therapeutic outcome. Clients must feel they will be believed before they will disclose their pain. The therapist's role is to remain neutral. However, it is comforting to know that the therapist understands that what the client is saying is true.

3. *Safety.* The therapist's office must be a safe haven where clients can tell their stories. Daily traumatizing events hinder the healing process and must be addressed. Supportive family and friends of the client are also important to the healing process because they provide a comforting support system outside the therapy office.

4. *The story.* Clients begin to tell their stories in their own way and in their own time. The completed story will often be told across multiple sessions. Clients are coming to terms with their experiences as they are telling the story and may need time to process what they are saying before they continue. The therapist's role is to listen and provide sympathetic understanding.

5. *Anger and sadness.* Incest victims come to associate emotion with deep pain and try to avoid feeling it at all costs. Survivors of incest have trouble processing and expressing emotions such as anger and sadness in a productive manner. If anger is not expressed in an appropriate manner, it can lead to a deep depression. If sadness and grief are not expressed in a healthy way, they can lead to an overwhelming feeling of pain. The therapist's role is to educate clients about the language of emotion and teach them how to express a range of emotions effectively. The therapist also encourages clients to express their anger and sadness outside the office in a way that keeps them and others safe.

6. *Mourning the losses.* Incest survivors have a lot to mourn, ranging from relationships to future possibilities. The relationships between the victim and the perpetrator, non-offending parents, siblings, other family members, and friends as well as future relationships may all be affected. The future for the child victim can change drastically, with upheavals occurring in everything from living arrangements to educational opportunities to the development of psychological difficulties. The client also mourns the hope that somehow the past can be made right. During this phase, which is often the most difficult stage of treatment, the therapist must be able to recognize and not flinch in the face of raw human emotion while remaining emotionally present for the client. The therapist is not able to lessen the pain experienced by the client and must accompany the client through this difficult process.

7. *Telling a new truth.* Clients begin to replace futile hopes of the past with new realistic hopes for the future. They must also face some new truths, such as the fact that no one is coming to rescue them, no one can make this better for them, life is not fair, and only the future—not the past—can be changed. The desire to seek justice and revenge is a common problem with which clients often struggle. However, seeking justice and revenge can serve as a road block to recovery. Sadly, many perpetrators are not held responsible for their

horrendous actions. It is important to relay to each client the idea that recovery and moving forward into a new life is more beneficial than revenge, no matter what outcome the perpetrator may face.

8. *Defining a new self.* This stage of therapy is characterized by self-discovery and introspection. Clients begin to ask questions about who they are, what they want from life, and what they can contribute to society. The therapist gives clients time to explore these questions and teaches them to begin sentences with the word "I."

9. *Social and spiritual reconnection.* Clients begin to integrate what they have learned in therapy and put it into practice. Incest isolates victims, who often feel alone and abnormal. This stage empowers clients to understand themselves and their relationships with others. In doing so, they begin to make healthy connections with family, friends, and the community. The therapist's role is to encourage and support the formation of positive relationships and explore spirituality, beliefs, and activities that sustain the soul.

10. *Saying good-bye.* Growth and development are lifelong pursuits; however, therapy must eventually come to an end. The process of termination of therapy should be discussed at the beginning of the therapeutic relationship as well as various points throughout the journey. It is important to celebrate with clients the hard work and accomplishments they have achieved since the beginning of therapy. It is also important to let clients know that there will be "bumps in the road" and that they can return for "booster" sessions if needed. As with any life passage, such as a graduation, the end of therapy can be thought of as a life transition, a point from which to move forward.

Another treatment program, a type of trauma-focused therapy as conceptualized by Lundberg-Love (1999), seeks to reduce social anxiety, depression, social and emotional alienation, and introversion among incest survivors. This program comprises four main stages: (1) anxiety management training, (2) the identification of feelings and salient therapeutic issues, (3) ventilation and assimilation surrounding the array of affective issues, and (4) the resolution of concurrent behavioral issues.

Anxiety management training teaches clients how to regulate their affect when experiencing strong and painful emotions. They learn how to control their bodies' reactions to anxiety-provoking stimuli and flashbacks. To this end, the therapist may teach the client progressive muscle relaxation, diaphragmatic breathing, metaphoric imagery, meditation, and verbal cueing. The use of these techniques outside the office can be both empowering and stress reducing.

During the *identification of feelings and salient therapeutic issues* stage of treatment, clients learn how to identify and label feelings and experiences associated with their past. Strategies to expand clients' emotional vocabulary include providing lists of verbal affective adjectives and pictorial representations of affective states to help them identify the emotions they are experiencing. Clients are also educated about possible cognitive distortions, faulty thought patterns, and ideas of which they were unaware that can arise from past experiences to create problems in the present. A common theme that incest survivors experience is that of powerlessness or lack of control, owing to the fact that they were unable to stop the incest. This theme is one of the most important therapeutic issues to address during treatment because its resolution generates empowerment and mastery within clients.

The *ventilation and assimilation surrounding the array of affective issues* stage of therapy employs symbolic/metaphoric techniques to enable survivors to express their feelings of anger, guilt, shame, sadness, and grief. Techniques commonly employed during this phase include drawing, painting, creating collages, sculpting, writing, and music. The success of these interventions depends on creative collaboration between the therapist and the client. The assimilation phase includes affective communication education such as techniques for assertiveness and conflict resolution.

The final stage of treatment, *resolution of concurrent behavioral issues*, addresses any additional problematic issues that exist, such as substance abuse, eating disorders, sexual dysfunction, relapse prevention, and prevention of revictimization. According to Lundberg-Love (1999), once trauma-related symptoms are resolved, the resolution of additional problems appears to be less complicated and more straightforward.

THE FAMILY

Incest has the power to affect the entire family and support system upon which the victim relies. It follows that the family also would benefit from education and treatment about incest and its consequences. Disclosed intrafamilial sexual abuse may slow the process of recovery for members of the family because the family dynamic has suddenly changed (Brohl & Potter, 2004). In addition, when the perpetrator is the parent primarily responsible for the family's financial security or discipline of the children, the roles for the non-offending parent are changed and any other children in the family must also make an adjustment.

The Non-offending Parent

It is widely accepted that the non-offending parent's care and support are important for the recovery of an incest victim. Discovering that someone in the family has sexually abused one's child is a traumatic experience that can lead to psychological disturbances and the questioning of one's sense of self. A parent in this situation experiences many different thoughts and emotions, and must make a variety of critical decisions. Many non-offending parents of incest victims experience numbness, shock, disbelief, and denial as immediate responses to their child's victimization (Brohl & Potter, 2004). Emotions commonly experienced by non-offending parents may also include guilt, depression, blame, shame, fear, grief, and anger. Some of these emotions can initially be motivating factors not only to report the incest, but also to remove the perpetrator from the victim's environment. Often, the non-offending parent blames himself or herself for not protecting the child from the perpetrator. This is especially true for mothers who bring a stepfather into a child's life, with the stepfather then becoming the perpetrator of sexual abuse. Sometimes, even though incest is the fault of the perpetrator, the non-offending parent must also take responsibility for ignoring or not actively being aware of clues that incest was occurring.

Relationships in the non-offending parent's life will change when sexual abuse is revealed, as will the relationships of the incest victim. A unique consequence of incest is how the loyalties between the child and the perpetrator are torn, because the person is not a stranger, acquaintance, or friend but often a close family member (Brohl & Potter, 2004). The relationship between the non-offending parent and the perpetrator, when he is a father or stepfather, also is riddled with complicated emotions and questions. If the perpetrator is the primary disciplinarian in the family, the absence of that parent places that responsibility on the non-offending parent, which acts as an added stressor in family life. If the perpetrator is the primary financial supporter for the family, it is sometimes tempting for the non-offending parent to deny that incest is occurring in an effort to maintain the financial security of the family. Nevertheless, it is in the child's best interest for the perpetrator to be removed from the home, no matter how much financial support that person is providing or how difficult it is to discipline the children.

Relationships with other family members also may change depending upon whether the child is believed. A supportive extended family will aid the child's recovery into adulthood. Conversely, relationships may change drastically for the worse when the family does not believe the child. Often, the non-offending parent must grieve not only for the child's experience but also for the disappointment and loss of his or her own relationship with the offender.

Secondary traumatic stress (STS), also known as compassion fatigue, may emerge when a non-offending parent or someone close to the child helps the incest victim through this crisis (Brohl & Potter, 2004). Often STS includes feelings such as confusion, helplessness, isolation, and excessive guilt and brings health consequences such as headaches, gastrointestinal difficulties, susceptibility to illness, high blood pressure, and sleep disturbances. STS is thought of as a variant of PTSD. Unlike PTSD, however, STS usually emerges and resolves relatively quickly.

Siblings

The sibling relationship is a very influential one, as is vividly demonstrated by the phenomenon of siblings modeling one another's behaviors. For example, children show improvement on cognitive tasks after observing a sibling perform the task (Wishart, 1986). Siblings also must share physical and emotional resources when they are limited (Baker, Tanis, & Rice, 2001). Examples of resources that are important to the sibling of an incest survivor include attention and support. It is important to remember that the incestuous abuse affects the siblings as well as the victim; thus the siblings should also be included in the treatment process.

It is very beneficial to include siblings in the learning and healing process for multiple reasons. Most importantly, incest has been linked to a dysfunctional family pattern (Herman, 1981). Because incest significantly alters the family dynamic, whether the dynamic was dysfunctional or not prior to the incestuous abuse, it is important to include the whole family in the intervention process (Baker et al., 2001). Another reason why siblings should be included in the therapy process is that they often feel distressed and torn in many different directions by the incest victim, other siblings, and the offending and non-offending parents. When a victim reveals the incest, the siblings may be somewhat ignored because much of the attention is directed toward the victim. This disparity can lead to feelings of resentment toward the victim. Such perceptions can greatly affect the sibling relationship with the victim, the relationship with the non-offending parent, and even subsequent adolescent and adult relationships.

The Family Learning Program is a center based in Florida (which also offers available online resources) where survivors of incest and their families can receive psychological treatment and support. This program provides support groups for all family members affected by incest, including the victim, the non-offending parents, the siblings, and even the perpetrator. Sibling groups were made available for many reasons. The safety of all children is of upmost importance. These groups educate the siblings about prevention, teach them to empathize with the victim instead of becoming or remaining resentful, and help them ward off feelings of neglect. The program also includes assertiveness training, techniques for anger management, conflict resolution, and social skills. In a study investigating the effectiveness of the sibling group, Baker, Tanis, and Rice (2001) found that all parents believed the group was beneficial to the siblings. Providing more complete treatment to the entire family is believed to be beneficial.

SUMMARY

This chapter has sought to provide the reader with information regarding incest: the numbers of individuals who have experienced incest, the psychological issues that can result from incest, the increased risk of revictimization that incest survivors face, expectations for treatment, and the importance of familial treatment. Not all incest victims heal at the same rate, of course. Some heal quickly. Some do not require psychotherapy, and exhibit little to no psychological disturbances in adulthood. Others heal slowly and manifest a plethora of psychological issues. In all cases, it is important to remember that incest is never the fault of the victim and that healing does occur. Psychotherapy enables an individual to resolve painful past experiences and empowers the person to thrive instead of merely survive, living fully and looking forward to the future.

REFERENCES

Alaggia, R., & Kirshenbaum, S. (2005). Speaking the unspeakable: Exploring the impact of family dynamics on child sexual abuse disclosures. *Families in Society, 86,* 227–234.

American Psychiatric Association (APA). (1994). *Diagnostic and statistical manual of mental disorders* (4th ed.). Washington, DC: Author.

Anda, R., Felitti, V., Bremner, J., Walker, J., Whitfield, C., Pery, B., Dube, S., & Giles, W. (2006). The enduring effects of abuse and related adverse experiences in childhood. *European Archives of Psychiatry and Clinical Neuroscience, 256,* 174–186.

Andersen, B., & Cyranowski, J. (1994). Women's sexual self-schema. *Journal of Personality and Social Psychology, 67,* 1079–1100.

Anderson, B., Rowan, D., Foy, W., Rodriguez, N., & Ryan, S. (1994). Posttraumatic stress disorder in a clinical sample of adults sexually abused as children. *Child Abuse and Neglect, 18,* 51–61.

Arata, C. (2002). Child sexual abuse and sexual revictimization. *Clinical Psychology: Science and Practice, 9,* 135–164.

Baker, J., Tanis, H., & Rice, J. (2001). Including siblings in the treatment of child sexual abuse. *Journal of Child Sexual Abuse, 10,* 1–16.

Baldo, T., Wallace, S., & O'Halloran, M. (1996). Effects of intrafamilial sexual assault on eating behaviors. *Psychological Reports, 79,* 531–536.

Bass, E., & Davis, L. (1988). *The courage to heal: A guide of women survivors of child sexual abuse.* New York: Perennial Library/Harper & Row.

Bolstad, B., & Zinbarg, R. (1997). Sexual victimization, generalized perception of control and posttraumatic stress disorder symptom severity. *Journal of Anxiety Disorders, 11,* 523–540.

Bowlby, J. (1969). *Attachment and loss: Attachment.* New York: Basic Books.

Briere, J., & Conte, J. (1993). Self-reported amnesia for abuse in adults molested as children. *Journal of Traumatic Stress, 6,* 21–31.

Brohl, K., & Potter, J. C. (2004). *When your child has been molested* (rev. ed.). San Francisco: Jossey-Bass.

Carter, J., Bewell, C., Blackmore, E., & Woodside, D. (2006). The impact of childhood sexual abuse in anorexia nervosa. *Child Abuse and Neglect, 30,* 257–269.

Classen, C., Koopman, C., & Spiegel, D. (1993). Trauma and dissociation. *Bulletin of the Menninger Clinic, 57,* 178–194.

Crowley, M., & Seery, B. (2001). Exploring the multiplicity of childhood sexual abuse with a focus on polyincestuous contexts of abuse. *Journal of Child Sexual Abuse, 10,* 91–110.

Cyranowski, J., & Andersen, B. (1998). Schemas, sexuality and romantic attachment. *Journal of Personality and Social Psychology, 74,* 1364–1379.

Davis, C. (2001). Women's accounts of resilience following child sexual abuse: A narrative study. *Dissertation Abstracts International: Section B: The Sciences and Engineering, 61*(12B), 6700.

DeAngelis, T. (2002, March). Promising treatments for anorexia and bulimia. *Monitor on Psychology.* Retrieved May 22, 2009, from www.apa.org/monitor/mar02/promising.html.

Edwards, C., Dunham, D., Ries, A., & Barnett, J. (2006). Symptoms of traumatic stress and substance use in a non-clinical sample of young adults. *Addictive Behaviors, 31,* 2094–2104.

Everett, B., & Gallop, R. (Eds.), *The link between childhood trauma and mental illness.* Thousand Oaks, CA: Sage.

Feiring, C., Simon, V., & Cleland, C. (2009). Childhood sexual abuse, stigmatization, internalizing symptoms and the development of sexual difficulties and dating aggression. *Journal of Consulting and Clinical Psychology, 77,* 127–137.

Fields, S., Malebranche, D., & Feist-Price, S. (2008). Childhood sexual abuse in Black men who have sex with men: Results from three qualitative studies. *Cultural Diversity and Ethnic Minority Psychology, 13,* 385–390.

Finkelhor, D. (1994). The international epidemiology of child sexual abuse. *Child Abuse and Neglect, 18,* 409–417.

Garnefski, N., & Arends, E. (1998). Sexual abuse and adolescent maladjustment: Differences between male and female victims. *Journal of Adolescence, 21,* 99–107.

Gibson, L., & Leitenberg, H. (2001). The impact of child sexual abuse and stigma on methods of coping with sexual assault among undergraduate women. *Child Abuse and Neglect, 25,* 1343–1361.

Glover, N., Janikowski, T., & Benshoff, J. (1996). Substance abuse and past incest contact: A national perspective. *Journal of Substance Abuse Treatment, 13,* 185–193.

Hanson, R., Borntrager, C., Self-Brown, S., Kilpatrick, D., Saunders, B., Resnick, H., & Amstadter, A. (2008). Relations among gender, violence exposure and mental health: The national survey of adolescents. *American Journal of Orthopsychiatry, 78,* 313–321.

Harvard Medical School. (2005). The biology of child maltreatment: How abuse and neglect of children leave their mark on the brain. *Harvard Mental Health Letter,* pp. 1–3.

Heim, C., & Nemeroff, C. (2001). The role of childhood trauma in the neurobiology of mood and anxiety disorders: Preclinical and clinical studies. *Biological Psychiatry, 49,* 1023–1039.

Herman, J. (1981). *Father–daughter incest.* Cambridge, MA: Harvard University Press.

Herman, J. (1992). Complex PTSD: A syndrome in survivors of prolonged and repeated trauma. *Journal of Traumatic Stress, 5,* 377–391.

Hetzel, M., & McCanne, T. (2005). The roles of peritraumatic dissociation, child physical abuse, and child sexual abuse in the development of posttraumatic stress disorder and adult victimization. *Child Abuse and Neglect, 29,* 915–930.

Holzer, S., Uppala, S., Wonderlich, S., Crosby, R., & Simonich, H. (2008). Mediational significance of PTSD in the relationship of sexual trauma and eating disorders. *Child Abuse and Neglect, 32,* 561–566.

Hunter, M. (1990). *Abused boys: The neglected victims of sexual abuse.* New York: Random House.

Hyde, M., & Kaufman, P. (1984). Women molested as children: Therapeutic and legal issues in civil actions. *American Journal of Forensic Psychiatry, 5,* 147–157.

Janikowski, T., & Glover-Graf, N. (2003). Qualifications, training and perceptions of substance abuse counselors who work with victims of incest. *Addictive Behaviors, 28,* 1193–1201.

Johnson, D., Pike, J., & Chard, K. (2001). Factors predicting PTSD, depression and dissociative severity in female treatment-seeking childhood sexual abuse survivors. *Child Abuse and Neglect, 25,* 179–198.

Kessler, B., & Bieschke, K. (1999). A retrospective analysis of shame, dissociation and adult victimization in survivors of childhood sexual abuse. *Journal of Counseling Psychology, 46,* 335–341.

Kim, J., Talbot, N., & Cichetti, D. (2009). Childhood abuse and current interpersonal conflict: The role of shame. *Child Abuse and Neglect, 33,* 362–371.

Kluft, R. (1990). Dissociation and subsequent vulnerability: A preliminary study. *Dissociation, 3,* 167–173.

Klump, M. (2006). Posttraumatic stress disorder and sexual assault in women. *Journal of College Student Psychotherapy, 21,* 67–83.

Koss, M., Bailey, J., & Yuan, N. (2003). Depression and PTSD in survivors of male violence: Research and training to facilitate recovery. *Psychology of Women Quarterly, 2,* 130–142.

Lundberg-Love, P. K. (1999). The resilience of the human psyche: Recognition and treatment of the adult survivor of incest. In M. Paludi (Ed.), *The psychology of sexual victimization* (pp. 4–30). Westport, CT: Greenwood.

Lundberg-Love, P. K. (2006). Adult survivors of child sexual and emotional abuse. In P. K. Lundberg-Love & S. Marmion (Eds.), *"Intimate" violence against women: When spouses, partners or lovers attack* (pp. 69–84). Westport, CT: Praeger.

Meston, C., Rellini, A., & Heiman, J. (2006). Women's history of sexual abuse, their sexuality and sexual self-schemas. *Journal of Consulting and Clinical Psychology, 74,* 229–236.

Mills, H., Reiss, N., & Dombeck, M. (2009). Stress reduction and management. *Mental Help.* Retrieved May 22, 2009, from http://mentalhelp.net/poc//.

Molnar, B., Buka, S., & Kessler, R. (2001). Child sexual abuse and subsequent psychopathology: Results from the national comorbidity study. *American Journal of Public Health 6,* 753–760.

Murray, C., & Waller, G. (2002). Reported sexual abuse and bulimic psychopathology among nonclinical women: The mediating role of shame. *Reported Sexual Abuse, 10,* 186–191.

National Institute of Health. (2008). The numbers count: Mental disorders in America. National Institute of Mental Health. Retrieved May 22, 2009, from http://www.nimh.nih.gov/health//.

Rhode, P., Ichikawa, L., Simon, G., Ludman, E., Linde, J., Jeffery, R., & Operskalski, B. (2008). Associations of child sexual and physical abuse with obesity and depression in middle-aged women. *Child Abuse and Neglect, 32,* 878–887.

Rohsenow, D., Corbett, R., & Devine, D. (1988). Molested as children: A hidden contribution to substance abuse? *Journal of Substance Abuse Treatment, 5,* 13–18.

Ruggiero, K., Smith, D., Hanson, H., Resnick, B., Saunders, D., Kilpatrick, D., et al. (2004). Is disclosure of childhood rape associated with mental health outcome? Results from the National Women's Study. *Child Maltreatment, 9,* 62–77.

Russell, D. (1986). *The secret trauma: Incest in the lives of girls and women.* New York: Basic Books.

Sanci, L., Cofy, L., Olsson, C., Reid, S., Carlin, J., & Patton, G. (2008). Childhood sexual abuse and eating disorders in females: Findings from the Victorian adolescent health cohort study. *Archives of Pediatrics and Adolescent Medicine, 162,* 261–267.

Saunders, B., Villeponteaux, L., Lipovsky, J., & Kilpatrick, D. (1992). Child sexual assault as a risk factor for mental disorders for women: A community survey. *Interpersonal Violence, 7,* 189–204.

Schaaf, K., & McCanne, T. (1998). Relationship of childhood sexual, physical and combined sexual and physical abuse to adult victimization and posttraumatic stress disorder. *Child Abuse and Neglect, 22,* 1119–1133.

Shalev, A. (1997). Acute to chronic: Etiology and pathophysiology of PTSD— a biopsychosocial approach. In C. Fullerton & R. Ursano (Eds.), *Posttraumatic stress disorder: Acute and long-term responses to trauma and disaster. Progress in Psychiatry Series* (pp. 209–240). Washington, DC: American Psychiatric Association.

Simmons, J., & Weinman, M. (1991). Self-esteem, adjustment and locus of control among youth in an emergency shelter. *Journal of Community Psychology, 19,* 277–280.

Sorsoli, L. (2004). Echoes of silence: Remembering and repeating childhood trauma. In A. Leblich, D. McAdams, & R. Josselson (Eds.), *Healing plots: The narrative basis of psychotherapy* (pp. 89–109). Washington, DC: American Psychiatric Association.

Spiegel, J. (2003). *Sexual abuse of males: The SAM model of theory and practice.* New York: Taylor & Francis.

Stahl, S. (2008). *Stahl's essential psychopharmacology: Neuroscientific basis and practical applications* (3rd ed.). Cambridge, UK: Cambridge University Press.

Tangney, J., & Dearing, R. (2002). *Shame and guilt.* New York: Guilford Press.

Teicher, M. (2000). Wounds that time wouldn't heal: The neurobiology of childhood abuse. *Cerebrum, 2,* 50–67.

Ullman, S., & Filipas, H. (2005). Gender differences in social reactions to abuse disclosures, post-abuse coping and PTSD of child sexual abuse survivors. *Child Abuse and Neglect, 29,* 767–782.

U.S. Department of Justice. (2000). *Sexual assault of young children as reported by law enforcement: Victim, incident, and offender characteristics.* Washington, DC: Department of Justice, Bureau of Justice Statistics.

Vogelanz, N., Wilsnack, S., Harris, T., Wilsnack, R., Wonderlich, S., & Krisjanson, A. (1999). Prevalence and risk factors for childhood sexual abuse in women: National survey findings. *Child Abuse and Neglect, 23,* 579–592.

Walsh, K., Blaustein, M., Knight, W., Spinazola, J., & van de Kolk, B. (2007). Resiliency factors in the relation between childhood sexual abuse and adulthood sexual assault in college-age women. *Journal of Child Sexual Abuse, 16,* 1–17,

Ward, C., & Lundberg-Love, P. (2006). Sexual abuse of women. In P. K. Lundberg-Love & S. Marmion (Eds.), *"Intimate" violence against women: When spouses, partners or lovers attack* (pp. 47–68). Westport, CT: Praeger.

Widom, C., Czaja, S., & Dutton, M. A. (2008). Childhood victimization and lifetime revictimization. *Child Abuse and Neglect, 32,* 785–796.

Wishart, J. (1986). Siblings as models in early infant learning. *Child Development, 57,* 1232–1240.

Wonderlich, S., Brewerton, T., Jocic, Z., & Dansky, B. (1997). Relationship of childhood sexual abuse and eating disorders. *American Academy of Child and Adolescent Psychiatry, 36,* 1107–1115.

Wyatt, G. (1985). The sexual abuse of Afro-American and white American women in childhood. *Child Abuse and Neglect, 9,* 507–519.

Chapter 8

A Review of Violence against Pregnant Women

Josephine C. H. Tan

Violence against women is a global problem. A study on intimate-partner violence (IPV) conducted by the World Health Organization (WHO) in 15 sites across 10 countries revealed that the lifetime prevalence of IPV ranged from 15 percent to 71 percent (Garcia-Moreno, Jansen, Ellsberg, Heise, & Watts, 2005, 2006). The cost of IPV is reflected in services (health care, social services, housing, legal expenses, criminal justice system), economy loss due to work absence, and human and emotional suffering (Walby, 2004). This cost is estimated at £23 billion per year for England and Wales. In the United States, the annual cost is estimated to exceed $5.8 billion, of which $4.1 billion is devoted to direct medical and mental health treatment (National Centre for Injury Prevention and Control, 2003). The Canadian estimate is $1.5 billion per year to cover dental and health (physical and psychological) services, utilization of shelters and crisis centers, and loss of work productivity (Health Canada, 1999).

Violence against women can also occur during pregnancy. In the United States, the Centers for Disease Control and Prevention's Pregnancy Risk Assessment Monitoring System (PRAMS) 1998 Surveillance Report reported rates ranging from 2.4 percent to 6.6 percent (U.S. General Accounting Office, 2002), whereas other studies showed a wider range of

0.9 percent to 20.1 percent, with most rates falling between 3.9 percent and 8.3 percent (Cokkinides, Coker, Sanderson, Addy, & Bethea, 1999; Gazmararian, Petersen, Spitz, Goodwin, Saltzman, & Marks, 1996). In Canada, the Maternity Experiences Survey drawn from the May 2006 Canadian Census showed that 10.9 percent of women reported experiencing physical and sexual abuse within the two years preceding the survey. One third of these women indicated that the abuse occurred during pregnancy (Chalmers, Dzakpasu, Heaman, & Kaczowski, 2008). The WHO study found a prevalence of IPV of 4 to 12 percent among ever-pregnant women who reported having experienced physical abuse during at least one pregnancy (Garcia-Moreno et al., 2005). By comparison, other studies have reported higher rates of pregnancy-related violence: 14.7 percent in South Carolina (Coker, Sanderson, & Dong, 2004); 15 percent in Pakistan (Fikree & Bhatti, 1999); 20 percent in Rio de Janeiro, Brazil (Moraes & Reichenheim, 2002); 21.5 percent in Lima, Peru (Perales, Cripe, Lam, Sanchez, Sanchez, & Williams, 2009); 22 percent (Purwar, Jeyaseelan, Varhadpande, Motgahare, & Pimplakute, 1999) to 28 percent in India (Nasir & Hyder, 2003); 25 percent (emotional abuse) and 35 percent (physical abuse) in Iran Republic (Salari & Nakhaee, 2008); and 34.5 percent in rural Haiti (Small, Gupta, Frederic, Joseph, Theodore, & Kershaw, 2008).

The variation in the prevalence rates across different studies may reflect a number of methodological factors, including sampling and measurement differences (see Ballard, Saltzman, Gazmararian, Spitz, Lazorick, & Marks, 1998; Campbell, Garcia-Moreno, & Sharps, 2004; Gazmararian, Lazorick, Spitz, Ballard, Saltzman, & Marks, 1996; Jasinski, 2004). Specifically, these factors focus on the type of sample (prenatal clinics, health clinics, hospitals, general community, population-based surveys, currently pregnant women, postpartum women, ever-pregnant women), age group of the sample, data collection procedures, assessment measures, index time frame (e.g., first trimester, immediate postpartum, 12 months previous to time of study, during most recent pregnancy), relationship of the perpetrator to the women, and recall accuracy.

Some researchers have looked at prevalence rates in association with ethnicity. In one U.S. study that used the PRAMS 2000–2003 population-based surveillance system, the researchers found that Native American women were at greater risk of abuse compared to other racial groups and that African American women were at higher risk than Caucasian or Asian/Pacific Islander women (Silverman, Decker, Reed, & Raj, 2006). However, another study using the PRAMS 1993–1997 data (Gilbert, Johnson, Morrow, Gaffield, Ahluwalia, & PRAMS Working Group, 1999) found that the differences related to ethnicity depended on the state assessed. In Alaska, Caucasian women reported the least amount of physical abuse during pregnancy compared to women from other ethnic groups. In Florida, Caucasian and African American women reported more physical abuse than other groups. In Washington, African American women reported more abuse than did Caucasian women. Finally, in Colorado, Hispanic women reported more physical abuse than did non-Hispanic women. These variations in ethnic-related prevalence rates might be linked to sociodemographic characteristics such as income, marital status, and age. Thus it would seem that, at least in the United States, ethnicity is not a reliable predictor of abuse. In Canada, Aboriginal women were found to be at higher risk of abuse during pregnancy (Heaman, 2005). Contributing factors have been cited as including a combination of colonization, poverty, substance use, and community stress that leads to high rates of family violence.

It is conceivable that the true prevalence of abuse during pregnancy might be under-reported for a number of reasons. Prevalence studies focus almost entirely on pregnancies that conclude with live births; in other words, pregnancies that terminate in fetal or maternal deaths are excluded. Some women do not disclose sexual violence because of social norms (Hussain & Khan, 2008). In addition, many women are more willing to disclose violence, especially that of a sexual nature, when asked about this issue by a female interviewer as compared to a male interviewer (Sorenson, Stein, Siegel, Golding, & Burnham, 1987). Fear that their babies will be taken from their care might lead to under-disclosure among some mothers (Bullock, Bloom, Davis, Kilburn, & Curry, 2006). Some cultural norms, prescriptions, and sanctions that govern women's movements and interactions with others might make it difficult for women in certain societies to discuss their experience with violence. For recommendations on how to safely collect reliable information in household interviews about violence against women, readers are directed to the work by Andersson et al. (2009); these researchers conducted a national survey of violence against women in Pakistan. A more detailed examination of cultural factors appears later in this chapter.

In several studies, the perpetrator of the abuse was identified as the current or previous partner (Alio, Nana, & Salihu, 2009; Chhabra, 2007; Coker et al., 2004; Dunn & Oths, 2004; Hammoury, Khawaja, Mahfoud, Afifi, & Madi, 2009; Quelopana, Champion, & Salazar, 2008; Quinlivan & Evans, 2005) or the biological father of the pregnancy (Fanslow, Silva, Robinson, & Whitehead, 2008). In other cases, family members may be involved. For example, a study conducted in India identified family perpetrators to include the mother-in-law, father-in-law, sister-in-law, and uncle (Chhabra, 2007).

DEFINITION AND ASSESSMENT

Three types of violence are typically assessed: physical, sexual, and emotional or psychological (e.g., see Alio et al., 2009; Harrykissoon, Rickert, & Wiemann, 2002; Quinlivan & Evans, 2001, 2005). The seriousness of physical abuse can range from minor (such as pushing) to severe (such as attacking with a weapon). Sexual abuse involves coerced sexual acts that involve anal, vaginal, or oral intercourse or other explicit sexual behaviors. Emotional or psychological abuse would include verbal humiliation or verbal threat to the woman or her family. There is a high association between verbal and physical abuse (Paterson, Feehan, Butler, Williams, & Cowley-Malcolm, 2007). In particular, verbal abuse often precedes physical abuse and its psychological consequences can be equally damaging (Mechanic, Weaver, & Resick, 2008; O'Leary, 1999; Tiwari et al., 2008).

Several screening tools for abuse are available. The most widely used is the Abuse Assessment Screen (AAS) created by Parker and McFarlane (1991), who also developed the Danger Assessment question-naire, which measures the risk of homicide. The AAS has been found to have test sensitivity of 31.9 percent and 61.4 percent for detecting minor and severe violence, respectively; as a consequence, it may fail to detect a number of positive cases and should not be used as a stand-alone tool (Reichenheim & Moraes, 2009). Ameh, Shittu, and Abdul (2008) developed a risk scoring tool for pregnancy-related abuse that was tested on 500 pregnant women in Nigeria; they reported excellent test sensitivity (96.6%) and low test specificity (11.8%). Another well-known tool for measuring different types of abuse is the Revised Conflict Tactics Scale (Straus, Hamby, Boney-McCoy, & Sugarman, 1996), which has strong psychometric properties (see Reichenheim & Moraes, 2009). Other tools include the Index of Spouse Abuse, which has excellent internal consistency (Hudson & McIntosh, 1981), and the Severity of Violence Against Women (Marshall, 1992).

PATTERNS OF ABUSE

Although several studies suggest that the *prevalence* of abuse decreases from the prepregnancy period to during pregnancy (Guo, Wu, Qu, & Yan, 2004; Saltzman, Johnson, Gilbert, & Goodwin, 2003; Topbaş, Ünsal, Çan, Bacak, & Özgün, 2008), the *severity* of abuse appears to increase over the same span (Burch & Gallup, 2004; Diaz-Olavarrieta, Paz, Abuabara, Martinez Ayala, Kolstad, & Palermo, 2007; Gielen, O'Campo, Faden, Kass, & Xue, 1994; Hussain & Khan, 2008; McFarlane, Parker, Soeken, Silva, & Reel, 1998). This increase is seen primarily in the form of psychological abuse (Castro, Peek-Asa, & Ruiz, 2003; Karaoglu et al., 2005); in contrast, the frequency of physical or sexual abuse decreases from the pre-pregnancy period to the actual pregnancy (Amaro, Fried, Cabral, & Zuckerman, 1990). It has been proposed that the increase in psychological abuse might be due to the women being less available physically or emotionally to their partners, who become increasingly insecure, jealous, and possessive (Bacchus, Mezey, & Bewley, 2006). The risk of abuse increases again in the few months postpartum from the pregnancy period (Bowen, Heron, Waylen, Wolke, & ALSPAC Study Team, 2005; Gielen et al., 1994; Guo et al., 2004; Harrykissoon et al., 2002; Macy, Martin, Kupper, Casanueva, & Guo, 2007). Macy et al. (2007) speculated that this increase might be related to the stress of having a newborn, such that sleepless nights and changes in the family dynamics contribute to increased family conflicts.

The areas of the body where the women are hit during pregnancy often involve the abdominal area (Fanslow et al., 2008; Garcia-Moreno et al., 2005; Hillard, 1985; Stewart & Cecutti, 1993), possibly reflecting a resentment of the partner toward the pregnancy (Bacchus et al., 2006; Campbell, Oliver, & Bullock, 1993), especially if it was unintended or if there is a doubt about paternity (Jasinski, 2004). Other studies report that the most common sites of physical violence are the face and neck regions as well as the limbs (Berenson, San Miguel, & Wilkinson, 1992; Bhandari, 2006; Hedin & Janson, 2000; Nannini et al., 2008; Tan & Gregor, 2006; Yang, Yang, Chou, Yang, Wei, & Lin, 2006). The risk of harm to the women during pregnancy abuse is considerable—the frequency and severity of injury have been found to be doubled in comparison to women who were abused outside of pregnancy. Amaro et al. (1990) noted that 36 percent of women in their study required medical attention for at least one violent incident and 10 percent required overnight hospitalization.

CORRELATES OF PREGNANCY-RELATED ABUSE

Certain universal factors are correlated with IPV across cultures. Unintended pregnancy has been consistently been found to be associated with an increased risk of pregnancy-related abuse (Chan, Brownridge, Tiwari, Fong, & Leung, 2008; Cripe, Sanchez, Perales, Lam, Garcia, & Williams, 2008; Fanslow et al., 2008; Gao, Paterson, Carter, & Iusitini, 2008; Gazmararian et al., 1995; Goodwin et al., 2000; Hammoury et al., 2009; Jasinski, 2004; Karaoglu et al., 2005; Kaye, Mirembe, Bantebya, Johansson, & Ekstrom, 2006; Martin, Kilgallen, Tsui, Maitra, Singh, & Kupper, 1999; Pallitto, Campbell, & O'Campo, 2005; Salari & Nakhaee, 2008; Silverman et al., 2006; Silverman, Gupta, Decker, Kapur, & Raj, 2007; Thananowan & Heidrich, 2008). Plausible explanations include the partner's jealousy toward the fetus, the perceptions that the pregnancy disrupts the woman's care-taking role toward the partner and that the pregnancy is something that is not under his control, and doubts about paternity (Bacchus et al., 2006; Campbell et al., 1993; Campbell, Harris, & Lee, 1995; Campbell, Pugh, Campbell, & Visscher, 1995; Jasinski, 2004). Unintended pregnancies might arise from low contraceptive use. For example, women who experience physical violence at the hands of their partners are less likely to use contraception and more likely to have an unwanted pregnancy (Stephenson, Koenig, Acharya, & Roy, 2008; Wingood & DiClemente, 1997). This low contraception use might, in part, reflect fear or difficulties in negotiating safe sex practices with the partner (Hussain & Khan, 2008; Martin, Matza, Kupper, Thomas, Daly, & Cloutier, 1999; Plichta & Abraham, 1996; Wingood & DiClemente, 1997).

Research also shows that women who were abused during pregnancy are likely to have experienced abuse prior to the pregnancy (Audi, Segall-Corrêa, Santiago, Andrade, & Pêrez-Escamilla, 2008; Diaz-Olavarrieta et al., 2007; Fanslow et al., 2008; Guo et al., 2004; Hammoury & Khawaja, 2007) or to have witnessed interpersonal violence (Audi et al., 2008; Castro et al., 2003). Indeed, abuse during pregnancy is often a continuation of abuse that occurred before the pregnancy (Castro et al., 2003; Diaz-Olavarrieta et al., 2007; Macy et al., 2007; Topbaş, Ünsal, Çan, Bacak, & Özgün, 2008), and is a strong predictor of abuse both during and after pregnancy (Guo et al., 2004).

Women who are unmarried tend to be at greater risk of pregnancy-related abuse (Goodwin et al., 2000; Heaman, 2005; Perales et al., 2009; Silverman et al., 2006; Thananowan & Heidrich, 2008; Torres et al., 2000). They also tend to be younger (Bullock et al., 2006; Chhabra, 2007; Datner, Wiebe, Brensinger, & Nelson, 2007; Goodwin, Gazmararian, Johnson, Gilbert, Saltzman, & PRAMS Working Group, 2000; Heaman, 2005; Reichenheim, Patricio, & Moraes, 2008; Silverman et al., 2006; Thananowan & Heidrich, 2008), possibly because of their inexperience with intimate relationships (Espinosa & Osborne, 2002; Wiemann, Agurcia, Berenson, Volk, & Rickert, 2000).

Low socioeconomic indicators are also correlated with abuse during pregnancy. These factors include illiteracy or low educational level (Audi et al., 2008; Bullock et al., 2006; Chan et al., 2009; Chhabra, 2007; Datner et al., 2007; Gilbert et al., 1999; Goodwin et al., 2000; Hammoury et al., 2009; Heaman, 2005; Perales et al., 2009; Silverman et al., 2006, 2007), financial dependence (Bullock et al., 2006; Chan, Brownridge, Tiwari, Fong, & Leung, 2008; Gilbert et al., 1999; Goodwin et al., 2000; Heaman, 2005; Karaoglu et al., 2005; Perales et al., 2009; Silverman et al., 2006, 2007), and living in crowded conditions (Peedicayil et al., 2004). The women who are abused during pregnancy also tend to use substances such as tobacco, alcohol, or illicit drugs (Bailey & Daugherty, 2007; Chan et al., 2008; Datner et al., 2007; Fanslow et al., 2008; Goodwin et al., 2000; Heaman, 2005; Karaoglu et al., 2005; Reichenheim et al., 2008). It is not clear whether substance use might be a cause or consequence of the abuse.

Multiparity also increases the risk of abuse during pregnancy (Chan et al., 2009; Cokkinides et al., 1999; Farid, Saleem, Karim, & Hatcher, 2008; Peedicayil et al., 2004; Persily & Abdulla, 2000). With every addition of a child to the family, the financial and emotional resources of the family become strained, especially under low socioeconomic conditions.

Alternatively, the higher parity might reflect the woman's lack of control in decision making regarding reproductive matters (Emenike, Lawoko, & Dalal, 2008) and low use of contraception.

The women who experience abuse during pregnancy also tend to have poor social support (Chan et al., 2009; Farid et al., 2008; Gielen et al., 1994; Jeanjot, Barlow, & Rozenberg, 2008; Peedicayil et al., 2004; Reichenheim et al., 2008). Lack of support makes it challenging for such women to disclose abuse and to leave the abusive relationship (Xu, 1997; Xu, Zhu, O'Campo, Koenig, Mock, & Campbell, 2005). Coohey (2007) found that mothers who were severely abused had limited social network and emotional support from friends, though not from family members. Thus it appears that the abusers might be more successful in disrupting friendships than family ties. Strong social support appears to be a protective factor against abuse (Farid et al., 2008; Gielen et al., 1994).

A similar profile seems to apply to the abusers of pregnant women. These individuals tend to have a low level of education (Haj-Yahia, 1998a; Karaoglu et al., 2005; Peedicayil et al., 2004; Torres et al., 2000), be unemployed or of low socioeconomic status (Audi et al., 2008; Leung, Leung, Lam, & Ho, 1999; Parish, Wang, Laumann, Pan, & Luo, 2004; Torres et al., 2000; Xu et al., 2005; Yick, 2000), are younger (Tang, 1999), use alcohol and/or drugs (Audi et al., 2008; Chan et al., 2008; Liu & Zhang, 2005; Parish et al., 2004; Peedicayil et al., 2004; Reichenheim et al., 2008; Stickley, Timofeeva & Sparén, 2008; Xu et al., 2005), have witnessed domestic violence in their childhood (Castro et al., 2003; Farid et al., 2008; Stickley et al., 2008), and suffer from sexual jealousy (Burch & Gallup, 2004; Parish et al., 2004).

Overall, it seems that young age, low education, poverty, multiple children, unintended pregnancy, risk behaviors (e.g., smoking, alcohol, illicit substance use), and being a witness to interpersonal violence when young in both the women and their partners are associated with pregnancy-related abuse. Some of these factors might play a contributing role to the abuse, some may be a consequence of the both, and some may serve both functions. The violence can compound the stress associated with poverty, pregnancy, and familial strain, which in turn might increase the risk of abuse. The mechanism by which being a witness to interpersonal violence when younger is linked to abuse in adulthood is believed to be explained by the social learning theory (Anderson & Kras, 2007).

CULTURAL FACTORS

Cultural beliefs that support male dominance over women and traditional wife/mother roles for women are linked to violence against women in general, as well as specifically during pregnancy. This relationship has been established in studies that were carried out in the United States

(Torres et al., 2000), Peru (Perales et al., 2009), China (Liu & Chan, 1999; Xu et al., 2005), Singapore (Choi & Edelson, 1996), Turkey (Ozcakir, Bayram, Ergin, Selimoglu, & Bilgel, 2008; Topbaş et al., 2008), India (Peedicayil et al., 2004), and the Middle East and North Africa (Boy & Kulczycki, 2008).

In Peru, employed women had higher risk of pregnancy abuse than those who were unemployed (Perales et al., 2009). This finding is consistent with other findings in patriarchal societies such as Peru (Flake, 2005). It has been proposed that men resort to violence to reassert control when they feel that they are losing their culturally sanctioned dominance over women (Jewkes, 2002; Jewkes, Levin, & Penn-Kekana, 2002; Straus, Gelles, & Steinmetz, 1980). Hence women who are employed and have some degree of financial independence are at risk (Flake, 2005). In China, which is a patrilineal and patriarchal society, abuse of women is linked to traditional cultural beliefs about male dominance and objectification of women as possessions (Liu & Chan, 1999). In a study that included groups of Mexican American, Puerto Rican, Cuban American, African American, Anglo American, and Central American immediate postpartum women, it was found that those with partners who had stronger beliefs in the wife/mother role for women were more susceptible to intimate-partner abuse (Torres et al., 2000). Moreover, some Pakistani Muslim men in the United Kingdom use their religion to justify violence against women (Macey, 1999).

Some abused women themselves adhere to traditional beliefs. In a study involving pregnant women recruited from two hospitals in Pakistan, more than 21 percent believed that their religion permitted their husbands to force sex upon them, and a much smaller percentage (4.9%) believed that their religion permitted physical beating by the husband even when the women were faithful (Shaikh, Shaikh, Kamal, & Masood, 2008). In a Turkish study, 20.9 percent of immediate postpartum women who experienced unwanted sex thought they had pleased their husband, and 4.9 percent thought they deserved physical abuse (Topbaş et al., 2008). One study with Chinese women showed that those who believed in the dominance of men were more likely to experience wife abuse (Xu et al., 2005).

In the West, the typical abuse scenario involves the male partner as the sole perpetrator. In Asia, it is not uncommon for other family members to become involved, such as the mother-in-law, who might also perpetrate abuse against the pregnant woman (Counts, Brown, & Campbell, 1999; Dasgupta, 2000; Fernandez, 1997; Leung et al., 1999; Ramanathan, 1996; Rianon & Shelton, 2003). Even in studies conducted in the United States with South Asian battered women, the findings showed that the in-laws might tolerate or even contribute to the violence against the women (Abraham, 1999; Mehotra, 1999; Rianon & Shelton, 2003; Supriya, 1996), with mothers-in-law and sisters-in-law being the more common perpetrators (Mehotra, 1999; Supriya, 1996). There appears to be a link between violence by the intimate partner and emotional abuse by the in-laws (Raj, Livramento, Santana, Gupta, & Silverman, 2006).

Studies with Chinese women who were abused during pregnancy found that they were more likely to report conflict with their parents-in-law in the year preceding the pregnancy and in their lifetime (Chan et al., 2009). Conflict with an in-law has also been found to be associated with violence by husbands (Chan, 2006; Meng, 2002) and with postpartum depression in the women (Lee, Yip, Leung, & Chung, 2004). Chan et al. (2008) explained two possible ways in which the partner's violence might be linked to in-laws' conflict with the women. Problems with the in-laws might intensify problems within the marital relationship itself, which would be increased even further should the conflict involve both sets of in-laws. If the man has a conflict with the woman's parents, there would be reduced contact with them, resulting in the isolation of the woman from her own family and subsequently decreased social support—a factor that is related to increased IPV.

Researchers have looked into the reasons for pregnancy-related abuse. A study carried out in seven sites in India revealed that the women who experienced moderate to severe violence during pregnancy reported being accused by their husband of being unfaithful or that their husband was having an affair, a husband having a low educational background, a husband being drunk regularly, dowry harassment, having three or more children, and household crowding (Peedicayil et al., 2004). In a study conducted with U.S. women (Campbell et al., 1993), the reasons for abuse included the partner's jealousy and anger toward the unborn child or perception of violence as "business as usual." In the Middle East, justification for violence against women included infidelity on the part of the woman (Haj-Yahia, 1998b, 2000), disobeying the husband (Amowitz, Kim, Reis, Asher, & Iacopino, 2004; Hortacsu, Kalaycioglu, & Rittersberger-Tilic, 2003), nagging or insulting the husband (Haj-Yahia, 2000; Hortacsu et al., 2003); neglecting the children, dishonoring the family, and kitchen-related problems such as burning the food (Haj-Yahia, 1998b; Khawaja, 2004).

OUTCOMES OF PREGNANCY-RELATED ABUSE

Several studies have examined the relationship between pregnancy-related abuse and outcomes for the pregnancy and for the mother. Some of the significant links include poor maternal health (anemia, hemorrhage, depression, hypertension, urinary tract infections, unhealthy diet, kidney infections, sexually transmitted diseases), maternal use of substances (alcohol, tobacco, drugs), poor weight gain, labor and delivery complications, low-birth-weight infants, fetal trauma (e.g., miscarriage, placental abruptions, fetal injury and death) and problems with breastfeeding

(Ahmed, Koenig, & Stephenson, 2006; Alio et al., 2009; Amaro et al., 1990; Brown, McDonald, & Krastev, 2008; Datner et al., 2007; Huth-Bocks, Levendosky, & Bogat, 2002; Jasinski, 2004; Jejeebhoy, 1998; Kaye et al., 2006; Kendall-Tackett, 2007; Maman, Campbell, Sewat, & Gielen, 2000; Martin, Kilgallen, Dee, Dawson, & Campbell, 1998; Petersen et al., 1997; Silverman et al., 2006). A review by Petersen et al. (1997) did not find any pregnancy outcome that could be consistently associated with abuse. However, a more recent review by Boy and Salihu (2004) found that compared to nonabused mothers, abused mothers are significantly more likely to have adverse pregnancy outcomes such as low birth weight and maternal and fetal mortality.

Homicide has been found to be the leading cause of maternal death in pregnancy (Campbell, Soeken, McFarlane, & Parker, 1998; Chang, Berg, Saltzman, & Herndon, 2005; Horon & Cheng, 2001; Shadigian & Bauer, 2005). A recent review concluded that intimate partners are responsible for as many as two thirds of all pregnancy-associated femicides in the United States (Martin, Macy, Sullivan, & Magee, 2007). In addition, suicide is a major cause of death among pregnant women and those who were recently pregnant (Shadigian & Bauer, 2005). Alio et al. (2009) analyzed data from the Cameroon Demographic Health Survey and concluded that recurrent fetal loss was related to spousal violence, in particular to emotional violence. This study has been lauded as important because of its examination of emotional violence—an aspect of abuse that has been relatively neglected in comparison to physical and sexual violence (Garcia-Moreno, 2009), and that has been found to have a strong link to poor mental health outcomes (Mechanic et al., 2008; O'Leary, 1999; Tiwari et al., 2008). Regardless of its frequency, the presence of emotional or psychological violence is closely associated with depression levels in pregnant women (Martin, Li, Casanueva, Harris-Britt, Kupper, & Cloutier, 2006).

Several studies have reported a delayed entry into prenatal care for women with pregnancy-related abuse (Bailey & Daugherty, 2007; Cripe et al., 2008; Espinosa & Osborne, 2002; Goodwin et al., 2000; Huth-Bocks et al., 2002; Quelopana et al., 2008). Reasons for late prenatal care initiation may include consideration of abortion (Johnson et al., 2003), psychological stress, and depression (Johnson et al., 2003; Quelopana et al., 2008). In addition the partner's jealousy and control over the woman's movements might potentially restrict her entry into prenatal care (Audi et al., 2008).

SCREENING FOR ABUSE

Only 27 percent of women who experience violence in pregnancy repeatedly seek counseling, social services, or other resources designed for women who experience violence (Quelopana et al., 2008). It has been proposed that appropriate identification and intervention in primary care settings might reduce the abuse suffered by this population by as much as 75 percent (Department of Health and Human Services, 1990, 1995; Rosenberg & Fenley, 1991).

Unfortunately, detection of abuse can be difficult for a number of reasons. As previously mentioned, women might be reluctant to disclose IPV because of social or cultural norms (Hussain & Khan, 2008), fear that their children might be removed by child protection services (Bullock et al., 2006), cultural sanctions that limit movement and interactions with others (Andersson et al., 2009), fear of retaliation by the abuser, feelings of responsibility for the abuse, denial, shame, embarrassment, and helplessness (Bacchus, Mezey, & Bewley, 2003; Parker & McFarlane, 1991; Peedicayil et al., 2004). Despite barriers to disclosure on the part of the women, research shows that 70 to 81 percent of abuse patients would like their health care providers to ask them questions privately about interpersonal violence (Caralis & Musialowski, 1997; McCauley, Yurk, Jenckes, & Ford, 1998).

In some cases, challenges in the screening and detection of abuse might lie within the health care system itself. Jeanjot et al. (2008) evaluated the attitude toward screening for domestic violence among a sample of health care providers who worked in a Department of Obstetrics in a public hospital. These researchers found that most of them (92.86%) screened for abuse only when their suspicions were aroused, such as by a patient's attitude, presence of bruises, or patient complaints of physical or psychosomatic symptoms. Questions were asked more often when the woman was alone, but sometimes the interview took place in the presence of the woman's companion and/or the companion was questioned. The health care providers cited barriers to detection that included language and cultural limitations, constant presence of the companion, the amount of time it took to complete the interview, their own discomfort and lack of training/education in asking questions about abuse, and lack of resources to offer the woman in the event of a positive detection. Two health care providers denied the existence of abuse in pregnancy. These barriers were also cited in a review of 12 studies that identified additional challenges, including fear of offending or endangering the patient, lack of effective interventions, and absence of complaints or disclosure on the part of the patient (Waalen, Goodwin, Spitz, Petersen, & Saltzman, 2000)

IMPLICATIONS FOR HEALTH CARE

The problem of violence against women and the need for screening has been acknowledged in the health care system for many years (American College of Obstetricians and Gynecologists, 1995; American Medical Association, 1992; Stevens, 2003; Washington State Department of Health, 2008). Screening guidelines have been developed by the American College of Obstetricians and Gynecologists (1995) and the Washington State Department of Health (2008).

Despite official recommendations, not every health professional undertakes screening on a routine basis. The percentage of physicians who routinely screen has been to found to be as low as 10 percent (Rodriguez, Bauer, McLoughlin, & Crumback, 1999). Although more 50 percent of primary physicians in a study estimated that at least 10 percent of their clients were abused, only 17 percent of them always screened for this possibility at the first prenatal visit, and only 5 percent screened for it at follow-up visits (Chamberlain & Perham-Hester, 2000). More encouraging statistics come from a study by Horan, Chapin, Klein, Schmidt, and Schulkin (1998), who observed that 39 percent of the obstetrician-gynecologists routinely screened for abuse at the first prenatal visit. The rate of screening increased with years since training and personal experiences with IPV on the part of the health care professional.

Goodwin et al. (2000) proposed that an important point of contact for screening and referral of abuse is during prenatal care. The development of specific protocols for screening and intervention in cases of abuse is essential; in fact, such protocols have been published (McFarlane & Parker, 1994; Warshaw, 1996). Some evidence indicates that the implementation of an abuse assessment protocol in prenatal clinics yields positive results. In one study, more pregnant women received screening and referral for abuse and medical documentation of the abuse increased (Wiist & McFarlane, 1999) even 15 months after initiation of the protocol. Similarly, another review reported that interventions with health care professionals such as provision of education and training for them, use of screening protocols, referral lists, and other aids improved their screening rates both within one year and within eight years of the initiation of intervention (Waalen et al., 2000).

McFarlane and Gondolf (1998) provided a comprehensive clinical protocol for pregnancy-related abuse that covered assessment, formulation of safety plans for the woman, evaluation of options for the future, intervention strategies that went beyond just referral and incorporated resource coordination and case management, and support for the health care provider (e.g., team conferences for support and generation of strategies). Heise, Ellsberg, and Gottemoeller (1999) offered intervention guidelines for health care providers that included asking the women about violence in ways that are helpful, offers of empathy and support, medical treatment and counseling, documentation of injuries, referral to legal assistance and support services, and reassurance to the women about the unacceptability of abuse. Health care service providers must be familiar with the reporting procedures within the jurisdiction that governs their practice (Parker & McFarlane, 1991) and need to be sensitized to pregnancy-related abuse; they must also be trained to undertake the assessment and intervention when needed. More recently, attention has been paid to clinical approaches that are sensitive to the processes involved in IPV, so that different stage-based interventions can be used with abused pregnant and postpartum women based on their level of readiness to make changes in their lives (Kramer, 2007).

Culture-appropriate assessments and interventions need to be developed in traditional communities with beliefs and practices that accept abuse against women. For example, screening and safety assessments could be expanded to a larger familial context when working with South Asian abused women (Raj et al., 2006). This effort would include identifying legal assistance and solutions for women who report abuse by in-laws, and educating the community on IPV in ways that also include discussions of abuse at the hands of the in-laws.

Antiviolence programs need to be developed, followed by evaluation of their effectiveness (Gazmararian et al., 2000). Effective innovative programs could coordinate community efforts from a variety of sources, including the legal, judicial, law enforcement, social services and medical realms (Cole & Flanagin, 1999). At present, health care providers remain challenged to move beyond the crisis management stage into interventions on an individual and societal level so that they can change attitudes and practices that are conducive to violence against women (McFarlane, 2007).

SUMMARY

Pregnancy-related abuse is a widespread problem with serious health consequences for both the women who experience the abuse and the outcomes of their pregnancies. Screening for abuse during pregnancy is critical; such screening must begin from the time the women enter into prenatal care and continue into the postpartum period, where the risk of abuse increases (Gielen et al., 1994; Guo et al., 2004; Harrykissoon et al., 2002; Macy et al., 2007). Although certain factors (e.g., age, marital status, socioeconomic indicators, multiparity, use of substances) are significantly associated with abuse, the screening has to be undertaken as a matter of routine care—not just when suspicions are aroused. It is also important to assess for psychological violence, given that its effects on mental health can be as deleterious as those of physical violence (Mechanic et al., 2008; O'Leary, 2001; Tiwari et al., 2008). In some cases, the partner of the pregnant woman is not the only abuser. Abuse by in-laws does occur sometimes in South Asian and traditional Chinese communities. Screening for psychological problems among pregnant women is also important because the presence of abuse might be manifested in the form of depression and feelings of stress. Screening protocols need to be developed within health care facilities visited by pregnant women, and health service providers need to be educated and trained not only to screen but also to intervene effectively in cases involving IPV. Finally, societal attitudes and practices by both men and women that tolerate abuse against women need to be targeted for change.

REFERENCES

Abraham, M. (1999). Sexual abuse in South Asian immigrant marriages. *Violence Against Women, 5*(6), 591–618. doi: 10.1177/10778019922181392.

Ahmed, S., Koenig, M. A., & Stephenson, R. (2006). Effects of domestic violence on perinatal and early-childhood mortality: Evidence from North India. *American Journal of Public Health, 96*(8), 1423–1428. doi: 10.2105/AJPH,2006.06 6316.

Alio, A. P., Nana, P. N., & Salihu, H. M. (2009). Spousal violence and potentially preventable single and recurrent spontaneous fetal loss in an African setting: Cross-sectional study. *Lancet, 373,* 318–324.

Amaro, H., Fried, L. W., Cabral, H., & Zuckerman, B. (1990). Violence during pregnancy and substance use. *American Journal of Public Health, 80*(5), 575–579.

Ameh, N., Shittu, S. O., & Abdul, M. A. (2008). Risk scoring for domestic violence in pregnancy. *Nigerian Journal of Clinical Practice, 11*(1), 18–21.

American College of Obstetricians and Gynecologists. (1995). ACOG technical bulletin Domestic Violence Number 209—August 1995 (Replaces Number 124, January 1989). *International Journal of Gynecology and Obstetrics, 51*(2), 161–170.

American Medical Association. (1992). Diagnostic and treatment guidelines on domestic violence. http://www.vahealth.org/Injury/projectradarva/documents/older/pdf/AMADiag&TreatGuide.pdf.

Amowitz, L., Kim, G., Reis, C., Asher, J., & Iacopino, V. (2004). Human rights abuses and concerns about women's health and human rights in southern Iraq. *Journal of the American Medical Association, 291*(12), 1471–1479. doi: 10.1001/jama.291.12.1471.

Anderson, J. F., & Kras, K. (2007). Revisiting Albert Bandura's social learning theory to better understand and assist victims of intimate personal violence. *Women & Criminal Justice, 17*(1), 99–124. doi: 10.1300/J012v17n01_05.

Andersson, N., Cockcroft, A., Ansari, N., Omer, K., Chaudhry, U. U., Khan, A., & Pearson, L. W. (2009). Collecting reliable information about violence against women safely in household interviews: Experience from a large-scale national survey in South Asia. *Violence Against Women, 15*(4), 482–496. doi: 10.1177/1077801208331063.

Audi, C. A. F., Segall-Corrêa, A. M., Santiago, S. M., Andrade, M. G. G., & Pêrez-Escamilla, R. (2008). Violence against pregnant women: Prevalence and associated factors. *Revista de Saúde Pública, 42*(5), 1–9.

Bacchus, L., Mezey, G., & Bewley, S. (2003). Experiences of seeking help from health professionals in a sample of women who experienced domestic violence. *Health & Social Care in the Community, 11*(1), 10–18.

Bacchus, L., Mezey, G., & Bewley, S. (2006). A qualitative exploration of the nature of domestic violence in pregnancy. *Violence Against Women, 12*(6), 588–604. doi: 10.1177/1077801206289131.

Bailey, B. A., & Daugherty, R. A. (2007). Intimate partner violence during pregnancy: Incidence and associated health behaviors in a rural population. *Maternal and Child Health Journal, 11*, 495–503. doi: 10.1007/s10995-007-0191-6.

Ballard, T. J., Saltzman, J. A., Gazmararian, J. A., Spitz, A. M., Lazorick, S., & Marks, J. S. (1998). Violence during pregnancy: Measurement issues. *American Journal of Public Health, 88*(2), 274–276.

Berenson, A. B., San Miguel, V. V., & Wilkinson, G. S. (1992). Prevalence of physical and sexual assault in pregnant adolescents. *Journal of Adolescent Health, 13*(6), 466–469.

Bhandari, M. (2006). Musculoskeletal manifestations of physical abuse after intimate partner violence. *Journal of Trauma, 61*(4), 1473–1479. doi: 10.1097/01.ta.0000196419.36019.5a.

Bowen, E., Heron, J., Waylen, A., Wolke, D., & ALSPAC Study Team. (2005). Domestic violence risk during and after pregnancy: Findings from a British longitudinal study. *BJOG: An International Journal of Obstetrics and Gynaecology, 112*, 1083–1089. doi: 10.1111/j.1471-0528.2005.00653.x.

Boy, A., & Kulczycki, A. (2008). What we know about intimate partner violence in the Middle East and North Africa. *Violence Against Women, 14*(1), 53–70. doi: 10.1177/1077801207311860.

Boy, A., & Salihu, H. M. (2004). Intimate partner violence and birth outcomes: A systematic review. *International Journal of Fertility, 49*(4), 159–163.

Brown, S. J., McDonald, E. A., & Krastev, A. H. (2008). Fear of an intimate partner and women's health in early pregnancy: Findings from the maternal health study. *Birth, 35*(4), 293–302.

Bullock, L., Bloom, T., Davis, J., Kilburn, E., & Curry, M. A. (2006). Abuse disclosure in privately and Medicaid-funded pregnant women. *Journal of Midwifery & Women's Health, 51*(5), 361–369. doi: 10.1016/j.jmwh.2006.02.012.

Burch, R. L., & Gallup, G. G. Jr. (2004). Pregnancy as a stimulus for domestic violence. *Journal of Family Violence, 19*(4), 243–247.

Campbell, J., García-Moreno, C., & Sharps, P. (2004). Abuse during pregnancy in industrialized and developing countries. *Violence Against Women, 10*(7), 770–789. doi: 10.1177/1077801204265551.

Campbell, J. C., Harris, M. J., & Lee, R. K. (1995). Violence research: An overview. *Scholarly Inquiry for Nursing Practice, 9*(2), 105–126.

Campbell, J. C., Oliver, C., & Bullock, L. (1993). Why battering during pregnancy? *AWHONNS Clinical Issues in Perinatal and Women's Health Nursing, 4*(3), 343–349.

Campbell, J. C., Pugh, L. C., Campbell, D., & Visscher, M. (1995). The influence of abuse on pregnancy intention. *Women's Health Issues, 5*(4), 214–223.

Campbell, J. C., Soeken, K., McFarlane, J., & Parker, B. (1998). Risk factors for femicide among pregnant and nonpregnant battered women. In J. C. Campbell (Ed.), *Empowering survivors of abuse: Health care for battered women and their children* (pp. 90–97). Thousand Oaks, CA: Sage.

Caralis, P., & Musialowski, R. (1997). Women's experiences with domestic violence and their attitudes and expectations regarding medical care of abuse victims. *Southern Medical Journal, 90*(11), 1075–1080.

Castro, R., Peek-Asa, C., & Ruiz, A. (2003). Violence against women in Mexico: A study of abuse before and during pregnancy. *American Journal of Public Health, 93*(7), 1110–1116.

Chalmers, B., Dzakpasu, S., Heaman, M., & Kaczowski, J. (2008). The Canadian Maternity Experiences Survey: An overview of findings. *Journal of Obstetrics and Gynaecology Canada, 30*(3), 217–228.

Chamberlain, L., & Perham-Hester, K. A. (2000). Physicians' screening practices for female partner abuse during prenatal visits. *Maternal and Child Health Journal, 4*(2), 141–148.

Chan, K. L. (2006). The Chinese concept of face and violence against women. *International Social Work, 49*(1), 65–73. doi: 10.1177/0020872806059402.

Chan, K. L., Brownridge, D. A., Tiwari, A., Fong, D. Y. T., & Leung, W. C. (2008). Understanding violence against Chinese women in Hong Kong: An analysis of risk factors with a special emphasis on the role of in-law conflict. *Violence Against Women, 14*(11), 1295–1312. doi: 10.1177/1077801208325088.

Chan, K. L., Tiwari, A., Fong, D. Y. T., Leung, W. C., Brownridge, D. A., & Ho, P. C. (2009). Correlates of in-law conflict and intimate partner violence against Chinese pregnant women in Hong Kong. *Journal of Interpersonal Violence, 24*(1), 97–110. doi: 10.1177/0886260508315780.

Chang, J., Berg, C. J., Saltzman, L. E., & Herndon, J. (2005). Homicide: A leading cause of injury deaths among pregnant and postpartum women in the United States, 1991–1999. *American Journal of Public Health, 95*(3), 471–477. doi: 10.2105/AJPH.2003.029868.

Chhabra, S. (2007). Physical violence during pregnancy. *Journal of Obstetrics and Gynaecology, 27*(5), 460–463. doi: 10.1080/01443610701406075.

Choi, A., & Edleson, J. L. (1996). Social disapproval of wife assaults: A national survey of Singapore. *Journal of Comparative Family Studies, 27*(1), 73–88.

Coker, A. L., Sanderson, M., & Dong, B. (2004). Partner violence during pregnancy and risk of adverse pregnancy outcomes. *Paediatric and Perinatal Epidemiology, 18*(4), 260–269.

Cokkinides, V. E., Coker, A. L., Sanderson, M., Addy, C., & Bethea, L. (1999). Physical violence during pregnancy: Maternal complications and birth outcomes. *Obstetrics and Gynecology, 93*(1), 661–666.

Cole, T. B., & Flanagin, A. (1999). What can we do about violence? *Journal of the American Medical Association, 282*(5), 481–483. doi: 10.1001/jama.282.5.481.

Coohey, C. (2007). The relationship between mothers' social networks and severe domestic violence: A test of the social isolation hypothesis. *Violence and Victims, 22*(4), 503–512.

Counts, D. A., Brown, J. K., & Campbell, J. (Eds.). (1999). *To have and to hit: Cultural perspectives on wife beating* (2nd ed.). Urbana, IL: University of Illinois Press.

Cripe, S. M., Sanchez, S. E., Perales, M. T., Lam, N., Garcia, P., & Williams, M. A. (2008). Association of intimate partner physical and sexual violence with unintended pregnancy among pregnant women in Peru. *International Journal of Gynecology and Obstetrics, 100*(2), 104–108. doi: 10.1016/j.ijgo.2007.08.003.

Dasgupta, S. D. (2000). Charting the course: An overview of domestic violence in the South Asian community in the United States. *Journal of Social Distress and the Homeless, 9*(3), 173–185.

Datner, E. M., Wiebe, D. J., Brensinger, C. M., & Nelson, D. B. (2007). Identifying pregnant women experiencing domestic violence in an urban emergency department. *Journal of Interpersonal Violence, 22*(1), 124–135. doi: 10.1177/0886260506295000.

Department of Health and Human Services. (1990). *Healthy people national health promotion and disease prevention objectives.* Washington, DC: Author.

Department of Health and Human Services. (1995). *Healthy people 2000: Midcourse review and 1995 revisions.* Washington, DC: Author.

Diaz-Olavarrieta, C., Paz, F., Abuabara, K., Martinez Ayala, H. B., Kolstad, K., & Palermo, T. (2007). Abuse during pregnancy in Mexico City. *International Journal of Gynecology and Obstetrics, 97*(1), 57–64. doi: 10.1016/j.ijgo. 2006.10.008.

Dunn, L. L., & Oths, K. S. (2004). Prenatal predictors of intimate partner abuse. *Journal of Obstetric, Gynecologic, and Neonatal Nursing, 33*(1), 54–63. doi: 10.1177/0884217503261080.

Emenike, E., Lawoko, S., & Dalal, K. (2008). Intimate partner violence and reproductive health of women in Kenya. *International Nursing Review, 55*, 97–102.

Espinosa, L., & Osborne, K. (2002). Domestic violence during pregnancy: Implications for practice. *Journal of Midwifery & Women's Health, 47*(5), 305–317.

Fanslow, J., Silva, M., Robinson, E., & Whitehead, A. (2008). Violence during pregnancy: Associations with pregnancy intendedness, pregnancy-related care, and alcohol and tobacco use among a representative sample of New Zealand women. *Australian and New Zealand Journal of Obstetrics and Gynaecology, 48*, 398–404. doi: 10.1111/j.1479-828X.2008.00890.x.

Farid, M., Saleem, S., Karim, M. S., & Hatcher, J. (2008). Spousal abuse during pregnancy in Karachi, Pakistan. *International Journal of Gynecology and Obstetrics, 101*(2), 141–145. doi: 10.1016/j.ijgo.2007.11.015.

Fernandez, M. (1997). Domestic violence by extended family members in India: Interplay of gender and generation. *Journal of Interpersonal Violence, 12*(3), 433–455.

Fikree, F. F., & Bhatti, L. I. (1999). Domestic violence and health of Pakistani women. *International Journal of Gynecology & Obstetrics, 65*, 195–201.

Flake, D. F. (2005). Individual, family, and community risk markers for domestic violence in Peru. *Violence Against Women, 11*(3), 353–373. doi: 10.1177/1077801204272129.

Gao, W., Paterson, J., Carter, S., & Iusitini, L. (2008). Intimate partner violence and unplanned pregnancy in the Pacific Islands Families Study. *International Journal of Gynecology and Obstetrics, 100*(2), 109–115. doi: 10.1016/j.ijgo. 2007.08.004.

Garcia-Moreno, C. (2009). Intimate-partner violence and fetal loss. *Lancet, 373*, 278–279.

Garcia-Moreno, C., Jansen, H. A., Ellsberg, M., Heise, L., & Watts, C. H. (2005). *WHO Multi-Country Study on Women's Health and Domestic Violence against Women: Initial results on prevalence, health outcomes, and women's responses.* Geneva, Switzerland: World Health Organization.

Garcia-Moreno, C., Jansen, H. A., Ellsberg, M., Heise, L., & Watts, C.H. (2006). Prevalence of intimate partner violence: Findings from the WHO Multi-Country Study on Women's Health and Domestic Violence. *Lancet, 368*, 1260–1269.

Gazmararian, J. A., Adams, M. M., Saltzman, L. E., Johnson, C. H., Bruce, F. C., Marks, J. S., Zahniser, S. C., & PRAMS Working Group. (1995). The relationship between pregnancy intendedness and physical violence in mothers of newborns. *Obstetrics & Gynecology, 85*(6), 1031–1038.

Gazmararian, J. A., Lazorick, S., Spitz, A. M., Ballard, T. J., Saltzman, L. E., & Marks, J. S. (1996). Prevalence of violence against pregnant women. *Journal of the American Medical Association, 275*(24), 1915–1920.

Gazmararian, J. A., Petersen, R., Spitz, A. M., Goodwin, M. M., Saltzman, L. E., & Marks, J. S. (2000). Violence and reproductive health: Current knowledge and future research directions. *Maternal and Child Health Journal, 4*(2), 79–84.

Gielen, A. C., O'Campo, P. J., Faden, R. R., Kass, N. E., & Xue, N. (1994). Interpersonal conflict and physical violence during the childbearing year. *Social Science and Medicine, 39*(6), 781–787.

Gilbert, B. J. C., Johnson, C. H., Morrow, B., Gaffield, M. E., Ahluwalia, I., & PRAMS Working Group. (1999). Prevalence of selected maternal and infant characteristics: Pregnancy Risk Assessment Monitoring System (PRAMS). *Morbidity and Mortality Weekly Report, 48*, SS5.

Goodwin, M. M., Gazmararian, J. A., Johnson, C. H., Gilbert, B. C. Saltzman, L. E., & PRAMS Working Group. (2000). Pregnancy intendedness and physical abuse around the time of pregnancy: Findings from the Pregnancy Risk Assessment Monitoring System, 1996–1997. *Maternal and Child Health Journal, 4*(2), 85–92.

Guo, S. F., Wu, J. L., Qu, C. Y., & Yan, R. Y. (2004). Physical and sexual abuse of women before, during, and after pregnancy. *International Journal of Gynecology and Obstetrics, 84*(3), 281–286. doi: 10.1016/j.ijgo.2003.08.019.

Haj-Yahia, M. M. (1998a). A patriarchal perspective of beliefs about wife beating among Palestinian men from the West Bank and the Gaza Strip. *Journal of Family Issues, 19*(5), 595–621. doi: 10.1177/019251398019005006.

Haj-Yahia, M. (1998b). Beliefs about wife beating among Palestinian women: The influence of their patriarchal ideology. *Violence Against Women, 4*(5), 533–558. doi: 10.1177/1077801298004005002.

Haj-Yahia, M. (2000). Wife abuse and battering in the sociocultural context of Arab society. *Family Process, 39*(2), 237–255.

Hammoury, N., & Khawaja, M. (2007). Screening for domestic violence during pregnancy in an antenatal clinic in Lebanon. *European Journal of Public Health, 17*(6), 605–606. doi: 10.1093/eurpub/ckm009.

Hammoury, N., Khawaja, M., Mahfoud, Z., Afifi, R. A., & Madi, H. (2009). Domestic violence against women during pregnancy: The case of Palestinian refugees attending an antenatal clinic in Lebanon. *Journal of Women's Health, 18*(3), 337–345. doi: 10.1089=jwh.2007.0740.

Harrykissoon, S. D., Rickert, V. I., & Wiemann, C. M. (2002). Prevalence and patterns of intimate partner violence among adolescent mothers during the postpartum period. *Archives of Pediatrics and Adolescent Medicine, 156*(4), 325–330.

Health Canada. (1999). Violence against women. http://www.hc-sc.gc.ca/hl-vs/pubs/women-femmes/violence-eng.php.

Heaman, M. I. (2005). Relationships between physical abuse during pregnancy and risk factors for preterm birth among women in Manitoba. *Journal of Obstetric, Gynecologic, and Neonatal Nursing, 34*, 721–731. doi: 10.1177/0884217505281906.

Hedin, L. W., & Janson, P. O. (2000). Domestic violence during pregnancy: The prevalence of physical injuries, substance use, abortions and miscarriages. *Acta Obstetrica et Gynecologica Scandinavica, 79*(8), 625–630. doi: 10.1034/j.1600-0412.2000.079008625.x.

Heise, L., Ellsberg, M., & Gottemoeller, M. (1999). Ending violence against women. In *Population Reports, Series L, No. 11* (pp. 1–43). Baltimore, MD: John Hopkins University School of Public Health, Population Information Program.

Hillard, P. J. A. (1985). Physical abuse in pregnancy. *Obstetrics & Gynecology, 66*(2), 185–190.

Horan, D. L., Chapin, J., Klein, L., Schmidt, L. A., & Schulkin, J. (1998). Domestic violence screening practices of obstetrician-gynecologists. *Obstetrics & Gynecology, 92*(5), 785–789.

Horon, I. L., & Cheng, D. (2001). Enhanced surveillance for pregnancy-associated mortality: Maryland, 1993–1998. *Journal of the American Medical Association, 285*(11), 1455–1459. doi: 10.1001/jama.285.11.1455.

Hortacsu, N., Kalaycioglu, S., & Rittersberger-Tilic, H. (2003). Intrafamily aggression in Turkey: Frequency, instigation, and acceptance. *Journal of Social Psychology, 143*(2), 163–184.

Hudson, W., & McIntosh, S. (1981). The assessment of spouse abuse: Two quantifiable dimensions. *Journal of Marriage and Family, 43*(4), 873–888.

Hussain, R., & Khan, A. (2008). Women's perceptions and experiences of sexual violence in marital relationships and its effect on reproductive health. *Health Care for Women International, 29*(5), 468–483. doi: 10.1080/073993 30801949541.

Huth-Bocks, A. C., Levendosky, A. A., & Bogat, G. A. (2002). The effects of domestic violence during pregnancy on maternal and infant health. *Violence and Victims, 17*(2), 169–185.

Jasinski, J. L. (2004). Pregnancy and domestic violence: A review of the literature. *Trauma, Violence Abuse, 5*(1), 47–64. doi: 10.1177/1524838003259322.

Jeanjot, I., Barlow, P., & Rozenberg, S. (2008). Domestic violence during pregnancy: Survey of patients and healthcare providers. *Journal of Women's Health, 17*(4), 557–567. doi: 10.1089/jwh.2007.0639.

Jejeebhoy, S. J. (1998). Associations between wife-beating and fetal and infant death: Impressions from a survey in rural India. *Studies in Family Planning, 29*(3), 300–308.

Jewkes, R. (2002). Intimate partner violence: Causes and prevention. *Lancet, 359*, 1423–1429.

Jewkes, R., Levin, J., & Penn-Kekana, L. (2002). Risk factors for domestic violence: Findings from a South African cross-sectional study. *Social Science & Medicine, 55*(9), 1603–1617.

Johnson, A. A., El-Khorazaty, M. N., Hatcher, B. J., Wingrove, B. K., Milligan, R., Harris, C., & Richards, L. (2003). Determinants of late prenatal care initiation by African American women in Washington, DC. *Maternal and Child Health Journal, 7*(2), 103–114.

Karaoglu, L., Celbis, O., Ercan, C., Ilgar, M., Pehlivan, E., Gunes, G., et al. (2005). Physical, emotional and sexual violence during pregnancy in Malatya, Turkey. *European Journal of Public Health, 16*(2), 149–156. doi: 10.1093/ eurpub/cki161.

Kaye, D. K., Mirembe, F. M., Bantebya, G., Johansson, A., & Ekstrom, A. M. (2006). Domestic violence during pregnancy and risk of low birth weight and maternal complications: A prospective cohort study at Mulago Hospital, Uganda. *Tropical Medicine and International Health, 11*(10), 1576–1584. doi: 10.1111/j.1365-3156.2006.01711.x.

Kendall-Tackett, K. A. (2007). Violence against women and the perinatal period: The impact of lifetime violence and abuse on pregnancy, postpartum, and breastfeeding. *Trauma, Violence, & Abuse, 8*(3), 344–353. doi: 10.1177/1524838007304406.

Khawaja, M. (2004). Domestic violence in refugee camps in Jordan. *International Journal of Gynecology and Obstetrics, 86*(1), 67–69. doi: 10.1016/j.ijgo.2004.04.008.

Kramer, A. (2007). Stages of change: Surviving intimate partner violence during and after pregnancy. *Journal of Perinatal and Neonatal Nursing, 21*(4), 285–295.

Lee, D. T. S., Yip, A. S. K., Leung, T. Y. S., & Chung, T. K. H. (2004). Ethnoepidemiology of postnatal depression: Prospective multivariate study of sociocultural risk factors in a Chinese population in Hong Kong. *British Journal of Psychiatry, 184*(1), 34–40.

Leung, W. C., Leung, T. W., Lam, Y. Y., & Ho, P. C. (1999). The prevalence of domestic violence against pregnant women in a Chinese community. *International Journal of Gynaecology and Obstetrics, 66,* 23–30.

Liu, M., & Chan, C. (1999). Enduring violence and staying in marriage: Stories of battered women in rural China. *Violence Against Women, 5*(12), 1469–1492. doi: 10.1177/10778019922183471.

Liu, M., & Zhang, L. (2005). Personal experiences and public attitudes: Findings from the national survey. In L. Huang & W. Rong (Eds.), *Combating domestic violence against women: China in action* (pp. 125–142). Beijing: China Social Sciences Press.

Macey, M. (1999). Religion, make violence, and the control of women: Pakistani Muslim men in Bradford, UK. *Gender and Development, 7*(1), 48–55.

Macy, R. J., Martin, S. L., Kupper, L. L., Casanueva, C., & Guo, S. (2007). Partner violence among women before, during, and after pregnancy. *Women's Health Issues, 17*(5), 290–299. doi: 10.1016/j.whi.2007.03.006.

Maman, S., Campbell, J. C., Sewat, M., & Gielen, A. C. (2000). The intersection of HIV and violence directions for future research and interventions. *Social Science and Medicine, 50*(4), 459–478.

Marshall, I. (1992). Development of the severity of violence against women scales. *Journal of Family Violence, 7*(2), 103–121.

Martin, S. L., Kilgallen, B., Dee, D. L., Dawson, S., & Campbell, J. C. (1998). Women in a prenatal care/substance treatment program: Links between domestic violence and mental health. *Maternal and Child Health Journal, 2*(2), 85–94.

Martin, S. L., Kilgallen, B., Tsui, A. O., Maitra, K., Singh, K. K., & Kupper, L. L. (1999). Sexual behaviors and reproductive health outcomes: Associations with wife abuse in India. *Journal of the American Medical Association, 282*(20), 1967–1972. doi: 10.1001/jama.282.20.1967.

Martin, S. L., Li, Y., Casanueva, C., Harris-Britt, A., Kupper, L. L., & Cloutier, S. (2006). Intimate partner violence and women's depression before and during pregnancy. *Violence Against Women, 12*(3), 221–239. doi: 10.1177/1077801205285106.

Martin, S. L., Macy, R. J., Sullivan, K., & Magee, M. L. (2007). Pregnancy-associated violent deaths: The role of intimate partner violence. *Trauma, Violence, & Abuse, 8*(2), 135–148. doi: 10.1177/1524838007301223.

Martin, S. L., Matza, L. S., Kupper, L. L., Thomas, J. C., Daly, M., & Cloutier, S. (1999). Domestic violence and sexually transmitted diseases: The experience of prenatal care patients. *Public Health Reports, 114*(3), 262–268.

McCauley, J., Yurk, R., Jenckes, M., & Ford, D. (1998). Inside "Pandora's box": Abused women's experiences with clinicians and health services. *Journal of General Internal Medicine, 13*(8), 549–555.

McFarlane, J. (2007). Pregnancy following partner rape: What we know and what we need to know. *Trauma, Violence, & Abuse, 8*(2), 127–134. doi: 10.1177/1524838007301222.

McFarlane, J., & Gondolf, E. (1998). Preventing abuse during pregnancy: A clinical protocol. *MCN: The American Journal of Maternal/Child Nursing, 23*(1), 22–26.

McFarlane, J., & Parker, B. (1994). Abuse during pregnancy: An assessment and intervention protocol. *MCN: The American Journal of Maternal/Child Nursing, 19*(6), 321–324.

McFarlane, J., Parker, B., Soeken, K., Silva, C., & Reel, S. (1998). Safety behaviours of abused women after an intervention during pregnancy. *Journal of Obstetric, Gynecologic, and Neonatal Nursing, 27*(1), 64–69. doi: 10.1111/j.1552-6909.1998.tb02592.x.

Mechanic, M. B., Weaver, T. L., & Resick, P. A. (2008). Mental health consequences of intimate partner abuse: A multidimensional assessment of four different forms of abuse. *Violence Against Women, 14*(6), 634–654. doi: 10.1177/1077801208319283.

Mehotra, M. (1999). The social construction of wife abuse: Experiences of Asian Indian women in the United States. *Violence Against Women, 5*(6), 619–640. doi: 10.1177/10778019922181400.

Meng, L. (2002). Rebellion and revenge: The meaning of suicide of women in rural China. *International Journal of Social Welfare, 11*(4), 300–309.

Moraes, C. L., & Reichenheim, M. E. (2002). Domestic violence during pregnancy in Rio de Janeiro, Brazil. *International Journal of Gynaecology and Obstetrics, 79*(3), 269–277.

Nannini, A., Lazar, J., Berg, C., Barger, M., Tomashek, K., Cabral, H., et al. (2008). Physical injuries reported on hospital visits for assault during the pregnancy-associated period. *Nursing Research, 57*(3), 144–149.

Nasir, K., & Hyder, A. A. (2003). Violence against pregnant women in developing countries: Review of evidence. *European Journal of Public Health, 13*(2), 105–107.

National Center for Injury Prevention and Control. (2003). *Costs of intimate partner violence against women in the United States.* Atlanta, GA: Centers for Disease Control and Prevention.

O'Leary, K. D. (1999). Psychological abuse: A variable deserving critical attention in domestic violence. *Violence and Victims, 14*(1), 3–24.

Ozcakir, A., Bayram, N., Ergin, N., Selimoglu, K., & Bilgel, N. (2008). Attitudes of Turkish men toward wife beating: A study from Bursa, Turkey. *Journal of Family Violence, 23*(7), 631–638. doi: 10.1007/s10896-008-9185-4.

Pallitto, C. C., Campbell, J. C., & O'Campo, P. (2005). Is intimate partner violence associated with unintended pregnancy? A review of the literature. *Trauma, Violence, & Abuse, 6*(3), 217–235. doi: 10.1177/1524838005277441.

Parish, W. L., Wang, T., Laumann, E. O., Pan, S., & Luo, Y. (2004). Intimate partner violence in China: National prevalence, risk factors and associated health problems. *International Family Planning Perspectives, 30*(4), 174–181.

Parker, B., & McFarlane, J. (1991). Identifying and helping battered pregnant women. *MCN: American Journal of Maternal Child Nursing, 16*(3), 161–164.

Paterson, J., Feehan, M., Butler, S., Williams, M., & Cowley-Malcolm, E. (2007). Intimate partner violence within a cohort of Pacific mothers living in New Zealand. *Journal of Interpersonal Violence, 22*(6), 698–721. doi: 10.1177/0886260507300596.

Peedicayil, A., Sadowski, L. S., Jeyaseelan, L., Shankar, V., Jain, D., Suresh, S., et al. (2004). Spousal violence against women during pregnancy. *BJOG: An International Journal of Obstetrics and Gynaecology, 111*(7), 682–687. doi: 10.1111/j.1471-0528.2004.00151.x.

Perales, M. T., Cripe, S. M., Lam, N., Sanchez, S. E., Sanchez, E., & Williams, M. A. (2009). Prevalence, types, and pattern of intimate partner violence among pregnant women in Lima, Peru. *Violence Against Women, 15*(2), 224–250. doi: 10.1177/1077801208329387.

Persily, C. A., & Abdulla, S. (2000). Domestic violence and pregnancy in rural West Virginia. *Online Journal of Rural Nursing and Health Care, 1*(3), 11–20.

Petersen, R., Gazmararian, J. A., Spitz, A. M., Rowley, D. L., Goodwin, M. M., Saltzman, L. E., & Marks, J. S. (1997). Violence and adverse pregnancy outcomes: A review of the literature and directions for future research. *American Journal of Preventive Medicine, 13*(5), 366–773.

Plichta, S. B., & Abraham, C. (1996). Violence and gynaecological health in women < 50 years old. *American Journal of Obstetrics and Gynecology, 174*(3), 903–907.

Purwar, M. B., Jeyaseelan, L., Varhadpande, U., Motgahare, V., & Pimplakute, S. (1999). Survey of physical abuse during pregnancy GMCH, Nagpur, India. *Journal of Obstetrics and Gynaecology Research, 25*, 165–171.

Quelopana, A. M., Champion, J. D., & Salazar, B. C. (2008). Health behavior in Mexican pregnant women with a history of violence. *Western Journal of Nursing Research, 30*(8), 1005–1018. doi: 10.1177/0193945908320464.

Quinlivan, J. A., & Evans, S. F. (2001). A prospective cohort study of the impact of domestic violence on young teenage pregnancy outcomes. *Journal of Pediatric and Adolescent Gynecology, 14*(1), 17–23.

Quinlivan, J. A., & Evans, S. F. (2005). Impact of domestic violence and drug abuse in pregnancy on maternal attachment and infant temperament in teenage mothers in the setting of best clinical practice. *Archives of Women's Mental Health, 8*, 191–199. doi: 10.1007/s00737-005-0079-7.

Raj, A., Livramento, K. N., Santana, M. C., Gupta, J., & Silverman, J. G. (2006). Victims of intimate partner violence more likely to report abuse from in-laws. *Violence Against Women, 12*(10), 936–949. doi: 10.1177/1077801206292935.

Ramanathan, S. (1996). Violence against women. *International Medical Journal, 3*, 145–148.

Reichenheim, M. E., & Moraes, C. L. (2009). Comparison between the abuse assessment screen and the revised conflict tactics scales for measuring physical violence during pregnancy. *Journal of Epidemiology and Community Health, 58*(6), 523–527. doi: 10.1136/jech.2003.011742.

Reichenheim, M. E., Patricio, T. F., & Moraes, C. L. (2008). Detecting intimate partner violence during pregnancy: Awareness-raising indicators for use by primary healthcare professionals. *Public Health, 122*, 716–724. doi: 10.1016/j.puhe.2007.09.016.

Rianon, N. J., & Shelton, A. J. (2003). Perception of spousal abuse expressed by married Bangladeshi immigrant women in Houston, Texas, U.S.A. *Journal of Immigrant Health, 5*(1), 37–44.

Rodriguez, M. A., Bauer, H. M., McLoughlin, E., & Crumback, K. (1999). Screening and intervention for intimate partner abuse: Practices and attitudes of primary care physicians. *Journal of the American Medical Association, 282*(5), 468–474. doi: 10.1001/jama.282.5.468.

Rosenberg, M., & Fenley, M. A. (1991). *Violence in America: A public health approach.* New York: Oxford University Press.

Salari, Z., & Nakhaee, N. (2008). Identifying types of domestic violence and its associated risk factors in a pregnant population in Kerman hospitals, Iran Republic. *Asia-Pacific Journal of Public Health, 20*(1), 49–55. doi: 10.1177/1010539507308386.

Saltzman, L. E., Johnson, C. H., Gilbert, B. C., & Goodwin, M. M. (2003). Physical abuse around the time of pregnancy: An examination of prevalence and risk factors in 16 states. *Maternal and Child Health Journal, 7*(1), 31–43.

Shadigian, E. M., & Bauer, S. T. (2005). Pregnancy-associated death: A qualitative systematic review of homicide and suicide. *Obstetrical and Gynecological Survey, 60*(3), 183–190.

Shaikh, M. A., Shaikh, I. A., Kamal, A., & Masood, S. (2008). Domestic violence and pregnancy: Perspective from Islamabad and Rawalpindi. *Journal of the College of Physicians and Surgeons Pakistan, 18*(10), 662–663.

Silverman, J. G., Decker, M. R., Reed, E., & Raj, A. (2006). Intimate partner violence victimization prior to and during pregnancy among women residing in 26 US states: Associations with maternal and neonatal health. *American Journal of Obstetrics and Gynecology, 195*(1), 140–188. doi: 10.1016/j.ajog.2005.12.052.

Silverman, J. G., Gupta, J., Decker, M. R., Kapur, N., & Raj, A. (2007). Intimate partner violence and unwanted pregnancy, miscarriage, induced abortion, and stillbirth among a national sample of Bangladeshi women. *BJOG: An International Journal of Obstetrics and Gynaecology, 114*(10), 1246–1252. doi: 10.1111/j.1471-0528.2007.01481.x.

Small, M. J., Gupta, J., Frederic, R., Joseph, G., Theodore, M., & Kershaw, T. (2008). Intimate partner and nonpartner violence against pregnant women in rural Haiti. *International Journal of Gynecology and Obstetrics, 102*(3), 226–231. doi: 10.1016/j.ijgo.2008.05.008.

Sorenson, S. B., Stein, J. A., Siegel, J. M., Golding J. M., & Burnham, M. A. (1987). The prevalence of adult sexual assault: The Los Angeles epidemiologic Catchment Area Project. *American Journal of Epidemiology, 126*(6), 1154–1164.

Stephenson, R., Koenig, M. A., Acharya, R., & Roy, T. K. (2008). Domestic violence, contraceptive use, and unwanted pregnancy in rural India. *Studies in Family Planning, 39*(3), 177–186.

Stevens, L. (2003). Improving screening of women for violence: Basic guidelines for physicians. http://cme.medscape.com/viewarticle/464417_print.

Stewart, D. E., & Cecutti, A. (1993). Physical abuse in pregnancy. *Canadian Medical Association Journal, 149*(9), 1257–1263.

Stickley, A., Timofeeva, I., & Sparén, P. (2008). Risk factors for intimate partner violence against women in St. Petersburg, Russia. *Violence Against Women, 14*(4), 483–495. doi: 10.1177/1077801208314847.

Straus, M. A., Gelles, R. J., & Steinmetz, S. K. (1980). *Behind closed doors: Violence in the American family.* New York: Anchor.

Straus, M. A., Hamby, S. L., Boney-McCoy, S., & Sugarman, D. B. (1996). The revised conflict tactics scales (CTS2) development and preliminary psychometric data. *Journal of Family Issues, 17*(3), 283–316. doi: 10.1177/ 019251396017003001.

Supriya, K. E. (1996). Confessionals, testimonials: Women's speech in/and contexts of violence. *Hypatia, 11*(4), 92–106.

Tan, J. C. H., & Gregor, K. V. (2006). Violence against pregnant women in northwestern Ontario. *Annals of the New York Academy of Sciences, 1087*, 320–338. doi: 10.1196/annals.1385.010.

Tang, C. S. K. (1999). Wife abuse in Hong Kong Chinese families: A community survey. *Journal of Family Violence, 14*(2), 173–191.

Thananowan, N., & Heidrich, S. M. (2008). Intimate partner violence among pregnant Thai women. *Violence Against Women, 14*(5), 509–527. doi: 10.1177/ 1077801208315525.

Tiwari, A., Chan, K. L., Fong, D., Leung, W. C., Brownridge, D. A., Lam, H., et al. (2008). The impact of psychological abuse by an intimate partner on the mental health of pregnant women. *BJOG: An International Journal of Obstetrics and Gynaecology, 115*, 377–384. doi: 10.1111/j.1471-0528.2007.01593.x.

Topbaş, M., Ünsal, M., Çan, G., Bacak, A., & Özgün, S. (2008). The effect of pregnancy on the physical and sexual abuse of women that presented to a state hospital in Trabzon, Turkey. *Turkish Journal of Medical Sciences, 38*(4), 335–342.

Torres, S., Campbell, J., Campbell, D. W., Ryan, J., King, C., Price, P., et al. (2000). Abuse during and before pregnancy: Prevalence and cultural correlates. *Violence and Victims, 15*(3), 303–321.

U.S. General Accounting Office. (2002). *Violence against women: Data on pregnant victims and effectiveness of prevention strategies are limited. Report to the Honorable Eleanor Holmes Norton, House of Representatives* (GAO-02-530). Washington, DC: Author. http://www.gao.gov/new.items/d02530.pdf.

Waalen, J., Goodwin, M. M., Spitz, A. M., Petersen, R., & Saltzman, L. E. (2000). Screening for intimate partner violence by health care providers: Barriers and interventions. *American Journal of Preventive Medicine, 19*(4), 230–237.

Walby, S. (2004). *The cost of domestic violence: Report prepared for the Women and Equality Unit*. London: Government Equalities Office. http://www .equalities.gov.uk/PDF/Cost%20of%20domestic%20violence%20(Walby) %20Sep%2004.pdf.

Warshaw, C. (1996). Identification, assessment and intervention with victims of domestic violence. In C. Warshaw (Ed.), *Identification, assessment and intervention with victims of domestic violence: Improving the healthcare response to domestic violence* (2nd ed., pp. 49–85). San Francisco, CA: Family Violence Prevention Fund.

Washington State Department of Health. (2008). *Domestic violence and pregnancy: guidelines for screening and referral*. Olympia, WA: Author. http://www.doh .wa.gov/CFh/mch/documents/DVPgGuide82008.pdf.

Wiemann, C. M., Agurcia, C. A., Berenson, A. B., Volk, R., & Rickert, V. I. (2000). Pregnant adolescents: Experiences and behaviour associated with physical assault by an intimate partner. *Maternal Child Health Journal, 4*, 93–101.

Wiist, W. H., & McFarlane, J. (1999). The effectiveness of an abuse assessment protocol in public health prenatal clinics. *American Journal of Public Health, 89*(8), 1217–1221.

Wingood, G. M., & DiClemente, R. J. (1997). The effects of an abusive primary partner on condom use and sexual negotiation practices of African-American women. *American Journal of Public Health, 87*(6), 1016–1018.

Xu, X. (1997). The prevalence and determination of wife abuse in urban China. *Journal of Comparative Family Studies, 28*(3), 280–303.

Xu, X., Zhu, F., O'Campo, P., Koenig, M. A., Mock, V., & Campbell, J. (2005). Prevalence of and risk factors for intimate partner violence in China. *American Journal of Public Health, 95*(1), 78–85. doi: 10.2105/AJPH.2003.023978.

Yang, M. S., Yang, M. J., Chou, F. H., Yang, H. M., Wei, S. L., & Lin, J. R. (2006). Physical abuse against pregnant aborigines in Taiwan: Prevalence and risk factors. *International Journal of Nursing Studies, 43*, 21–27. doi: 10.1016/j.ijnurstu.2004.12.005.

Yick, A. G. (2000). Predictors of physical spousal/intimate violence in Chinese American families. *Journal of Family Violence, 15*(3), 249–267.

Chapter 9

Power, Violence, and HIV Risk in Women

Monica D. Ulibarri, Lekeisha A. Sumner,
Ajitha Cyriac, and Hortensia Amaro

Human immunodeficiency virus (HIV) infection is a serious public health concern for women, who account for more than one fourth of all new diagnoses of HIV infection and acquired immune deficiency syndrome (AIDS) in the United States (Camacho, Brown, & Simpson, 1996; Centers for Disease Control and Prevention [CDC], 2008). In 2006, HIV infection was the fifth leading cause of death among all U.S. women aged 35 to 44 years and the sixth leading cause of death among all women aged 25 to 34 years, with only cancer and heart disease causing more deaths of women due to illness (National Center for Injury Prevention and Control, 2009). High-risk heterosexual contact is the leading cause of HIV infection among women ages 20 to 34 years (82%), with injection drug use ranking second (12% to 18%) (CDC, 2007).

Ethnic minority women are disproportionately affected by the HIV epidemic. African American and Latina women represent 24 percent of all U.S. women, but they accounted for 82 percent of the estimated total of AIDS diagnoses for women in 2005 (CDC, 2008). In recent years, HIV infection was the third leading cause of death for African American women aged

25 to 34, and it was the fourth leading cause of death for Latina women aged 35 to 44 (National Center for Injury Prevention and Control, 2009).

Women infected with HIV report multiple overlapping risk factors, such as lack of HIV knowledge, substance abuse, psychological issues, and socioeconomic stresses (CDC, 2008). Threats of gender-based violence or violence against women and unequal relationship power dynamics also play key roles in women's sexual risk. This chapter focuses on gender-based violence such as violence against women by past and current male intimate partners and on child sexual abuse in girls, as these are the most pervasive forms of gender-based violence women experience and those on which the published literature has focused.

Some women in current abusive relationships or with a history of abuse do not insist on condom use because they fear that their partners will physically abuse them or leave them (Suarez-Al-Adam, Raffaelli, & O'Leary, 2000). Moreover, gender inequalities, coupled with socially and culturally sanctioned violence against women, may hinder women's ability to modify high-risk behavior and serve to maintain women's socioeconomic subservient position. Although agencies such as the National Institutes of Health and the Centers for Disease Control and Prevention recognize the importance of incorporating culture- and gender-relevant material into HIV prevention interventions (CDC, 2008; National Institutes of Health and Office of AIDS Research, 2009a, 2009b), most behavioral risk-reduction interventions to date have not fully and comprehensively addressed these issues.

This chapter provides an overview of the literature pertaining to gender-based violence and women's HIV risk, identifies gaps in the research, and offers suggestions for future HIV prevention research and interventions targeting women with histories of violence. It focuses primarily on the U.S. literature, as the nature of women's risk in other countries involves other considerations beyond the scope of this chapter.

To date, the majority of behavioral studies on HIV risk among women have mainly focused on individual-level factors, such as knowledge about and intentions to use contraception; they have also relied on cognitive theories of health (e.g., social cognitive theory), which focus on behavior that is under the control of the individual (see the review by Herbst, Kay, Passin, Lyles, Crepaz, & Marín, 2007). While these cognitive theories are well known and have demonstrated limited effectiveness in reducing HIV risk behavior, relationship power dynamics and sociocultural contextual factors should also be considered in addressing this issue (Amaro, 1995; Amaro & Raj, 2000; Beadnell, Baker, Morrison, & Knox, 2000; Singer & Clair, 2003). Therefore, women's power in interpersonal relationships and society (e.g., cultural influences on gender roles and policies that structure the social status of women) as it relates to HIV risk is emphasized throughout this chapter.

The chapter begins with an overview of theories and empirical findings related to the associations between gender-based violence and women's risk for HIV. Next, it examines the relationships among violence, co-occurring psychological symptoms and disorders, and HIV risk. Finally, it concludes with a brief review of the literature on effective HIV prevention interventions for women that have addressed gender-based violence, trauma, and gender and power issues.

THEORETICAL PERSPECTIVES

Although the causal links between violence and HIV infection have not been established, several theoretical perspectives have been proposed. Maman, Campbell, Sweat, and Gielen (2000) suggested that gender-based violence is linked to women's HIV risk through forced or coercive sexual intercourse with an HIV-infected partner, social and interpersonal limitations placed on women that limit their ability to negotiate safe sexual behaviors, and established patterns of sexual risk taking among individuals who are assaulted in childhood and adolescence.

Several long-term effects are associated with childhood sexual abuse (CSA) and violence against women, including substance abuse, psychopathology (e.g., depression), and sexual dissatisfaction and dysfunction (e.g., an inability to sustain intimate relationships, fear of sexual intimacy) and increased sexual risk taking (e.g., unprotected sex, participation in sex work) (Beitchman, Zucker, Hood, & DaCosta, 1992; Browne, Finkelhor, Chess, Thomas, & Hertzig, 1988; Goodman, Koss, Fitzgerald, Russo, & Keita, 1993; Goodman, Koss, & Russo, 1993; Polusny & Follette, 1995). In an effort to elucidate the relationship between early sexual abuse and HIV risk among women, Miller (1999) developed a theoretical model that includes many of these negative health sequelae associated with CSA. In addition, the model includes a possible causal pathway between history of sexual abuse and HIV risk via social network membership (e.g., membership in social networks composed primarily of drug users), the support of network members, and subjective feelings of social isolation. This model proposes that women with histories of abuse may deny or inaccurately perceive the risks involved in relationships and not implement risk-reduction strategies or engage in self-protective behaviors as a result of mental health disorders, other psychosocial effects of abuse, or a pattern of unhealthy relationships developed in response to a history of abuse.

The theory of gender and power (Connell, 1987; Wingood & DiClemente, 2000), as applied to the context of HIV risk, posits that gender-based power inequities in society and in heterosexual relationships may contribute to a reduction in women's control over their sexual relationships and use of condoms, thereby increasing their risk for HIV. This theory suggests that a male-dominated society, which condones male-perpetrated violence against women, limits women's ability to negotiate safer sex practices and increases the risk of HIV acquisition.

Singer (1996) termed the interaction among substance abuse, violence, and AIDS the "SAVA (substance abuse, violence, and AIDS) syndemic"; according to this model, mutually reinforcing connections between these conditions contribute to excess burden of disease (i.e., HIV/AIDS) in a population. Syndemics theory posits that endemic and epidemic conditions such as violence, substance abuse, and AIDS in disadvantaged populations reflect the interplay of broader political, economic, and social factors (Singer, 1994). These larger forces then further complicate individuals' attempts to engage in healthy behaviors. For example, even if an individual attempts to practice risk reduction, avoiding HIV-risk behaviors may come secondary to the need for using drugs as a method of self-medication for psychological symptoms of violence trauma, or avoiding pain from alcohol or drug withdrawal if the person is addicted. Likewise, women at risk for violence may forgo requesting condoms in fear of violent retribution from abusive partners.

Similarly, Newcomb, Locke, and Goodyear (2003) developed an expanded model of HIV risk based on Szapocznik and Coatsworth's (1999) ecodevelopmental perspective and Bronfenbrenner's (1979) structural eco-systems theory. Their model takes into consideration multiple levels of social and environmental influence on an individual's behavior (e.g., microsystems, mesosystems, exosystems), but adds aspects of interpersonal and individual functioning such as psychological distress and drug use. These authors evaluated their model of HIV risk with a sample of predominantly Mexican American adolescent women. During this investigation, they found that both psychological distress and drug use were directly related to HIV risk and mediated the relationship between history of abuse (e.g., childhood maltreatment and neglect) and later HIV risk. Thus considering gender-based violence is important when examining more proximal influences on HIV–sex risk behavior such as psychological distress and drug use.

Research has identified gender-based violence in adulthood (e.g., intimate-partner violence [IPV]) and history of childhood abuse as correlates of HIV risk among women (Gielen, Ghandour, Burke, Mahoney, McDonnell, & O'Campo, 2007; Malow, Devieux, & Lucenko, 2006; Senn, Carey, & Vanable, 2008); unfortunately, longitudinal studies tracking the development of HIV risk behaviors subsequent to gender-based violence are lacking. Future research in this area could provide essential information about mediating variables amenable to change that can be targeted in HIV-prevention interventions. Nonetheless, many studies have consistently found evidence linking gender-based violence to HIV risk behaviors for women, establishing it as an important contextual factor to consider when working with women to reduce their HIV risk behaviors.

Review of Literature on Gender-Based Violence and Women's Risk for HIV

History of Sexual Abuse in Childhood and Adolescence and HIV Risk

Childhood and adolescent sexual abuse (collected under the acronym CSA) has been defined and measured in a variety of ways in psychological research. Some utilize self-reports and dichotomize groups into those who have been abused and those who have not; others focus on the age at which the abuse occurred, with the cut-off age typically ranging from 12 to 20 years old; and some take into account the severity of the experiences and include noncontact experiences such as being forcibly exposed to nudity or pornographic materials (see the review in Roosa, Reyes, Reinholtz, & Angelini, 1998). To encompass a wide range of CSA literature (Malow, Devieux, & Lucenko, 2006), this chapter uses the broad definition of CSA suggested by Browne and Finkelhor (1986)—forced or coerced sexual activity and/or sexual activity between a child and an older person.

In a review of the literature investigating the relation between CSA and subsequent sexual risk behaviors, Senn, Carey, and Vanable (2008) concluded that CSA has consistently been associated with higher rates of sexual risk behaviors, particularly sex trading, multiple sexual partners, and an earlier age of first intercourse for general and high-risk (e.g., women who traded sex, or women who had a male sex partner who injected drugs) samples of women. Likewise, in a meta-analysis of studies investigating CSA and sexual risk behavior among women, Arriola, Louden, Doldren, and Fortenberry (2005) found a small positive association between CSA and unprotected sex, multiple partners, and sex trading. Other high-risk sexual behaviors shown to be associated with a history of CSA include increased alcohol and illegal drug use (Bensley, Eenwyk, & Simmons, 2000; Johnsen & Harlow, 1996); and increased likelihood of having a sexually transmitted disease (STD), history of anal sex, and physically abusive sexual partners (Wingood & DiClemente, 1997). Further evidence is provided by a recent study (Stockman, Campbell, & Celentano, 2009) of a nationally representative sample of women in the United States, which found that history of a coerced first sexual intercourse as well as sexual coercion after sexual debut were both significantly associated with increased HIV-related risk behaviors.

Despite the robust findings of the association between CSA and high-risk sexual behavior, the existing literature on adult sexual risk behavior suffers from some limitations—namely, lack of a consistent definition of CSA among researchers, failure to investigate gender as a moderator, failure to examine other types of abuse (e.g., physical abuse, IPV), confounding CSA experiences with sex risk behavioral outcomes, and dependence on correlational data, which then limits the study's ability to draw conclusions about causality (Senn et al., 2008). Additional research is needed to identify possible mediating and moderating factors such as drug use, sex trading, and IPV that can be targeted for intervention. Without addressing history of gender-based violence and its subsequent negative outcomes, it is likely that HIV-prevention programs targeting at-risk women will be less effective and relevant (Malow, Devieux, & Lucenko, 2006).

Intimate-Partner Violence and HIV Risk

Extensive data gathered in the United States across the last decade document that women with a history of IPV are at increased risk for HIV due to lower rates of condom use and condom negotiation, higher numbers of sex partners, and increased likelihood of sex trade involvement, as well as being more likely to have a sexually transmitted infection (STI) and HIV. Studies have documented the relationship between IPV and HIV risk among heterosexual women in different international settings (Dude, 2007; Gonzalez-Guarda, Peragallo, Urrutia, Vasquez, & Mitrani, 2008; Jewkes, Levin, & Penn-Kekana, 2003; Silverman, Decker, Saggurti, Balaiah, & Raj, 2008); in women from various U.S. ethnic backgrounds (Beadnell et al., 2000; El-Bassel, Gilbert, Rajah, Foleno, & Frye, 2000; Raj, Silverman, & Amaro, 2004); among adolescent girls (Decker, Silverman, & Raj, 2005); and among older women (Sormanti, Wu, & El-Bassel, 2004; see also the review by Campbell, Baty, Ghandour, Stockman, Francisco, & Wagman, 2008). Research has identified specific HIV risk behaviors associated with IPV, such as having multiple partners, history of STIs, inconsistent use or non-use of condoms, and increased likelihood of engaging in sex with a partner with known risk factors such as being HIV infected or using injection drugs (El-Bassel, et al., 2007; Panchanadeswaran et al., 2008; Sareen, Pagura, & Grant, 2009; Wu, El-Bassel, Witte, Gilbert, & Chang, 2003). Furthermore, these risk factors may be exacerbated for drug-involved women (El-Bassel, Gilbert, Wu, Go, & Hill, 2005).

Gender-based power imbalances may also play a role in HIV risk by constraining women's ability to negotiate condom use out of fear of violent retribution. When male-perpetrated violence occurs in the context of a romantic relationship, this violence is often used as a means of establishing, asserting, or protecting the man's power (Marin & Russo, 2003). The decreased relationship power among women who are in relationships characterized by IPV (Pulerwitz, Gortmaker, & DeJong, 2000) often diminishes women's consistency in using condoms with their partners (Pulerwitz, Amaro, De Jong, Gortmaker, & Rudd, 2002).

Gender-based violence such as sexual coercion and IPV within heterosexual relationships is likely a mechanism for increasing the risk of contracting HIV among women with abusive male partners as a function of their partners' risky sexual behaviors. Consistent with these findings, growing research with men documents an association between IPV perpe-tration and STI/HIV risk (Decker et al., 2009; El-Bassel, Fontdevila, Gilbert, Voisin, Richman, & Pitchell, 2001; Raj, Santana, La Marche, Amaro, Cranston, & Silverman, 2006). Studies in South Asia and South Africa have demonstrated that male IPV perpetrators are significantly more likely to be infected with STIs or HIV and to have been clients of female sex workers compared to men who did not report perpetrating IPV (Decker, Miller, Kapur, Gupta, Raj, & Silverman, 2008; Dunkle et al., 2006; Silverman, Decker, Kapur, Gupta, & Raj, 2007). To date, however, research in the United States among males on IPV and STI/HIV risk is lacking. In one of the few studies conducted among men in the United States, Raj et al. (2008) found that IPV perpetration was significantly associated with recent STI/HIV diagnosis, unprotected anal sex, and buying sex; the sample in this study consisted of African American men presenting for clinical care in an urban setting. This finding was consistent with previous research conducted in the United States with predominantly Latino and African American male samples, which ascertained that male perpetrators of IPV were more likely to engage in unprotected sex (El-Bassel et al., 2001; Raj et al., 2006). Implica-tions from these studies support previous research that women experienc-ing IPV are at increased risk for HIV due to the risk posed by their abusive male partners.

VIOLENCE, PSYCHOLOGICAL DISORDERS, AND HIV RISK

The relationship between violence, co-occurring psychological disor-ders, and HIV risk is multidirectional and complex. Women with histories of gender-based violence (e.g., child sexual abuse, IPV) have been shown to experience increased risk for developing psychological disorders and symptoms of severe emotional distress including depression (Browne & Finkelhor, 1986; Burnam et al., 1988; Winfield, George, Swartz, & Blazer, 1990), post-traumatic stress disorder (PTSD; Engstrom, El-Bassel, Go, & Gilbert, 2008; Koopman et al., 2005), personality disorders and dissocia-tion (Breslau, Davis, Andreski, & Peterson, 1991; Winfield, George, Swartz, & Blazer, 1990), and substance use and abuse (Collins, Ellickson, Orlando, & Klein, 2005; El-Bassel et al., 2000). For many women, violence precedes mental health symptoms and substance abuse (Kilpatrick, Acierno, Resnick, Saunders, & Best, 1997); however, women also experi-ence violence subsequent to mental illness and substance use (RachBeisel, Scott, & Dixon, 1999).

Violence and co-occurring disorders have been shown to be associated with HIV risk factors among women (Dunkle, Jewkes, Brown, Gray, McIntryre, & Harlow, 2004; Latkin & Mandell, 1993; Maman et al., 2000). Those population subgroups at highest risk for HIV infection are often the same groups characterized by especially high rates of violence—for example, young women, women living in poverty, and those who use illegal drugs (Gielen et al., 2007). These women have a higher likelihood of contracting STDs, report less frequent condom use, have a greater engagement in sex work, and often experience co-occurring psychological disorders (Gilbert et al., 2000; Maman et al., 2000; Miller, 1999; Wingood & DiClemente, 1997).

Depression

The higher prevalence of depression in women relative to men (Kessler & Frank, 2000) and the association between gender-based violence and depression have been well documented (Burnam et al., 1988; Mullen, Martin, Anderson, Romans, & Herbison, 1993; Resnick, Kilpatrick, Dansky, Saunders, & Best, 1993; Winfield et al., 1990). In addition, depression has been associated with HIV drug and sexual risk behaviors among community samples comprising women (Morokoff et al., 2009), high-risk samples of ethnic minority women (Klein, Elifson, & Sterk, 2008; Sterk, Theall, & Elifson, 2006), and injection-drug-using women (Braine, Jarlais, Goldblatt, Zadoretzky, & Turner, 2005). Among drug users, depression has been found to discriminate between those who participate in HIV drug and sex risk behaviors and those who do not (Camacho et al., 1996; El-Bassel et al., 1997; Hartgers, Van den Hoek, Coutinho, & Van der Pligt, 1992). In addition, results from prospective studies with cohorts of drug users and young adults have linked depression to HIV risk behaviors, such as the frequency of injection, participation in sex work, and choosing risky sex partners (e.g., an intravenous drug user) over time (Latkin & Mandell, 1993; Stiffman, Dore, Earls, & Cunningham, 1992).

Depression increases HIV risk behaviors through a variety of mechanisms, including participation in self-destructive behaviors (e.g., sharing syringes with HIV-infected drug injectors, unprotected sex with HIV-infected partners) and increases drug-related risk behaviors (e.g., increased sexual risk taking related to drug use, sharing syringes, trading sex for drugs) (Browne & Finkelhor, 1986; Parillo, Freeman, Collier, & Young, 2001; Van der Kolk, Perry, & Herman, 1991). The proclivity to engage in high-risk drug and sex risk behaviors among depressed women may be directly connected to depression, given that depression affects women's overall sense of agency as evidenced by the ability to leave or keep oneself safe in a relationship due to the feelings of helplessness and hopelessness associated with depression.

Post-traumatic Stress Disorder

The associations between post-traumatic stress disorder (PTSD) and IPV, sexual gender-based violence, and history of childhood abuse among women is well documented (Brand, 2003; Breslau et al., 1991; Cortina &

Kubiak, 2006; Resnick et al., 1993; Winfield et al., 1990). Some evidence suggests that PTSD has a negative impact on adherence to treatment regimens among HIV-positive individuals with histories of gender-based violence and childhood trauma (Cohen, Alfonso, Hoffman, Milau, & Carrera, 2001; Whetten, Reif, Whetten, & Murphy-McMillan, 2008). As yet, however, little research has examined the relationship between PTSD and HIV drug and sex risk behavior.

Some research has focused on the relationship between PTSD and HIV risk among drug-using and incarcerated women. Plotzker, Metzger, and Holmes (2007) found that PTSD mediated the relationship between childhood sexual abuse and HIV drug and sex risk among a sample of women injection drug users. Roberts, Wechsberg, Zule, and Burroughs (2003) found that symptoms of PTSD were associated with higher sex risk among crack-abusing African American women. In a study of incarcerated women, PTSD was associated with increased sex risk behavior and prostitution practiced in the five years prior to incarceration (Hutton et al., 2001).

Several studies have documented the relationship between PTSD and increased drug use or substance use disorders among women with histories of gender-based violence (Brady, Dansky, Lewis-Hall, Williams, Panetta, & Herrera, 2002; Hien, Brady, Back, & Greenfield, 2009; McCauley, Amstadter, Danielson, Ruggiero, Kilpatrick, & Resnick, 2009; Sullivan & Holt, 2008). Thus PTSD may be especially important to consider among drug-using women at high risk for HIV. Self-medication to alleviate psychiatric symptoms associated with PTSD may represent a potent mechanism underlying HIV–drug risk behaviors among abused women.

Further research is needed to examine how symptoms of PTSD influence HIV drug and sex risk among women. Future HIV-prevention interventions should strongly consider including assessment and treatment of PTSD symptoms, especially among women with histories of gender-based violence and substance use disorders.

Substance Use and Abuse

The relevance of violence to substance use among women has also been well documented in the literature. Studies in the United States have found that women who are exposed to emotional, physical, and sexual intimate-partner gender-based violence are more likely to abuse alcohol and illicit substances, potentially as a coping mechanism (Beadnell et al., 2000; Gilbert et al., 2000; Wingood, DiClemente, & Raj, 2000).

The link between substance abuse and HIV can be attributed to two major mechanisms: exposure to a contaminated needle during intravenous drug use (IDU), and high-risk sexual behavior, such as unprotected sex (Leigh & Stall, 1993; Santibanez, Garfein, Swartzendruber, Purcell, Paxton, & Greenberg, 2006). Alcohol or drug use may place women at greater risk for HIV infection by decreasing their ability to make and implement informed decisions while under their influence (Clapper & Lipsitt, 1991; Nyamathi & Vasquez, 1989). For example, in a sample of women in drug treatment, those who reported recently experiencing IPV also reported low rates of condom use, reduced sexual decision-making power, and reduced motivation to use condoms compared to those who did not report IPV (El-Bassel et al., 2000). Also, women may be sexually assaulted or physically attacked in the process of obtaining or using drugs (Falck, Wang, Carlson, & Siegal, 2001; Goodman, Dutton, & Harris, 1995).

Together, a history of gender-based violence and resulting increased likelihood of substance use—both factors that are linked to increased sexual risk taking among women—appear likely to result in a multiplicative risk for HIV. For example, results from a longitudinal study among youth at high risk for HIV infection indicated that participants with a history of physical and sexual abuse reported even greater HIV–drug risk behaviors compared to those with no such gender-based violence histories (Cunningham, Stiffman, Doré, & Earls, 1994).

Other Mental Health Disorders

Persons with serious mental illness (e.g., schizophrenia, bipolar disorder, and other major chronic affective disorders) and personality disorders have disproportionate rates of HIV seroprevalence and risk behaviors (Carey, Carey, Maisto, Schroder, Vanable, & Gordon, 2004; Meade & Sikkema, 2005; Singh, Ochitill, Fernandez, & Ruiz, 2006). Reported estimates of HIV seroprevalence range from 4 percent to 23 percent among seriously mentally ill adults (Malow, Devieux, Martinez, Peipman, Lucenko, & Kalichman, 2006).

Factors associated with HIV risk among adults with serious mental illness include substance use, coerced sex, trading sex for money or goods, multiple sex partners, and sex with injection drug users (Otto-Salaj, Heckman, Stevenson, & Kelly, 1998). In a study of seriously mentally ill women, nearly two thirds had not used condoms during sexual intercourse in the past three months, more than two thirds had sex with multiple partners, and almost one third had been treated for a sexually transmitted infection in the past year (Randolph et al., 2007). Substance use disorders and history of abuse frequently co-occur among the seriously mentally ill and may exacerbate HIV risk behavior. For example, in a study of history of traumatic abuse (emotional, physical, and sexual) and HIV risk among severely mentally ill, substance-abusing adults, those with a history of abuse reported significantly greater lifetime and current psychiatric symptoms, recent unprotected sexual intercourse, and illegal drug use compared to their nonabused counterparts (Malow, Devieux, Martinez, et al., 2006). Among bipolar individuals with co-occurring substance use disorders, independent correlates of total HIV risk included recent manic episode, lower psychiatric severity, and greater drug severity (Meade, Graff, Griffin, & Weiss, 2008). Both bipolar and substance use disorders are associated with impulsivity, impaired judgment, and risk taking.

Although persons with personality disorders (e.g., borderline personality disorder, antisocial personality disorder) are disproportionately represented among those living with and at risk for HIV, research in this area is relatively sparse (Singh et al., 2006). Some research has focused on borderline personality disorder (BPD); it indicates that women with BPD are significantly more likely to have histories of gender-based violence than are women without such a diagnosis (Battle et al., 2004; Bradley, Jenei, & Westen, 2005; Sansone, Songer, & Miller, 2005). In turn, several characteristics of BPD overlap with HIV risk behaviors such as participation in self-damaging sex and drug use behaviors (American Psychiatric Association, 2000).

In addition, psychological dissociation, which is one of the possible symptoms of BPD, is hypothesized to lead to a numbing of responsiveness among women with a history of gender-based violence. Psychological dissociation may increase HIV risk among women with BPD and other psychological disorders in which dissociation can occur (e.g., PTSD). For example, women may sense that they cannot exercise control in a sexually risky situation and may activate dissociative coping mechanisms to protect their psychological or physical integrity in the short term rather than resist or experience physical or psychological violence (Walker, 2000).

Although the association between psychological disorders and HIV risk is relatively understudied, research consistently documents high HIV risk rates among women with depression, PTSD, and other serious mental illnesses. Moreover, substance use and history of gender-based violence frequently co-occur in persons with psychological disorders, further exacerbating HIV-related risk behaviors. Results from existing studies underscore the importance of addressing abuse history and substance use in HIV prevention interventions in this underserved, highly at risk population.

HIV BEHAVIORAL RISK-REDUCTION INTERVENTIONS

The description of interventions presented in this section is not intended as a definitive review of HIV behavioral risk-reduction interventions for all women, but rather as a sampling of interventions that have achieved some success in reducing risk behaviors among selected populations of women (e.g., drug-using women, women with histories of gender-based violence) in the United States. While the micro- and macro-level gender inequalities inherent in HIV transmission and risk-reduction interventions are certainly complex, in the interest of brevity this section highlights selected behaviorally focused interventions for reducing the risk of HIV in women that address gender issues, history of gender-based violence, and/or co-occurring substance use and psychological disorders.

Historically, HIV risk-reduction interventions were grounded in frameworks that focused on individual factors and did not consider the gendered dynamics of sexual behaviors and risk-reduction negotiation (Amaro, 1995). The exclusion of women's unique needs has prompted funding agencies to issue a call for the development of effective behavioral interventions to combat the spread of HIV and the development of gender-tailored interventions (National Institutes of Health and Office of AIDS Research, 2009b). As a result, in recent years, gender-specific interventions that integrate the role of power dynamics in sexual negotiation and HIV risk reduction have emerged (Amaro, Dai, et al., 2007; DiClemente & Wingood, 1995; El-Bassel et al., 2003; Lauby, Smith, Stark, Person, & Adams, 2000; Wingood et al., 2004; Wyatt et al., 2004). Based on this growing body of empirical evidence, it is recommended that HIV prevention interventions for women be developed within a sociocultural framework and address the psychological distress and gender-related violence that often increase women's risk of HIV infection.

Published reviews of U.S.-based HIV risk-reduction interventions that have targeted women have underscored the importance of utilizing culturally relevant theory- and gender-tailored curricula (Amaro, Raj, & Reed, 2001; Crepaz et al., 2009; Logan, Cole, & Leukefeld, 2002; Raj, Amaro, Reed, Kazarian, & Evans, 2001). Logan and colleagues (2002) conducted a review of the literature on social and contextual factors that contribute to HIV risk and a meta-analysis of HIV behavioral prevention interventions that targeted adult heterosexual women. According to this meta-analysis, the interventions demonstrated time-limited effectiveness in reducing risky sexual behavior. The authors recommend that interventions should be more comprehensive, incorporate methods of female-controlled sexual protection (e.g., microbicides), and attempt to influence social and cultural norms regarding sex. They noted that while the majority of interventions were grounded in theory, none of the commonly used interventions relied on theories that were gender relevant. In a meta-analysis of HIV/STI behavioral interventions for African American women in the United States, Crepaz et al. (2009) noted that greater intervention efficacy was observed in studies that used gender- or cultural-specific materials and addressed empowerment issues. The results from these meta-analyses underscore the importance of developing culturally relevant curricula that address gender and empowerment in HIV prevention interventions for heterosexual women in the United States. As yet, however, it has not become common practice to include these issues in behavioral interventions designed for women.

The CDC, in partnership with the Academy for Educational Development (AED) Center on AIDS and Community Health (COACH), has identified several scientifically proven effective HIV prevention interventions for women that are included in the Diffusion of Effective Behavioral Interventions (DEBI) project (CDC and AED, 2009). [See also Lyles et al. (2007) for a list of best-evidence HIV behavioral interventions.] The goal of the DEBI project is to enhance the capacity to implement effective, science-based, community, group, and individual interventions at the state and local levels to reduce the spread of HIV and STDs (CDC and AED, 2009). However, only a few of the best-evidence interventions for women specifically address issues of gender and power.

One example of a HIV-prevention intervention grounded in theory and gender-relevant concepts included in the DEBI project is the Women's Health Promotion (WHP) program. The WHP program was tailored for Spanish- speaking, heterosexual, HIV negative Latina women. Developed by Raj, Amaro, and colleagues (2001) and based on the tenets of social cognitive theory, the theory of reasoned action, and the health belief model within a gender context, this intervention sought to reduce risky sexual behavior. Unique features of the study were early and sustained collaboration with community leaders in the development and implementation of the intervention and a focus on partner communication, mental health, and social justice. Findings from the evaluation of this program indicated that women in the WHP group demonstrated substantial increases in condom use at the three-month follow-up compared to women in the wait-list control group.

Other DEBI project interventions that specifically address gender and power issues unique to women include El-Bassel et al.'s (2003) HIV-prevention intervention for heterosexual women and their main partners (CONNECT), DiClemente and Wingood's (1995) program for African American women based on the theory of gender and power (SISTA), and Sterk, Theall, and Elifson's (2003) female and culturally specific negotiation intervention for African American female drug injectors and crack cocaine smokers. The CDC (2009) website provides a complete listing of the best-evidence interventions.

BRIDGING THE GAP: ADDRESSING VIOLENCE AND PSYCHOSOCIAL DISTRESS

It is not uncommon for women—especially those with few social and material resources—to suffer the ills of gender-based violence alone and to cope with resultant psychological distress with unhealthy strategies, including substance use and risky sexual behaviors. HIV risk-reduction interventions that have addressed violence and psychological symptoms have demonstrated success in reducing psychological distress and HIV-risky behaviors.

Wyatt and colleagues (2004) developed the U.S.-based Enhanced Sexual Health Intervention (ESHI), a community-integrated behavioral prevention intervention for 147 African American and Latina HIV-positive women with histories of childhood sexual abuse. Using a randomized design guided by cognitive behavioral approaches incorporating cultural and gender-specific concepts, the ESHI sought to increase safe-sex behaviors, medication adherence, and psychological functioning. The curriculum highlighted three culturally related themes: interconnectedness, body awareness, and sexual ownership. The impact of CSA on personal decision making was emphasized throughout the sessions as an important connection between past traumatic experiences, HIV infection, and current functioning. Essential components of CSA treatment were included, such as short-term trauma-focused groups and peer modeling of disclosure, with a focus on tension reduction, normalization of CSA sequelae, and affect regulation. While only results from a pre- and post-test comparison have been published, these preliminary findings showed improvements in medication adherence and psychological distress at immediate follow-up and at six months' follow-up (Wyatt et al., 2004).

Using data from the Boston study site of the Women, Co-Occurring Disorders and Violence Study (WCDVS), Amaro, Larson, and colleagues (2007) examined whether an intervention that addressed trauma symptoms would reduce unprotected sex among women with co-occurring psychiatric and substance use disorders and a history of sexual or physical abuse. Women in the comparison group received standard treatment for substance abuse. Those in the intervention group participated in the Trauma Recovery and Empowerment Model (TREM)—a series of 25 psycho-educational group sessions that addressed trauma, empowerment and coping skills, safety, and increasing awareness of the association between substance abuse, mental health problems, and trauma. This intervention was augmented with components on sexual negotiation with partners and sexual safety (El-Bassel & Schilling, 1992). Women in the comparison group had 2.8 times the likelihood of having had unprotected sex at 6 months' follow-up relative to the women in the intervention group. At 12 months' follow-up, women in the intervention group continued to demonstrate reduced sexual risk behaviors relative to the control group. Moreover, at 12 months' follow-up, women in the comparison group were 4.5 times more likely to have engaged in unprotected sex than women in the intervention group. Among women in recent relationships, those with higher relationship power scores were less likely to engage in unprotected sex than women with lower scores.

Taken together, these results indicate that a comprehensive intervention addressing trauma history and psychological distress symptoms in substance abuse treatment is effective in reducing long-term, high-risk sexual behaviors. The finding that increased relationship power reduced unprotected sex indicates that relationship power, including economic skills, should be addressed in HIV risk-reduction interventions with women. Further, the intervention also produced other related advantages over standard substance abuse treatment, include ng significantly greater reductions in psychological distress symptoms and drug abstinence (Amaro, Dai, et al., 2007) and increased length of treatment stay (Amaro, Chernoff, Brown, Arevalo, & Gatz, 2007).

Economic and social empowerment interventions aimed at reducing IPV and HIV infection rates among women, which have been used primarily outside the United States, have also demonstrated remarkable success. Pronyk and colleagues (2006) tested whether a microfinance-based intervention that emphasized HIV risk and prevention, gender norms, sexuality, and IPV would result in improved economic well-being, empowerment, and reductions in IPV among rural South African women. Using a cluster-randomized trial design, the Intervention with Microfinance for AIDS and Gender Equity (IMAGE) project integrated a microfinance component that consisted of a savings and credit program that gave loans to women and a participatory learning program that was gender focused. The Sisters-for-Life component consisted of two phases: (1) 10 one-hour training sessions that addressed gender and cultural norms, relationship communication, IPV, and HIV risk and (2) a wider community mobilization phase that incorporated community leaders to educate women. The authors found that although the intervention did not decrease unprotected sexual intercourse with nonspousal partners, women in the intervention group experienced reductions in physical or sexual IPV in the past year by greater than half compared to women in the control group. Findings from this study and similar trials that have been conducted in Asia (Ramsay, Rivas, & Feder, 2005) demonstrate that women's empowerment and economic literacy, when combined with a culturally tailored curriculum and community involvement, can demonstrably reduce IPV among women.

In summary, incorporating concepts of gender pride and empowerment within relevant sociocultural contexts can be helpful in HIV behavioral risk-reduction interventions for women. To broaden the impact of such interventions for women with histories of abuse, programs should routinely screen for gender-based violence and incorporate treatment for trauma. Also, given the well-documented impact of male-perpetrated IPV on women's HIV risk, further research is needed to develop and evaluate interventions with male partners and couples. El-Bassel and colleagues (2003) have demonstrated that couples-based HIV interventions can be successful so long as precautions are taken to ensure women's safety. Women with abusive partners are not only at increased risk for HIV as a result of reduced sexual decision-making power common to relationships characterized by IPV, but also as a result of being with a partner who is more likely to engage in behaviors associated with greater risk of HIV infection (Decker et al., 2009; El-Bassel et al., 2001; Raj et al., 2006, 2008).

CONCLUSION AND FUTURE DIRECTIONS

Since the beginning of the HIV/AIDS epidemic in the United States, when women accounted for only a small proportion of those diagnosed with AIDS, the proportion of women with AIDS and living with HIV has significantly increased. Initially, HIV prevention was based largely on approaches that did not address gender dynamics in transmission of HIV. More recently, however, increased attention to specific barriers and the context of HIV infection in women has resulted in research that has documented the role of violence as a factor that contributes to women's risk of HIV infection. More specifically, interventions that integrate the role of violence in women's lives have emerged and appear promising. It has become evident that especially for women with a history of abuse, HIV intervention approaches need to address issues of trauma and relationship power as risk factors that can directly affect women's ability to engage in sexually protective behaviors with their male partners. Advances have also been made in the articulation of gender-specific theoretical frameworks for reduction of HIV risk in women.

It is also evident that important gaps continue to exist in our understanding of the causal relationship between history of abuse and HIV risk behaviors and HIV infection, as well as in the development of interventions to reduce HIV risk in women with a history of abuse and/or trauma. In the area of interventions, for example, studies utilizing more diverse and larger samples are needed to test the complex relationships in intervention efficacy. Similarly, longer follow-up periods are needed as part of studies, so that researchers can assess the lasting effects of interventions with this population. Interventions that test the effectiveness of community-based approaches and economic policy interventions are also needed. Emerging research on microfinance as a means of improving women's social status and sexual health agency may prove helpful in the United States, as it has been in international settings (Pronyk et al., 2006; Swendeman, Basu, Das, Jana, & Rotheram-Borus, 2009). In addition, studies that test culturally tailored and language-appropriate interventions with various demographic, clinical, and cultural groups will be important, given that as the populations most disproportionately affected by HIV/AIDS are often the most disenfranchised.

There is also much work that needs to be done with respect to implementation of efficacious approaches to prevention of HIV infection in women with a history of abuse. For example, the use of screening tools to assess violence exposure in women and HIV risk needs to be integrated consistently through health and social services as well as in substance abuse and mental health treatment settings. Training of front-line health and social service providers will be a critical component of identification and appropriate referral and intervention with women at risk. Further, mechanisms for broad dissemination and implementation of efficacious approaches will need to be developed so that advances in the science of prevention of HIV can be translated into programs for women with a history of abuse, both to benefit those women and to reduce the risk of HIV in communities most affected by HIV/AIDS and violence toward women.

SUMMARY

A wealth of literature has documented the devastating effects of violence against women on women's health and the recognition that violence against women is both a consequence and a cause of gender inequality (World Helath Organization, 2005). For many women, HIV infection is one of those health consequences. To be effective in the long run, interventions to reduce the risk of HIV infection in women must address gender-based violence and gender inequity as important underlying interpersonal dynamics. Individual interventions have an important role in HIV prevention; however, socially based gender inequities will also need to be addressed through larger social programs, economic interventions, and policies.

ACKNOWLEDGMENTS

Monica D. Ulibarri was supported in part by grants from the National Institute of Mental Health (R01 MH65849-S1) and the National Institute on Drug Abuse Center for HIV/AIDS Minority Pipeline in Substance Abuse Research (R25 DA025571). Lekeisha A. Sumner received support from the National Institute of Mental Health–funded Grant Collaborative Center for Trauma and Mental Health Disparities (CCTMHD) 1P50MH073453: 010A1, the Pittsburgh Mind–Body Center (PMBC; NIH grants HL076852/076858), the University of California–Los Angeles (UCLA) AIDS Institute, and the UCLA Center for AIDS Research (AI28697). Ajitha Cyriac was supported by the Canadian Institutes for Health Research (Institute of Infection and Immunity), Doctoral Research Award (IDR147157). The authors would like to thank Anita Raj from Boston University School of Public Health and Liz Reed from George Washington University for their comments and suggestions on previous drafts of this chapter.

REFERENCES

Amaro, H. (1995). Love, sex, and power: Considering women's realities in HIV prevention. *American Psychologist, 50*(6), 437–447.
Amaro, H., Chernoff, M., Brown, V., Arevalo, S., & Gatz, M. (2007). Does integrated trauma-informed substance abuse treatment increase treatment retention? *Journal of Community Psychology, 35,* 845–862.

Amaro, H., Dai, J., Arevalo, S., Acevedo, A., Matsumoto, A., Nieves, R., et al. (2007). Effects of integrated trauma treatment on outcomes in a racially/ethnically diverse sample of women in urban community-based substance abuse treatment. *Journal of Urban Health: Bulletin of the New York Academy of Medicine, 84*(4), 508–522.

Amaro, H., Larson, M. J., Zhang, A., Acevedo, A., Dai, J., & Matsumoto, A. (2007). Effects of trauma intervention on HIV sexual risk behaviors among women with co-occurring disorders in substance abuse treatment. *Journal of Community Psychology, 35*(7), 895–908.

Amaro, H., & Raj, A. (2000). On the margin: Power and women's HIV risk reduction strategies. *Sex Roles, 42*(7), 723–749.

Amaro, H., Raj, A., & Reed, E. (2001). Women's sexual health: The need for feminist analyses in public health in the Decade of Behavior. *Psychology of Women Quarterly, 25*(4), 324–334.

American Psychiatric Association. (2000). *Diagnostic and statistical manual of mental disorders* (4th ed., text revision ed.). Washington, DC: Author.

Arriola, K. R., Louden, T., Doldren, M. A., & Fortenberry, R. M. (2005). A meta-analysis of the relationship of child sexual abuse to HIV risk behavior among women. *Child Abuse & Neglect, 29*(6), 725–746.

Battle, C. L., Shea, M. T., Johnson, D. M., Yen, S., Zlotnick, C., Zanarini, M. C., et al. (2004). Childhood maltreatment associated with adult personality disorders: Findings from the collaborative longitudinal personality disorders study. *Journal of Personality Disorders, 18*(2), 193–211.

Beadnell, B., Baker, S. A., Morrison, D. M., & Knox, K. (2000). HIV/STD risk factors for women with violent male partners. *Sex Roles, 42*(7), 661–689.

Beitchman, J. H., Zucker, K. J., Hood, J. E., & DaCosta, G. A. (1992). A review of the long-term effects of child sexual abuse. *Child Abuse & Neglect, 16*(1), 101–118.

Bensley, L. S., Eenwyk, J. V., & Simmons, K. W. (2000). Self-reported childhood sexual and physical abuse and adult HIV-risk behaviors and heavy drinking. *American Journal of Preventive Medicine, 18*(2), 151–158.

Bradley, R., Jenei, J., & Westen, D. (2005). Etiology of borderline personality disorder: Disentangling the contributions of intercorrelated antecedents. *Journal of Nervous and Mental Disease, 193*(1), 24–31.

Brady, K. T., Dansky, B. S., Lewis-Hall, F., Williams, T. S., Panetta, J. A., & Herrera, J. M. (2002). Effects of victimization and posttraumatic stress disorder on substance use disorders in women. In *Psychiatric illness in women: Emerging treatments and research.* (pp. 449–466). Arlington, VA: American Psychiatric Publishing.

Braine, N., Jarlais, D. C. D., Goldblatt, C., Zadoretzky, C., & Turner, C. (2005). HIV risk behavior among amphetamine injectors at U.S. syringe exchange programs. *AIDS Education and Prevention, 17*(6), 515–524.

Brand, B. (2003). Trauma and women. *Psychiatric Clinics of North America, 26*(3), 759–779.

Breslau, N., Davis, G. C., Andreski, P., & Peterson, E. (1991). Traumatic events and posttraumatic stress disorder in an urban population of young adults. *Archives of General Psychiatry, 48*(3), 216–222.

Bronfenbrenner, U. (1979). *The ecology of human development: Experiments by nature and design.* Cambridge, MA: Harvard University Press.

Browne, A., & Finkelhor, D. (1986). Impact of sexual abuse: A review of the research. *Psychological Bulletin, 99*, 66–77.

Browne, A., Finkelhor, D., Chess, S., Thomas, A., & Hertzig, M. (1988). Impact of child sexual abuse: A review of the research. In S. Chess (Ed.), *Annual progress in child psychiatry and child development, 1987* (pp. 555–584). Philadelphia: Brunner/Mazel.

Burnam, M. A., Stein, J. A., Golding, J. M., Siegel, J. M., Sorenson, S. B., Forsythe, A. B., et al. (1988). Sexual assault and mental disorders in a community population. *Journal of Consulting and Clinical Psychology, 56*(6), 843–850.

Camacho, L. M., Brown, B. S., & Simpson, D. D. (1996). Psychological dysfunction and HIV/AIDS risk behavior. *Journal of Acquired Immune Deficiency Syndromes and Human Retrovirology, 11*(2), 198–202.

Campbell, J. C., Baty, M. L., Ghandour, R. M., Stockman, J. K., Francisco, L., & Wagman, J. (2008). The intersection of intimate partner violence against women and HIV/AIDS: A review. *International Journal of Injury Control and Safety Promotion, 15*(4), 221–231.

Carey, M. P., Carey, K. B., Maisto, S. A., Schroder, K. E. E., Vanable, P. A., & Gordon, C. M. (2004). HIV risk behavior among psychiatric outpatients: Association with psychiatric disorder, substance use disorder, and gender. *Journal of Nervous and Mental Disease, 192*(4), 289–296.

Centers for Disease Control and Prevention (CDC). (2007). HIV/AIDS surveillance in women. Retrieved September 10, 2009, from http://www.cdc.gov/hiv/topics/surveillance/resources/slides/women/index.htm.

Centers for Disease Control and Prevention (CDC). (2008). HIV/AIDS among women. *CDC HIV/AIDS Fact Sheet.* http://www.cdc.gov/hiv/topics/women/resources/factsheets/women.htm.

Centers for Disease Control and Prevention (CDC). (2009). Best-evidence interventions. Retrieved September 15, 2009, from http://www.cdc.gov/hiv/topics/research/prs/best-evidence-intervention.htm.

Centers for Disease Control and Prevention (CDC) & Academy for Educational Development (AED). (2009). The Diffusion of Effective Behavioral Interventions (DEBI) project. Retrieved September 15, 2009, from http://www.effectiveinterventions.org/.

Clapper, R. L., & Lipsitt, L. P. (1991). A retrospective study of risk-taking and alcohol-mediated unprotected intercourse. *Journal of Substance Abuse, 3*(1), 91–96.

Cohen, M. A., Alfonso, C. A., Hoffman, R. G., Milau, V., & Carrera, G. (2001). The impact of PTSD on treatment adherence in persons with HIV infection. *General Hospital Psychiatry, 23*(5), 294–296.

Collins, R. L., Ellickson, P. L., Orlando, M., & Klein, D. J. (2005). Isolating the nexus of substance use, violence and sexual risk for HIV infection among young adults in the United States. *AIDS and Behavior, 9*(1), 73–87.

Connell, R. W. (1987). *Gender and power: Society, the person and sexual politics.* Palo Alto, CA: Stanford University Press.

Cortina, L. M., & Kubiak, S. P. (2006). Gender and posttraumatic stress: Sexual violence as an explanation for women's increased risk. *Journal of Abnormal Psychology, 115*(4), 753–759.

Crepaz, N., Marshall, K. J., Aupont, L. W., Jacobs, E. D., Mizuno, Y., Kay, L. S., et al. (2009). The efficacy of HIV/STI behavioral interventions for African American females in the United States: A meta-analysis. *American Journal of Public Health, 99*(11), 2069–2078.

Cunningham, R. M., Stiffman, A. R., Doré, P., & Earls, F. (1994). The association of physical and sexual abuse with HIV risk behaviors in adolescence and young adulthood: Implications for public health. *Child Abuse & Neglect, 18*(3), 233–245.

Decker, M. R., Miller, E., Kapur, N. A., Gupta, J., Raj, A., & Silverman, J. G. (2008). Intimate partner violence and sexually transmitted disease symptoms in a national sample of married Bangladeshi women. *International Journal of Gynaecology and Obstetrics, 100*(1), 18–23.

Decker, M. R., Seage, G. R., Hemenway, D., Raj, A., Saggurti, N., Balaiah, D., et al. (2009). Intimate partner violence functions as both a risk marker and risk factor for women's HIV infection: Findings from Indian husband–wife dyads. *Journal of Acquired Immune Deficiency Syndromes, 51*(5), 593–600.

Decker, M. R., Silverman, J. G., & Raj, A. (2005). Dating violence and sexually transmitted disease/HIV testing and diagnosis among adolescent females. *Pediatrics, 116*(2), e272–e276.

DiClemente, R. J., & Wingood, G. M. (1995). A randomized controlled trial of an HIV sexual risk-reduction intervention for young African-American women. *Journal of the American Medical Association, 274*(16), 1271–1276.

Dude, A. (2007). Intimate partner violence and increased lifetime risk of sexually transmitted infection among women in Ukraine. *Studies in Family Planning, 38*(2), 89–100.

Dunkle, K. L., Jewkes, R. K., Brown, H. C., Gray, G. E., McIntryre, J. A., & Harlow, S. D. (2004). Gender-based violence, relationship power, and risk of HIV infection in women attending antenatal clinics in South Africa. *Lancet, 363* (9419), 1415–1421.

Dunkle, K. L., Jewkes, R. K., Nduna, M., Levin, J., Jama, N., Khuzwayo, N., et al. (2006). Perpetration of partner violence and HIV risk behaviour among young men in the rural Eastern Cape, South Africa. *AIDS, 20*(16), 2107–2114.

El-Bassel, N., Fontdevila, J., Gilbert, L., Voisin, D., Richman, B. L., & Pitchell, P. (2001). HIV risks of men in methadone maintenance treatment programs who abuse their intimate partners: A forgotten issue. *Journal of Substance Abuse, 13*(1), 29–43.

El-Bassel, N., Gilbert, L., Rajah, V., Foleno, A., & Frye, V. (2000). Fear and violence: Raising the HIV stakes. *AIDS Education and Prevention, 12*(2), 154–170.

El-Bassel, N., Gilbert, L., Wu, E., Chang, M., Gomes, C., Vinocur, D., et al. (2007). Intimate partner violence prevalence and HIV risks among women receiving care in emergency departments: Implications for IPV and HIV screening. *Emergency Medicine Journal, 24*(4), 255–259.

El-Bassel, N., Gilbert, L., Wu, E., Go, H., & Hill, J. (2005). HIV and intimate partner violence among methadone-maintained women in New York City. *Social Science & Medicine, 61*(1), 171–183.

El-Bassel, N., & Schilling, R.F. (1992). 15-month follow-up of women methadone patients taught skills to reduce heterosexual HIV transmission. *Public Health Reports, 107*(5), 500–504.

El-Bassel, N., Schilling, R. F., Irwin, K. L., Faruque, S., Gilbert, L., Von Bargen, J., et al. (1997). Sex trading and psychological distress among women recruited from the streets of Harlem. *American Journal of Public Health, 87*(1), 66–70.

El-Bassel, N., Witte, S. S., Gilbert, L., Wu, E., Chang, M., Hill, J., et al. (2003). The efficacy of a relationship-based HIV/STD prevention program for heterosexual couples. *American Journal of Public Health, 93*(6), 963–969.

Engstrom, M., El-Bassel, N., Go, H., & Gilbert, L. (2008). Childhood sexual abuse and intimate partner violence among women in methadone treatment: A direct or mediated relationship? *Journal of Family Violence, 23*(7), 605–617.

Falck, R. S., Wang, J., Carlson, R. G., & Siegal, H. A. (2001). The epidemiology of physical attack and rape among crack-using women. *Violence and Victims, 16*(1), 79–89.

Gielen, A. C., Ghandour, R. M., Burke, J. G., Mahoney, P., McDonnell, K. A., & O'Campo, P. (2007). HIV/AIDS and intimate partner violence: Intersecting women's health issues in the United States. *Trauma, Violence, & Abuse, 8*(2), 178–198.

Gilbert, L., El-Bassel, N., Rajah, V., Foleno, A., Fontdevila, J., Frye, V., et al. (2000). The converging epidemics of mood-altering-drug use, HIV, HCV, and partner violence: A conundrum for methadone maintenance treatment. *Mount Sinai Journal of Medicine, New York, 67*(5–6), 452–464.

Gonzalez-Guarda, R. M., Peragallo, N., Urrutia, M. T., Vasquez, E. P., & Mitrani, V. B. (2008). HIV risks, substance abuse, and intimate partner violence among Hispanic women and their intimate partners. *Journal of the Association of Nurses in AIDS Care, 19*(4), 252–266.

Goodman, L. A., Dutton, M. A., & Harris, M. (1995). Episodically homeless women with serious mental illness: Prevalence of physical and sexual assault. *American Journal of Orthopsychiatry, 65*(4), 468–478.

Goodman, L. A., Koss, M. P., Fitzgerald, L. F., Russo, N. F., & Keita, G. P. (1993). Male violence against women: Current research and future directions. *American Psychologist, 48*(10), 1054–1058.

Goodman, L. A., Koss, M. P., & Russo, N. F. (1993). Violence against women: Physical and mental health effects: II. Research findings. *Applied & Preventive Psychology, 2*(2), 79–89.

Hartgers, C., Van den Hoek, J. A., Coutinho, R. A., & Van der Pligt, J. (1992). Psychopathology, stress and HIV-risk injecting behaviour among drug users. *British Journal of Addiction, 87*(6), 857–865.

Herbst, J. H., Kay, L. S., Passin, W. F., Lyles, C. M., Crepaz, N., & Marín, B. V. (2007). A systematic review and meta-analysis of behavioral interventions to reduce HIV risk behaviors of Hispanics in the United States and Puerto Rico. *AIDS and Behavior, 11*(1), 25–47.

Hien, D., Brady, K. T., Back, S. E., & Greenfield, S. F. (2009). Trauma, posttraumatic stress disorder, and addiction among women In K. Brady, S. Back & S. Greenfield (Eds.), *Women and addiction: A comprehensive handbook* (pp. 242–256). New York: Guilford Press.

Hutton, H. E., Treisman, G. J., Hunt, W. R., Fishman, M., Kendig, N., Swetz, A., et al. (2001). HIV risk behaviors and their relationship to posttraumatic stress disorder among women prisoners. *Psychiatric Services, 52*(4), 508–513.

Jewkes, R. K., Levin, J. B., & Penn-Kekana, L. A. (2003). Gender inequalities, intimate partner violence and HIV preventive practices: Findings of a South African cross-sectional study. *Social Science & Medicine, 56*(1), 125–134.

Johnsen, L. W., & Harlow, L. L. (1996). Childhood sexual abuse linked with adult substance use, victimization, and AIDS risk. *AIDS Education and Prevention, 8*(1), 44–57.

Kessler, R. C., & Frank, E. (2000). Gender differences in major depression: Epidemiological findings. In E. Franks (Ed.), *Gender and its effects on psychopathology* (pp. 61–84). Arlington, VA: American Psychiatric Publishing.

Kilpatrick, D. G., Acierno, R., Resnick, H. S., Saunders, B. E., & Best, C. L. (1997). A 2-year longitudinal analysis of the relationships between violent assault and substance use in women. *Journal of Consulting and Clinical Psychology, 65* (5), 834–847.

Klein, H., Elifson, K. W., & Sterk, C. E. (2008). Depression and HIV risk behavior practices among at risk women. *Women & Health, 48*(2), 167–188.

Koopman, C., Palesh, O., Marten, B., Thompson, B., Ismailji, T., Holmes, D., et al. (2005). Child abuse and adult interpersonal trauma as predictors of post-traumatic stress disorder symptoms among women seeking treatment for intimate partner violence. In *Focus on posttraumatic stress disorder research* (pp. 1–16). Hauppauge, NY: Nova Science.

Latkin, C. A., & Mandell, W. (1993). Depression as an antecedent of frequency of intravenous drug use in an urban, nontreatment sample. *International Journal of the Addictions, 28*(14), 1601–1612.

Lauby, J. L., Smith, P. J., Stark, M., Person, B., & Adams, J. (2000). A community-level HIV prevention intervention for inner-city women: Results of the women and infants demonstration projects. *American Journal of Public Health, 90*(2), 216–222.

Leigh, B. C., & Stall, R. (1993). Substance use and risky sexual behavior for exposure to HIV: Issues in methodology, interpretation, and prevention. *American Psychologist, 48*(10), 1035–1045.

Logan, T. K., Cole, J., & Leukefeld, C. (2002). Women, sex, and HIV: Social and con-textual factors, meta-analysis of published interventions, and implications for practice and research. *Psychological Bulletin, 128*(6), 851–885.

Lyles, C. M., Kay, L. S., Crepaz, N., Herbst, J. H., Passin, W. F., Kim, A. S., et al. (2007). Best-evidence interventions: Findings from a systematic review of HIV behavioral interventions for US populations at high risk, 2000–2004. *American Journal of Public Health, 97*(1), 133–143.

Malow, R. M., Devieux, J. G., & Lucenko, B. A. (2006). History of childhood sexual abuse as a risk factor for HIV risk behavior. *Journal of Psychological Trauma, 5*(3), 13–32.

Malow, R. M., Devieux, J. G., Martinez, L., Peipman, F., Lucenko, B. A., & Kalichman, S. C. (2006). History of traumatic abuse and HIV risk behaviors in severely mentally ill substance abusing adults. *Journal of Family Violence, 21*(2), 127–135.

Maman, S., Campbell, J., Sweat, M. D., & Gielen, A. C. (2000). The intersections of HIV and violence: Directions for future research and interventions. *Social Science & Medicine, 50*(4), 459–478.

Marin, A., & Russo, N. F. (2003). Feminist perspectives on male violence against women. In M. Coleman & L. Ganong (Eds.), *Points and counterpoints: Controversial relationship and family issues in the 21st century (an anthology)* (pp. 97–105). Los Angeles, CA: Roxbury.

McCauley, J. L., Amstadter, A. B., Danielson, C. K., Ruggiero, K. J., Kilpatrick, D. G., & Resnick, H. S. (2009). Mental health and rape history in relation to non-medical use of prescription drugs in a national sample of women. *Addictive Behaviors, 34*(8), 641–648.

Meade, C. S., Graff, F. S., Griffin, M. L., & Weiss, R. D. (2008). HIV risk behavior among patients with co-occurring bipolar and substance use disorders: Associations with mania and drug abuse. *Drug and Alcohol Dependence, 92*(1), 296–300.

Meade, C. S., & Sikkema, K. J. (2005). Voluntary HIV testing among adults with severe mental illness: Frequency and associated factors. *AIDS and Behavior, 9*(4), 465–473.

Miller, M. (1999). A model to explain the relationship between sexual abuse and HIV risk among women. *AIDS Care, 11*(1), 3–20.

Morokoff, P. J., Redding, C. A., Harlow, L. L., Cho, S., Rossi, J. S., Meier, K. S., et al. (2009). Associations of sexual victimization, depression, and sexual assertiveness with unprotected sex: A test of the multifaceted model of HIV risk across gender. *Journal of Applied Biobehavioral Research, 14*(1), 30–54.

Mullen, P. E., Martin, J. L., Anderson, J. C., Romans, S. E., & Herbison, G. P. (1993). Childhood sexual abuse and mental health in adult life. *British Journal of Psychiatry: Journal of Mental Science, 163*, 721–732.

National Center for Injury Prevention and Control. (2009). WISQARS leading causes of death reports 1999–2004. Retrieved Septemer 10, 2009, from http://webapp.cdc.gov/sasweb/ncipc/leadcaus10.html.

National Institutes of Health and Office of AIDS Research. (2009a). Fiscal year 2009 trans-NIH olan for HIV-related research. Retrieved February 19, 2008, from www.oar.nih.gov/public/pubs/fy2009/Preface.pdf.

National Institutes of Health and Office of AIDS Research. (2009b). Fiscal year 2010 trans-NIH plan for HIV-related research Retrieved September 14, 2009, from www.oar.nih.gov.

Newcomb, M. D., Locke, T. F., & Goodyear, R. K. (2003). Childhood experiences and psychosocial influences on HIV risk among adolescent Latinas in Southern California. *Cultural Diversity and Ethnic Minority Psychology, 9*(3), 219–235.

Nyamathi, A., & Vasquez, R. (1989). Impact of poverty, homelessness, and drugs on Hispanic women at risk for HIV infection. *Hispanic Journal of Behavioral Sciences, 11*(4), 299–314.

Otto-Salaj, L. L., Heckman, T. G., Stevenson, L. Y., & Kelly, J. A. (1998). Patterns, predictors and gender differences in HIV risk among severely mentally ill men and women. *Community Mental Health Journal, 34*(2), 175–190.

Panchanadeswaran, S., Johnson, S. C., Sivaram, S., Srikrishnan, A. K., Latkin, C., Bentley, M. E., et al. (2008). Intimate partner violence is as important as client violence in increasing street-based female sex workers' vulnerability to HIV in India. *International Journal on Drug Policy, 19*(2), 106–112.

Parillo, K. M., Freeman, R. C., Collier, K., & Young, P. (2001). Association between early sexual abuse and adult HIV-risky sexual behaviors among community-recruited women. *Child Abuse & Neglect, 25*(3), 335–346.

Plotzker, R. E., Metzger, D. S., & Holmes, W. C. (2007). Childhood sexual and physical abuse histories, PTSD, depression, and HIV risk outcomes in women injection drug users: A potential mediating pathway. *American Journal on Addictions, 16*(6), 431–438.

Polusny, M. A., & Follette, V. M. (1995). Long-term correlates of child sexual abuse: Theory and review of the empirical literature. *Applied & Preventive Psychology, 4*(3), 143–166.

Pronyk, P. M., Hargreaves, J. R., Kim, J. C., Morison, L. A., Phetla, G., Watts, C., et al. (2006). Effect of a structural intervention for the prevention of intimate-partner violence and HIV in rural South Africa: A cluster randomised trial. *Lancet, 368*(9551), 1973–1983.

Pulerwitz, J., Amaro, H., De Jong, W., Gortmaker, S. L., & Rudd, R. (2002). Relationship power, condom use and HIV risk among women in the USA. *AIDS Care, 14*(6), 789–800.

Pulerwitz, J., Gortmaker, S. L., & DeJong, W. (2000). Measuring sexual relationship power in HIV/STD research. *Sex Roles, 42*(7), 637–660.

RachBeisel, J., Scott, J., & Dixon, L. (1999). Co-occurring severe mental illness and substance use disorders: A review of recent research. *Psychiatric Services, 50*(11), 1427–1434.

Raj, A., Amaro, H., Cranston, K., Martin, B., Cabral, H., Navarro, A., et al. (2001). Is a general women's health promotion program as effective as an HIV-intensive prevention program in reducing HIV risk among Hispanic women? *Public Health Reports (Washington, DC: 1974), 116*(6), 599–607.

Raj, A., Amaro, H., Reed, E., Kazarian, S. S., & Evans, D. R. (2001). Culturally tailoring HIV/AIDS prevention programs: Why, when, and how. In S. Kazanan & D. Evans (Eds.), *Handbook of cultural health psychology* (pp. 195–239). San Diego, CA: Academic Press.

Raj, A., Reed, E., Welles, S. L., Santana, M. C., & Silverman, J. G. (2008). Intimate partner violence perpetration, risky sexual behavior, and STI/HIV diagnosis among heterosexual African American men. *American Journal of Men's Health, 2*(3), 291–295.

Raj, A., Santana, C., La Marche, A., Amaro, H., Cranston, K., & Silverman, J. G. (2006). Perpetration of intimate partner violence associated with sexual risk behaviors among young adult men. *American Journal of Public Health, 96*(10), 1873–1878.

Raj, A., Silverman, J. G., & Amaro, H. (2004). Abused women report greater male partner risk and gender-based risk for HIV: Findings from a community-based study with Hispanic women. *AIDS Care, 16*(4), 519–529.

Ramsay, J., Rivas, C., & Feder, G. (2005). Interventions to reduce violence and promote the physical and psychosocial well-being of women who experience partner violence: A systematic review of controlled evaluations. Retrieved January 15, 2009, from http://www.dh.gov.uk/en/Publicationsandstatistics/Publications/PublicationsPolicyAndGuidance/DH_4126266.

Randolph, M. E., Pinkerton, S. D., Somlai, A. M., Kelly, J. A., McAuliffe, T. L., Gibson, R. H., et al. (2007). Severely mentally ill women's HIV risk: The influence of social support, substance use, and contextual risk factors. *Community Mental Health Journal, 43*(1), 33–47.

Resnick, H. S., Kilpatrick, D. G., Dansky, B. S., Saunders, B. E., & Best, C. L. (1993). Prevalence of civilian trauma and posttraumatic stress disorder in a representative national sample of women. *Journal of Consulting and Clinical Psychology, 61*(6), 984–991.

Roberts, A. C., Wechsberg, W. M., Zule, W., & Burroughs, A. R. (2003). Contextual factors and other correlates of sexual risk of HIV among African-American crack-abusing women. *Addictive Behaviors, 28*(3), 523–536.

Roosa, M. W., Reyes, L., Reinholtz, C., & Angelini, P. J. (1998). Measurement of women's child sexual abuse experiences: An empirical demonstration of the impact of choice of measure on estimates of incidence rates and of relationships with pathology. *Journal of Sex Research, 35*(3), 225–233.

Sansone, R. A., Songer, D. A., & Miller, K. A. (2005). Childhood abuse, mental healthcare utilization, self-harm behavior, and multiple psychiatric diagnoses among inpatients with and without a borderline diagnosis. *Comprehensive Psychiatry, 46*(2), 117–120.

Santibanez, S. S., Garfein, R. S., Swartzendruber, A., Purcell, D. W., Paxton, L. A., & Greenberg, A. E. (2006). Update and overview of practical epidemiologic aspects of HIV/AIDS among injection drug users in the United States. *Journal of Urban Health, 83*(1), 86–100.

Sareen, J., Pagura, J., & Grant, B. (2009). Is intimate partner violence associated with HIV infection among women in the United States? *General Hospital Psychiatry, 31*(3), 274–278.

Senn, T. E., Carey, M. P., & Vanable, P. A. (2008). Childhood and adolescent sexual abuse and subsequent sexual risk behavior: Evidence from controlled studies, methodological critique, and suggestions for research. *Clinical Psychology Review, 28*(5), 711–735.

Silverman, J. G., Decker, M. R., Kapur, N. A., Gupta, J., & Raj, A. (2007). Violence against wives, sexual risk and sexually transmitted infection among Bangladeshi men. *Sexually Transmitted Infections, 83*(3), 211–215.

Silverman, J. G., Decker, M. R., Saggurti, N., Balaiah, D., & Raj, A. (2008). Intimate partner violence and HIV infection among married Indian women. *Journal of the American Medical Association, 300*(6), 703–710.

Singer, M. (1994). AIDS and the health crisis of the U.S. urban poor: The perspective of critical medical anthropology. *Social Science & Medicine, 39*(7), 931–948.

Singer, M. (1996). A dose of drugs, a touch of violence, a case of AIDS: Conceptualizing the SAVA syndemic. *Free Inquiry in Creative Sociology, 24*(2), 99–110.

Singer, M., & Clair, S. (2003). Syndemics and public health: Reconceptualizing disease in bio-social context. *Medical Anthropology Quarterly, 17*(4), 423–441.

Singh, K., Ochitill, H., Fernandez, F., & Ruiz, P. (2006). Personality disorders. In F. Fernandez & P. Ruiz (Eds.), *Psychiatric aspects of HIV/AIDS* (pp. 101–110). Philadelphia: Lippincott Williams & Wilkins.

Sormanti, M., Wu, E., & El-Bassel, N. (2004). Considering HIV risk and intimate partner violence among older women of color: A descriptive analysis. *Women & Health, 39*(1), 45–63.

Sterk, C. E., Theall, K. P., & Elifson, K. W. (2003). Effectiveness of a risk reduction intervention among African American women who use crack cocaine. *AIDS Education and Prevention, 15*(1), 15–32.

Sterk, C. E., Theall, K. P., & Elifson, K. W. (2006). The impact of emotional distress on HIV risk reduction among women. *Substance Use & Misuse, 41*(2), 157–173.

Stiffman, A. R., Dore, P., Earls, F., & Cunningham, R. (1992). The influence of mental health problems on AIDS-related risk behaviors in young adults. *Journal of Nervous and Mental Disease, 180*(5), 314–320.

Stockman, J. K., Campbell, J., & Celentano, D. D. (2009, September 3). Sexual violence and HIV risk behaviors among a nationally representative sample of heterosexual American women: The importance of sexual coercion. *Journal of Acquired Immune Deficiency Syndromes* [Electronic publication ahead of print].

Suarez-Al-Adam, M., Raffaelli, M., & O'Leary, A. (2000). Influence of abuse and partner hypermasculinity on the sexual behavior of Latinas. *AIDS Education and Prevention, 12*(3), 263–274.

Sullivan, T. P., & Holt, L. J. (2008). PTSD symptom clusters are differentially related to substance use among community women exposed to intimate partner violence. *Journal of Traumatic Stress, 21*(2), 173–180.

Swendeman, D., Basu, I., Das, S., Jana, S., & Rotheram-Borus, M. J. (2009). Empowering sex workers in India to reduce vulnerability to HIV and sexually transmitted diseases. *Social Science & Medicine (1982), 69*(8), 1157–1166.

Szapocznik, J., & Coatsworth, J. D. (1999). An ecodevelopmental framework for organizing the influences on drug abuse: A developmental model or risk and protection. In M. D. Glantz & C. R. Hartel (Eds.), *Drug abuse origins and interventions* (pp. 331–366). Washington, DC: American Psychological Association.

Van der Kolk, B. A., Perry, J., & Herman, J. L. (1991). Childhood origins of self-destructive behavior. *American Journal of Psychiatry, 148*(12), 1665–1671.

Walker, L. E. (2000). *The battered woman syndrome* (2nd ed.). New York: Springer.

Whetten, K., Reif, S., Whetten, R., & Murphy-McMillan, L. K. (2008). Trauma, mental health, distrust, and stigma among HIV positive persons: Implications for effective care. *Psychosomatic Medicine, 70*(5), 531–538.

Winfield, I., George, L. K., Swartz, M., & Blazer, D. G. (1990). Sexual assault and psychiatric disorders among a community sample of women. *American Journal of Psychiatry, 147*(3), 335–341.

Wingood, G. M., & DiClemente, R. J. (1997). Child sexual abuse, HIV sexual risk, and gender relations of African-American women. *American Journal of Preventive Medicine, 13*(5), 380–384.

Wingood, G. M., & DiClemente, R. J. (2000). Application of the theory of gender and power to examine HIV-related exposures, risk factors, and effective interventions for women. *Health Education & Behavior, 27*(5), 539–565.

Wingood, G. M., DiClemente, R. J., Mikhail, I., Lang, D. L., McCree, D. H., Davies, S. L., et al. (2004). A randomized controlled trial to reduce HIV transmission risk behaviors and sexually transmitted diseases among women living with HIV: The WiLLOW program. *Journal of Acquired Immune Deficiency Syndromes (1999), 37*(suppl 2), S58–S67.

Wingood, G. M., DiClemente, R. J., & Raj, A. (2000). Adverse consequences of intimate partner abuse among women in non-urban domestic violence shelters. *American Journal of Preventive Medicine, 19*(4), 270–275.

World Health Organization (WHO). (2005). *WHO Multi-Country Study on Women's Health and Domestic Violence against Women: Summary report of initial results on prevalence, health outcomes and women's responses.* Geneva, Switzerland: Author.

Wu, E., El-Bassel, N., Witte, S. S., Gilbert, L., & Chang, M. (2003). Intimate partner violence and HIV risk among urban minority women in primary health care settings. *AIDS and Behavior, 7*(3), 291–301.

Wyatt, G. E., Longshore, D., Chin, D., Carmona, J. V., Loeb, T. B., Myers, H. F., et al. (2004). The efficacy of an integrated risk reduction intervention for HIV-positive women with child sexual abuse histories. *AIDS and Behavior, 8*(4), 453–462.

Chapter 10

Creeps and Casanovas: Experiences, Explanations, and Effects of Street Harassment

Harmony B. Sullivan, Tracy L. Lord, and Maureen C. McHugh

On a daily basis, women in public places are the targets of catcalls, unwanted touches, crude comments about their appearance or sexual predilections, and all other manner of harassment. Two of the first scholars to study the phenomenon of gender-based street harassment, Cheryl Benard and Edit Schlaffer (1981), found that women on the streets of Vienna were harassed regardless of their age, weight, clothing, or race by men of every different race and socioeconomic level. Carol Gardner found the same thing to be true in the United States when she interviewed hundreds of men and women on the streets of Indianapolis. She eloquently defined street harassment as "that group of abuses, harryings, and annoyances characteristic of public places and uniquely facilitated by communication in public" (1995, p. 4). These researchers have described street harassment as a violation of a woman's right to walk down the street unmolested and without being constantly reminded of men's position of privilege. The prevailing societal opinion on street harassment, however, is that it is annoying but not really such a big deal. It is just "boys being boys."

This chapter offers support for Carol Gardner, Cheryl Benard, Edit Schlaffer, and the other researchers, theorists, and activists who emphatically refuse to dismiss street harassment as a trivial fact of life for women. The fact that street harassment is a daily reality for most women does not make it trivial. No one would claim that daily physical or emotional abuse is trivial. Indeed, research shows that the effects of long-term, daily abuse are often more harmful than the effects of a single trauma. The reader may laugh uneasily and say, "Oh, but being catcalled is not the same as being raped!"—and the reader would be right: they are different. Even so, both events exist on a continuum of violence against women, with mundane street harassment at one end and rape on the other. This chapter presents empirical and theoretical evidence suggesting that street harassment causes serious and insidious negative effects on a woman's emotional well-being and causes her to feel unsafe and unwelcome in her own world. It also discusses personal and collective responses to street harassment with the conviction that societal change is possible.

CONCEPTUALIZING STREET HARASSMENT

Although street harassment is directed toward individuals belonging to various groups, including people of ethnic minorities, those with disabilities, and those who identify as gay, lesbian, and transgender (Fogg-Davis, 2006; Gardner, 1995), this chapter focuses on gender-based street harassment, referred to hereafter simply as "street harassment" for the sake of space.

This category encompasses many different types of harassing behaviors, ranging from staring openly at a woman's breasts to complimenting her on her breasts to grabbing her breasts. Verbal comments can seem flattering, such as telling a woman that she is beautiful, or they can appear flirtatious, such as asking a woman for her telephone number. They can also be blatantly hostile, such as calling a woman a bitch or a whore. However, the characteristics that unite all of these behaviors under the banner of street harassment are the following: (1) the targets of street harassment are usually female; (2) the harassers are usually male; (3) the harassers are unacquainted with their targets; (4) the encounter is of a face-to-face nature; (5) the forum is a public one, such as a street, sidewalk, bus, bus station, taxi, or other place to which the public generally has access; but (6) the content of the speech, if any, is not intended as public discourse. Rather, the remarks are aimed at the individual (although the harasser may intend that they be overheard by comrades or passersby), and they are objectively degrading, objectifying, humiliating, and frequently threatening in nature (Bowman, 1993, p. 524).

In a study by Tracy Lord (2009), female undergraduates at a public university in the mid-Atlantic region were asked to provide examples of harassment they had experienced. Many of the women reported being the targets of whistling, being followed (on foot or in a car), purposeful and "accidental" touching, staring, and horn honking. Several participants reported that unwanted touching came from patrons at their places of employment, particularly if they worked as restaurant servers. Participants also specified that unwanted touching frequently occurred at parties. Some women described a frightening escalation of the harassment when they tried to ignore the initial "compliments." The harassers moved quickly from these purported compliments to shouted insults.

In her ground-breaking ethnographic study of street harassment, Carol Gardner (1995) identified specific types and subtle characteristics of harassment. After interviewing 506 targets and perpetrators of street harassment, Gardner concluded that harassment can be categorized as an "access information intrusion," an "exploitation of presence," a "street remark," or a combination of all three. Harassment that attempts to access a woman's information can range in severity from asking for a woman's phone number on a busy street to following her at night for many blocks. Exploitation of presence violates a woman's physical space and ruffles her calm, dignified exterior. Examples of this type of harassment include blocking a woman's path, touching, hitting, tripping, or poking. Street remarks are most often evaluative and sometimes come in the form of eloquent innuendos, effectively redefining a mundane activity or situation by giving it sexual undertones.

Obviously, these categories of harassment are not mutually exclusive; a harassing behavior may entail a combination of these types. For example, by following a woman, a harasser both intrudes on her private information, by seeking to know where she is going or where she lives, and exploits her presence in public. What does seem common to all types of street harassment is that it is often "stealthy, quick, silent and unseen" (Gardner, 1995, p. 148). As a consequence, the target's attention is often diverted and the harassment comes too unexpectedly and quickly for a woman to react satisfactorily. When harassment is more overt, harassers often inject humor into their behavior, thereby making the woman the butt of the joke and leaving her unable to make a serious or satisfactory response. It also depoliticizes the harassing behavior, making it seem lighthearted and nonthreatening (Gardner).

Another defining characteristic of street harassment is that it occurs in public spaces where specific, unspoken codes define appropriate behavior between strangers so that people can move about in public without feeling threatened. One of these social norms, described in detail by Erving Goffman (1963), is the norm of "civil inattention." Civil inattention generally forbids strangers from paying one another too much attention in public. Although strangers may say certain legitimate phrases to one another when passing on the street, such as a brief greeting or asking for the time, all other speech is discouraged. The unspoken code of civil inattention also dictates how much eye contact is appropriate; when walking past a stranger on the street, we look each at each other for only a brief moment and then only in the face. Any additional eye contact causes us to feel uneasy or uncomfortable. In sum, civil inattention allows individuals to maintain a sense of privacy and to feel protected from the intrusion of strangers into their private space (Goffman).

When a man makes a sexually suggestive comment to or about a female stranger on the street, looks fixedly at her body as she walks past him, or reaches out to touch her, such behavior is a blatant violation of the social norm of civil inattention. If street harassment does, in fact, violate a social norm, then it would stand to reason that harassers form a special category of men and that such behavior is abnormal and infrequent. Interestingly, neither of these things appears to be true. Although most women and men alike assume that the majority of perpetrators of street harassment are working-class and of a minority race, interviews with perpetrators and targets indicate that harassers are men of every race, age, socioeconomic status, and cultural background (Gardner, 1995; Benard & Schlaffer, 1981).

PREVALENCE

Based on the authors' own experiences and our conversations with women friends and colleagues, street harassment seems to be a common experience that occurs quite often. Everyone has at least one personal story to tell about it. Unfortunately, empirical data about the frequency of street harassment are sparse. The only two large-scale surveys measuring the frequency of street harassment of women found that between 85 percent and 91 percent of the Canadian women sampled had experienced some type of street harassment after the age of 16, and 36 percent reported experiencing it in the last year (Lenton, Smith, Fox, & Morra, 1999; Macmillan, Nierobisz, & Welsh, 2000). Both of these surveys defined street harassment more narrowly than the definition used in this chapter; therefore, these numbers probably underestimate the real frequency.

After interviewing 100 women recruited from public spaces (in the United States), Nielsen (2000) found that 61 percent reported being made the target of sexually suggestive comments "every day" or "often." Most men (86%), by comparison, heard such comments only "sometimes," "rarely," or "never." Nielsen also found that nearly one fourth of women of color reported hearing suggestive comments on a daily basis, compared to only 14 percent of White women. As part of an anti-street harassment campaign, a group of female teenagers of varied races and ethnicities surveyed peers in their urban neighborhood and found that 36 percent of teenagers surveyed said that they were catcalled every day and often multiple times per day (Roberson, 2005).

In a recent study of street harassment, Tracy Lord (2009) surveyed 130 female undergraduate students about harassing behaviors they had experienced and their feelings about these behaviors. The behaviors ranged from subjectively mild (e.g., being stared at in a way that made the women uncomfortable) to more severe (e.g., indecent exposure, being followed, or unwanted touching). Each woman reported being subjected to at least two forms of harassing behavior, and each of the eight harassing behaviors was endorsed by at least 42 percent of the women. Results indicated that women of color are harassed significantly more frequently than are White women.

With the results from these various surveys indicating that most women experience harassing behavior from male strangers in public at least once in their lifetime and as often as every day, it would seem that street harassment is an accepted behavior guided by a separate code of conduct from the code of civil inattention. Goffman (1963) explained that although civil inattention discourages people from giving strangers too much attention, certain kinds of strangers may be exempt from this rule. He described these people as "open people." Examples of open people include children, people accompanied by children or pets, or someone wearing a funny costume. Individuals who do not meet society's standards for what is ideal may also fall into the open person category. Perhaps men have learned to treat women as open persons. Treating women differently than men in public simply because they are women seems to be the definition of sexism.

STREET HARASSMENT AS PROBLEM

Although most girls and women have experienced street harassment repeatedly, they are not encouraged to confront street harassers or to take harassment seriously. For example, Gardner (1995) described the ways in which women have been taught to interpret street harassment experiences. Gardner found that many women were likely to interpret public harassment from a romanticized perspective, in which street harassment was viewed as harmless or even complimentary. In this view, the comments, looks, and whistles are just men's ways of voicing their appreciation or approval of the way women look. In reality, not all the comments are complimentary; Gardner notes that even people with a romantic outlook on public harassment cannot always classify harassment as flattery.

As Natalie Nichols (2006) argues, harassment implies that men on the street have been accorded the opportunity to evaluate women's bodies and appearance: "Their 'compliments' make me feel angry and violated. I resent their sense of entitlement to comment on my body, to demand any piece of *my* mind" (www.LACITY.BEAT.com). Street commentary on women's attractiveness or lack of attractiveness places them in a beauty pageant on a daily basis, a pageant they have not agreed to enter. Every man or any man can appoint himself the judge, and for every pageant winner there are losers. This aspect of harassment implies that women are in competition for men's attention, and that men have the right to judge women on their appearance in any and every context of their lives. Thus, even if public harassment is flattering and makes some women feel better about themselves, it reinforces traditional gender norms and the division of power between men and women. Moreover, it reinforces the view that men have the right to comment on a woman's appearance. Many women can attest to the fact that an initial compliment can easily become vulgar or turn into a different form of harassment (e.g., stalking, touching), or the ostensible compliment can be rescinded if the harasser does not get the response he wants.

Other women hold a politicized view (Gardner, 1995) in which public harassment is comparable to both racial comments and gay bashing in public and to workplace and school harassment. "Sexual harassment has been a dirty little secret for generations, an unacknowledged barrage of intrusive, threatening male behaviors that has limited women's freedoms and violated even their simple human right to ride a bus or walk down the street in peace" (Langelan, 1993, p. 22). Gender-based street harassment is seen as evidence of men's power over women in a male-dominated society. Lenton and her colleagues (1999) described harassment as a phenomena linked to power and control. They argue that street harassment—as a form of sexual harassment—is part of a larger structure in which men and women have unequal power because men have access to more resources (e.g., physical, political) than women do. Society is structured such that men have more power than women, and public harassment is a demonstration of men's power and privilege. For example, the website Holla Back NYC (www.hollabacknyc.blogspot.com) argues that "at its [street harassment's] core is a power dynamic that constantly reminds historically subordinated groups (women and LGBTQ folks, for example) of their vulnerability to assault in public spaces. Further, it reinforces the ubiquitous sexual objectification of these groups in everyday life." Street harassment is a reflection of and serves to perpetuate gender roles. Gender roles place males in a superior, dominant position to females. Our culture socializes men to be aggressive, dominant, and sexual, and women to be more submissive.

Moreover, street harassment is implicitly and explicitly heterosexist; the practice is based on assumptions of heteronormity—that is, the assumption that everyone is heterosexual. Harassers publicly display their own heterosexuality and act on the assumption that women on the street are heterosexual and are concerned with their (male) attraction to them.

Women's perceptions of and reactions to men's attention in public vary depending on their own personal history with violence and the context in which the harassment occurs. Other factors include: what men are doing, age differences, race differences/similarities, socio-economic differences, and how safe they feel at the time. No woman wants to be insulted, groped, stalked, or assaulted. Many women do not want to be bothered at all. Girls and women should have just as much right as boys and men to be in public spaces without being treated as public property and worse (http://www.stopstreetharass ment.com).

STREET HARASSMENT AS EVERYDAY SEXISM

One way to think about street harassment is as a type of mundane sexist event that is one of innumerable hassles women go through on a daily basis. While major life events, such as the death of a family member or the loss of a job have long been thought to cause physical and mental illness, in the past few decades researchers have come to view smaller-scale, daily annoyances as potentially more detrimental to long-term health and well-being. Researchers studying daily hassles define them as "irritating, frustrating, distressing, demands that to some degree characterize every-day transactions with the environment" (Kanner, Coyne, Schaefer, & Lazarus, 1981, p. 3). They consistently find that the more daily hassles a person endures, the more vulnerable he or she is to psychological distress and psychiatric symptoms (Evans, Jacobs, Dooley, & Catalano, 1987; Kanner et al., 1981; Weiten, 1998).

Not surprisingly, data from large-scale epidemiological surveys have shown that women experience significantly more daily hassles than do men (Kessler & McLeod, 1984). Hope Landrine and Elizabeth Klonoff (1997) proposed that one reason for this difference may be women's daily exposure to nonviolent sexist events, including "being ignored, treated as if they are stupid, excluded, ridiculed, called names, and treated in unfair ways by their families, lovers, employers, and coworkers" (p. 17). The two researchers began testing their theory by asking women about the "worst thing that [had] ever happened to or been done to them because they are women" (p. 12). They then used these data to create a quantitative mea-sure of the frequency of both recent and lifelong exposure to daily sexist events, which they called the Schedule of Sexist Events (SSE). Using the SSE, Landrine and Klonoff found that 99 percent of women sampled, regardless of their educational attainment or income level, reported experiencing a sexist event at some point in their lifetime; an almost equally large percentage reported experiencing such an event in the past year. The authors also found that when using both the SSE and a measure of non-gender-related daily stressors, the SSE was the single best predic-tor of psychiatric and physical symptoms. Specifically, the more sexist events a woman went through on a daily basis, the more likely she was to report symptoms of anxiety, depression, obsessive-compulsive disorder, and even menstrual pain.

The theory that exposure to day-to-day sexism increases a woman's vulnerability to symptoms of anxiety, depression, and physical pain has been supported and expanded in the years since Landrine and Klonoff introduced it. Using a particularly innovative method, Janet Swim and her colleagues instructed women and men to keep daily diaries in which they described events perceived to be sexist as well as their own emotional reactions to those events. Because it is difficult to think back about events that occurred weeks, months, or even decades ago, diaries are useful in allowing the writer to more easily describe the details of experiences and emotional responses that occurred that day. The results from the diary studies indicated that sexist hassles are a common experience for women; these events occur on average once or twice a week for college-age women (Swim, Hyers, Cohen, & Fergusan, 2001). The authors categorized the experiences as involving one or more of three types of incidents: (1) traditional gender role prejudice, (2) demeaning and derogatory comments and behavior, or (3) sexual objectification. Although male participants also reported experiencing sexist events, the frequency of women's experiences was much higher than that of men, especially in terms of sexual objectification. Perhaps most important finding was that the most common emotional response to sexist events was anger and the frequency of sexist events was positively correlated with higher levels of anger, depression, and feelings of discomfort.

What does all of this have to do with street harassment? Simply put, if street harassment is classified as a sexist event, then the frequency of these events could partially explain why women are so much more likely to suffer from clinical depression and anxiety than are men. In other words, perhaps being catcalled on a regular basis as a woman walks to work or waits for a friend on the sidewalk is more than just annoying; perhaps it causes psychological damage. For general sexist events, researchers have hypothesized that the pressure women feel to brush such behavior off as trivial causes even more damage because it forces women to disregard their own anger, discomfort, and immense frustration. This is certainly true of societal responses to street harassment. In fact, the mundane nature of such events makes them even more impactful.

STREET HARASSMENT AS VIOLENCE AGAINST WOMEN

A mounting body of evidence suggests that street harassment causes women to feel more aware of their sexual vulnerability and, therefore, more afraid of being raped. Using data from the 1993 Violence Against Women Survey of 12,300 Canadian women, Ross Macmillan and his colleagues (2000) found that the more experiences a woman had being harassed in public and the more varied these experiences, the less safe she felt in public. In fact, stranger harassment had a much larger effect on women's perception of safety than did sexual harassment in the workplace. Stranger harassment was associated with increased fears about safety while walking alone at night, using public transportation, and walking alone in a parking garage. As a result of the harassment, nearly half of the women began using personal safety strategies such as bringing a companion or dog with them when they went out, avoiding certain places or men, staying more alert, or checking their cars before getting in. These authors argue that street harassment causes women to feel less safe in public because it entails a unique combination of unwanted sexualized interactions with people who are unknown. This factor may cue women to perceive the male harassers as potential rapists rather than as potential guardians, leading women to be aware of their own sexual vulnerability and, therefore, feel unsafe in public spaces (Macmillan et al., 2000).

Women are significantly more afraid than men of being the victims of crime (Gordon & Riger, 1989; Rozee, 2000). This discrepancy occurs despite clear evidence that men are actually more at risk than women of being robbed, murdered, assaulted, and victimized in countless other ways (Ferraro, 1996; Lenton et al., 1999). When studies control for the fear of rape and focus on fears of other crime, however, they find that men are actually more afraid of murder and assault than are women (Ferraro). It appears that the fear of rape actually causes women to fear all crime more because any face-to-face crime against women, such as burglary, could theoretically lead to rape. Warr (1985) surveyed urban women and found that young women fear rape more than any other criminal offense including murder, assault, and robbery. This fear causes women to take certain lifestyle precautions, such as limiting where and when they go out and whether they go places alone.

Although the fear of rape is a completely rational fear of men's violence, and one that develops from both personal and societal history of violence toward women in the home, workplace, and public, it is also inflamed and manipulated by the media, advertising, and society at large (Stanko, 1995). Women receive messages from the time they are quite young to both fear rape and to avoid situations that could lead to rape. Because rape is not under their control, this barrage of messages leads to a constant low-level fear whenever they leave the house (Gordon & Riger, 1989). It is probably for this reason that men are not aware of the fear that street harassment triggers. They simply do not have the same reasons to fear it because they are not socialized to fear rape.

Medea and Thompson (1974) referred to public harassment experiences as "little rapes" that psychologically undermine women's resistance to sexual assault. In their early analysis of the impact of daily harassment, Medea and Thompson argued that women are trained how to (not) respond to such male transgressions. Women are socialized to not call attention to themselves, to be easily embarrassed in public, to avoid confrontation, and to ignore street harassment. They are taught to avert their eyes in public, to ignore street harassment, to walk quickly away from harassers, and to avoid streets and other public areas where harassment might occur. Although women are not encouraged to object to street harassment, they are expected to object strenuously—even violently—to sexual assault. Medea and Thompson argued that women's gender socialization in general, and their socialized responses to street harassment in particular, leave women vulnerable when a serious sexual assault occurs. Women who immediately resist rapists are less likely to be raped, but it is difficult to know that a man is planning to rape until it is too late. Therefore, attending to intuition and gut reactions is an important survival skill (Gordon & Riger, 1989). Unfortunately, women are also taught to ignore such reactions of fear, anger, and discomfort when they are harassed by unknown men on the street. This places women in a horrible double bind: if they react based on their feelings, they are discredited and often ridiculed; if they do not react and suppress those feelings, they disconnect themselves from important inner cues and may put themselves at risk for victimization (Bowman, 1993).

In their phone survey of 1,990 randomly selected Canadian women aged 18 to 65, Rhonda Lenton and her colleagues (1999) asked about the frequency of victimization of several types of crime, including harassment by unknown men in public. They also asked women about their fear of crime and strategies used to protect themselves. Of the 91 percent of sampled women who reported experiencing street harassment, 75 percent reported feeling fear immediately following the harassment; 20 percent reported feeling angry; and only 2.9 percent reported feeling nothing. Almost 20 percent reported still feeling upset or afraid about harassment that had occurred years before. In addition, the most commonly reported behavioral reaction to the harassment was an alteration of the woman's own behavior to reduce the risk of future victimization (Lenton et al.).

Harassment forces some women out of the public sphere, which men consider their territory, and back into the private sphere. Street harassment then becomes an expression of patriarchal power that can serve to constrain women's mobility. Lenton and her colleagues (1999) reported on research that supported the conclusion that harassment is related to the social control of women, with many of their respondents experiencing fear and limiting their activities as a result of being harassed. Similarly, Gardner (1995) found that women used multiple strategies to cope with being in public and experiencing public harassment, including staying home, not going out in public, and avoiding multiple arenas. McHugh (1996) argued that agoraphobia may not always be an irrational fear of public spaces, but rather a reasonable response to street harassment.

In Lord's study of undergraduate women, negative feelings about being harassed were also associated with increasing avoidance of going out alone in public. Lord's research supported the proposition that street harassment may cause women to experience negative emotional reactions, including anger, discomfort, and fear, and that harassment may trigger women's awareness of their vulnerability to sexual assault.

Lenton and her colleagues (1999) argued that harassment is a "means of social control that serves to reproduce and maintain the status quo of male dominance" (p. 520). "It is seen as a micro-inequity, not a big deal," said Maggie Hadleigh-West, whose 1998 documentary *War Zone* detailed her personal encounters with street harassers. Nevertheless, street harassment, because it induces a kind of anxiety in women akin to the fear of rape, is not just an annoyance for Hadleigh-West but a real threat. Hawley Fogg-Davis (2006) eloquently states:

> Just as rape is not about sex, street harassment is not about flirtation or courtship. Both acts are meant to assert male dominance over women in situations where women appear vulnerable, and both leave psychological wounds on women's lives that are rarely tended to, let alone acknowledged. (p. 65)

STREET HARASSMENT AS OBJECTIFICATION

In addition to the stress associated with daily hassles and reminding women about their sexual vulnerability, street harassment may also lead women to feel self-conscious and be concerned or embarrassed about their appearance. Feminist theory has discussed at length how the feeling of self-consciousness about one's body and appearance can be problematic for women. When a woman is regularly reminded that her appearance is the most important thing about her and that this appearance does not match the societal ideal, she may suffer a range of negative consequences.

In modern society, maintaining physical attractiveness is a daily obsession for many women. In the past, researchers and theorists speculated that this focus on maintaining one's beauty was due to women's innate narcissism; more recently, research has clarified that the cause lies not in women themselves but in the societal pressures placed upon them (Frederickson & Roberts, 1997; Kilbourne & Jhally, 2001). In particular, women face a daily onslaught of sexual objectification wherein they are viewed as a collection of physical attributes and body parts valued only in terms of how much pleasure they provide the viewer (Bartkey, 1990). One can readily see this perspective by flipping through the pages of a magazine or turning on the television where images of headless, faceless women accentuating breasts, legs, and buttocks are regularly used to draw the viewer in and sell products. Objectification also occurs in interpersonal encounters, such as when a man looks at the breasts of the woman with whom he is speaking instead of into her eyes. Many types of street harassment are also clearly intended as sexually objectifying behaviors, such as when men comment on a woman's breasts or buttocks as she walks by on the street.

When a woman is sexually objectified, she loses the complexity that is common to all people and becomes simply a body to be ogled or derided. Although men can be sexually objectified, it is by and large women who are the victims of this behavior. Whether this pattern arises because objectification perpetuates societal norms regarding male dominance or whether it results from evolutionary directives is open for debate. What is clear is that women experience a constant onslaught of objectification, whether it occurs in the media (Kilbourne & Jhally, 2001) or takes place in interpersonal encounters (Frederickson & Roberts, 1997). In short, they are constantly reminded that their level of physical attractiveness has an enormous impact on their success in life, love, and the workplace.

Because sexual objectification becomes an unavoidable part of a woman's daily life when she reaches puberty, it negatively affects her budding identity and, consequently, her mental and physical well-being. According to Barbara Fredrickson and Tomi-Ann Roberts (1997), pioneers in the study of objectification, "[A] critical repercussion of being viewed by others in sexually objectifying ways is that, over time, individuals may be coaxed to internalize an observer's perspective on self" (p. 179), a phenomenon they label "self-objectification." When a woman self-objectifies, she sees herself as a body to be seen and evaluated instead of as an agent of action. Competency becomes less important than beauty, and the woman spends an inordinate amount of mental energy monitoring her body for flaws.

At the core of self-objectification is a comparison between one's own body and the cultural ideal. Unfortunately, this ideal is very rarely achieved. As a consequence, such a comparison often leads to shame and a constant preoccupation with minimizing the discrepancy between one's own body and the cultural ideal. The shame and anxiety that self-objectification causes women to feel, along with its taxing of their mental energy, might explain the higher base rates of depression and anxiety disorders among women. According to Barbara McKinley and Janet Hyde (1996, p. 183):

Constant self-surveillance, seeing themselves as others see them, is necessary to ensure that women comply with cultural body standards and avoid negative judgments. Women's relationship to their bodies becomes that of object and external onlooker; they exist as objects to themselves. Women learn to associate body surveillance with self-love, health, and individual achievement.

Barbara Fredrickson and her colleagues came up with a particularly ingenious way to study self-objectification (Fredrickson, Roberts, Noll, Quinn, & Twenge, 1998). In their experiment, male and female college students were randomly assigned to try on either a swimsuit or a sweater alone in a room with a full-length mirror and, while in the dressing room, were then asked to take a food taste test and a math test. Results showed that wearing a swimsuit caused both men and women to score significantly higher on measures of self-objectification. While this state of self-objectification caused men to feel silly and awkward, it caused women to feel disgust, revulsion, and body shame. In addition, the women who had tried on a bathing suit scored significantly worse on the math test and displayed more restrained eating than women wearing a sweater. No such differences were found for men. The authors concluded from these results that the negative consequences of self-objectification are not part of a general human condition but rather are socialized to primarily affect young women because of the cultural focus on objectification of the female body. In addition, they concluded that certain situations prime women to self-objectify and to feel "on display" (Fredrickson et al., 1998).

The subsequent results from a multitude of studies using various techniques to evoke self-objectification have supported the premise that self-objectification has negative effects on the well-being of women. In addition to causing shame and decreasing cognitive ability, self-objectification seems to be a contributing factor in the development of mood and eating disorders in women (Greenleaf & McGreer, 2006; Moradi, Dirks, & Matteson, 2005).

Inherent in objectification theory is the idea that self-objectification occurs when young women begin to internalize the male gaze. Feminist theorists describe the male gaze as the objectifying gaze that women endure daily and that they learn to anticipate and prepare for (Bartkey, 1990). Rachel Calogero (2004) sought to experimentally test the power of the male gaze by telling female participants that they were either going to meet with a male experimenter or a female experimenter or telling them nothing. Amazingly, the mere *anticipation* of talking to a man caused women to endorse significantly higher levels of body shame and social physique anxiety than women in the other two groups. Calogero concluded that these women anticipated the male gaze and, therefore, began self-objectifying so as to monitor their appearance in preparation.

Although no experimental studies have as yet investigated the effects of street harassment on self-objectification, the previous studies do suggest that street harassment increases self-objectification. The male gaze is inextricably linked to street harassment, as is the impression that women targets are on display. Certainly, male harassers sexually objectify their targets, either by ogling them or by verbally evaluating the target's body parts. The hypothesized connection between harassment and objectification was partly supported by the results of Lord's recent study (2009), in which she surveyed undergraduate women. This researcher found that the more harassing behaviors undergraduate women reported experiencing, the more likely they were to report having a negative reaction, such as anger or fear. Also, the more negatively the women felt about being harassed, the more likely they were to report lower self-esteem, unhappiness with their appearance, and preoccupation with their weight.

What about the remarks made by strangers on the street that might be interpreted as complimentary? Do they cause harmful effects? Although no one has specifically studied the results of complimentary street remarks, Rachel Calogero and her colleagues have studied the effects of complimentary remarks made by acquaintances to women about their bodies and appearance. Results showed that both strong positive feelings about compliments and strong negative feelings about criticisms were associated with increased body dissatisfaction and body surveillance (Calogero, Herbozo, & Thompson, 2009). The findings from this study suggest that compliments about a woman's weight, shape, or appearance are associated with body dissatisfaction both among women who identify appearance as centrally important to their identity and among women who do not. Even when women feel good about the appearance compliment, such comments do not appear to have a beneficial effect on body image or satisfaction about one's appearance. Therefore, remarks by strangers on the street that appear to compliment a woman's appearance probably have a similarly—if not more severe—negative effect.

RESPONDING TO STREET HARASSMENT

Street harassment as an everyday form of sexism may feel normal or expected for many women. Women often report that they feel like they have *learned to live with* street harassment. In this chapter and elsewhere, women have asked, How does "living with" street harassment affect us? According to Cathy Ramos (n.d), "Living with street harassment means having to take the message about our bodies that harassers bring. It means accepting assault and disrespect as normal." Ramos, like Medea and Thompson (1974), notes that women are taught not to respond to harassers, to pretend the abuse is not happening. When women do say something or object to street harassment, they may be called a "bitch" or threatened with violence. "Living with street harassment means learning that in uncomfortable sexual situations, you should do nothing. It means that when you walk outside you do not walk with freedom. It means you have to come to expect and accept disrespect. Street harassment changes who you are and how you are allowed to live" (Ramos, n.d.).

In the classroom, this chapter's co-author Maureen McHugh invites young women to relate their own past responses to street harassment and to carefully consider alternative responses to street harassment. Students typically report responses such as ignoring the behavior, yelling back or making rude gestures, or making a (loud) joke about the harasser. Using an assertiveness training approach, McHugh helps students to classify responses as passive, aggressive, passive-aggressive, or assertive. In the class, the students analyze responses to harassment using a behavioral analysis. What are the likely outcomes and costs of each response type? Traditionally taught responses such averting one's eyes or ignoring the harassment are passive and are not effective in terms of expressing the individual's feelings or reducing the likelihood of harassment in the future. When women pretend to ignore harassment, there is no consequence created for harassers. As a consequence of passivity, women may feel powerless and angry. Nevertheless, a passive or do-nothing response may, in some circumstances, be the safest course of action. When women do not respond or communicate their feelings, the harassers may continue to believe that their comments or actions are harmless or are appreciated. Certainly, the traditional passive responses have not curbed or extinguished street harassment.

Women may feel better when they make aggressive responses such as yelling obscenities at the harassers. These responses communicate to harassers that women do not find what is happening to be "cute," "fun," or "desired." Responding with an obscenity communicates women's anger and refusal to take harassment. Sometimes women report such incidents to their friends, proud of their resistance to being victimized. Confronting discrimination has the potential to decrease discrimination, but also poses possible threats (Dodd, Giuliano, Boutell, & Moran, 2001). For example, aggressive responses may result in an escalation of the aggression and they generally do not diminish the antagonistic attitudes of the harassers. Ramos (n.d.). notes that sometimes harassers get angrier or become threatening when women refuse to act politely—a response that reveals the coercive elements present in street harassment.

Although women may say that they would react with anger to sexual harassment, recent research suggests that there is a gap between what women *claim* they would do about confronting sexism in their lives and what they *actually* do when experiencing sexism (Swim & Hyers, 1999). The difference between women's endorsement of confrontational responses and their actual behavior may reflect the reality that women's safety or well-being feels threatened in some instances of sexism such as street harassment. Self-defense training suggests that any response, including defensive aggression, must be practiced extensively if it is to be enacted effectively in a threatening situation. Silence has often been the reinforced and encouraged response, and speaking up requires practice and encouragement. Some women report that they have been actively discouraged from expressing angry feelings or acting aggressively in response to public gender harassment.

Influenced by both women's self-defense approaches and principles of nonviolence, one strategy for direct action emphasizes assertiveness over aggressiveness or passivity. Advocates see this method as allowing women to take control away from harassers. Under the assertiveness training model used in the 1970s, both passive and aggressive responses were viewed as less than optimal. Assertiveness involves requesting what one wants, refusing what one does not want, and expressing positive and negative messages to others (Crawford, 1995); assertiveness training encouraged speakers to use "I" statements, to make direct requests without giving reasons, and to make repeated requests. Thus an assertive response would be one that conveys the woman's own feelings without being hostile or derogatory to the harasser. A typical nonviolent confrontation might go something like this: "Whistling at women when they walk by is disrespectful. No one likes it. Don't ever whistle at another woman you don't know again."

The difficulty of making an honest and assertive response can dissuade women from a romanticized perspective on harassment. If there is no negative intention in harassment, then why not relate to the harasser your authentic reaction to his intrusion? The political view of street harassment encourages women to recognize the dehumanizing aspects of harassment, and the assertive approach encourages them to state their feelings, thereby turning the harassment into a more human interaction. A few students have reported communicating their feelings directly to the harassers about their comments. In many harassing situations, however, it may not be feasible to say, "Your comments are offensive to me." For example, it is difficult to effectively state one's feelings to construction workers making catcalls from atop building sites. When might women be able to use an assertive strategy? Considering the possibility allows women to understand the power dynamics operating in the harassment situation and helps them to consider the complexities of each situation. What is the woman feeling? Does she feel safe? How might the harasser respond to her assertions?

Assertive and nonviolent strategies are sometimes endorsed as the "correct" response to street harassment. For example, the website Harassment 101 advocates a direct and assertive response to harassment. Marty Langelan (1993), in *Back Off*, provides an analysis and a guide to street harassment with details on this strategy and self-defense. The D.C. Anti-Street Harassment Squad, a new activist organization of women, promotes nonviolent confrontation techniques (http://lists.mutualaid.org/mailman/listinfo/dontcallmebaby). This organization and Langelan provide workshops and training on these techniques.

Conversely, Crawford (1995) concludes that assertion in some real-life situations may result in negative reactions, and that nonassertion may in some situations be a "positive and adaptive strategy for women" (p. 65).

Research by Ayers, Friedman, and Leaper (2009) indicates that confronting unwanted sexual attention, especially from unfamiliar others, is very difficult for girls and young women. Women respondents in their research perceived that confronting sexism in certain situations would compromise their physical safety. Further, Ayers and her co-authors conclude that confronting sexism is not always the best or most adaptive coping response.

While endorsing assertive responses, a behavioral analysis does not make prescriptive statements regarding reactions but rather encourages women to carefully consider the costs and consequences of their responses. Women do not make the decision to confront discrimination lightly but need to consider the costs and benefits of such confrontation (Swim & Hyers, 1999). What price do they pay for their passivity? How much risk is involved with confrontation of everyday sexism? Will confrontation result in women being disliked, derogated, or attacked? Will the harassment escalate? Even if women continue to avert their eyes and avoid confrontation, this response may result in different personal reactions if they make a careful and deliberate decision to not address the comments or actions of a complete stranger on the street. Women are less likely to feel powerless if they have decided not to invest their energy into such interaction on a particular day in a particular situation.

Counter-harassment is another tactic that has been used by women in groups. This strategy involves women heckling or harassing the harassers. For example, The Street Harassment Project (http://wwwstreetharas smentproject.org) conducts a version of this strategy, in which groups of 4 to 10 women go to different parts of the city and walk around. When a woman is harassed, she yells out for others and everyone surrounds the harasser. This gives women a safe and powerful context in which to perform resistance. Another form of collective action is a formal petition or boycott. If harassment occurs at a construction site, for example, a group of local women can call the building owners (e.g., a local bank) and threaten not to use their services or to write to the local paper if the harassment does not stop.

Women do not feel encouraged to report public harassment. In the past, authorities may have ridiculed or ignored women's reports of harassment. For example, the police failed to intervene when women were being harassed in Central Park during the Puerto Rican Day in New York City. Increasingly, however, some forms of public harassment such as frottage (rubbing against a person's body in public), exhibitionism (showing one's genitals to others in a public setting), and voyeurism (peeping on others in a state of undress or sexual activity) are becoming more likely to be viewed as harmful and prosecuted. Research indicates that these forms of harassment are a serious form of fetishism and have been associated with both pedophilia and sexual assault.

In 2006, police went undercover to arrest and charge 13 individuals with lewdness on New York subways (Lee, 2006). While public lewdness on the subway has been a problem for years, the police campaign came in the wake of increasing publicity in recent months over sexual misconduct, especially in Manhattan. In a number of cases, women used cell phone cameras to take pictures of people who harassed them and posted them on the Internet. These women's active resistance to being harassed, in turn, prompted the police action. Women subway riders said cases of indecent exposure on the trains were commonplace, describing their own experiences when men either touched themselves or women.

NEW ALTERNATIVE RESPONSES

In *War Zone*, a documentary film, Maggie Hadleigh-West (1998) introduced a new approach to addressing street harassment. Hadleigh-West took a video camera to the streets of New York City and turned the lens on the creeps and Casanovas who harassed her as she walked the streets of her neighborhood. The documentary detailed her personal encounters with street harassers. "It is seen as a micro-inequity, not a big deal," says Hadleigh-West, but "the violence and disrespect experienced daily by countless people in public spaces is a serious problem with real, material consequences."

In her documentary, Hadleigh-West provides an elaborate analysis of the effects of street harassment on herself and other women. For example, she contends that the passivity most women demonstrate in response to public harassment results in feeling stifled. "You have to allow yourself to feel what you're feeling," she says. "It is the intent behind words, behavior, gestures that we are responding to." Hadleigh-West connects harassment to women's anxieties about sexual assault and to feelings of anger and powerlessness. She uses the camera to turn the gaze back on men's bad behavior. Her documentary can be used to educate men and women about the impact of street harassment and has provided women with an alternative to passive acceptance of being accosted on the streets.

HollaBackNYC is a project that similarly uses the camera to confront street harassment. This blog is dedicated to the proposition that women do not have to put up with men's propositions. (www.hollabacknyc .blogspot.com). Holla Back! is one of several websites that encourage street-harassed women—in New York and numerous other places—to snap a photo of their harassers and post the phone online with a report of the incident. HollaBackNYC is a collective of men and women who believe in creating a community where everyone feels comfortable, safe, and respected. Many people, particularly men, are unaware of the frequency and severity of disrespect and intimidation that women experience in public spaces on a daily basis. HollaBackNYC aims to expose and combat street harassment as well as provide an empowering forum in this struggle. On HollaBackNYC, women use their cell phones as weapons and as tools for social change. This website offers an outlet for women to vent and an education for the men who are oblivious to how often women get sexually intimidated on the street—and how it makes them feel. It connects the personal experience with political awareness. The stories of women's experiences bring awareness to the issue and keep everyone focused on the goal of ending street harassment (May, 2009).

Beyond its networking capacities, the blogosphere serves the movement against street harassment with a form of vigilantism. Here, the anonymous gaze is female and women become private perpetrators who publicly objectify harassers. "Some men assume they have a right to comment out loud about a woman, and we're supposed to just shrug it off," says the founder of Holla Back San Francisco. Jessica started the blog site (www.sfgate.com) as a result of her own frustration over the catcalls and kissing noises she received on the streets of her neighborhood. The point of Holla Back is to shift the power dynamic so that women have an alternative to simply hanging their heads and walking away (Adler, 2006). In Adler's piece on National Public Radio (NPR), Monica Cumming reported that her anger is subsiding now that she has a place to vent about the daily comments she gets on her way to work and school in Oakland. "Now the whole dynamic is less passive," Cumming said. "It can be risky to say something back when it happens, but now I have a way to deal with it that is more entertaining."

Internet reporter Natalie Nichols (2006) described HollaBack.com as "just a little patch of empowering catharsis in a woman's world besieged by subway flashers, tongue-waggers, boob-oglers, butt-eyeballers, and path-blockers." "We're trying to create a community where women feel safe speaking out against street harassment," said Emily May, one of the site's founders. "I think that's been exceptionally empowering for a lot of women."

CONCLUSION

On June 11, 2000, 1 million people participated in the Puerto Rican Day Parade in New York City. Although as many as 4,000 officers were assigned throughout the city and surrounded Central Park, none intervened when as many as 50 women found themselves surrounded by men who drenched them with water, grabbed at them, pulled off their clothes, and sexually assaulted them. The women who went to the police were ignored and ridiculed. How was this incident different from many other examples of street harassment and assault of women? More than 30 amateur videotapes of the incidents were turned into the police, turned over to media sources, and made available online. Based on the videos, more than 30 young men were arrested.

The release of the tapes not only resulted in arrests and prosecution, it provoked a national discussion about the harassing behavior that in many circumstances had been ignored or viewed as normal. This incident may be a watershed moment in our society. It may come to represent the time when a substantial change began: when the public started to realize that it is not okay for random men to touch and comment on women's bodies. In this era, many women are putting harassers on their cell phones and on notice. Increasingly, women are refusing to tolerate sex harassment in any form. The change has been a long time in coming.

REFERENCES

Adler, M. (2006). On the issues. National Public Radio. http://www.npr.org/templates/story/story.php?storyId=6177409.

Ayers, M. M., Friedman, C. K., & Leaper, C. (2009). Individual and situational factors related to young women's likelihood of confronting sexism in their everyday lives. *Sex Roles, 61*, 449–460.

Bartkey, S. L. (1990). *Femininity and domination: Studies in the phenomenology of oppression.* New York: Routledge.

Benard, C., & Schlaffer, E. (1981). The man on the street: Why he harasses. *Ms Magazine, 9*, 18–19.

Bowman, C. G. (1993). Street harassment and the informal ghettoization of women. *Harvard Law Review, 106*(3), 517–580.

Calogero, R. M. (2004). A test of objectification theory: The effect of the male gaze on appearance concerns in college women. *Psychology of Women Quarterly, 28*, 16–21.

Calogero, R. M., Herbozo, S., & Thompson, J. K. (2009). Complimentary weightism: The potential costs of appearance-related commentary for women's self-objectification. *Psychology of Women Quarterly, 33*, 120–132.

Crawford, M. (1995). *Talking difference: On gender and language.* London: Sage.

Dodd, E. H., Giuliano, T. A., Boutell, J. M., & Moran, B. E. (2001). Respected or rejected: Perceptions of women who confront sexist remarks. *Sex Roles, 45*, 567.

Evans, G. W., Jacobs, S. V., Dooley, D., & Catalano, R. (1987). The interaction of stressful life events and chronic strains on community mental health. *American Journal of Community Psychology, 15*, 23–34.

Ferraro, K. F. (1996). Women's fear of victimization: Shadow of sexual assault? *Social Forces, 75*(2), 667–690.

Fogg-Davis, H. G. (2006). Theorizing Black lesbians within Black feminism: A critique of same-race street harassment. *Politics & Gender, 2*, 57–76.

Frederickson, B. L., & Roberts, T. (1997). Objectification theory: Toward understanding women's lived experiences and mental health risks. *Psychology of Women Quarterly, 21*, 173–206.

Fredrickson, B. L., Roberts, T. A., Noll, S. M., Quinn, D. M., & Twenge, J. M. (1998). That swimsuit becomes you: Sex differences in self-objectification, restrained eating, and math performance. *Journal of Personality and Social Psychology, 75,* 269–284.

Gardner, C. B. (1995). *Passing by: Gender and public harassment.* Los Angeles: University of California Press.

Goffman, E. (1963). *Behavior in public places: Notes on the social organization of gatherings.* New York: Macmillan.

Gordon, M. T., & Riger, S. (1989). *The female fear.* New York: Free Press.

Greenleaf, C., & McGreer, R. (2006). Disordered eating attitudes and self-objectification among physically active and sedentary female college students. *Journal of Psychology, 140,* 187–198.

Hadleigh-West, M. (creator/director), & Levine, H. (producer). (1998). *War zone* [motion picture]. Available from Media Education Foundation, 60 Masonic St., Northampton, MA, 01060.

Kanner, A. D., Coyne, J. C., Schafer, C., & Lazarus, R. S. (1981). Comparison of two modes of stress measurement: Daily hassles and uplifts versus major life events. *Behavioral Medicine, 4*(4), 1–39

Kessler, R. C., & McLeod, J. D. (1984). Sex differences in vulnerability to undesirable life events. *American Sociological Review, 49,* 620–631.

Kilbourne, J. (creator), & Jhally, S. (producer/director). (2001). *Killing us softly: Advertising's image of women* [motion picture]. Available from Media Education Foundation, 60 Masonic St., Northampton, MA, 01060.

Landrine, H., & Klonoff, E. (1997). *Discrimination against women: Prevalence, consequences, remedies.* Thousand Oaks, CA: Sage.

Langelan, M. (1993). *Back off! How to confront and stop sexual harassment and harassers.* New York: Simon & Schuster.

Lee, J. (2006, June 23). Undercover police charge 13 with lewdness on subways. *New York Times.* Retrieved on 4/21/10 from http://www.nytimes.com/2006/06/23/nyregion/23expose.html?_r=1

Lenton, R., Smith, M. D., Fox, J., & Morra, N. (1999). Sexual harassment in public places: Experiences of Canadian women. *Canadian Review of Sociology and Anthropology, 36*(4), 517–540.

Lord, T. (2009). *The relationship of gender-based public harassment to body image, self-esteem, and avoidance behavior.* Doctoral dissertation, Indiana University of Pennsylvania, Pennsylvania. Retrieved November 7, 2009, from *Dissertations & Theses: Full Text* (Publication No. AAT 3369986).

MacMillan, R., Nierobisz, A., & Welsh, S. (2000). Experiencing the streets: Harassment and perceptions of safety among women. *Journal of Research in Crime and Delinquency, 37*(3), 306–322.

May, E. (2009). Gender harassment: From our revolution to yours. *On the Issues Magazine.* http://www.ontheissuesmagazine.com/cafe2/article/37.

McHugh, M. C. (1996). A feminist approach to agoraphobia: Challenging the traditional views of women at home. In J. C. Chrisler, C. Golden, & P. D. Rozee (Eds.), *Lectures on the psychology of women* (2nd ed.) (pp. 339–357). New York: McGraw-Hill.

McKinley, N. M., & Hyde, J. S. (1996). The objectified body consciousness scale: Development and validation. *Psychology of Women Quarterly, 20,* 181–215.

Medea, A., & Thompson, K. (1974). *Against rape.* New York: Farrar, Straus & Giroux.

Moradi, B., Dirks, D., & Matteson, A. V. (2005). Roles of sexual objectification experiences and internalization of standards of beauty in eating disorder symptomatology: A test and extension of objectification theory. *Journal of Counseling Psychology, 52,* 420–428.

Nichols, N. (2006, September 14). Hey baby. *LA City Beat.* http://www.lacitybeat.com/cms/story/detail/?id=4341&IssueNum=171.

Nielsen, L. B. (2000). Situating legal consciousness: Experiences and attitudes of ordinary citizens about law and street harassment. *Law and Society Review, 34*(4), 1055–1090.

Ramos, C. (n.d.). A feminist guide to analysis and direct action. http://www.ffiles.net/activism.html.

Roberson, A. (2005). Anti-street harassment. *Off Our Backs,* May–June, p. 48.

Rozee, P. D. (2000). Freedom from fear of rape: The missing link in women's freedom. In J. C. Chrisler, C. Golden, & P. D. Rozee (Eds.), *Lectures on the psychology of women* (2nd ed.) (pp. 255–269). New York: McGraw-Hill.

Stanko, E. A. (1995). Women, crime, and fear. *Annals of the American Academy of Political and Social Sciences, 539,* 46–58.

Swim, J. K., & Hyers, L. L. (1999). Excuse me—What did you just say?!: Women's public and private reactions to sexist remarks. *Journal of Experimental Social Psychology, 35,* 68–88.

Swim, J. K., Hyers, L. L., Cohen, L. L., & Fergusan, M. J. (2001). Everyday sexism: Evidence for its incidence, nature, and psychological impact from three daily diary studies. *Journal of Social Science, 57,* 31–53.

Tiggemann, M., & Williamson, S. (2004). The role of body objectification in disordered eating and depressed mood. *British Journal of Clinical Psychology, 43,* 299–311.

Warr, M. (1985). Fear of rape among urban women. *Social Problems, 32,* 238–252.

Weiten, W. (1998). Pressure, major life events, and psychological symptoms. *Journal of Social Behavior & Personality, 13,* 51–64.

Chapter 11

How Abusive Husbands and Sexual Harassers Infer Women's Thoughts and Feelings

William E. Schweinle and Betty A. Hulse

INTRODUCTION

This chapter describes a series of four studies of men who maltreat women. More specifically, it addresses the social cognition of men who abuse their wives and men who sexually harass women. Social cognition is the area of psychology that is concerned with how people perceive, interpret, process, encode, store, retrieve, and apply information from other people (see Fiske & Taylor, 2007, for a thorough and well-written review of social cognition theory and research). This chapter focuses on the ways in which men who maltreat women perceive and interpret women's thought and feelings.

The studies described here evolved from a simple question that grew from Holtzworth-Munroe's (1992) application of McFall's (1982) social information processing theory to research on abusive men. Holtzworth-Munroe theorized that abusive men are deficient in their ability to effectively receive, interpret, or act on social information. The research question was, "Are abusive husbands more or less accurate than nonabusive husbands when they infer women's thoughts and feelings?"

The findings from these four studies help us understand how abusive men perceive women's thoughts and feelings, how abusive men sustain those perceptions and how those perceptions lead to abusive behavior. However and perhaps more importantly, the studies discussed below offer insight into abusive men and that insight may inform interventions designed to reduce men's abusive behavior. The findings may also offer some important cues by which abusive men can be identified before they abuse women.

STUDY I: EMPATHIC ACCURACY IN HUSBAND-TO-WIFE AGGRESSION—THE OVERATTRIBUTION BIAS

Several authors have reported that abusive husbands tend to be hyper-vigilant for signs of women's criticism and rejection (Berry, 1998; Deschner, 1984; Downey, Feldman, & Ayduk, 2000; Dutton, 1995, 1998; Jacobson & Gottman, 1998; Nelson, 1997; Walker, 1979). The scientific literature has also tentatively suggested that this hypervigilance results in biased and inaccurate inferences about women's critical or rejecting thoughts and feelings.

However, this assumption had never actually been tested. In fact, a plausible argument based on the some social psychology literature could be made in favor of the hypothesis that abusive men are unusually accurate when they infer criticism or rejection.

Schweinle, Ickes, and Bernstein (2002) set out to scientifically test these competing notions: hyperaccuracy versus biased inaccuracy. More specifically, Schweinle et al. designed a study to determine whether abusive men are hyperaccurate, rather than unusually biased and inaccurate, when they infer women's critical/rejecting thoughts and feelings.

To resolve this issue, Schweinle, Ickes, and Bernstein recruited 86 married men to participate in a modified version of the standardized *empathic accuracy* (EA) paradigm. The EA paradigm (described in more detail later in this section) is a valid reliable method that was originally developed by Ickes and his colleagues for measuring the accuracy with which people infer others' thoughts and feelings (Marangoni, Garcia, Ickes, & Teng, 1995; see also Ickes, 1997, 2003). The EA paradigm has been used in basic and applied studies. For the purposes here, key studies with this paradigm include research demonstrating that people with borderline personality characteristics are *not* more empathically accurate than other people (Flury, Ickes, & Schweinle, 2008) and a study demonstrating that greater EA in married couples is associated with better supportive behavior between married partners (Verhofstadt, Buysse, Ickes, Davis, & Devoldre, 2008).

In the Schweinle et al. (2002) study of abusive men, participants were shown videotapes of three women in a simulated individual therapy session. The therapy sessions were simulated only insofar as they were videotaped. On the videotapes, the female therapy clients spoke with a male Rogerian therapist about real problems or concerns. The women expressed a wide range of emotions and thoughts about their recent divorce, their pending divorce, or their conflicting roles as a professional and a mother. After each woman's therapy session, she was shown the videotape of her own therapy session and asked to write down in sentence form the specific content of the thoughts and feelings that she remembered having during her therapy session. The women were also asked to indicate the exact time point on the videotape when the thought or feeling occurred. These videotapes, along with the women's written thoughts and feelings, were then reviewed by eight independent women raters, who determined whether the thoughts and feelings written and expressed by the female therapy clients were critical or rejecting.

The 86 married male participants were invited to the University of Texas at Arlington Social Interaction Lab individually. Each was seated alone in a cubicle when he arrived. The men were asked to complete a battery of instruments, including a demographic questionnaire, a measure of the men's marital satisfaction (RDAS; Busby, Christensen, Crane, & Larson, 1995) and a measure of the men's socially desirable response bias (M-C 1[10], Strahan & Gerbasi, 1972). After they completed the questionnaires, the men were shown the women's therapy videotapes.

While the male participants were viewing the videotapes, the experimenter paused the tape at the exact point on the tape that the woman therapy client had remembered a specific thought or feeling. The men then wrote in sentence form their inferences of the woman's thoughts and feelings and indicated whether the inferred thought that thought or feeling was critical or rejecting. This procedure yielded a data set that included (1) the men's inferences about whether the women therapy clients' thoughts or feelings were critical or rejecting and (2) whether the women's thoughts and feelings actually were critical or rejecting.

Schweinle et al. (2002) used signal detection analyses to determine each of the men's degree of inferential bias (Donaldson, 1992) to infer the women's criticism or rejection. Signal detection analysis was also used to score the accuracy (i.e., "sensitivity," or d in signal detection terms) of the men's inferences.

After the inference phase of the procedure, the men completed a final questionnaire that included the Conflict Tactics Scale (Straus, 1979), which is a widely used self-report measure of men's wife-directed aggression. The men's social desirability response scores were used to adjust their scores on the Conflict Tactics Scale using a regression method described by Saunders (1991).

Schweinle et al. (2002) looked at the relationship between the men's inferential bias scores, the accuracy scores, and the adjusted scores on the Conflict Tactics Scale (Straus, 1979) while statistically controlling for the men's marital satisfaction, their length of marriage, and their estimate of the stability of their marriages. These control variables were used to reduce the chance that these factors—as opposed to the men's wife-directed aggression alone—were related to the men's inferential bias and/or accuracy.

The results indicated that the more aggressive husbands were perceptually biased to overattribute critical/rejecting thoughts and feelings to women. This phenomenon has been termed the *critical/rejecting overattribution bias* (C/R-O bias). Conversely, the more abusive men were not unusually able to correctly identify women's critical/rejecting thoughts and feelings. In fact, the more biased the men were, the less accurate their inferences were. This pattern of results clearly indicated that abusive men are biased to over-infer women's criticism or rejection. The more abusive men were not unusually accurate in this regard.

In summary, Schweinle et al. (2002) demonstrated that abusive men are inclined to inaccurately take offense in the form of women's criticism or rejection even when no criticism, rejection, or offense is intended by women. Perhaps the more important moral or forensic implication of these results is that abusive men, through their perceptual bias to overattribute critical/rejection thoughts and feelings to their female partners, are capable of providing their own provocation for aggression.

STUDY 2: EMPATHIC ACCURACY OF INTIMATE PARTNERS IN VIOLENT VERSUS NONVIOLENT RELATIONSHIPS

An important issue with the Schweinle, Ickes, and Bernstein (2002) study was that it relied on men's self-reported levels of aggression and did not compare a sample of known violent men to men who were known to be nonviolent. Because batterers and nonbatterers have been addressed in the scientific literature as distinct populations (see Johnson, 1995), it was important to compare the empathic accuracy of samples of men from each of these populations. Clements, Holtzworth-Munroe, Schweinle, and Ickes (2007) designed a follow-up study to expand on the findings reported by Schweinle et al. (2002) and to test whether known abusive men were unique from nonabusive men in their ability to infer their wives' and other women's thoughts and feelings.

This study used a standardized version of the empathic accuracy paradigm described previously and the dyadic EA paradigm. In the dyadic EA paradigm, pairs of participants—male and female partners, in this case—interacted with each other while being unobtrusively videotaped. After the interaction session, the participants independently viewed the videotape of their interaction and wrote their own specific thoughts and feelings. The participants then viewed the videotape a second time and inferred the content of their interaction partners' thoughts and feelings when the experimenter paused the tape. The experimenter paused the videotape at the exact times when the participant's partner had reported a specific thought or feeling. The participants' actual thoughts and feelings and their partners' concordant inferences were then rated for similarity by a team of independent raters, which resulted in an empathic accuracy score for each participant.

Whereas the Schweinle, Ickes, and Bernstein (2002) study tested men's ability to determine whether a woman's thought or feeling was critical or rejecting, the dependent variable of interest in the Clements et al. (2007) study was empathic accuracy. Empathic accuracy refers to the accuracy with which a person infers the *actual content* of another person's thoughts and feelings. The goal of this study was to compare the empathic accuracy of male and female partners between three groups of couples: (1) couples who were experiencing violence in their relationship, (2) couples who were not experiencing violence but were having relationship distress, and (3) couples who were nonviolent and nondistressed.

Clements et al. (2007) found that violent husbands were significantly less accurate than nonviolent, nondistressed men at inferring the actual content of their female partner's thoughts and feelings. In fact, when inferring their own partners' thoughts and feelings, violent men were significantly less accurate than objective observers, who did not even know the men's female partners. This effect was not attributable to group differences in the clarity with which the women expressed their own thoughts and feelings, because there were no group differences in objective observers' empathic accuracy for the female partners' thoughts and feelings.

The level of the men's physical violence—but not their level of relationship satisfaction—was a significant predictor of men's empathic accuracy for their female partner's thoughts and feelings. Increasing levels of male violence predicted decreased levels of men's empathic accuracy for their female partners. These findings confirmed that male intimate-partner violence is related to inaccuracy in men's inferences about their female partner's thoughts and feelings. This pattern of findings also supported the conclusions of Schweinle et al. (2002) that abusive men are deficient in their ability to infer the theme of women's thoughts and feelings.

STUDY 3: THE ROLE OF MEN'S CRITICISM AND REJECTION OVERATTRIBUTION BIAS, AFFECT, AND ATTENTIONAL DISENGAGEMENT IN MARITAL AGGRESSION

The primary goal of Schweinle and Ickes's (2007) study grew from the question, "How, in the light of the social information available to them, are aggressive men able to make such consistently biased and inaccurate inferences about women's thoughts, feelings, criticism and rejection?" Specifically, these researchers explored abusive men's affective reactions to women and abusive men's attention to women's expressions as factors that could potentially "enable" and sustain the men's C/R-O bias. More specifically, this study explored the possibility that abusive men's negative affective reactions to women and attentional disengagement might be mechanisms by which aggressive men maintain their biased inaccurate inferential style, which leads to abusive behavior.

According to a tradition of social cognition research and theory, affective responses precede social cognition and social judgment. Social cognition and judgment, in turn, influence social behavior (Feshbach & Singer, 1957; Schachter, 1959). Other findings support the hypothesized causal sequence in which negative emotion precipitates biased inference making, and biased inferences, in turn, precipitate aggression (Fincham & Bradbury, 1992; Karney, Bradbury, Fincham, & Sullivan, 1994). Abusive men are more likely than nonabusive men to have angry reactions to women (Holtzworth-Munroe & Smutzler, 1996; Jacobson & Gottman, 1998). Based on these reports, Schweinle and Ickes hypothesized that abusive men's angry reactions to women precipitate abusive men's biased and inaccurate inferences, which then precipitate the men's aggression.

Other findings support the conclusion that more aggressive or abusive husbands may be less willing to engage emotionally with women who express their relationship-related distress (Holtzworth-Munroe & Smutzler, 1996; Sillars, Roberts, Leonard, & Dun, 2000). Also, men's attentional disengagement or "tuning out" may forestall a sympathetic identification with women's relationship distress. Following this logic, if more aggressive husbands disengage their attention from their wives' expressions, they may remain ignorant of the women's expressions and effectively sustain their inaccurate bias to overattribute criticism or rejection to women and respond with more aggression.

To test these hypotheses, Schweinle and Ickes (2007) recruited a sample of 80 married men through newspaper ads. They then used a uniquely modified version of the standardized EA paradigm as part of their study design.

The male participants were shown a tape of one woman in a therapy session and asked to infer whether her specific thoughts and feelings were critical or rejecting, just as in the Schweinle et al. (2002) study. These inferences were analyzed with signal detection methods to arrive at bias and accuracy scores for the men. Again, this procedure was very similar to the one used by Schweinle et al. (2002).

One major procedural difference occurred in the Schweinle and Ickes (2007) study, however. In this adaptation of the EA paradigm, a small camera was hidden in the test cubicle and focused on the men's faces while the men were viewing the stimulus tape and making their inferences. The tapes of the men's facial expressions, which included the woman inference target's audio track, were played to the men after the men had viewed the therapy tape and made their inferences.

At the exact points when the woman's therapy tape had been paused, the men's tape was paused by the experimenter. The men indicated on a mood-adjective checklist the feeling closest to the one that they remembered having at that moment. The mood-adjective choices were *irritated, annoyed, sympathetic, concerned, indifferent, unaffected, insulted, contempt, uncaring,* and *sad*. Within this limited range, the procedure revealed what the men were feeling when they were making an inference of the woman's thought or feeling.

Two independent raters then viewed the tapes of the men's facial expressions and recorded the amount of time that the men were not attending to the videotape of the woman's therapy session.

These two procedures resulted in two important measures: (1) what the men were feeling at the time they made an inference about whether the woman on the video was having a critical or rejecting thought or feeling and (2) an objective measure of the amount of attention that the men were paying to the woman on the therapy tape while she was talking with the therapist.

The results replicated the important finding reported by Schweinle et al. (2002): husbands' aggression toward their own wives was positively correlated with the strength of each husband's C/R-O bias, but not with hyperaccuracy or hypersensitivity on the husbands' part. This provides converging evidence that the abusive men's wife-directed aggression probably derives at least in some part from the social cognition of the men themselves, and not necessarily from provocation by abusive men's female partners.

Consistent with predictions, the men's feelings of contempt for the woman in the stimulus videotape served as a mediating mechanism by which the men were able to sustain their biased inferences about the woman's criticism and rejection. This finding implies that abusive men are able to make their biased inaccurate inferences by not identifying with women and instead by responding to women with feelings of contempt. The results also indicated that attentional disengagement is a another independent mediating mechanism by which abusive men are able to avoid making more accurate inferences about the nature of women's thoughts and feelings. Together, these results suggest abusive men's contempt for women and abusive men's attentional disengagement from women are important markers of their propensity for wife-directed aggression.

In summary, this study demonstrated that abusive husbands prejudge women's thoughts and feelings as critical or rejecting and that abusive husbands behave aggressively to the extent that they can sustain this biased prejudgment through feelings of contempt for women or by ignoring the social cues that might reveal what a woman actually thinks and feels.

STUDY 4: MEN'S EMPATHIC BIAS, EMPATHIC ACCURACY, AND SEXUAL HARASSMENT

The fourth study grew from another simple question, "How would a man be likely behave if he were biased *against* inferring women's criticism or aggression?" The intuitive answer naively assumed that men's sexual harassment of women is motivated by seduction. After reviewing the relevant literature, however, Schweinle, Cofer, and Schatz (2009) were able to form and test three competing hypotheses. According to the first hypothesis, if sexual harassment represents inept seduction, then sexual harassers would be expected to be biased against inferring women's criticism or rejection. Following this logic, if a man were able to accurately infer women's criticism or rejection, he could use this information to make his behavior more appropriate. According to the second hypothesis, if sexual harassment is a form of sexual aggression against women (as theorized by O'Leary-Kelly, Patezold, & Griffin, 2000), then sexual harassers may be like abusive husbands in their bias to overattribute criticism to women. Finally, according to the third hypothesis, there are two types of sexual harassers: seduction-minded men who are unable to accurately infer when women are rejecting them and misogynistic aggressive sexual harassers who harass as a form of retaliation for a perceived slight (i.e., criticism or rejection from women).

The participants for this study included the 80 married men included in the study by Schweinle and Ickes (2007). The men were asked to complete a self-report measure of their behaviors that women tend to find sexually harassing. The men's scores on this measure were compared to their sensitivity and bias when inferring women's criticism and rejection.

The results clearly supported the second hypothesis—namely, that men's sexual harassment behavior is positively associated with the level of the men's bias to over-infer women's criticism and rejection and negatively associated with men's accuracy in making this inference. Further, the more aggressive the man is toward his wife, the more sexual harassment behavior he tends to exhibit.

In summary, these findings indicate that men who are prone to engaging in sexual harassment are biased to infer women's criticism and rejection, and these men tend to make this inference at the wrong times (i.e., when women do not have critical or rejecting thoughts or feelings). This social cognitive characteristic—men's C/R-O bias—is also associated with men's wife-directed aggression. Finally, this study offers some strong evidence that sexual harassment may be, at least in terms of men's social cognition, a way in which men retaliate for the erroneously perceived slight of women's criticism or rejection.

SUMMARY

This chapter briefly summarized four studies in a program of research that explored the social cognition of men who abuse their wives and men who sexually harass women. The findings across these four studies supported four main ideas:

1. Men who abuse their wives tend to inaccurately infer the content of women's thoughts and feelings.
2. These men also tend to be biased to over-infer criticism or rejection in women's thoughts and feelings, and this bias is enabled by the men's contemptuous affective reactions to women and by their attentional disengagement from women's expressions.
3. Abusive men tend to sexually harass women.
4. Men who are prone to sexually harassing women tend to have the same critical/rejecting overattribution bias that is characteristic of abusive husbands.

Taken together, these findings suggest that men's critical/rejecting overattribution bias, men's deficient ability to accurately infer women's thoughts and feelings, men's contemptuous reactions toward women, and men's attentional disengagement from women play important roles in at least two ways that men maltreat women: wife abuse and sexual harassment.

The findings in these studies have important therapeutic implications. This research has revealed characteristics of abusive men that may lead to a reliable system for identifying these men before they abuse women. Furthermore, the development of therapeutic interventions that are aimed at reducing abusive men's C/R-O bias may prevent or reduce men's abusive behavior, although this notion has not been empirically tested. Future research should continue to investigate the relationship between men's C/R-O bias and other ways in which men may mistreat women and look for ways in which to reduce men's abusive behavior.

REFERENCES

Berry, D. (1998). *The domestic violence sourcebook*. Los Angeles: Lowell House.

Busby, D. M., Christensen, C., Crane, D. R., & Larson, J. H. (1995). A revision of the dyadic adjustment scale for use with distressed and nondistressed couples: Construct hierarchy and multidimensional scales. *Journal of Marital and Family Therapy, 21*(3), 289–308.

Clements, K., Holtzworth-Munroe, A., Schweinle, W., & Ickes, W. (2007). Empathic accuracy of intimate partners in violent versus nonviolent relationships. *Personal Relationships, 14*, 369–388.

Deschner, J. (1984). *How to end the hitting habit*. New York: Free Press.

Donaldson, W. (1992). Measuring recognition memory. *Journal of Experimental Psychology: General, 121*(3), 275–277.

Downey, G., Feldman, S., & Ayduk O. (2000). Rejection sensitivity and male violence in romantic relationships. *Personal Relationships, 7*, 54–61.

Dutton, D. G. (1995). *The batterer: A psychological profile*. New York: Basic Books.

Dutton, D. G. (1998). *The abusive personality*. New York: Guilford Press.

Feshbach, S., & Singer, R. (1957). The effects of fear arousal and suppression of fear upon social perception. *Journal of Abnormal and Social Psychology, 55*, 283–288.

Fincham, F., & Bradbury, T. (1992). Assessing attributions in marriage: The relationship attribution measure. *Journal of Personality and Social Psychology, 62*(3), 457–468.

Fiske, S., & Taylor, S. (2007). *Social cognition, from brains to culture.* New York: McGraw-Hill.

Flury, J., Ickes, W., & Schweinle, W. (2008). The borderline empathy effect: Do high BPD individuals have greater empathic ability? Or are they just more difficult to "read"? *Journal of Research in Personality, 42,* 312–332.

Holtzworth-Munroe, A. (1992). Social skill deficits in maritally violent men: Interpreting the data using a social information processing model. *Clinical Psychology Review, 12,* 605–617.

Holtzworth-Munroe, A., & Smutzler, N. (1996). Comparing the emotional reactions and behavioral intentions of violent and nonviolent husbands to aggressive, distressed, and other wife behaviors. *Violence and Victims, 11*(4), 319–339.

Ickes, W. (Ed.). (1997). *Empathic accuracy.* New York: Guilford Press.

Ickes, W. (2003). *Everyday mindreading.* Amherst, NY: Prometheus Books.

Jacobson, N., & Gottman, J. (1998). *When men batter women.* New York: Simon and Schuster.

Johnson, M. (1995). Patriarchal terrorism and common couple violence: Two forms of violence against women. *Journal of Marriage & the Family, 57*(2), 283–294.

Karney, B., Bradbury, T., Fincham, F., & Sullivan, K. (1994). The role of negative affectivity in the association between attributions and marital satisfaction. *Journal of Personality and Social Psychology, 66*(2), 413–424.

Marangoni, C., Garcia, S., Ickes, W., & Teng, G. (1995). Empathic accuracy in a clinically relevant setting. *Journal of Personality and Social Psychology, 68,* 854–869.

McFall, R. (1982). A review and reformulation of the concept of social skills. *Behavioral Assessment, 4,* 1–33.

Nelson, N. (1997). *Dangerous relationships.* New York: Plenum.

O'Leary-Kelly, A., Patezold, R., & Griffin, R. (2000). Sexual harassment as aggressive behavior: An actor based perspective. *Academy of Management Review, 25*(2), 372–388.

Saunders, D. G. (1991). Procedures for adjusting self-reports of violence for social desirability bias. *Journal of Interpersonal Violence, 6*(3), 336–344.

Schachter, S. (1959). *The psychology of affiliation.* Palo Alto, CA: Stanford University Press.

Schweinle, W., Bernstein, I., & Ickes, W. (2002). Empathic accuracy in husband to wife aggression: The overattribution bias. *Personal Relationships, 9,* 141–158.

Schweinle, W., Cofer, C., & Schatz, S. (2009). Men's empathic bias, empathic inaccuracy and sexual harassment. *Sex Roles, 60,* 142–150.

Schweinle, W., & Ickes, W. (2007). The role of men's critical/rejecting overattribution bias, affect, and attentional disengagement in marital aggression. *Journal of Social and Clinical Psychology, 26,* 173–198.

Sillars, A., Roberts, L., Leonard, K., & Dun, T. (2000). Cognition during marital conflict: The relationship of thought and talk. *Journal of Social and Personal Relationships, 17*(4–5), 479–502.

Strahan, R., & Gerbasi, K. (1972). Short homogeneous versions of the Marlowe–Crowne social desirability scale. *Journal of Clinical Psychology, 28,* 191–193.

Straus, M. A. (1979). Measuring intrafamily conflict and violence: The conflict tactics (CT) scale. *Journal of Marriage and Family, 41,* 75–88.

Verhofstadt, L., Buysse, A., Ickes, W., Davis, M., & Devoldre, I. (2008). Support provision in marriage: The role of emotional similarity and empathic accuracy. *Emotion, 8*(6), 792–802.

Walker, L. (1979). *The battered woman.* New York: Harper & Row.

Chapter 12

Sexual Harassment of Women Employees

NiCole T. Buchanan, Isis H. Settles, Krystle C. Woods, and Brian K. Colar

Approximately half of all women will experience sexual harassment over the course of their working lives (Ilies, Hauserman, Schwochau, & Stibal, 2003), resulting in many negative health, work, and psychological outcomes (Willness, Steel, & Lee, 2007). The frequency of harassment and the severity of its consequences necessitate that women, and the organizations in which they work, better understand which behaviors constitute harassment and how to reduce their incidence. To this end, the current chapter provides an overview of the literature on the sexual harassment of working women, focusing on the legal and psychological definitions of sexual harassment, theories of why harassment occurs, and concerns specific to racial and sexual minority women. Emphasis is placed on the negative work, health, and psychological outcomes experienced by sexually harassed women and the coping strategies they use.

HOW CAN ONE RECOGNIZE SEXUAL HARASSMENT?

Psychological Definitions of Sexual Harassment

Sexual harassment has been defined as both a psychological and a legal phenomenon. Psychologists define sexual harassment as unwanted gender-based comments and behaviors that are appraised as offensive, exceed one's available coping resources, or are perceived to be a threat to the individual's well-being (Fitzgerald, Swan, & Magley, 1997). Generally, sexual harassment is divided into three subtypes (Fitzgerald et al., 1988; Fitzgerald, Gelfand, & Drasgow, 1995). *Gender harassment* includes negative nonsexual, gender-based comments and behaviors, such as statements that women are less intelligent than men or that women cannot do certain jobs because they are "men's work." *Unwanted sexual attention* includes verbal and nonverbal unsolicited comments, gestures, or attempts at physical contact, such as attempts to touch or kiss someone or repeated requests for dates. *Sexual coercion* encompasses any job-related threats or benefits that are contingent upon compliance with sexual demands, such as a supervisor promising to promote a worker only if she is sexually cooperative, or threatening to terminate employment if she refuses sexual advances. *Contrapower sexual harassment* is another form that may include any of the three previously mentioned subtypes, but involves a subordinate (e.g., undergraduate) sexually harassing his or her superior (e.g., a professor; Rospenda, Richman, & Nawyn, 1998).

Legal Definitions of Sexual Harassment

Legal definitions outline two forms of sexual harassment: quid pro quo and hostile environment. *Quid pro quo* is the legal equivalent of sexual coercion and includes any attempt to coerce sexual interactions by threatening one's employment. A *hostile work environment* is created when unwanted gender-based behaviors become sufficiently pervasive that an employee either perceives the general work environment to be hostile or his or her job performance is negatively affected as a result of the poor climate (Equal Employment Opportunity Commission, 1980). Frequently, a hostile work environment includes behaviors that fall under the psychological definitions of gender harassment and unwanted sexual attention.

WHY DOES SEXUAL HARASSMENT OCCUR?

Sociocultural and organizational theories have been the primary explanations put forth regarding antecedents of sexual harassment. Eventually, they were combined by Louise Fitzgerald and colleagues to form the integrated process theory of sexual harassment. These three theories are summarized in this section.

Sociocultural Theories of Harassment

One sociocultural theory asserts that sexual harassment is an extension of gender socialization processes. Men are socialized and rewarded for engaging in "dominance, sexual initiative, and self-interest," whereas women are socialized for "submissiveness, sexual gatekeeping," and self-sacrifice (Tangri & Hayes, 1997, p. 121). These learned gender-role norms are carried into the workplace, such that women are socialized to submit to dominant men, and men are socialized to assert their dominance by using gender-based comments and by reducing women to purely sexual beings. By building on socialized roles, sexual harassment functions to maintain male power—both economic and social—by intimidating women in the workplace.

Building on gender-role socialization theory, sex-role spillover theory suggests that gender-based expectations for behavior are brought into the workplace (Gutek & Morasch, 1982). Because of the salience of gender, individuals are seen as male or female before they are seen in terms of their work identity. Further, coworkers respond to one another according to gender roles rather than work roles. This theory suggests that the impact of sex-role spillover for women is that they may be treated differently than their male coworkers—treated in a feminized or sexualized manner—thereby increasing the likelihood that they will be subjected to sexually harassing behaviors. Such dynamics are exacerbated in male-dominated workplaces, which increases both hostility toward and sexual harassment of women who defy gendered work norms (Berhdahl, 2007a; Morgan & Gruber, 2005).

Organizational Theories of Harassment

Organizational theories focus on differences in the relative status and organizational power between men and women. Men typically hold formal power in organizations, including positions higher in the organizational hierarchy as well as positions with greater relevance to the central mission of the organization. Even when women have comparable positions to men in the organization, men frequently have more informal power, which includes access to support from peers, mentoring, and those who make decisions (DiTomaso, 1989; Ragins & Sundstrom, 1989). According to organizational theories, sexual harassment is an extension of an organizational culture that grants male workers formal and informal power over their female colleagues; this greater power may be used by men to sexually intimidate female workers (Cleveland & Kerst, 1993) as a means of maintaining their higher status.

Integrated Process Theory of Harassment

The sociocultural and organizational theories explain the function of harassment in some cases, but not all. For example, socialization and sex-role spillover theories do not explain why some men harass and others do not, and theories of formal and informal organizational power do not fully account for the fact women are harassed by colleagues and subordinates, as well as by supervisors (Wayne, 2000). To address these limitations, Fitzgerald, Drasgow, Hulin, Gelfand, and Magley (1997) and Fitzgerald, Hulin, and Drasgow (1995) developed a comprehensive model addressing both sociocultural and organizational factors involved in sexual harassment in the workplace.

Fitzgerald, Drasgow, Hulin, Gelfand, and Magley (1997) and Fitzgerald, Hulin, and Drasgow (1995) posit that workplace sexual harassment is the result of both the organizational climate and the job-gender context; they suggest that this condition has detrimental implications for work, psychological, and physical health outcomes (see Figure 12.1). Organizational climate refers to the degree to which the organization is tolerant of sexual harassment (e.g., harassment is modeled by superiors, harassers are not reprimanded). Job-gender context refers to the gender ratio of the

Figure 12.1
Expansion of the integrated process model of the antecedents and outcomes of sexual harassment in organizations. The original model is shown in white; the shaded boxes represent expanded components of the model. (Adapted from Fitzgerald, Drasgow, Hulin, Gelfand, & Magley, 1997; Fitzgerald, Hulin, & Drasgow, 1995.)

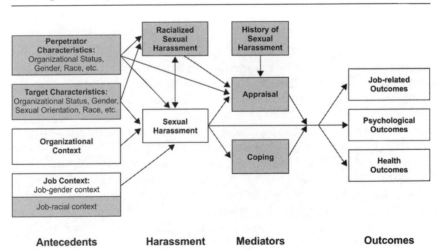

work group and recognition of the job as a traditionally male or female occupation. Organizations with a climate that is more tolerant of sexual harassment and those with more male job-gender contexts are theorized to be associated with more prevalent sexual harassment for women. Greater sexual harassment is, in turn, theorized to lead to three types of negative outcomes: job-related outcomes, psychological outcomes, and health outcomes.

SUPPORT FOR THE INTEGRATED PROCESS THEORY OF SEXUAL HARASSMENT: PREVALENCE, ANTECEDENTS, AND OUTCOMES OF SEXUAL HARASSMENT

As noted earlier, half of working women experience sexual harassment prior to retirement (Fitzgerald & Shullman, 1993; Ilies et al., 2003). In the United States, the Equal Employment Opportunity Commission (EEOC) is charged with investigating employment discrimination allegations. In 2008, this agency received 13,867 complaints of workplace sexual harassment, more than 80 percent of which were filed by women (EEOC, 2009). Consistent with the integrated process theory of sexual harassment, some workplaces are associated with higher rates of sexual harassment than others, particularly those with a job-gender context that is highly masculinized or jobs that are traditionally deemed "men's work." For example, 65 to 79 percent of female military personnel report experiencing sexual harassment within a one-year period (Department of Defense, 2004; Department of Defense Inspector General, 2005; Fitzgerald, Magley, Drasgow, & Waldo, 1999; Hansen, 2004), and higher rates of sexual harassment have been reported among female police officers (Collins, 2004; Martin, 1994; Texeira, 2002), blue-collar workers (Gruber, 1998, 2003; Gruber & Smith, 1995), medical faculty (Carr et al., 2000), and natural scientists and engineers (Settles, Cortina, Malley, & Stewart, 2006).

Individuals within male-dominated organizations and those who hold traditionally male jobs frequently have more negative attitudes toward women, and their organizations are often perceived as being high in their tolerance of sexual harassment (Gutek & Morasch, 1982; Sadler, Booth, Cook, Torner, & Doebbeling, 2001; Vogt, Bruce, Street, & Stafford, 2007). As predicted by the integrated process theory of sexual harassment, organizations that rate high in sexual harassment tolerance have elevated rates of not only sexual harassment (Hulin, Fitzgerald, & Drasgow, 1996; Low, Radhakrishnan, Schneider, & Rounds, 2007; Williams, Fitzgerald, & Drasgow, 1999), but also other forms of harassment (Buchanan & Fitzgerald, 2008). Decreasing the perceived tolerance of sexual harassment (e.g., conveying that harassment is unacceptable, reprimanding offenders) reduces the overall rate of harassment and increases the likelihood that a target will report the incident, which provides the organization with an opportunity to stop the harassment and reduce its liability (Bell, Cycyota, & Quick, 2002; Gruber, 1998).

Effect of Harassment on Job Outcomes

Experiences of sexual harassment have been linked to negative work-related outcomes for both those targeted by such behavior and for those who witness or are aware of the harassment (Glomb, Richman, Hulin, Drasgow, Schneider, & Fitzgerald, 1997; Hitlan, Schneider, & Walsh, 2006; Low et al., 2007). Studies have found that sexually harassed women report lower job satisfaction, work productivity, and supervisor satisfaction, and demonstrate increased absenteeism, work withdrawal, and intentions to quit (Langhout, Bergman, Cortina, Fitzgerald, Drasgow, & Williams, 2005; Lapierre, Spector, & Leck, 2005; O'Connell & Korabik, 2000; Stockdale, 1998). Women who have been sexually harassed are more likely to withdraw from work by being arriving late or actively looking for another job (Kath, Swody, Magley, Bunk, & Gallus, 2009) and their job performance is negatively affected by their difficulty concentrating due to the harassment (Glomb, Munson, Hulin, Bergman, & Drasgow, 1999). Targets of harassment have reported higher turnover rates and lower levels of organizational commitment (Munson, Hulin & Drasgow, 2000; Schneider, Swan, & Fitzgerald, 1997; Sims, Drasgow, & Fitzgerald, 2005). Sexual harassment has also been shown to negatively affect work engagement—that is, the commitment to one's employer—which results in decreased motivation to fulfill work goals (Cogin & Fish, 2009).

Effect of Harassment on Psychological Outcomes

The negative effect of sexual harassment on mental health outcomes has also been well documented (see Woods & Buchanan, in press, for a review). Meta-analytic reviews have found significant associations between sexual harassment and psychological well-being indicators such as depression, anxiety, post-traumatic stress disorder, and disordered eating (Cantisano, Dominguez, & Depolo, 2008; Chan, Lam, Chow, & Cheung, 2008; Willness et al., 2007). Some sexually harassed women also show an increased use of prescription drugs, drinking to intoxication, and escapist drinking motives (e.g., drinking to decrease tension, escape problems, feel better, forget painful memories or worries; Richman, Rospenda, Flaherty, Freels, & Zlatoper, 2004). Victims of sexual harassment may turn to prescription drugs and alcohol in an effort to self-medicate, which places them at increased risk for alcohol abuse or dependence and more serious psychological problems over time. These negative effects frequently persist long after the harassment has ended. For example, in a longitudinal study on the effects of harassment, Glomb and colleagues (1999) found that two years after the sexual harassment ended, targets reported lower psychological well-being, less satisfaction with life, and more post-traumatic symptoms compared to women who had not experienced prior sexual harassment.

The negative impact of sexual harassment on psychological outcomes has been supported across a wide variety of populations, including former military reservists (Street, Gradus, Stafford, & Kelly, 2007), women in both the U.S. (Bergman & Drasgow, 2003) and Swedish armed forces (Estrada & Berggren, 2009), female employees of the U.S. federal judicial circuit (Lim & Cortina, 2005), physicians (Shrier, Zucker, Mercurio, Landry, Rich, & Shrier, 2007), police officers (Dowler & Arai, 2008), lesbian/bisexual women (Szymanski, 2005), and Latina (Cortina, 2004), Asian (Patel, 2008), and Black women (Buchanan & Fitzgerald, 2008).

Effect of Harassment on Physical Outcomes

Sexual harassment is also sufficiently stressful as to result in declines in affected individuals' physical health, such as stress-induced physiological changes, suppressed immune system functioning, inflammation, gastrointestinal problems, fatigue, headaches, sleep problems, and back pain (Cleary, Schmieler, Parscenzo, & Ambrosio, 1994; Dansky & Kilpatrick, 1997; Smith, 2006; van Roosmalen & McDaniel, 1998; Woods & Buchanan, in press). Meta-analyses indicate that a perceived lack of control, chronic stress, and threats tied to social identity are important in increasing levels of cortisol, which is a biomarker for stress (Dickerson & Kemeny, 2004; Michaud, Matheson, Kelly, & Anisman, 2008; Miller, Chen, & Zhou, 2007). Bodily systems that usually serve to adaptively cope with isolated stressors, such as the hypothalamic–pituitary–adrenal axis and the sympathetic arousal system (Goldstein & McEwen, 2002; Sapolsky, Romero, & Munck, 2000), may become overtaxed when a person experiences a chronic stressor such as harassment, resulting in negative health outcomes (McEwen, 2000, 2003). In addition, pervasive harassment may lead the targeted individual to engage in behaviors that are counter to positive health outcomes, such as neglecting self-care and health-sustaining behaviors (e.g., exercise, healthy eating, and regular sleeping patterns), which in turn may result in a plethora of health problems (Zucker & Landry, 2007).

EXPANSION OF THE INTEGRATED PROCESS THEORY OF SEXUAL HARASSMENT: OTHER FACTORS INVOLVED IN SEXUAL HARASSMENT

Building on the integrated model, several other factors related to the target and perpetrator have been considered in research on sexual harassment. The expansion of the original integrated model (see Figure 12.1) incorporates these research developments. This section provides a brief overview of the expanded model of sexual harassment, and then discuss in greater detail those components of the model that have received somewhat less attention in the literature to date (i.e., four target characteristics and racialized sexual harassment).

In addition to the organizational climate and the job-gender context as influences on sexual harassment, the expanded model includes the job-racial context, several target characteristics (e.g., race, sexual orientation), and several perpetrator characteristics (e.g., race, organizational status) as antecedents of sexual harassment frequency. In terms of the job context, the racial demography of the organization is relevant, particularly in regard to the harassment experiences of women of color, who may be at greater risk of sexual harassment as racial minorities (Berdahl & Moore, 2006; Buchanan & Woods, 2009). Further, researchers have recently begun to consider characteristics of the perpetrator as influences on sexual harassment. For example, research shows that sexual harassment is often perpetrated by men of a higher organizational status (Berdahl, 2007) and that the perpetrator's organizational status (Buchanan, Settles, & Woods, 2008; Langhout et al., 2005) and race influence how targets appraise the harassment (Woods, Buchanan, & Settles, 2009).

Additionally, because the presence of one form of harassment increases the likelihood that other forms will be present, racialized sexual harassment and sexual harassment are theorized to influence the frequency of each other. The impact of sexual harassment on outcomes is theorized to be mediated by two factors: the individual's coping responses and his or her appraisal of the harassment experience. Coping can refer to any cognitive or behavioral strategy used to reduce the stress of a traumatic event (Lazarus & Folkman, 1984), such as sexual harassment. The type of coping method employed can be influenced by characteristics of the target, the harassing event, and culture. Also, the findings of several studies (e.g., Buchanan, Settles, & Langhout, 2007; Cortina & Wasti, 2005) confirm Lazarus and Folkman's (1984) theory that coping strategies may diversify as stressor severity increases and may also reflect that coping with sexual harassment is a dynamic process in which women adapt their strategies over time depending on their usefulness in ending the harassment (Magley, Fitzgerald, & Buchanan, 2000). Women's appraisal of the harassment has also been shown to mediate the relationship between sexual harassment and mental health outcomes. Specifically, women who appraise harassment as being more severe or more pervasive are likely to have worsened psychological, work, and physical health outcomes compared to women with similar experiences who appraise the harassment as less severe and a relatively rare occurrence (Dambrun, 2007; Langhout et al., 2005).

The expanded model suggests that appraisal is influenced by the presence of racialized sexual harassment, perpetrator characteristics, and the target's past history of sexual harassment. Research has found, for example, that a past history of sexual harassment is associated with more negative outcomes following subsequent harassment because of more negative appraisals of current harassment (Langhout et al., 2005). Similarly, cross-racial sexual harassment has been associated with more negative appraisals of the harassment and worsened outcomes (Woods et al., 2009).

Target Characteristics: Is Sexual Harassment Different Depending on Women's Organizational Status?

Demographic factors have recently been identified as important predictors of the prevalence of sexual harassment and as relevant to harassment outcomes. One such factor that may influence the frequency of sexual harassment is organizational status. High organizational status is protective with regard to a variety of negative workplace behaviors, such as incivility and sexual harassment (Cortina, Magley, Williams, & Langhout, 2001). Conversely, individuals with lower organizational status are more frequently targets of sexual harassment, particularly those working in male-dominated organizations (e.g., Buchanan, Settles, & Woods, 2008; Gruber, 1998, 2003). Organizational status also influences sexual harassment outcomes, such that sexual harassment involving perpetrators of higher status (Buchanan et al., 2008; Langhout et al., 2005) is associated with more negative appraisals of the harassment and more psychological distress.

Target Characteristics: Is Sexual Harassment Different for Sexual Minorities?

One's sexual orientation influences a variety of experiences and interactions (Bilimoria & Stewart, 2009; Cochran, 2001), including sexual harassment. In addition to the traditional forms of gender harassment, unwanted sexual attention, and sexual coercion, heterosexist harassment is common (Silverschanz, Cortina, Konik, & Magley, 2008). Heterosexism refers to a preference for heterosexuality as a norm that systematically disparages, oppresses, or denies the existence of lesbian, gay, bisexual, and transgendered (LGBT) people (Herek, 1990). Heterosexist harassment is a manifestation of heterosexism and includes negative comments about LGBT people, harassing behaviors directed toward those perceived to be LGBT, and similar behaviors directed at heterosexuals that imply the individual is LGBT or engaging in a nontraditional gender role.

When Siverschanz and colleagues (2008) conducted a study of verbal and symbolic heterosexist behaviors among heterosexual and LGBT college students, these researchers found that 58 percent of LGBT students and 39 percent of heterosexual students directly experienced heterosexist harassment and 53 percent and 47 percent, respectively, witnessed such acts. Workplace studies have found similarly high rates of heterosexist harassment such that individuals who openly identify as LGBT experience more harassment than other employees (Badgett, 2003; McDermott, 2006; Waldo, 1999). This harassment is often done publically and without consequence to the harasser.

As has been found with other forms of sexual harassment, heterosexist harassment and discrimination are associated with detrimental effects on individuals' academic, work, physical, and psychological well-being. Such experiences are associated with poorer physical health and life satisfaction, as well as with greater depression and anxiety (Waldo, 1999). Negative job and career attitudes (Ragins & Cornwell, 2001), higher organizational withdrawal, and lower satisfaction with one's work, coworkers, and supervisors have also been associated with heterosexist harassment (Waldo, 1999). Although much of the research in this area to date has focused on the effects of these experiences on LGBT people, Silverschanz and colleagues (2008) were the first to demonstrate that even heterosexuals experience negative psychological and academic outcomes after witnessing heterosexist harassment targeted toward others—demonstrating that this should be an area of focus for employers regardless of the sexual orientation of their workers.

Target Characteristics: Can Men Be Sexually Harassed?

The vast majority of sexual harassment research has been dedicated to uncovering the experiences of women. Given the prevalence of harassment among women and its negative effects on their well-being, this focus on women is understandable. Nevertheless, men do experience sexual harassment—yet little attention has been paid to the similarities and differences in men and women's experiences. Some evidence suggests that men are harassed at much higher rates than previously believed (Antecol & Cobb-Clark, 2001; Berdahl, Magley, & Waldo, 1996). For example, nearly 20 percent of the sexual harassment complaints filed with the EEOC were filed by men (EEOC, 2009). More than 35 percent of male military personnel have reported sexual harassment (Antecol & Cobb-Clark, 2001). Among civilians, approximately 15 percent of men have had at least one experience of sexual harassment at work (U.S. Merit Systems Protection Board, 2004).

Overwhelming evidence demonstrates that those who sexually harass other men or women are generally male (Huerta, Cortina, Pang, Torges, & Magley, 2006; Ménard, Nagayama Hall, Phung, Erian, & Martin, 2003; Rospenda, Richman, & Nawyn, 1998; Stockdale, Visio, & Batra, 1999; Waldo, Berdahl, & Fitzgerald, 1998) and perceive themselves as having higher status, either formally (e.g., one's boss) or informally (e.g., a coworker who believes he has greater social status than a coworker. Sexual harassment of men frequently focuses on pressuring men to conform to gender-role stereotypes in a variety of ways. For example, in their review of sexual harassment case law involving male targets, Waldo and colleagues found that in the vast majority of cases, men were targeted due to their perceived sexual orientation or expression of masculinity (Waldo et al., 1998). Such "not man enough" harassment can include enforcing the traditional heterosexual male gender role (e.g., accusing someone of not being a real man if he leaves work for traditionally female activities, such as cooking dinner or picking up children; calling him a "fag" or "gay"). Although less common, men do also experience the other forms of sexual harassment, such as unwanted sexual attention and sexual coercion. Regardless of the differences, the sexual harassment of men serves similar purposes as that of women—it is a way to exert power, dominance, and control over another person (Berdahl, 2007; Morgan & Gruber, 2005).

Target Characteristics: Is Sexual Harassment Different for Women of Color?

Theoretical and empirical work addressing the sexual harassment experiences of women of color is emerging (e.g., Berdahl & Moore, 2006; Buchanan, 2005; Buchanan & Fitzgerald, 2008; Buchanan & Ormerod, 2002; Buchanan et al., 2008; Cortina, 2004; Cortina, Fitzgerald, & Drasgow, 2002; Martin, 1994; Mecca & Rubin, 1999; Moradi & Subich, 2003; Muliawan & Kleiner, 2001; Rederstorff, Buchanan, & Settles, 2007; Texeira, 2002; Whitson, 1997; Wyatt & Reiderle, 1995; Yoder & Aniakudo, 1996, 1997), but remains sparse. This body of research theorizes that factors such as being both a minority and female (double jeopardy; Beal, 1970) and race-specific sexual stereotypes influence the prevalence and type of sexual harassment experienced among minority women. Consistent with the theory, empirical studies have found that the harassment experiences of ethnic minority and Caucasian women do differ in a number of ways, including women of color reporting higher prevalence (Berdahl & Moore, 2006; Cortina, Swan, Fitzgerald, & Waldo, 1998) and greater severity (e.g., gender harassment versus unwanted sexual attention; Cortina et al., 1998; Nelson & Probst, 2004) associated with their sexual harassment experiences. Additionally, the experience of sexual harassment for women of color may depend on the race of the perpetrator. For example, Woods and colleagues (2009) found that Black women reported more symptoms of post-traumatic stress when harassed by a White man than when harassed by a Black man. More research is needed to determine how perpetrator characteristics influence target harassment experiences.

Racialized Sexual Harassment

Minority women experience sexual racism (Essed, 1992) and racialized sexual harassment (Buchanan, 2005; Buchanan & Ormerod, 2002; Texiera, 2002) as unique forms of harassment that combine racial and gender-based harassment simultaneously (see Figure 12.2). While much of the harassment literature has described sexual and racial harassment as distinct, actual experiences of harassment are often fused in such a way that the two forms become indistinguishable from each other (see Buchanan & Ormerod, 2002; Collins, 2000; Essed, 1992). Studies of Black, Filipino, and Latina working women offer evidence for the presence of these behaviors (Buchanan & Ormerod, 2002; Cortina et al., 2002; Texiera, 2002; Welsh, Carr, MacQuarrie, & Huntley, 2006). These examples call upon sexualized stereotypes of minority women (i.e., being called "mamacita" or a "geisha") and physical features thought to vary by race (e.g., comments about a Black woman's "large black behind").

Although the negative work and psychological outcomes of sexual harassment have been well studied, outcomes resulting from racialized sexual harassment are less well known. Nevertheless, the empirical evidence suggests that racialized sexual harassment is present across a variety of institutions, is associated with higher rates of sexual harassment (Buchanan & Woods, 2009), is associated with more negative appraisals of the harassment and greater post-traumatic stress symptoms (Woods et al., 2009), and can be

Figure 12.2
Racialized sexual harassment. (Buchanan, 2005; Buchanan & Ormerod, 2002.)

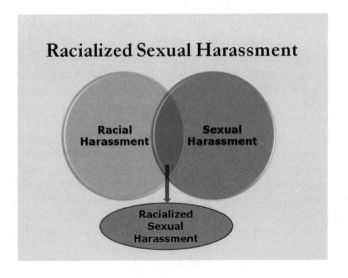

merged with harassment that targets other marginalized dimensions for women of color (e.g., lesbian women of color; Bowleg, Huang, Brooks, Black, & Burkholder, 2003; DeFour, David, Diaz, & Thompkins, 2003).

SUMMARY

Sexual harassment research has sought to define harassment, explain why it occurs, and explore the associated risk factors and outcomes. Lower job satisfaction, diminished work productivity, negative psychological sequelae, and stress-related health problems have all been associated with sexual harassment, making it costly for women who are targeted and the organizations within which they work. Once harassed, women employ a variety of methods to cope with this stressor, especially as the harassment increases in severity. Long overdue is greater attention to the needs of marginalized workers, such as women of color and lesbians, who often experience double or triple jeopardy. Future research must begin to concentrate on these issues to provide effective solutions and a secure working environment for all working women.

REFERENCES

Antecol, H., & Cobb-Clark, D. (2001). Men, women, and sexual harassment in the U.S. military. *Gender Issues, 19*, 3–18.

Badgett, M. V. L. (2003). Employment and sexual orientation: Disclosure and discrimination in the workplace. In L. D. Garnets & D. C. Kimmel (Eds.), *Psychology perspectives on lesbian, gay, and bisexual experiences* (pp. 327–348). New York: Columbia University Press.

Beal, F. (1970). Double jeopardy: To be Black and to be female. In T. Cade (Ed.), *The Black woman: An anthology* (pp. 90–100). New York: New American Library.

Bell, M. P., Cycyota, C. S., & Quick, J. C. (2002). An affirmative defense: The preventative management of sexual harassment. In D. L. Nelson & R. J. Burke (Eds.), *Gender, work stress, and health* (pp. 191–210). Washington, DC: American Psychological Association.

Berdahl, J. L. (2007). Harassment based on sex: Protecting social status in the context of gender hierarchy. *Academy of Management Review, 32*, 641–658.

Berdahl, J. L., Magley, V., & Waldo, C. R. (1996). The sexual harassment of men? Exploring the concept with theory and data. *Psychology of Women Quarterly, 20*, 527–547.

Berdahl, J. L., & Moore, C. (2006). Workplace harassment: Double jeopardy for minority women. *Journal of Applied Psychology, 91*(2), 426–436.

Bergman, M. E., & Drasgow, F. (2003). Race as a moderator in a model of sexual harassment: An empirical test. *Journal of Occupational Health Psychology, 8*(2), 131–145.

Bilimoria, D., & Stewart, A. J. (2009). "Don't ask, don't tell": The academic climate for lesbian, gay, bisexual, and transgender faculty in science and engineering. *National Women's Studies Association Journal, 21*(2), 85–103.

Bowleg, L., Huang, J., Brooks, K., Black, A., & Burkholder, G. (2003). Triple jeopardy and beyond: Multiple minority stress and resilience among Black lesbians. *Journal of Lesbian Studies, 7*, 87–108.

Buchanan, N. T. (2005). The nexus of race and gender domination: The racialized sexual harassment of African American women. In P. Morgan & J. Gruber (Eds.), *In the company of men: Re-discovering the links between sexual harassment and male domination* (pp. 294–320). Boston: Northeastern University Press.

Buchanan, N. T., & Fitzgerald, L. F. (2008). The effects of racial and sexual harassment on work and the psychological well-being of African American women. *Journal of Occupational Health Psychology, 13(2)*, 137–151.

Buchanan, N. T., & Ormerod, A. J. (2002). Racialized sexual harassment in the lives of African American women. *Women & Therapy, 25*, 107–124.

Buchanan, N. T., Settles, I. H., & Langhout, R. D. (2007). Black women's coping styles, psychological well-being, and work-related outcomes following sexual harassment. *Black Women, Gender and Families, 1*, 100–120.

Buchanan, N. T., Settles, I. H., & Woods, K. C. (2008). Comparing sexual harassment subtypes for Black and White women: Double jeopardy, the Jezebel, and the cult of true womanhood. *Psychology of Women Quarterly, 32*, 347–361.

Buchanan, N. T., & Woods, K. C. (2009, November). Racialized sexual harassment: Conceptualizing workplace harassment as a function of race and sex. In M. E. Bergman (Chair), *Workplace mistreatment and social identity: An exploration across different types of diversity.* Symposium conducted at the meeting of the International Conference on Occupational Stress and Health in San Juan, Puerto Rico.

Cantisano, G. T., Dominguez, J. F. M., & Depolo, M. (2008). Perceived sexual harassment at work: Meta-analysis and structural model of antecedents and consequences. *Spanish Journal of Psychology, 11(1)*, 207–218.

Carr, P. L., Ash, A. S., Friedman, R. H., Szalacha, L., Barnett, R. C., Palepu, A., et al. (2000). Faculty perceptions of gender discrimination and sexual harassment in academic medicine. *Annals of Internal Medicine, 132*, 889–896.

Chan, D. K. S., Lam, C. B., Chow, S. Y., & Cheung, S. F. (2008). Examining the job-related, psychological, and physical outcomes of workplace sexual harassment: A meta-analytic review. *Psychology of Women Quarterly, 32*, 362–376.

Cleary, J. S., Schmieler, C. R., Parascenzo, L. C., & Ambrosio, N. (1994). Sexual harassment of college students: Implications for campus health promotion. *Journal of American College Heath, 43*, 3–10.

Cleveland, J. N., & Kerst, M. E. (1993). Sexual harassment and perceptions of power: An under-articulated relationship. *Journal of Vocational Behavior, 42(1)*, 46–67.

Cochran, S. D. (2001). Emerging issues in research on lesbians' and gay men's mental health: Does sexual orientation really matter? *American Psychologist, 56*, 932–947.

Cogin, J. A., & Fish, A. (2009). An empirical investigation of sexual harassment and work engagement: Surprising differences between men and women. *Journal of Management & Organization, 15*, 47–61.

Collins, P. H. (2000). *Black feminist thought: Knowledge, consciousness, and the politics of empowerment* (2nd ed.). New York: Routledge.

Collins, S. C. (2004). Sexual harassment and police discipline: Who's policing the police? *Policing: An International Journal of Police Strategies and Management, 27*, 512–538.

Cortina, L. M. (2004). Hispanic perspectives on sexual harassment and social support. *Personality and Social Psychology Bulletin, 30*(5), 570–584.

Cortina, L. M., Fitzgerald, L. F., & Drasgow, F. (2002). Contextualizing Latina experiences of sexual harassment: Preliminary tests of a structural model. *Basic and Applied Social Psychology, 24*, 295–311.

Cortina, L. M., Magley, V. J., Williams, J. H., & Langhout, R. D. (2001). Incivility in the workplace: Incidence and impact. *Journal of Occupational Health Psychology, 6*, 64–80.

Cortina, L. M., Swan, S., Fitzgerald, L. F., & Waldo, C. (1998). Sexual harassment and assault: Chilling the climate for women in academia. *Psychology of Women Quarterly, 22*, 419–441.

Cortina, L. M., & Wasti, S. A. (2005). Profiles in coping: Responses to sexual harassment across persons, organizations, and cultures. *Journal of Applied Psychology, 90*(1), 182–192.

Dambrun, M. (2007). Gender differences in mental health: The mediating role of perceived personal discrimination. *Journal of Applied Social Psychology, 37*(5), 1118–1129.

Dansky, B. S., & Kilpatrick, D. G. (1997). Effects of sexual harassment. In W. O'Donohue (Ed.), *Sexual harassment: Theory, research and treatment* (pp. 5–28). Needham Heights, MA: Allyn & Bacon.

DeFour, D. C., David, G., Diaz, F. J., & Thompkins, S. (2003). The interface of race, sex, sexual orientation, and ethnicity in understanding sexual harassment. In M. A. Paludi & C. Paludi (Eds.), *Academic and workplace sexual harassment: A handbook of cultural, social science, management, and legal perspectives* (pp. 31–45). Westport, CT: Praeger/Greenwood.

Department of Defense. (2004, April). *Task force report on care for victims of sexual assault*. Washington, DC: Author.

Department of Defense Inspector General. (2005). *Report on sexual harassment and assault at the U.S. Air Force Academy*. Washington, DC: Department of Defense.

Dickerson, S. S., & Kemeny, M. E. (2004). Acute stressors and cortisol responses: A theoretical integration and synthesis of laboratory research. *Psychological Bulletin, 130*, 355–391.

DiTomaso, N. (1989). Sexuality in the workplace: Discrimination and harassment. In J. Hearn, D. L. Sheppard, P. Tancred-Sheriff, & G. Burrell (Eds.), *The sexuality of organizations* (pp. 71–90). Newbury Park, CA: Sage.

Dowler, K., & Arai, B. (2008). Stress, gender and policing: The impact of perceived gender discrimination on symptoms of stress. *International Journal of Police Science & Management, 10*(2), 123–135.

Equal Employment Opportunity Commission (EEOC). (1980). Guidelines on discrimination because of sex. *Federal Regulations, 43*, 74676–74677.

Equal Employment Opportunity Commission (EEOC). (2009). *Sexual Harassment Charges: EEOC & FEPAs Combined: FY 1997–FY 2008*. Retrieved October 1, 2009, from http://www.eeoc.gov/stats/harass.html.

Essed, P. (1992). Alternative knowledge sources in explanations of racist events. In M. J. Cody & M. L. McLaughlin (Eds.), *Explaining one's self to others: Reason-giving in a social context* (pp. 199–224). Hillsdale, NJ: Lawrence Erlbaum Associates.

Estrada, A. X., & Berggren, A. W. (2009). Sexual harassment and its impact for women officers and cadets in the Swedish Armed Forces. *Military Psychology, 21*(2), 162–185.

Fitzgerald, L. F., Drasgow, F., Hulin, C. L., Gelfand, M. J., & Magley, V. J. (1997). Antecedents and consequences of sexual harassment in organizations: A test of an integrated model. *Journal of Applied Psychology, 82*, 578–589.

Fitzgerald, L. F., Gelfand, M. J., & Drasgow, F. (1995). Measuring sexual harassment: Theoretical and psychometric advances. *Basic and Applied Social Psychology, 17*, 425–427.

Fitzgerald, L. F., Hulin, C. L., & Drasgow, F. (1995). The antecedents and consequences of sexual harassment in organizations. In G. Keita & J. H. Jr. (Eds.), *Job stress in a changing workforce: Investigating gender, diversity, and family issues* (pp. 55–73). Washington, DC: American Psychological Association.

Fitzgerald, L. F., Magley, V. J., Drasgow, F., & Waldo, C. R. (1999). Measuring sexual harassment in the military: The Sexual Experiences Questionnaire (SEQ-DoD). *Military Psychology, 11*, 243–263.

Fitzgerald, L. F., & Shullman, S. L. (1993). Sexual harassment: A research analysis and agenda for the 1990s. *Journal of Vocational Behavior, 42*, 5–27.

Fitzgerald, L. F., Shullman, S. L., Bailey, N., Richards, M., Swecker, J., Gold, Y., et al. (1988). The incidence and dimensions of sexual harassment in academia and the workplace. *Journal of Vocational Behavior, 32*, 152–175.

Fitzgerald, L., Swan, S., & Fischer, K. (1995). Why didn't she just report him? The psychological and legal implications of women's responses to sexual harassment. *Journal of Social Issues, 51*, 117–38.

Fitzgerald, L. F., Swan, S., & Magley, V. J. (1997). But was it really sexual harassment? Legal, behavioral, and psychological definitions of the workplace victimization of women. In W. O'Donohue (Ed.), *Sexual harassment: theory, research, and treatment* (pp. 5–28). Needham Heights, MA: Allyn & Bacon.

Glomb, T. M., Munson, L. J., Hulin, C. L., Bergman, M. E., & Drasgow, F. (1999). Structural equation models of sexual harassment: Longitudinal explorations and cross-sectional generalizations. *Journal of Applied Psychology, 84*, 14–28.

Glomb, T. M., Richman, W. L., Hulin, C. L., Drasgow, F., Schneider, K. T., & Fitzgerald, L. F. (1997). Ambient sexual harassment: An integrated model of antecedents and consequences. *Organizational Behavior and Human Decision Processes, 71*, 309–328.

Goldstein, D. S., & McEwen, B. (2002) Allostasis, homeostasis, and the nature of stress. *Stress, 5*, 5–58.

Gruber, J. E. (1998). The impact of work environments and organizational policies on women's experiences of sexual harassment. *Gender and Society, 12*, 301–320.

Gruber, J. E. (2003). Sexual harassment in the public sector. In M. Paludi & C. Paludi (Eds.), *Academic and workplace sexual harassment: A handbook of cultural, social science, management, and legal perspectives* (pp. 49–75). Westport, CT: Praeger/Greenwood.

Gruber, J. E., & Smith, M. D. (1995). Women's responses to sexual harassment: A multivariate analysis. *Basic and Applied Social Psychology, 17*, 543–562.

Gutek, B. A., & Morasch, B. (1982). Sex-ratios, sex-role spillover, and sexual harassment of women at work. *Journal of Social Issues, 38*, 55–74.

Hansen, C. (2004, March/April). Filing a flight plan: Policy and social change to address sexual violence in the military. *Sexual Assault Report, 7*, 60–62.

Herek, G. M. (1990). The context of anti-gay violence: Notes on cultural and psychological heterosexism. *Journal of Interpersonal Violence, 5*, 316–333.

Hitlan, R. T., Schneider, K. T., & Walsh, B. M. (2006). Upsetting behavior: Reactions to personal and bystander sexual harassment experiences. *Sex Roles, 55,* 187–195.

Huerta, M., Cortina, L. M., Pang, J. S., Torges, C. M., & Magley, V. J. (2006). Sex and power in the academy: Modeling sexual harassment in the lives of college women. *Personality and Social Psychology Bulletin, 32,* 616–628.

Hulin, C., Fitzgerald, L. F., & Drasgow, F. (1996). Organizational influences on sexual harassment. In M. S. Stockdale (Ed.), *Sexual harassment in the workplace: Perspectives, frontiers, and response strategies* (pp. 127–150). London: Sage.

Ilies, R., Hauserman, N., Schwochau, S., & Stibal, J. (2003). Reported incidence rates of work-related sexual harassment in the United States: Using meta-analysis to explain reported rate disparities. *Personnel Psychology, 56*(3), 607–631.

Kath, L. M., Swody, C. A., Magley, V. J., Bunk, J. A., & Gallus, J. A. (2009). Cross-level, three-way interactions among work-group climate, gender, and frequency of harassment on morale and withdrawal outcomes of sexual harassment. *Journal of Occupational and Organizational Psychology, 82,* 159–182.

Langhout, R. D., Bergman, M. E., Cortina, L. M., Fitzgerald, L. F., Drasgow, F., & Williams, J. H. (2005). Sexual harassment severity: Assessing situational and personal determinants and outcomes. *Journal of Applied Social Psychology, 35*(5), 975–1007.

Lapierre, L. M., Spector, P. E., & Leck, J. D. (2005). Sexual versus nonsexual workplace aggression and victims' overall job satisfaction: A meta-analysis. *Journal of Occupational Health Psychology, 10,* 155–169.

Lazarus, R. S., & Folkman, S. (1984). *Stress, appraisal, and coping.* New York: Springer.

Lim, S., & Cortina, L. M. (2005). Interpersonal mistreatment in the workplace: The interface and impact of general incivility and sexual harassment. *Journal of Applied Psychology, 90*(3), 483–496.

Low, K. S. D., Radhakrishnan, P., Schneider, K. T., & Rounds, J. (2007). The experiences of bystanders of workplace ethnic harassment. *Journal of Applied Social Psychology, 37*(10), 2261–2297.

Magley, V. J., Fitzgerald, L. F., & Buchanan, N. T. (2000, April). Assessing coping with sexual harassment over time. In V. J. Magley (Chair), *Coping with sexual harassment: Layers of meaning.* Symposium conducted at the annual meeting of the Society for Industrial and Organizational Psychology, New Orleans, LA.

Martin, S. E. (1994). "Outsider within" the station house: The impact of race and gender on Black women police. *Social Problems, 41,* 383–400.

McDermott, E. (2006). Surviving in dangerous places: Lesbian identity performances in the workplace, social class and psychological health. *Feminism & Psychology, 16,* 193–211.

McEwen, B. S. (2000). Allostasis and allostatic load: Implications for neuropsychopharmacology. *Neuropsychopharmacology, 22,* 108–124.

McEwen, B. S. (2003). Mood disorders and allostatic load. *Biological Psychiatry, 54,* 200–207.

Mecca, S. J., & Rubin, L. J. (1999). Definitional research on African American students and sexual harassment. *Psychology of Women Quarterly, 23,* 813–817.

Ménard, K. S., Nagayama Hall, G. C., Phung, A. H., Erian, M. F., & Martin, L. (2003). Gender differences in sexual harassment and coercion in college students: Developmental, individual, and situational determinants. *Journal of Interpersonal Violence, 18,* 1222–1239.

Michaud, K., Matheson, K., Kelly, O., & Anisman, H. (2008). Impact of stressors in a natural context on release of cortisol in healthy adult humans: A meta-analysis. *Stress, 11*(3), 177–197.

Miller, G. E., Chen, E., & Zhou, E. (2007). If it goes up, must it come down? Chronic stress and the hypothalamic–pituitary–adrenal axis in humans. *Psychological Bulletin, 133,* 25–45.

Moradi, B., & Subich, L. M. (2003). A concomitant examination of the relations of perceived racist and sexist events to psychological distress for African American women. *Counseling Psychologist, 31,* 451–469.

Morgan, P., & Gruber, J. (2005). *In the company of men: Re-discovering the links between sexual harassment and male domination.* Boston: Northeastern University Press.

Muliawan, H., & Kleiner, B. H. (2001). African-American perception of sexual harassment. *Equal Opportunities International, 20*(5–7), 53–58.

Munson, L. J., Hulin, C., & Drasgow, F. (2000). Longitudinal analysis of dispositional influences and sexual harassment: Effects on job and psychological outcomes. *Personnel Psychology, 53,* 21–46.

Nelson, N. L., & Probst, T. M. (2004). Multiple minority individuals: Multiplying the risk of workplace harassment and discrimination. In J. L. Chin (Ed.), *The psychology of prejudice and discrimination: Ethnicity and multiracial identity* (pp. 193–217). Westport, CT: Praeger/Greenwood.

O'Connell, C. E., & Korabik, K. (2000). Sexual harassment: The relationship of personal vulnerability, work context, perpetrator status, and type of harassment to outcomes. *Journal of Vocational Behavior, 56*(3), 299–329.

Patel, N. (2008). Racialized sexism in the lives of Asian American women. In C. Raghavan, A. E. Edwards, & K. M. Vas (Eds.), *Benefiting by design: Women of color in feminist psychological research* (pp. 116–128). Cambridge, UK: Scholars.

Ragins, B. R., & Cornwell, J. M. (2001). Pink triangles: Antecedents and consequences of perceived workplace discrimination against gay and lesbian employees. *Journal of Applied Psychology, 86,* 1244–1261.

Ragins, B. R., & Sundstrom, E. (1989). Gender and power in organizations: A longitudinal perspective. *Psychological Bulletin, 105,* 51–88.

Rederstorff, J. C., Buchanan, N. T., & Settles, I. H. (2007). The moderating roles of race and gender role attitudes in the relationship between sexual harassment and psychological well-being. *Psychology of Women Quarterly, 31,* 50–61.

Richman, J. A., Rospenda, K. M., Flaherty, J. A., Freels, S., & Zlatoper, K. (2004). Perceived organizational tolerance for workplace harassment and distress and drinking over time. *Women & Health, 40*(4), 1–23.

Rospenda, K. M., Richman, J. A., & Nawyn, S. J. (1998). Doing power: The confluence of gender, race, and class in contrapower sexual harassment. *Gender & Society, 12,* 40–60.

Sadler, A. G., Booth, B. M., Cook, B. L., Torner, J. C., & Doebbeling, B. N. (2001). The military environment: Risk factors for women's non-fatal assaults. *Journal of Environmental Medicine, 43,* 325–334.

Sapolsky, R. M., Romero, L. M., & Munck, A. U. (2000). How do glucocorticoids influence stress responses? Integrating permissive, suppressive, stimulatory, and preparative actions. *Endocrine Reviews, 21,* 55–89.

Schneider, K. T., Swan, S., & Fitzgerald, L. F. (1997). Job-related and psychological effects of sexual harassment in the workplace: Empirical evidence from two organizations. *Journal of Applied Psychology, 82,* 401–415.

Settles, I. H., Cortina, L. M., Malley, J., & Stewart, A. J. (2006). The climate for women in academic science: The good, the bad, and the changeable. *Psychology of Women Quarterly, 30*(1), 47–58.

Shrier, D. K., Zucker, A. N., Mercurio, A. E., Landry, L. J., Rich, M., & Shrier, L. A. (2007). Generation to generation: Discrimination and harassment experiences of physician mothers and their physician daughters. *Journal of Women's Health, 16*(6), 883–894.

Silverschanz, P., Cortina, L. M., Konik, J., & Magley, V. J. (2008). Slurs, snubs, and queer jokes: Incidence and impact of heterosexist harassment in academia. *Sex Roles, 58,* 179–191.

Sims, C. S., Drasgow, F., & Fitzgerald, L. F. (2005). The effects of sexual harassment on turnover in the military: Time-dependent modeling. *Journal of Applied Psychology, 90*(6), 1141–1152.

Smith, T. W. (2006). Personality as risk and resilience in physical health. *Current Directions in Psychological Science, 15,* 227–231.

Stockdale, M. S. (1998). The direct and moderating influences of sexual harassment pervasiveness, coping strategies, and gender on work-related outcomes. *Psychology of Women Quarterly, 22,* 521–535.

Stockdale, M. S., Visio, M., & Batra, L. (1999). The sexual harassment of men: Evidence for a broader theory of sexual harassment and sex discrimination. *Psychology, Public Policy, and the Law, 5,* 630–664.

Street, A. E., Gradus, J. L., Stafford, J., & Kelly, K. (2007). Gender differences in experiences of sexual harassment: Data from a male-dominated environment. *Journal of Consulting and Clinical Psychology, 75*(3), 464–474.

Szymanski, D. M. (2005). Heterosexism and sexism as correlates of psychological distress in lesbians. *Journal of Counseling & Development, 83,* 355–360.

Tangri, S., & Hayes, S. M. (1997). Theories of sexual harassment. In W. O'Donohue (Ed.), *Sexual harassment: Theory, research, and treatment* (pp. 112–128). Needham Heights, MA: Allyn & Bacon.

Texeira, M. T. (2002). "Who protects and serves me?" A case study of sexual harassment of African American women in one U.S. law enforcement agency. *Gender & Society, 16,* 524–545.

U.S. Merit Systems Protection Board. (2004). Issues of merit. Retrieved October 12, 2009, from http://www.mspb.gov/netsearch/viewdocs.aspx?docnumber =255805&version=256094&application=ACROBAT.

van Roosmalen, E., & McDaniel, S. A. (1998). Sexual harassment in academia: A hazard to women's health. *Women & Health, 28,* 33–54.

Vogt, D., Bruce, T. A., Street, A. E., & Stafford, J. (2007). Attitudes toward women and tolerance for sexual harassment among reservists. *Violence Against Women, 13,* 879–900.

Waldo, C. (1999). Working in a majority context: A structural model of heterosexism as minority stress in the workplace. *Journal of Counseling Psychology, 46,* 218–232.

Waldo, C. R., Berdahl, J. L., & Fitzgerald, L. F. (1998). Are men sexually harassed? If so, by whom? *Law and Human Behavior, 22,* 59–79

Wayne, J. H. (2000). Disentangling the power bases of sexual harassment: Comparing gender, age and position power. *Journal of Vocational Behavior, 57,* 301–325.

Welsh, S., Carr, J., MacQuarrie, B., & Huntley, A. (2006). "I'm not thinking of it as sexual harassment": Understanding harassment across race and citizenship. *Gender & Society, 20*(1), 87–107.

Whitson, M. H. (1997). Sexism and sexual harassment: Concerns of African American women of the Christian Methodist Episcopal Church. *Violence Against Women, 3*(4), 382–400.

Williams, J. H., Fitzgerald, L. F., & Drasgow, F. (1999). The effects of organizational practices on sexual harassment and individual outcomes in the military. *Military Psychology, 11*, 303–328.

Willness, C. R., Steel, P., & Lee, K. (2007). A meta-analysis of the antecedents and consequences of workplace sexual harassment. *Personnel Psychology, 60*, 127–162.

Woods, K. C., & Buchanan, N. T. (2010). Discrimination, harassment, and women's physical and mental health. In M. Paludi (Ed.), *Feminism and women's rights worldwide* (pp. 235–251). Westport, CT: Praeger.

Woods, K. C., Buchanan, N. T., & Settles, I. H. (2009). Sexual harassment across the color line: Experiences and outcomes of cross- vs. intra-racial sexual harassment among Black women. *Cultural Diversity and Ethnic Minority Psychology, 15*(1), 67–76.

Wyatt, G. E., & Reiderle, M. (1995). The prevalence and context of sexual harassment among African American and White American women. *Journal of Interpersonal Violence, 10*(3), 309–321.

Yoder, J. D., & Aniakudo, P. (1996). When pranks become harassment: The case of African American and women firefighters. *Sex Roles, 35*, 253–270.

Yoder, J. D., & Aniakudo, P. (1997). "Outsider within" the firehouse: Subordination and difference in the social interaction of African American women. *Gender & Society, 11*(3), 324–341.

Zucker, A. N., & Landry, L. J. (2007). Embodied discrimination: The relation of sexism and distress to women's drinking and smoking behaviors. *Sex Roles, 56*, 193–203.

Chapter 13

Bullying as Gender-Based Sexual Harassment

Susan Strauss

Sexual harassment, although a new term coined in 1975 (Farley, 1978), is an old phenomenon whose roots date back to when women first appeared in the marketplace in the nineteenth century (Bullough, 1990). The term "sexual harassment" was created by American women to describe their experiences at work, but the phenomenon is not unique to the United States. Beginning in 1975, this term has gradually been applied to define women's academic and education harassment experiences worldwide, and it is recognized as a human rights issue (DeSouza & Solberg, 2003; Gruber, 1997; Webb, 1994).

A specific form of sexual harassment—gender harassment—is the most frequently occurring sexual harassment (Fitzgerald, Swan, & Fischer, 1995), yet it has been the focus of little empirical study. Gender harassment is behavior that does not have to be sexual in nature but occurs due to one's gender; it is characterized by hostile and degrading comments, jokes, and

This chapter was adapted from Strauss, S. (2007). *Quantitative and qualitative analysis of physician abuse as gender harassment to female and male registered nurses in the operating room.* Doctoral dissertation, St. Mary's University, 2007. Retrieved from *ProQuest Digital Dissertations* (DAI 3290679).

body language, usually directed toward women, about women, or toward a particular woman; however, men may also be targets of the misconduct.

Literature on workplace abuse, sometimes referred to as bullying, suggests that this phenomenon shares certain similarities with gender harassment, particularly in relation to the abuse of power as a likely cause, the types of abusive behavior that characterize it, and the effects of the abuse on the victim and the organization (Lee, 2001, 2002). Even though the workplace bullying literature has discussed the gender of both the target and the abuser, with only one exception found (Lee, 2001, 2002), it does not address gender dynamics, which means it fails to acknowledge this factor as a salient issue in abusive workplace behavior.

DEFINING ABUSIVE WORKPLACE BEHAVIOR

Mistreatment of employees in the workplace is labeled by various terms in the literature depending on the country in which the author resides and the perspective from which the construct is studied—for example, a psychological, sociological, or business approach. Terminology defining the phenomenon varies, with different countries attributing different labels. Researchers in Germany, Austria, and Scandinavia, for example, refer to the behavior as mobbing (Lee, 2000; Zapf, 1999), and those in the United Kingdom, Ireland, and the United States call it bullying (Adams, 1997; Cusack, 2000; Lee, 2000; Rayner & Cooper, 1997; Smith, 1997). Other terms used to define the mistreatment include victimization (Aquino & Byron, 2002), abuse (Bassman, 1992; Braun, Christle, Walker, & Tiwanak, 1991; Byrne, 1997; Cook, Green, & Topp, 2001; McGuinness, 1992; Rosenstein, 2002), violence (Baron & Neuman, 1996); hostility (Folger & Baron, 1996), aggression (Baron & Neuman, 1996; Baron, Neuman, & Geddes, 1999; Bjorkqvist, Osterman, & Hjelt-Back, 1994; Buss, 1961; Einarsen, 1999; Harvey & Keashly, 2003; Infante, Riddle, Hovath, & Tumlin, 1992; Kivimaki, Elovainio, & Vahtera, 2000; Liefooghe & Olafsson, 1999; Rayner, 1999; Schat & Kelloway, 2003), mistreatment (Aquino & Byron, 2002; Spratlen, 1994), deviant behavior (Griffin, O'Leary-Kelly, & Collins, 1998), incivility (Anderson & Pearson, 1999; Cortina, Magley, Williams, & Langhout, 2001; Pearson, Anderson, & Porath, 2000), conflict (Ayoko, Callan, & Hartel, 2003), counterproductive behaviors (Ayoko et al., 2003), disempowering acts (Young , Vance, & Ensher, 2003), dysfunctional behavior (Griffin et al., 1998), psychological terror (Leymann, 1990), and petty tyranny (Ashforth, 1994). For the purposes of this chapter, the terms "abuse" and "bullying" will be used interchangeably to refer to the misconduct.

While the country of residence and the academic perspective may define the authors' labels, there is no consistent definition of the construct across the literature (Cusack, 2000; Einarsen, 1999; Kivimaki et al., 2000; Rayner, 1999; Spurgeon, 1997). Nevertheless, some common threads are interwoven within the definitions—for example, repeated and/or severe, unwelcome, hostile, oppressive, controlling, and abusive behavior directed from one or more individuals to others. Examples of specific behaviors identified in the literature include rudeness (Pearson et al., 2000); demeaning language or offensive remarks (Einarsen, 2000; Pearson et al., 2000); disregard of others (Kivimaki et al., 2000; Pearson et al., 2000); disrespectful treatment (Pearson et al., 2000), berating (Pearson et al., 2000); exclusion, isolation, or silence (Baron & Neuman, 1996; Cusack, 2000; Einarsen, 1999, 2000; Keashley, 1998; Kivimaki et al., 2000; Pearson et al., 2000; Smith, 1997); threats (Cusack, 2000; Einarsen, 1999; Kivimaki et al., 2000); belittling, ridiculing, or insulting (Adams, 1997; Baron & Neuman, 1996; Cusack, 2000, Einarsen, 1999); public humiliation (Cusack, 2000; Einarsen, 1999); shouting or angry outbursts (Adams, 1997; Ayoko et al., 2003; Baron & Neuman, 1996; Einarsen, 1999; Keashley, 1998); offensive language (Adams, 1997); over-monitoring (Adams, 1997); nit-picking over trivia (Adams, 1997); aggressive eye contact (Ayoko et al., 2003); name calling (Brodsky, 1976; Keashley, 1998; Smith, 1997); scapegoating (Brodsky, 1976), physical violence (Baron & Neuman, 1996; Einarsen, 1999; Smith, 1997); and micromanagement and gossip (Einarsen, 2000; Kivimaki et al., 2000; Smith, 1997).

Aggression can be both generic and specific (Brodsky, 1976), and exists along a continuum ranging from subtler behavior such as deliberately ignoring someone to more severe behavior such as physical attacks. Buss's (1961) framework for categorizing forms of aggression differentiates among the sometimes subtle behaviors, such as gossip, over-monitoring, and silent treatment, to the more egregious forms, such as threats, insults, and physical violence. This author defined aggression as the behavioral expression of hostility, and classified the behavior into three categories: physical and verbal, active and passive, and direct and indirect. Buss then combined elements of the categories together. For example, *active* aggression inflicts injury on an individual through the performance of specific behavior, while *passive* aggression may entail withholding some action such as praise. Therefore, if using the passive-verbal combination, one would be aggressive by failing to inform a colleague of an important meeting (withholding communication); active-verbal aggression is demonstrated by insulting remarks. In another example, *direct aggression* is aimed at the victim directly, while *indirect* aggression is aimed at harming the victim through a third party or by injuring an item of value to the victim. An example of indirect-verbal aggression is gossip, and an example of direct verbal aggression is offensive language directed toward someone. Baron and Neuman (1996) found that most aggression at work is verbal, indirect, and passive rather than physical, direct, and active.

Brodsky (1976) further categorized aggression as *subjective*, referring to whether the victim is actually aware of the aggression, or *objective*, which refers to aggression that is evident to others who witness the situation. These concepts depend on the perception(s) of the individual(s). "The eye of the beholder" may confound the concept when the same or similar treatment is directed to several individuals, such that some feel bullied whereas others do not. Brodsky's theory is comparable to the "reasonable person" standard used in sexual harassment law (Drobac, 2005) and is similar to the concept of ambient sexual harassment (Glomb, Richman, Hulin, Drasgow, Schneider, & Fitzgerald, 1997), both of which are described in more detail later in this chapter.

Research

The empirical examination of bullying behavior first began in Scandinavian schools in the 1970s (Olweus, 1978; Smith, 1997). Scandinavian researchers were also the pioneers in exploring bullying in workplaces among adults (Cortina et al., 2001; Smith, 1997). Soon investigators in other countries in Europe, such as those in the United Kingdom, France, and Germany, began examining the phenomenon empirically and governments began passing legislation outlawing the behavior at work (Kivimaki et al., 2000; Lee, 2000; Vartia, 1996).

Research findings regarding the rates of abuse in the workplace vary considerably depending on the various definitions, the types of measurement instruments used, the country in which the study occurred, and the time frames in which the study participants experienced the abuse. Einarsen and Raknes (1997) demonstrated that 75 percent of Norwegian engineers were subjected to generalized harassment during the previous six months. Fifty-five percent of female employees and 30 percent of male employees at a Finnish university experienced similar behaviors at least occasionally during the same time frame (Bjorkqvist, Osterman, & Hjelt-Back, 1994). In contrast, Scandinavian research suggested lower rates of bullying, ranging from 3 percent to 4 percent (Leymann, 1992, cited in Hoel , Rayner, & Cooper, 1999). A study done in an English health care service found 38 percent of employees were bullied within the previous year and that 42 percent of employees were witnesses to the bullying of others (Quine, 1999). Leymann (1992, cited in Hoel et al., 1999) estimated that 25 percent of the Swedish workforce experienced aggression at some point in their working lives. A U.S. study conducted by Northwestern National Life Insurance Company (1993) concluded that 2.2 million U.S. workers were attacked physically, 6.3 million were threatened, and 16.1 million were harassed during a 12-month period.

Impact of Workplace Abuse

The impact of workplace abuse on its victims (including witnesses) can be devastating (Brodsky, 1976). Examples of its effects include loss of self-esteem; feelings of helplessness and revenge (Brodsky, 1976); increased illnesses such as hypertension, insomnia, gastrointestinal problems, and accidents (Brodsky, 1976); depression (Bjorkqvist et al., 1994; Zapf, 1999); anger, rage, and hostility (Brodsky, 1976); post-traumatic stress disorder (PTSD) (Bjorkqvist, Osterman, & Hjelt-Back, 1994; Zapf, 1999); feelings of alienation (Brodsky, 1976); increased use of alcohol (Brodsky, 1976); feelings of confusion, isolation, and paranoia; panic attacks or anxiety (Zapf, 1999); increased stress (Einarsen & Raknes, 1991, cited in Hoel et al., 1999); and attempted suicide and heart attacks. Zapf (1999) found that when a person is attacked by a bully, the strongest effect occurs in relation to the target's psychological health. The effects of bullying on women seem to be greater than the effects of bullying on men (Leymann, 1992, cited in Hoel et al., 1999; Niedl, 1996), with women being especially likely to report musculoskeletal pain, other somatic symptoms, and depression.

Workplace aggression affects not only the victim, but also the organization as a whole (Bassman, 1992). Pearson, Anderson, and Porath (2000) contended that 12 percent of victims quit their jobs as a result of such aggression, 52 percent lost work time due to worrying about the incidents to which they were subjected, and 22 percent decreased their work effort. These results translate into organizational expenses such as medical, disability, and legal costs. Bassman (1992) identified a second category of costs related to workplace aggression—declining quality and customer service, increased absenteeism, turnover, and revenge or sabotage. The third cost discussed by Bassman is the lost opportunity to become a truly quality company owing to the loss of employee involvement and creativity, which disappear in a culture of mistrust.

The Etiology of Abusive Workplaces

According to Davenport, Schwartz, and Elliot (2002), workplace abuse is too complex a phenomenon to place the blame on a single cause—for example, poor management. Their approach instead focuses on a web of causative factors, all of which interact to reinforce one another. Zapf (1999) segregated the causes of bullying into four categories: the perpetrator, the organization, the victim, and the social system. In contrast, according to Baron and Neuman (1996), the causes of workplace aggression are employee diversity, reengineering, downsizing, budget cuts, autocratic work environments, pressure to produce, and part-time employees. Frustration from a perceived sense of injustice was Folger and Baron's (1996), and Baron, Neuman, and Geddes's (1999) thesis, as these researchers suggested yet another causal variable in workplace aggression. Vartia (1996) found that envy, a weak boss, and competition were the perceived reasons why people bully. Her study also characterized the work environment where bullying occurred as strained and competitive, with employees looking out for themselves and their own personal and professional interests. Einarsen and Skogstad (1996) suggested that lack of parity between two parties, such that one party exerts power over the other, causes aggression; conversely, if there is equal strength in their conflict, it is not considered bullying.

Other authors have explored aggression from a psychological perspective. Buss (1961) explored numerous theories of aggression including discussions of Sigmund Freud's writings on libido and psychosexual development, Alfred Adler's early beliefs of aggression as being biological in origin, and Karen Horney's attribution of aggression to anxiety from a hostile childhood. According to Buss, aggression may be a symptom of psychopathology such as psychosis, manic depression, and maladjustment. He posited that the aggressor is angry, is in conflict, and may be prejudiced. According to this theory, aggression is a catharsis, a way of "draining of the reservoir ... the less that remains ... the less pressure is exerted by impulses seeking release" (Buss, 1961, p. 75). Brodsky (1976) also described the abuser's behavior as pathological or indicative of a personality disorder.

The organization and its culture have been identified as potential factors in workplace abuse by additional scholars. Einarsen, Raknes, and Matthiesen (1994) discovered that bullying is correlated with several different environmental factors: low satisfaction with leadership, work control, social climate, and role conflict. In their study, both the victim and the bystanders of bullying reported a low-quality work environment and both suffered from the abuse. Einarsen and Skogstad (1996) found that large organizations, male-dominated environments, and industrial organizations had the highest incidence of bullying. According to Robinson and O'Leary-Kelly (1998), the social context of the work group is a catalyst in terms of whether and when employees will engage in antisocial behaviors.

Characteristics of the Abuser

Bjorkqvist, Osterman, and Hjelt-Back (1994) posited that the aggressor behaves in ways that will harm the victim while taking great care to risk as few negative consequences to self as possible. They referred to this relationship as the effect/danger ratio, which incorporates the aggressor's subjective estimate of the two variables. According to these authors, the aggressor will not bully if the possibility of danger to self is greater than the desired effect on the victim. Verbal and passive forms of aggression maximize this ratio.

According to Baumeister, Smart, and Boden (1996), some aggression is the result of a threat to the aggressor's ego. These authors suggest that when others view the aggressor unfavorably, that perspective is contrary to the aggressor's own self-image, deflates the aggressor's belief in his or her sense of superiority, and results in the aggressor directing anger outward as a coping mechanism to avoid introspection of self.

Malamuth and Thornhill (1994) demonstrated that *hostile masculinity* or *hostile dominance* is a characteristic of men who are both sexually and nonsexually aggressive toward women. Three components make up the construct of hostile masculinity: hostility toward women, dominance in sexual relationships, and attitudes of acceptance of violence toward women, but not toward men.

One of the threads most commonly observed in the literature is the recognition of the abuse of power, often from management, in precipitating aggressive behavior. According to Brodsky (1976), the belief that "rank has its privilege" (p. 107) is an inherent belief of the aggressor—that is, the aggressor would not attempt to bully the boss, but believes he or she has the right to pick on subordinates. This approach supports Bassman's (1992) discussion of the abuse of power, and the positional power that is often demonstrated in the hierarchical structure of many work environments (Brodsky 1976; Cortina et al., 2001; Pearson et al., 2000). Ayoko, Callan, and Hartel (2003) and Rayner (1999) found that the majority of respondents to their studies perceived their managers as bullies. Ashforth (1994) used the term "petty tyrant" to describe tyrannical behaviors of management in which the manager "lords his or her power over others" (p. 772), thereby causing low self-esteem, high frustration, stress, work alienation, and helplessness among subordinates. He concluded that the tyranny catalyzes a vicious cycle that sustains the misconduct and makes it difficult to change. Interestingly, Einarsen and Skogstad (1996) found that those in management were no more likely to bully than were colleagues.

Often the aggressor is the organization itself (Bassman, 1992; Brodsky, 1976; Folger & Baron, 1996). Aggressive organizational behavior may include increased/excessive work demands, raising the CEO's salary while downsizing, imposed change, lack of safety protocols, instilling fear, psychological testing, and hiring and retaining bully bosses, among others. Vartia (1996) found that an environment that was authoritative, competitive, and unable to influence the culture, and that showed a poor flow of information, poor attitude toward innovation, and lack of effective communication was characteristic of aggressive organizations.

Institutionalized Abuse

According to Brodsky (1976), "Harassment [bullying] has been institutionalized as a way in which persons in certain roles should relate to each other. As such, it is not an aberration of human behavior, but a formula for interacting" (p. 5). She cited the origins of workplace aggression as dating back to the time when the stratification of work and society emerged, with some individuals gaining more power, privilege, and status than others. Slavery represents one of the most egregious types of workplace aggression in its time. Over the years, the concepts of human rights, children's rights, women's rights, and workers' rights (e.g., worker's compensation, unions) emerged to influence society's thinking, and embrace of those rights ultimately enhanced working conditions. Yet, workplace abuse still exists and is allowed to fester because the organizational culture both permits and rewards it. Cowie, Naylor, Rivers, Smith, and Pereira (2002) argued that abuse has become an accepted aspect of some organizational cultures and, indeed, has even been encouraged. Crawford (1997) posited that abuse is so endemic that it is interwoven into the very fabric of work, a symptom of organizational dysfunction, and that it is "sadism protected by positions of power" (p. 221). According to Adams (1997), the organization has become a "conspiracy of silence" (p. 178) that filters information related to abuse from the top down and threatens the potential of the organization.

Characteristics of the Victim

Abusive behavior may occur between managers and their staff as well as between colleagues (Einarsen & Skogstad, 1996; Rayner, 1997). Some abuse is directed to individuals, while other workers are bullied in groups (Rayner, 1997). The victims of the abusive behavior include not just the intended target(s), but the bystander(s) as well (Cusack, 2000). Einarsen and Skogstad (1996) found that to be a victim of bullying, one must feel inferior in defending oneself. They also discovered that older workers (age greater than 45 years) were more likely to be victimized than younger workers. Younger employees admitted to being more aggressive than their older colleagues (Baron et al., 1999). This finding stands in contrast to the results of Einarsen and Raknes' (1995) study, which demonstrated that among male workers, older men were less likely to be abused than the younger men. National cultural differences may account for some of the variation in findings (Einarsen & Skogstad, 1996; Hoel et al., 1999).

The Role of Gender

The literature includes mixed results regarding the role of gender in bullying and scant data exploring the gender dynamics inherent in the construct. Vartia (1996) and Cusack (2000) found that there was no correlation between gender and bullying. Leymann (1992, cited in Hoel et al., 1999) and Einarsen et al. (1994) found that men are predominantly bullied by other men, and women are bullied by both men and women, though more frequently by other women. Einarsen and Skogstad (1996) noted that women were more likely to be bullied by a man, which they attributed to women's inferior position in the hierarchy of the organization. These authors also discovered that men are more likely to bully in groups. Bjorkqvist, Osterman, and Hjelt-Back (1994) and Cortina et al. (2001) discovered that women are the most frequent victims of bullying, with 25 percent of Bjorkqvist et al.'s respondents having indicated that gender was the cause of their victimization. Bjorkqvist, Osterman, and Lagerspetz (1994) likewise found not only that women were more likely to be the gender abused, but also that they were bullied more often and more severely than men. In Rayner's (1997) study, there were no significant gender differences in experiences of bullying, but men were the more likely gender to bully. Baron, Neuman, and Geddes (1999) found that males engaged in aggressive behavior more often than did women; moreover, women were bullied by both men and women, whereas women rarely bullied men. Although gender was identified as a variable in these authors' work, gender dynamics were not examined.

Hofstede (1980) found that organizations in Sweden, Finland, and Norway, where the bulk of the research on this issue has been done, typically exhibit less power differentiation, lower masculinity, more feminine values, and individualism. These characteristics place a high value on the individual worker's well-being and lead to a negative view of abuse of power. Because feminine values are the foundation of their culture, domination, and aggression are not supported. In these Scandinavian countries, individuals value more fluid sex roles and demonstrate a higher level of equality between the sexes than do other countries; as a result, there is less tolerance for aggression and abuse of power.

The perception of abusive behavior has also been studied. The results of Harris and Knight-Bohnhoff's (1996) study, for example, suggest that women view abusive behavior more seriously than do men. Their study participants viewed male aggression, particularly toward a female, negatively. Women were found to be more offended than men when measuring their perception of *disempowering acts* directed toward other women and toward men (Young et al., 2003).

Both men and women prefer to use covert aggression tactics, with women being more likely to use social manipulation as compared to men (Bjorkqvist, Osterman, & Lagerspetz, 1994). Covert aggression by both genders entails an attempt to disguise the abusive behavior in hopes of preventing retaliation or social ostracism. As in Bjorkqvist et al.'s work, covert aggression was found to be the more prevalent form of aggression in Baron and Neuman (1996) study.

While scholars have found that men and women can be both victims and perpetrators of workplace abuse, most researchers have failed to examine the gender politics within the dynamic of this phenomenon. Lee (2002) stated, "It is highly unlikely that abuse of organizational power would not be gendered "(p. 207). According to Halford and Leonard (2001), "organizational structures do not come to reproduce male power unwittingly, but are in fact designed for this purpose, or at least, actively maintained with this in mind" (p. 50).

Lee's (2003) qualitative research suggested that failure of the target of the behavior to conform to gender stereotypes was the foundation of gendered bullying. In her report, she provided examples of women who were bullied because they failed to adhere to *appropriate* female workplace conduct. In some cases, the bullying resulted in low performance-related pay and promotions. Other examples suggested that women who were assertive were bullied, whereas women who were perceived as compliant and quiet—characteristics associated with femininity—were treated more favorably. Lee also examined workplace bullying that targeted men who were treated less favorably than other men because they did not conform to stereotypical male appearance and behavior.

Simpson and Cohen (2004) investigated the role of gender in bullying in higher education. They argued that bullying cannot be separated from gender and that the construct of bullying requires its relationship to gender. Like others who have studied gender in organizations (Evans, 1997; Halford & Leonard, 2001; Johnson, 1997; Lee, 2002), these researchers found that a masculine infrastructure is the framework for a culture of bullying.

Women were more likely than men to perceive abusive behavior as unwelcome and threatening, were more likely to be targeted by bullies for unfair criticism and intimidation, and were significantly more likely to have their decisions overruled (Simpson & Cohen, 2004). Women were also more likely than men to report bullying to their managers than they were to report it to human resources personnel. Men were more likely to tie bullying into the management style of the organization and were also more likely to label behavior as bullying when they were the targets.

DEFINITION OF SEXUAL HARASSMENT

Defining sexual harassment can be a challenge, because this behavior is often discussed as a legal phenomenon yet it emanates from a social experience with a resulting psychological effect (Fitzgerald, Swan, & Magley, 1997). The psychological and social perspectives are broader constructs than the legal parameters, which are continuously evolving with emerging sexual harassment case law. Women may experience a myriad of sexual and gender-based offensive conduct, yet the behavior may not meet the legal definition of sexual harassment.

Fitzgerald et al. (1997) defined sexual harassment psychologically as "unwanted sex-related behavior at work that is appraised by the recipient as offensive, exceeding her resources, or threatening her well-being" (p. 15). According to these authors, numerous elements influence the target's evaluation of the behavior: (1) objective factors, such as the frequency, intensity, and duration of the acts; (2) individual factors, including the target's resources, attitude, control, and the history of the victimization; (3) contextual factors, such as bystander stress, gender ratio of the work group, organizational climate, management norms, policies and procedures, and the presence of other types of harassment; (4) the target's subjective appraisal as to whether the behavior was offensive, upsetting, embarrassing, and frightening; and (5) a variety of potential outcomes that may be psychological, health or organization related.

While various definitions of sexual harassment have been proposed, the Equal Employment Opportunity Commission (EEOC)—the federal agency whose task is to oversee enforcement of the Civil Rights Act, Title VII, which prohibits discrimination based on race, gender, religion, national origin and other protected classes—defines the term as follows:

> Unwelcome sexual advances, requests for sexual favors, and other verbal or physical conduct of a sexual nature constitutes sexual harassment when (1) submission to such conduct is made either explicitly or implicitly a term or conduction of an individual's employment, (2) submission to or rejection of such conduct by an individual is used as the basis for employment decisions affecting such individuals, or (3) such conduct has the purpose or effect of unreasonably interfering with an individual's work performance or creating an intimidating, hostile, or offensive work environment. (Code of Federal Regulations, 2002, p. 186)

The first two examples of the EEOC's definition have historically been referred to as *quid pro quo*—a Latin term meaning "this for that"—and always involve a person in positional power over the target of the harassment (Code of Federal Regulations, 2002). The third example is commonly called the *hostile environment* segment of the law. In a hostile environment incident of harassment, the harasser may be a coworker, vendor, client, patient, student, physician, or one's supervisor.

Isolated incidents of misconduct do not reach the threshold of sexual harassment (EEOC, 1990). The unwelcome behavior must be severe and/or pervasive enough that a *reasonable person*, in the same or similar environment or circumstances, would find it created a hostile or abusive environment. As stated, the context in which the harassment occurred should be considered, recognizing that the behavior does not occur in a vacuum.

The "reasonable person" standard recognizes that even if offensive conduct is the norm, it may still constitute a hostile work environment; even if the majority of workers state that the conduct is to be expected, is part of the job, or is harmless. Using the "reasonable person" standard represents an objective view of the behavior (Wiener & Hurt, 1999). Wiener and Hurt argue, however, that "the law adopts a point of view that does not take into consideration the idiosyncratic sensitivities of the complainant; it falls far short of operationalizing the construct of sexual harassment with the specificity commonly found in social science research" (p. 573).

According to the *Ellison v. Brady* (924 F.2d 872; 9th Cir.1991) opinion, the "reasonable person" standard fails to recognize the divergent views between most women and men about what constitutes appropriate social sexual conduct at work. Instead, this standard reflects the perspective of appropriateness through a hidden male-biased lens and fails to recognize the salient fact that most victims of sexual harassment are women. As a result, a "reasonable woman" standard was considered an appropriate alternative in this case, which has since been analyzed and debated at length by both legal and social scholars (Drobac, 2005).

The EEOC (1990) lists numerous factors that courts should examine in determining whether the misconduct was so offensive that it becomes actionable according to the law: (1) the type of conduct—verbal, physical, or both; (2) the frequency of the behavior; (3) the degree to which the conduct was hostile or offensive; (4) others' willingness to join in with the harasser; (5) the position of the harasser—supervisor or coworker; and (6) the number of people who experienced the harassment.

Although Title VII was enacted in 1964 to combat discrimination in general, it was not until 1980 that the EEOC developed the previously given definition for sexual harassment. While the definition of sexual harassment has remained constant within Title VII, the courts have continued to interpret the sexual harassment laws (providing new case law) to further refine the legal definition of sexual harassment (Fitzgerald et al., 1997). A Washington, D.C., federal court was the first to recognize quid pro quo harassment as a legal issue in 1976 (*Williams v. Saxbe*, 413 F. Supp. 654; D.C. Cir. 1976). Five years later, in 1981, the concept of hostile environment sexual harassment was accepted by another federal court in *Bundy v. Jackson* (641 F.2d 934; D.C. Cir. 1981).. Shortly after the *Bundy* opinion, the courts, in *Henson v. City of Dundee* (682 F. 2d 897; 1982), rendered the following opinion:

> Sexual harassment which creates a hostile or offensive environment for members of one sex is every bit the arbitrary barrier to sexual equality at the workplace that racial harassment is to racial equality. Surely, a requirement that a man or a woman run a gauntlet of sexual abuse in return for the privilege of being allowed to work and make a living can be as demeaning and disconcerting as the harshest of racial epithets. (p. 902)

Several other landmark cases further helped to define sexual harassment. A year following the *Bundy* decision, in *Barnes v. Costle* (561 F. 2d 983; D.C. 1977), the judge ruled that *but for* the plaintiff's sex, the behavior would not have occurred. The first U.S. Supreme Court sexual harassment opinion in 1986, in *Meritor Savings Bank v. Vinson* (477 U.S. 57), stated that sexual harassment was a violation of Title VII and, therefore, constituted a form of sex discrimination. This was the first case that identified the relationship between sexual harassment and Title VII. It was not until 1993 that the U.S. Supreme Court would hear its next sexual harassment case, *Harris v. Forklift Systems* (510 U.S. 17). With this opinion, the Court established additional parameters under which the harassing behavior must exist for it to rise to the level of legally recognized sexual harassment. To constitute sexual harassment, the behavior must be severe and/or pervasive enough to interfere with an employee's ability to do her or his work and create a hostile, offensive, and intimidating work environment based from the perspective of any reasonable person.

In 1998, the U.S. Supreme Court heard three workplace sexual harassment cases. The *Oncale v. Sundowner Offshore Services* (523 U.S. 75) decision determined that same-sex sexual harassment is actionable under Title VII, emphasizing that men can also be victims of sexual harassment. In *Faragher v. City of Boca Raton* (524 U.S. 775) and *Burlington Industries, Inc. v. Ellerth* (524 U.S. 742), the Court opined that an employer may vicariously be held liable for harassment based on race, color, sex (whether or not of a sexual nature), religion, national origin, age, or disability, if a supervisor subjects the victim to employment actions such as a demotion, termination, or change in responsibilities. Even if the victim does not suffer any tangible employment action, the employer is liable unless it can demonstrate that it took action to both prevent and correct incidents of sexual harassment by a supervisor, and if the victim failed to utilize whatever measures existed within the organization to address the harassment, such as the use of the organization's policy.

Ambient Sexual Harassment

Most research devoted to sexual harassment has focused on the target of the behavior and paid little attention to the witnesses who are indirectly exposed to it (Glomb et al., 1997). Glomb and colleagues term the witnessing of sexual harassment "ambient sexual harassment," which they define as "the general or ambient level of sexual harassment in a work group as measured by the frequency of sexually harassing behaviors experienced by others in a woman's work group" (p. 309). These researchers further suggest that ambient sexual harassment results in similar psychological, health, and job outcomes to the witness as direct sexual harassment does to the target. Following her study, Schneider (1996) suggested that women's mental health deteriorated and that the women had less satisfaction with their colleagues and also with their life following ambient sexual harassment. She also found that men who witnessed the harassment of coworkers were negatively affected—specifically, they experienced stress as a result of this event.

Glomb et al. (1997) studied ambient sexual harassment from the perspective of workplace stress. These researchers suggested that coworkers are cognizant of sexual harassment not only from observing it, but also from hearing about it or knowing about colleagues who have been harassed. This indirect exposure to sexual harassment functions as a job stressor, as workers worry about the possibility of their own victimization, feel powerless to influence the harassing climate, and are aware of the lack of support by the organization. According to these investigators, "indirect exposure within the context of the work group exerts a detrimental influence on job satisfaction and psychological conditions" (p. 322).

The results of Glomb et al.'s (1997) study suggest that ambient sexual harassment might lead to a legal remedy for victims who are members of a workgroup in which a hostile work environment exists as a result of sexual harassment. These data provide statistical evidence that a person does not need to be the direct recipient of the harassment to feel harassed and experience negative consequences.

Effects of Sexual Harassment

The negative effects of sexual harassment on targets' health have been thoroughly researched and include psychological disturbances such as depression, anger, fear of losing one's job and income, anxiety, loss of self-esteem and confidence, and a sense of helplessness (Hamilton, Alagna, King, & Lloyd, 1987). Dansky and Kilpatrick (1997) noted that PTSD was experienced by sexual harassment victims, indicating that such abuse has a long-lasting impact. Gutek (1985) suggested that victims may also report irritability, shame, alienation, and vulnerability as a result of such abuse.

Physical symptoms of abuse, including a broad range of gastrointestinal disturbances, headaches, weight loss, jaw clenching, teeth grinding, anorexia, fatigue, diminished libido, and urinary tract infections, were reported by Lenhart (1996). Gutek (1985) found additional health impairment in the form of fatigue, sleep disturbances, and dental problems. In addition, women reported diminished work relationships (Culberston, Rosenfeld, Booth-Kewley, & Magnusson, 1992; Gutek, 1985), an increase in absenteeism (U.S. Merit Systems Protection Board [USMSPB], 1981, 1988, 1995), decreased motivation to work (Jensen & Gutek, 1985), less satisfaction with their jobs (Culbertson et al., 1992; Gruber & Bjorn, 1986), diminished job performance (Crull, 1982; Gutek, 1985), and an interruption in their careers (Livingston, 1982).

Despite these effects of sexual harassment, few victims report the problem because they fear (1) they will be blamed, (2) they will not be believed, (3) nothing will change, and (4) they will experience retaliation

(Fitzgerald & Ormerod, 1993; Fitzgerald, Swan, & Fischer, 1995; Terpstra & Baker, 1986).

Women's Responses to Sexual Harassment

Initially, most women ignore sexual harassment (Fitzgerald et al., 1988; Fitzgerald, Swan & Fischer, 1995; Gutek, 1985) and avoid the harasser (Culbertson et al., 1992; USSMSPB, 1981, 1988, 1995). Reporting the harasser or the harassing behavior is not a common response by most women for a variety of reasons (Fitzgerald et al., 1988; Gutek, 1985). One of the most common reasons is fear—of being labeled a troublemaker, of not being believed, and of retaliation. Additionally, most women become somewhat protective of the harasser himself and do not want him to have to suffer any negative repercussions of his behavior. Victims may also be embarrassed about their victimization, and believe that coming forward with their complaint will not result in any changes.

Many women are reluctant to label themselves as victims, which may diminish the likelihood of them reporting their victimization (Koss, 1990). Minimizing her sexual harassment experience often provides a woman with a false sense of safety to protect her sense of vulnerability. When women decide to complain, their coworkers often do not support them, their complaints may be trivialized, and they are often blamed, leading to feelings of betrayal. Livingston (1982) and Jensen and Gutek (1982) suggested that women who do file formal complaints or seek legal assistance may experience an increase in both psychological and physical symptoms. This may be due, in part, to continued harassment or retaliation that occurs following the complaint (Crull, 1982).

Characteristics of the Sexual Harasser

A review of the literature examining sexual harassers is scarce. Early studies suggested that the sexual harasser tended to be a married, older man in a more powerful position than the victim within the organization (O'Hare & O'Donahue, 1998). Pryor (1987) assumed that sexual harassment existed as part of a continuum, with the extreme endpoint being rape. In Malamuth's (1981) work on the likelihood of men to rape, Pryor developed a survey instrument to measure the likelihood of a man to sexually harass. His Likelihood to Sexually Harass (LSH) questionnaire measured severe forms of sexual abuse that correlated with Malamuth's Likelihood to Rape (LR) scale and Burt's (1980) Adversarial Sexual Beliefs and Rape Myth Acceptance scales. As a result, Pryor's assumption of the connection between sexual harassment and rape was supported.

Three types of harassers were identified by Lengnick-Hall (1995): hard-core, opportunist, and insensitive. The *hard-core* harasser actively seeks out opportunities to harass, and is probably the least likely of the three to stop his behavior when confronted by the victim. Such an individual tends to have an affinity toward sexual harassment and other types of dysfunctional behavior owing to his personality type or past experiences. The *opportunist* is the typical sexual harasser in the general population, considering personality traits and past experiences. He does not specifically seek out opportunities to sexually harass; however, if an opportunity presents itself, he will take advantage of the situation. The *insensitive* individual is not cognizant of how his behavior affects others. Like the opportunist, this individual does not seek out opportunities to sexually harass; neither the insensitive harasser nor the opportunist will continue with their harassing conduct if confronted.

Pryor and Whalen (1997), and Lengnick-Hall (1995) found that both the person and the situation are important factors in sexual harassment. Pryor and Whalen (1997) suggested that men who are sexist in their beliefs about women—that is, men demonstrate misogyny by viewing women as the *outgroup* when they divide the world into males and females—are more likely to demonstrate hostility toward women in the workplace. Both men and women who feel hostility toward women were likely to be more tolerant of sexual harassment, according to Russell and Trigg (2004). The sexual harasser's framework is based on interpersonal aggression, according to O'Leary-Kelly, Paetzold, and Griffin (2000). These authors assert that using an aggression concept in researching sexual harassers provides an innovative approach. Their research suggests that the harasser may be merely pursuing goals of "retributive justice and self presentation" (p. 384). This motivation manifests itself when the harasser uses sexual harassment as a means of reprisal toward the target for a perceived injustice that the target directed toward the harasser. At other times, the sexual harasser engages in abuse while attempting to present himself as more manly to his coworkers.

Characteristics of the Target of Sexual Harassment

Any woman in any profession or industry may experience sexual harassment, and certain conditions within her occupation may increase the likelihood of being subjected to it. Although men can be victims of sexual harassment (Grieco, 1987; USMSPB, 1981, 1988, 1995), women are the most frequent targets of such behavior (Fitzgerald et al., 1988; Gutek, 1985). Younger women (younger than 35 years) who are single or divorced and working in a predominantly male work environment are more likely to experience the behavior (Lengnick-Hall, 1995). Persons who are well educated, who are newly employed, and whose supervisor is the opposite sex are often targeted as well (USMSPB, 1981, 1988, 1995). Single, young, and minority women tend to experience more severe and frequent sexual harassment (Gruber & Bjorn, 1986; Gutek & Nakamura, 1980). Other researchers have found that single women are more likely to experience harassment and bullying (Fain & Anderton, 1987; Greico, 1987; O'Connell & Korabik, 2000). Previous victimization from rape, battering, or sexual abuse and harassment may increase the risk of subsequent abuse, although it is not understood why this relationship occurs (Dansky & Kilpatrick, 1997; Fitzgerald et al., 1997).

Race and Sexual Harassment

Race and gender discrimination are not separate issues for African American workers; they are integrated into an abusive work environment, yet the effects of race and sexual harassment are not clear (Adams, 1997). Not only culture but also the minority status of women influence both their perceptions and their experiences of harassing behavior. Measuring culture and one's membership in an ethnic minority with the relationship to sexual harassment is challenging because of the influence of the different norms from the variety of cultures and countries. The USMSPB (1981, 1988) findings revealed only a small difference in the amount of sexual harassment experienced by White and non-White women. Black women were more likely to be pressured for a date, leered at, and targeted with sexual gestures (Fain & Anderton, 1987). Niebuhr and Boyles (1991) found that White women were more likely to be harassed than non-White women, a finding that contrasts with the results obtained by Mansfield, Koch, Henderson, Vicary, Cohn, and Young (1991), who found that Black women were significantly more likely to be sexually harassed.

Sexual Harassment of Men

An under-researched aspect of sexual harassment is the sexual harassment of men. The USMSPB surveys (1981, 1988, 1995) provide data on the sexual harassment of both women and men. According to these surveys, 14 to 19 percent of men working for the federal government experienced a minimum of one incident of sexual harassment in the two years before the survey was conducted, with these incidents consisting most often of unwanted sexual teasing and jokes. Twenty-one percent of the men experienced sexual harassment by other men, whereas only 2 percent of women experienced sexual harassment by other women. Fitzgerald and her colleagues (1988) found that men were much less likely than women to be sexually harassed. According to Donovan and Drasgow (1999), men do not experience gender harassment in the same way as women. Berdahl, Magley, and Waldo (1996) likewise found that the behaviors that men define as sexual harassment have not been identified as such by women and that the behaviors women identify as harassing, men experience as less threatening. Stockdale (2005) argued that the sexual harassment of men may be underestimated partly because survey instruments are written to reflect the sexual harassment behaviors toward women.

Stockdale, Wood, and Batra (1999) examined the sexual harassment experiences of men by comparing their harassment by other men with incidents in which women were the harassers. The harassment of men by women tended to incorporate sexual hostility when the women made sexist comments or putdowns, or offered unwanted sexual attention such as attempts to date and to touch in a sexual way (Stockdale et al., 1999). Same-sex harassment—male to male—demonstrated sexist hostility in the form of crude comments, jokes, and pictures. Research conducted by Stockdale and Motoike (2000) found that men were more likely to experience teasing, insults or threats from (1) both genders, (2) men, and (3) women, in that order. Dirty jokes and putdowns because of being male were most likely delivered by (1) both genders, (2) women, and (3) men, in that order. Thus Stockdale and her colleagues categorized the men's experiences as resulting from one of two motives for sexual harassment—approach-based and rejection-based sexual harassment.

Approach-based sexual harassment, in which the abuse of power *may* be the catalyst, generally represents behaviors that are based on sexual attraction, even though the advances are unwelcome (Stockdale et al., 1999). Rejection-based harassment has a more malicious intent—namely, to demean and ridicule the target. Stockdale and her colleagues argue that:

> Rejection-based sexual harassment is conducted to enforce preferred heterosexist, hypermasculine gender-role behavior. Men who do not live up to their tormentors' masculinity standards are targeted for harassment. For example, men who appear to be effeminate, gay, or in other ways not sufficiently masculine . . . are likely targets . . . Rejection-based sexual harassment is sexist because it serves to exalt hypermasculinity and diminish femininity. (1999, p. 124)

According to these authors, the theory of approach–rejection sexual harassment represents masculine hegemony and demonstrates that men can be victims of sexual harassment including gender harassment. As Stockdale (2005) has stated, "[M]ale dominance and masculine hegemony remain the root cause of sexual harassment for both women and men" (p. 139).

If a male is sexually harassed by his female supervisor, she is abusing the power of her position but is not using her gender privilege because she does not have it to use (Johnson, 1997). This is contrary to what occurs when a male supervisor sexually harasses one of his female direct reports—he is abusing the privileges of his position *and* his gender, resulting (according to Johnson) in his harassment of her being more harmful. The male supervisor's gender privilege automatically places a social context around his harassment of the female subordinate that a female supervisor cannot do when she harasses a male subordinate.

Female-to-Female Harassment

When women bully, sabotage, gossip, or undermine one another, does this behavior always rise to the level of gender-based sexual harassment? Is the abusive behavior that women typically perpetrate on one another the same behavior they would direct to one of their male colleagues? These questions require scholarly and legal examination to resolve them.

Simpson and Cohen (2004) acknowledged that women can be bullies. These authors recognized the issue of gender within their framework, thereby supporting the potential of female-to-female harassment:

> Rather than challenging the masculine hegemony of management, some women—particularly those who employ bullying tactics— may be conforming to the masculine ethic that underpins many management practices. On this basis, while men and women may be involved as perpetrators in bullying situations, and while, irrespective of gender, much bullying involves the abuse of power, such behavior cannot be divorced from gender considerations. (p. 182)

Women complain about working with other women; call their colleagues sex-specific sexual epithets such as "bitch," "cunt," and "whore"; gossip about those who got the promotion because they "slept their way to the top"; and give the silent treatment to their female peers. According to Mizrahi (2004), this type of female-to-female workplace hostility may be actionable under Title VII of the Civil Rights Act of 1964 and, therefore, constitute sexual harassment.

The Supreme Court, in its ruling in *Meritor Savings Bank v. Vinson*, established that victims could demonstrate sexual harassment if they were subjected to a hostile or abusive work environment *because of their sex*, and if the behavior was severe or pervasive enough to interfere with their working conditions. Mizrahi (2004) concluded:

> When the *reason* for the harassment [bullying] is female-specific, the same "but for" test can be used to determine that the "because of sex" element has been satisfied: If only a woman could be targeted for the harassment, it is by definition sex-based. For example, when a woman harasses a female coworker out of jealousy regarding a female-specific trait, the harassment can be considered sex-based. (p. 1617)

In *Oncale v. Sundowner Offshore Services, Inc.*, the Supreme Court acknowledged that sexual desire is not required for to warrant a finding of sex discrimination and harassment. Following the Court's opinion in this case, scholars and courts have focused on male-to-male harassment, while "nonsexualized female-on-female harassment remains invisible as well as undertheorized" (Mizrahi, 2004).

Schultz (1998) contended that nonsexual gender hostility impedes a woman's ability to professionally advance in her career. One catalyst for gender hostility is workplace sex segregation, which establishes a workplace structure and environment in which women undercut one another. Sex segregation, both horizontal and vertical, is the norm in most workplaces. In horizontal segregation, both women and men work predominantly with members of their own gender. Men generally hold the top executive positions and women the lower positions, thereby creating a vertical segregation, even in predominantly female occupations (Mizrahi, 2004). According to Mizrahi, "sex segregation leads to sex being salient, so that women are more likely to compare themselves to each other along gendered lines than they would be in an integrated environment" (p. 1617). Additionally, these segregations reinforce sex-role stereotypes that create barriers for women attempting to advance into senior leadership positions, which are typically held by men. Double standards are then applied to the woman who is pursuing, or has already attained, the leadership role, resulting in female (and male) hostility toward her (Strauss, 2008). When women are hostile toward one of their female peers who is pursuing a promotion, they are responding to lack of organizational power within their sex-segregated work environment (Mizrahi, 2004; Strauss, 2008).

Women tend to have healthier positive relationships among themselves when the workplace features a significant number of women in positions of power. Conversely, when women work in a male-dominated environment, the women may gossip, undermine, and badmouth their female coworkers to separate themselves from the other women in their workgroup, thereby allowing themselves to be perceived in a more favorable light with their male peers. This outcome is reflective of Kanter's (1977a, 1977b) theory of tokenism (a "token" woman working with men) in which women work to dissociate themselves from their female peers so that they will be accepted by their predominantly male coworkers.

In researching female-to-female sexual harassment cases, Mizrahi (2004) found 50 cases. Of this number, 27 comprised sexualized behavior (which did not include hostility) involving lesbians, homoerotic behavior, or sexual advances. The other 23 cases were hostility based and included behaviors such as shouting, invading personal space, requiring work on regular days off, refusing to let the female worker play the radio, and reprimanding her for idleness. Some of these cases were granted summary judgments because many courts still require sexualized behavior to allow an actionable Title VII lawsuit.

Another notable aspect of female-to-female harassment is oppression. One element of oppression is a phenomenon called horizontal violence (HV), which is exhibited in female-to-female hostility, bullying, and aggression (Dunn, 2003). HV occurs when the oppressed (women) direct their anger and sense of helplessness and hopelessness about their oppression toward members of their own group. This behavior results from the oppressed group's inability to exhibit feelings of aggression against the dominant group—often men and managers—for fear of reprisal. The oppressed also tend to lack pride in their own female group, and are hesitant to align themselves with those members who have the least power within their group. Such a perspective can result in self-hatred—an example of internalized oppression, in which the women are unable to challenge the patriarchal system and its male privilege; they may not even see patriarchy as a problem because it is part of the job (Johnson, 1997).

THEORIES OF ETIOLOGY OF SEXUAL HARASSMENT

Natural/Biological Model

Several models have been suggested to explain the causes of sexual harassment, with no one model being sufficient by itself to fully explain the behavior (Tangri & Hayes, 1997). One of the models examined is the natural/biological model described by Tangri, Burt, and Johnson (1982). This model suggests that sexual harassment does not actually exist but instead posits that behaviors labeled as such merely reflect the natural sexual tension and attraction between men and women. As a result, the behavior is neither sexist nor discriminatory. The basis of this model is the assumption that men do not have any intention or maliciousness to harass, but because they have a stronger libido than women, they are just naturally more sexually aggressive. If this model were valid, one could expect that complaints and lawsuits would reflect male harassers to be fall within the age group with the highest sex drive; in reality, harassers are characterized by a variety of ages, positions, and statuses.

Organizational Model

A second model was called the "organizational model" by Tangri et al. (1982). Gruber (1998), Gruber and Bjorn (1986), and Gutek (1985) identified specific organizational characteristics that contribute to sexual harassment, such as occupational norms, the amount of contact with the opposite gender, the ratio of males to females, and job functions, to name a few. This model argues that it is the organization itself that supports sexual harassment via its hierarchy, which is represented by the stratification of power within the organization. According to this model, abuse often plays itself out when someone in a position of authority uses sexual harassment to intimidate and control those who are subordinate to him or him. The misuse of power is the common theme of this model.

Bargh and Raymond (1995) contend that "having power within a situation automatically and nonconsciously triggers a sexuality schema, just as racial or gender features automatically trigger stereotypes of that group" (p. 85). These researchers found that men with power lacked awareness of the role their power played in their interactions with women at work, and denied that their behavior, including sexual harassment, was a misuse of power.

"Contrapower sexual harassment" was the term used by Rospenda, Richman, and Nawyn (1998) when defining harassment by a perpetrator with less organizational power than the target. The authors posited that power dynamics are broader than the organizational model, which fails to take into consideration class, race, and gender as salient elements individually as well as when they intersect. According to these authors, when organizational models fail to recognize the role of these other social characteristics in organizational power dynamics, they assume that men perpetrate abuse merely because they have higher positions in the organizational hierarchy (Tangri et al., 1982). Acker (1990) argues that women are excluded from the male power bastion because of organizational design, which she asserted is male based. Ragins and Sundstrum (1989) found that "the path to power for women resembles an obstacle course" (p. 51).

MacKinnon (1979) claims that men use power to gain sex, as evidenced in quid pro quo sexual harassment. In contrast to MacKinnon's theory, Wise and Stanley (1987) argue that men use sex to maintain power, which they do not imply is based on positional quid pro quo. Cleveland and Kerst's (1993) research has explored the role of power among coworkers considering the context of the situation and the level and the sources of power. These authors challenge the idea that misuse of power, while an important ingredient in the etiology of coworker sexual harassment, cannot be viewed as a sufficient explanation. They acknowledge the multifaceted aspects of sexual harassment and the need for further research, particularly in regard to coworker power differentials and sexual harassment.

Both work environment and job context set the norms and affect perceptions regarding appropriate and inappropriate behaviors and, therefore, demonstrate whether there is organizational tolerance and/or tacit approval of the abuse and harassment (Fitzgerald et al., 1997; Gutek, 1985). A culture that permits and rewards abuse or harassment plays a prominent role in the degree to which such behavior is allowed to flourish (Ashforth, 1994; Brodsky, 1976; Einarsen, 2000). Keashley (1998) found that health care settings may have different norms from other settings regarding what is considered appropriate workplace behavior.

Environments that are considered disrespectful and unprofessional and in which stereotypes are reinforced are examples of environmental antecedents to sexual harassment (Lundberg-Love & Marmion, 2003). O'Hare and O'Donohue (1998) identified environments that devalue and dominate women as inferior or as sex objects to be perpetrating a harassing climate.

Sociocultural Model

The sociocultural model—the third model identified by Tangri and her colleagues (1982)—recognizes that sexual harassment does not exist in a vacuum but rather encompasses society's values, norms, and mores of patriarchy (MacKinnon, 1979; Wise & Stanley, 1988). This model purports that gender socialization establishes male dominance over women, rewards males for aggression, and socializes females to be passive and to avoid conflict. In addition, women are taught to regard men's sexual attention as flattery, to be sexually attractive, and to blame themselves when they are victimized. The sociocultural model assumes a feminist perspective of patriarchy (McKinnon, 1979; Wise & Stanley, 1988), in that sexual harassment is viewed as intimidating women while providing an avenue for men to maintain dominance. It also has face value considering that most sexual harassment is directed by men toward women (Gutek, 1985; Tangri et al., 1982). According to Franke (1997), "Sexual harassment is the technology of sexism in that it enforces these norms either through enacting them in the more traditional male as harasser and female as victim cases or, 'by punishing gender nonconformists' " (p. 763).

Sex-Role Spill-Over Model

Sex-role spill-over theory constitutes the fourth model of sexual harassment etiology (Gutek, 1985; Gutek & Morasch, 1982). Researchers who advocate this model have found that sexual harassment is a spill-over of society's gender expectations into the workplace. Organizations where the sex ratio is skewed toward one gender or the other are the most likely to exemplify the sex-role spill-over theory.

According to this theory, women employed in male-dominated or female-dominated work often find that their sex role is a salient aspect of their position. For example, a woman's gender singles her out in the male-dominated workplace, where she is perceived as a female before being seen as a worker. Women in these positions are aware of this different treatment but attribute it to being different as an individual woman rather than as a woman in a male role. Female-dominated/traditional jobs generally build on women's stereotypical roles as nurturer and helper (nurse, teacher, secretary), or sex object (waitress), thereby integrating the sex role into the actual job. These women experience the sex role spill-over from a different perspective—their sex role and their work role are nearly identical. These women are treated basically the same as other female workers in the same job so they are not aware that their treatment is based on a sex role. As a result, they believe their treatment is an aspect of their job, indicating that the job itself is sexualized (Gutek, 1985; Gutek & Morasch, 1982).

Gutek's model (1985) combines elements of both the organizational model and the sociocultural model. The sociocultural and sex-role spillover models recognize gender as the foundation of power differences between women and men (Rospenda et al., 1998). Because O'Hare and O'Donohue (1998) recognized the strengths and limitations of these models, they developed a four-factor model that they posited as a better predictor of sexual harassment.

Four-Factor Model

The four-factor model incorporates specific aspects of the previous four models into one comprehensive model (O'Hare & O'Donohue, 1998). This model identifies four key elements that are critical for sexual harassment to occur: (1) motivation in the form of sexual attractiveness, anger toward women, or the misuse of power; (2) overcoming internal inhibitions against harassment such as empathizing with the victim; perceiving sexual harassment as either immoral, illegal, or both; fear of rejection, and any other potential outcomes construed by the harasser; (3) overcoming external inhibitions against harassment—for example, the organization's harassment policy and grievance procedure, the privacy of the work space, sexist attitudes, a skewed sex ratio, and potential consequences to the harasser; and (4) overcoming victim resistance to the harasser via the victim communicating that the behavior must stop. The authors asserted that all four factors must be met for behavior to constitute sexual harassment.

According to Lengnick-Hall (1995), few theories have received adequate testing to support these proposed causal relationships. O'Hare and O'Donohue (1998), however, researched sexual harassment risk factors using the previously described four-factor model approach. They found sexist attitudes, lack of knowledge about grievance procedures, and an unprofessional atmosphere to be the strongest risk factors for sexual harassment. Understanding these risk factors provides a guideline for organizations in prioritizing their sexual harassment prevention and intervention strategies.

Patriarchy and Oppression

Patriarchy and oppression may be the underlying basis for all of the other models introduced so far. Patriarchy, however, is rarely included in discussions regarding gender violence and harassment, with the exception of some feminist analysis (Johnson, 1997; Paludi, 1990). According to Johnson (1997), "a society is patriarchal to the degree that it is *male-dominated, male-identified,* and *male-centered*" (p. 5). He explains that the oppression of women lies at the core of patriarchy, that the work in which women are engaged tends to be devalued, and the inherent sexism within patriarchy promotes male privilege and women's inferiority. Patriarchy, however, is not just about the male–female dynamic, but rather is a system that encompasses "an entire world organized around principles of control, domination, and competition" (p. 51). As a result, it can make oppression appear as an everyday reality, as normal, and as acceptable.

Patriarchy emphasizes male aggression and contrasts it with female caring, nurturance, and subordination to men (Johnson, 1997). It includes "power over" as a culturally positive masculine characteristic; thus those who lack this power are viewed as weak or feminine. Male aggression is at the heart of the patriarchal system, and violence toward women is both accepted and normalized. Patriarchy is a hegemonic masculinity that has destructive consequences for not only women, but also for men, in that it defines *real* men as aggressive and full of machismo. Johnson argues that the status quo will continue if society continues to ignore the patriarchal system as the social force of gendered violence. Violence (including bullying and harassment) toward women, because they are women, is a symptom of the oppression of women as a group.

SEXUAL HARASSMENT: A MULTIDIMENSIONAL CONSTRUCT

Sexual harassment has evolved from a single construct to a multidimensional phenomenon. Gruber (1992) outlined a typology of sexual harassment based on both a review of the literature and an analysis of case law. His model comprises three categories of harassment: verbal requests, verbal comments, and nonverbal displays. Each of the three major categories consists of a number of subcategories identifying types of behavior that may range from more to less severe. Verbal requests include sexual bribery, sexual advances, relational advances, and subtle pressures/advances. Verbal comments encompass personal remarks, objectification, and sexual remarks. Nonverbal behavior includes sexual assault, sexual touching, sexual posturing, and sexual materials.

Following research conducted by Till (1980), Fitzgerald and her colleagues (Fitzgerald et al., 1988; Fitzgerald, Gelfand, & Drasgow, 1995) proposed that sexual harassment falls within one of three dimensions: sexual coercion (sexual bribery for sexual activity), unwanted sexual attention (leering and touching), and gender harassment (sexist or misogynist comments). Their approach to studying sexual harassment has become a frequent springboard for empirical research. Like Gruber's (1992) approach, these authors' approach offers a detailed conceptualization through which to study the sexual harassment framework.

Gender harassment encompasses insulting, degrading, and hostile behaviors directed toward a woman, a group of women, or about women, thereby creating environmental harassment (Fitzgerald, Gelfand, & Drasgow, 1995; Gruber, 1992; Piotrkowski, 1998). Unwanted sexual attention is comprises both verbal and nonverbal communication, including repeatedly asking for dates, offensive emails, touching and grabbing, and cornering or blocking, to name a few. Both implicit and explicit threats and/or bribes for sexual relations, dates, or other forms of sexual activity in exchange for job-related benefits constitute sexual coercion. These three dimensions of sexual harassment often coexist. Because gender harassment may be severe or pervasive enough to interfere with a woman's ability to do her job, such behavior meets the legal standard for employment discrimination (Piotrkowski, 1998).

Frequency of Sexual Harassment

The EEOC collects annual statistics of complaints filed through state and federal agencies, but these data represent only a fraction of the actual number of sexual harassment incidents that occur throughout the United States each year. Fitzgerald and her colleagues (1988) estimated that approximately 5 percent of victims report their harassment to their supervisor or to human resources personnel, and even fewer file formal charges or lawsuits.

Research studies provide a more accurate picture of the extent of sexual harassment in U.S. workplaces. Studies by the U.S. Merit Systems Protection Board, along with many university-based scholarly studies, suggest that 42 to 80 percent of American women have experienced sexual harassment (DeSouza & Solberg, 2003; Fitzgerald, 1993; Fitzgerald et al., 1988; Gutek, 1985; USMSPB, 1981, 1988, 1995). Gruber (1990) summarized 18 studies from the literature in which the median percentage of women reporting sexual harassment was 44 percent.

GENDER HARASSMENT

The *Policy Guidance on Current Issues of Sexual Harassment* from the EEOC (1990) recognizes that harassment directed toward an individual based on her or his sex violates Title VII even if the harassment is not sexual in nature. Fitzgerald and her colleagues (1995) refer to this type of sexual harassment as gender harassment. Gender harassment is defined as behavior that is directed toward a woman or a group of women that is hostile and degrades women (or men, but more likely women), such as sexist and derogatory comments, jokes demeaning to women, sexual epithets and slurs, pornography, gender-based hazing, and comments that question women's competence. With gender harassment, however, the less that the conduct is actually sex based, the less likely that a court will interpret the harassment as *based on sex* and, therefore, in violation of Title VII.

Despite the damage to individuals and its potential legal consequences, gender harassment is not specifically seen as negative by some (Parker & Griffin, 2002). The derogatory name calling, sexist comments, and jokes that constitute gender harassment are often perceived by perpetrators as "just male fun" (Stanko, 1988, p. 98) or viewed as the typical interaction between men and women. Men's and women's perceptions about gender harassment vary, with men being less likely to consider the behaviors as harassment (Wiener & Hurt, 1999).

Fitzgerald and her colleagues (1995) were not the only researchers to approach nonsexual sexual harassment with the label "gender harassment." Miller (1997), separately, coined the phrase in her study of gender harassment as a form of protest for Army men toward Army women. Labeling the behavior was viewed as important by Monson (1997) as part of an effort to implement strategies to prevent it. She observed that some women view the everyday sexism as everyday rudeness and fail to see the social injustices in the behavior. Epstein (1997) argued that the phrase "sexual harassment" fails to identify a broader range of women's experiences that she labeled *sexist* harassment. She believed that this term would make visible the unwelcome male conduct toward women that is not understood with the term "sexual harassment." Lee's (2001) qualitative study demonstrated that women want to make the distinction between sexual harassment, sexism, and a sexualized environment based on, among other variables, whether they perceive the situation to indicate unwelcome sexual desire.

Gender harassment is a form of sexual harassment characterized by unwanted behavior that creates a negative (hostile) work environment and can be psychologically injurious (Fitzgerald & Hesson-McInnis, 1989; Lee, 2001; Piotrkowski, 1998; Yoder & Aniakudo, 1996). The hostile work environment classification of sexual harassment is surrounded by ambiguity, however (Fitzgerald & Ormerod, 1993). Yoder and Aniakudo (1996) and others (Schultz, 1998; Wiener & Hurt, 1999) suggested that it is not the behavior alone that determines if the incidents are hostile, but rather consideration of the environmental context is required to make the determination. Yoder and Aniakudo posited that "the gender-typing of an occupation, the gender composition of the work groups, and the organizational climate regarding gender, all may impact on what is perceived as harassing behavior" (1996, p. 254). The authors stated that these issues are broader than the workplace and reflect societal factors.

Prevalence of Gender Harassment

Research on gender harassment is scarce, with most sexual harassment research examining the *typical* types of harassment such as sexually offensive jokes, comments, touch, and bribery, and the prevalence, causes, and impact of the behavior on the victim (Welsh, 1999). Schultz (1998) stated, "Of course making a woman the object of sexual attention can also undermine her image and self-confidence as a capable worker. Yet, much of the time, harassment assumes a form that has little or nothing to do with sexuality but everything to do with gender" (p. 1687).

Using Fitzgerald, Gelfand, and Drasgow's (1995) three-dimensional approach to examining sexual harassment, gender harassment appears to be the most common form of harassment, as demonstrated by several studies (Fitzgerald et al., 1988; Fitzgerald & Hesson-McInnis, 1989; Fitzgerald, Swan, & Fischer, 1995; O'Hare & O'Donohue, 1998; Vaux, 1993). Piotrkowski (1998) found that 72 percent of her study participants had experienced gender harassment at some time in their careers. This result is consistent with that of Vaux (1993), who found 60 to 76 percent of women had experienced such abuse. These may be conservative findings, as Gruber (1992) argued that studies have underestimated the prevalence of sexual harassment.

In examining the relationship of the work context, the status of the perpetrator, and the vulnerability of the victim, O'Connell and Korabik (2000) found gender harassment to be the most prevalent form of sexual harassment. Likewise, gender harassment was most likely to be experienced in a study of women from the former Soviet Union, Canada, and the United States (Gruber, Smith, & Kauppinen-Toropainen, 1996). Another cross-cultural study with French, Spanish, and English women obtained similar results (Rubenstein, 1992).

Few studies dealing with sexual harassment of African American women have been conducted (Gruber & Bjorn, 1986; Piotrkowski, 1998; Yoder & Aniakudo, 1996). Yoder and Aniakudo (1996) conducted both quantitative and qualitative research of women firefighters, showing that 77 percent of the women had been sexually harassed at some point during their careers. The women were subjected to being called derogatory names such as "bitch," "rebel," and "troublemaker," as well as being told they were militant and difficult to work with. It is often reported that women who are targets of gender harassment are told that they should "learn to take a joke" and not be so sensitive (Fitzgerald & Ormerod, 1993). These women may be the targets of abusive behavior that the authors describe as fraternity pranks. For example, men placed eggs and syrup in female firefighters' boots, flashed the women, dispersed their gear, and balanced pails of water on their lockers (Yoder & Aniakudo, 1996). One woman got written up for missing a call because she could not find her gear. Another slipped on the water that spilled when she opened her locker, injured her knee, and required surgery. The women also shared stories of being ignored, having their competence questioned, and the application of a work double standard between the men and women.

O'Connell and Korabik's (2000) study provided the first look at various gender harassment antecedent variables such as the context of the work and the vulnerability of the victim; the outcome variables included in this investigation were psychological, physical, and work related. The relationship between the perpetrator and the victim was also considered—specifically, their difference in status.

O'Connell and Korabik (2000) studied two variables dealing with sexual harassment. The first variable examined was sexual harassment by higher-level men using Fitzgerald et al.'s (1995) three forms of sexual harassment. Among the three forms, gender harassment was the most prevalent, particularly toward younger, better-educated women, who worked with a high proportion of men as coworkers, and in work environments that were perceived to provide minimal organizational sanctions for the behavior. Women who were 35 years of age and younger were most likely to experience gender harassment, followed by women between the ages of 45 and 49. Women 56 years of age and older were the least likely to be subjected to gender harassment. Victims of gender harassment reported less satisfaction with their work, more stress and turnover, and a negative mood.

The second variable of O'Connell & Korabik's (2000) study related to gender harassment by higher-level men and demonstrated that gender harassment was more prevalent toward women with less education and lower incomes, who worked primarily with women, were mentored by women, and had a negative perception of organizational sanctions. These lower-educated women did not appear to be affected as negatively as the higher-educated women and reported only decreased work satisfaction. These two variables demonstrated a relationship among the status of the men, the characteristics of the targets, and the work context.

Gender harassment and unwanted sexual attention were demonstrated by equal-level men toward younger, well-educated (with postgraduate degrees) women working in an environment that provided them with ample opportunities to interact with their male peers (O'Connell & Korabik, 2000). Women with salaries between $60,000 and $90,000 were most vulnerable, followed by women earning less than $30,000. Those women earning between $30,000 and $60,000 experienced the least amount of gender harassment and unwanted sexual attention.

At lower levels of the organization, men subjected women with higher incomes and experience to gender harassment as the most frequent type of sexual harassment (O'Connell & Korabik, 2000). These targets were more likely to have women mentors, to work with a higher proportion of men, and to have increased opportunities to interact with men who were at lower levels than the women. Again, younger women (younger than 35 years) were most likely to be targeted, followed by women between the ages of 50 and 55. Those 56 years of age and older were the least likely targets of gender harassment. Women with only some high school education were less likely to be targets of gender harassment; those with technical training were most likely to report gender harassment, followed by women with bachelor and postgraduate degrees. None of the outcomes that were demonstrated as a result of harassment by higher-level men were evident in the analysis of the lower-level men. The authors suggest this outcome reflects the targets not experiencing a long-lasting negative impact from the abuse, perhaps because these men, by virtue of their status, held less formal power over the women they harassed.

Contrary to the findings of Thacker and Gohmann (1996), who claimed that gender harassment (hostile environment harassment in their study) does not result in psychological trauma, O'Connell and Korabik's (2000) study demonstrated that gender harassment resulted in several negative outcomes to the victims. These outcomes included decreased work satisfaction, increased stress, and increased turnover. These results closely mirrored those of Piotrkowski (1998) and Schneider, Swan, and Fitzgerald (1997). The latter author group indicated that "harassment does not have to be particularly egregious to result in negative consequences" (p. 142).

Parker and Griffin (2002) determined that one example of the harm gender harassment does toward women is making them feel they need to overperform to be accepted and recognized by the organization. For men, however, gender-harassing behaviors were not associated with psychological distress over performance demands. Instead, for men, the harassing behavior was viewed as being accepted within the masculine culture. This stands a sharp contrast to women's perceptions that the behavior is threatening, especially when they are in the minority.

The gender harassment literature discussed to this point in the chapter has reflected a more narrow view of the construct than some other authors have posited. Wise and Stanley (1987), for example, have discussed sexual harassment from a feminist perspective: "Male behaviour forced on women, whether it's in the form of unwanted sexual advances or of demands for time, attention and sympathy, is what we, in contrast to the much narrower and specifically sexual conventional view that has come into existence, see as the essential feature of sexual harassment" (p. 4). These authors argue that sexual harassment is "any and all unwanted and intrusive [behaviors] . . . that aren't 'sexual' in any way other than that one sex, male, does them to another sex, female" (p. 8). They disagree with the typical mainstream definitions of sexual harassment that define the behavior as sexual, which is carried out by "atypical men" and at work (p. 72). Instead, these authors define sexual harassment as "behaviors linked by the way they represent *an unwanted and unsought intrusion by men* into women's feelings, thoughts, behaviours, space, time, energies and bodies" (p. 72). This all-encompassing definition embraces gender harassment beyond the workplace, and argues that it is not just atypical men who are guilty of the behavior.

Schultz (1998), a Yale law professor, has approached gender harassment from a legal perspective, arguing that the courts are too narrow in
their conception of a hostile work environment when the focus is on sexual harassment as sexual abuse. Wiener and Hurt (1999) agree with
Schultz, noting that the courts have failed to ask pertinent questions in
cases that will regulate social sexual conduct in the workplace. Schultz
refers to this approach as the *sexual desire-dominance* paradigm. She argues
that this approach negates the nonsexual forms of mistreatment based on
gender—that is, gender harassment. Schultz suggests an alternative paradigm that more accurately defines the workplace inequalities that women
face—namely, a *competence-centered* perspective. This approach is not
based on sexual desire but rather on maintaining the masculinity of men's
work along with the status associated with it. According to Schultz, the
harassing man's "actions are an abuse of his power and an abuse of her
sex" (p. 7).

Schultz (1998) asserts that the range of behaviors intended to protect
the bastions of masculinity, via the gender harassment of women (and
some men who threaten the masculine stereotype), include the following:
(1) disparaging women's work performance; (2) tendering patronizing
offers of help; (3) withholding training, information, or other opportunities to learn; (4) sabotaging work; (5) providing sexist evaluations of
women's performance or denying them deserved promotions; (6) isolating women from social networks that confer a sense of belonging; (7)
assigning women stereotyped tasks; (8) engaging in taunting, pranks,
and other misconduct designed to remind women they are *different*; and
(9) assaulting or threatening to assault women who dare to fight back.
As is evident from these examples, frequently harassment has nothing to
do with sex and much to do with gender.

Schultz (1998) has challenged the courts' handling of hostile work environment sexual harassment cases (e.g., the Seventh Circuit's decision in
King v. Board of Regents of the University of Wisconsin System [898 F. 2d 533;
1990]; the U.S. Supreme Court's decision in *Harris v. Forklift Systems* and
Meritor Savings Bank v. Vinson) when they distinguished sexual misconduct
from nonsexual treatment by determining that the nonsexual treatment
was disparate treatment and not a hostile work environment. Courts have
failed to consider whether both the sexual and nonsexual misconduct,
when taken together, created a hostile work environment. Instead, they
have analyzed each incident separately. Schultz argues that many courts
have applied the law from a narrow, sexualized perspective:

To a large extent, the courts have restricted their conception of hostile
work environment harassment to male–female sexual advances and other
explicitly sexualized actions perceived to be driven by sexual designs. In
doing so, they have created a framework that is under-inclusive. By defining the essence of harassment as sexual advances, this paradigm has

obscured—and excluded—some of the most pervasive forms of gender hostility experienced on a day-to-day basis by many women (and men) in the workplace (Schultz, 1998, p. 16).

The U.S. courts have traditionally segregated sexual misconduct from gender-based misconduct that is viewed as nonsexual, according to Schultz (1998). These decisions recognize sexual misconduct as a hostile work environment and nonsexual gender-based misconduct as disparate treatment. Taken together, the courts' opinions demonstrate the adaptation of the sexual desire-dominance paradigm and ignore gender-based problems in the workplace. Such an approach distorts the hostile work environment by failing to perceive the culture of the workplace, thereby trivializing both the disparate treatment and hostile work environment claims. By failing to view both sexual and gender-based abuse together, the court may conclude that the behavior was not severe or pervasive enough to constitute sexual harassment. According to Schultz:

> It is not enough to focus on the harm to women as sexual beings; the law must also address women's systematic disadvantages—and facilitate women's equal empowerment—as creative, committed workers. We need an account of hostile work environment harassment that highlights its dynamic relationship to larger forms of gender hierarchy at work. (1998, p. 6)

Put simply, U.S. courts have failed to understand that the gender stratification of work, and the marginalization that results from this stratification, works to women's disadvantage as much as sexual misconduct.

Not all courts have emphasized sexual behavior as the only valid misconduct that defines sexual harassment (Schultz, 1998). In 1985, the Court of Appeals for the District of Columbia Circuit decided in *McKinney v. Dole* (765 F. 2d 1129) that physical violence that is not sexual may qualify as sex-based harassment if it demonstrates unequal treatment that would not have taken place if not for the employee's gender. This opinion was the first to introduce the concept of gender-based sexual harassment, meaning that if a hostile environment exists for one gender, even if the hostility is not sexual in nature, it may constitute sexual harassment. Following the *McKinney* ruling, other courts responded similarly (e.g., *Berkman v. City of New York* [705 F.2d 584; 2d Cir.1983]). However, *McKinney* carried little weight in influencing the law. Many courts of appeals ignored the case and continue to use the sexual desire-dominance paradigm as the basis for their decisions, thereby pushing gender into the background.

A 2005 gender harassment hostile environment decision supported the *McKinney* ruling. In *EEOC v. National Education Association* (422 F. 3d 840), a male supervisor in an Alaska National Education Association office used foul language, yelled at female employees, invaded their space, regularly startled them, and publicly reprimanded them. The EEOC filed claims against the National Education Association for maintaining a sex-based hostile work environment. A lower court granted the National Education Association a summary judgment without a trial, finding that the case did not fall within the purview of Title VII because it was not sexual in nature. The 9th Circuit Court of Appeals disagreed, however, ruling that there is no legal requirement that hostile acts have to be overtly sexual or gender specific. The court explained that the ultimate question was whether one sex was subjected to a disadvantage in employment when the opposite sex was not. As a result, the case was remanded back to the lower court for further proceedings. A review of case law has not resulted in any further findings at the time of this writing.

In February 2005, the 10th Circuit Court of Appeals, ruling in *Chavez v. New Mexico* (397 F. 3d 826), reversed a lower court's grant of summary judgment in favor of the defendants in a case alleging hostile environment gender harassment conduct. The conduct consisted primarily of derogatory comments both about women in general and directed specifically toward the plaintiffs. No further information about the case was available at the time of this chapter's writing.

Comparing and Contrasting Workplace Abuse and Gender Harassment

This review of the literature of workplace abuse and sexual/gender harassment has demonstrated that the two constructs are analogous in the following elements: (1) their proposed causes—for example, the abuse of power, the recognition of organizations as gendered, gender stereotypes, and a hierarchical and a male dominated infrastructure; (2) the adverse physical and psychological effects on both targets and bystanders; (3) the negative response by targets and bystanders to their job and their organization; (4) the detrimental consequences to the organization; (5) the role that management/organization assumes in establishing a norm in which the misconduct is accepted; (6) the recognition that the perpetrator is usually a male and the victim is usually a female; (7) the fact that women experience the behaviors as more severe than do men; (8) recognition of the "eye of the beholder" as a factor in determining harassment; (9) the tendency of male perpetrators to exhibit hostile masculinity; and (10) the behaviors themselves, though gender harassment *may* also include sexist and misogynist language.

The primary differences between workplace abuse and gender harassment rest in the legal parameters. Workplace abuse is not illegal in the United States, whereas gender/sexual harassment is considered a violation of civil rights law. Within this realm is another discrepancy between the two constructs: gender harassment must be based on the target's gender, whereas workplace abuse does not require that gender is the basis for the behavior.

A RESEARCH CASE STUDY

Strauss's (2007) study was the first to examine whether bullying behavior constituted gender-based sexual harassment. She studied the construct by investigating whether the abuse physicians direct to female and male registered nurses (RN) in the operating room (OR) met the legal parameters of sexual harassment. Legal parameters were built into the study to make the findings relevant to Title VII law, including examining welcomeness, determining whether the behavior was severe or pervasive enough to interfere with the nurses' work and work environment, and identifying whether it was gender based. The study also examined the role that the gender of the nurse played in witnessing abusive behavior. Exploring both the personal experiences and the witnessing of the abuse together helped to examine the pervasiveness of the misconduct.

Reasonableness was a construct that could not be measured with this study; indeed, it is a difficult construct to define and research. The reasonable person/woman/victim (Drobac, 2005) standard is used to determine whether the behavior is severe or pervasive enough to rise to the threshold of sexual harassment. Even though reasonableness is considered an objective aspect of the law, it contains subjectivity—what is reasonable? Justice Sandra Day O'Connor, writing in the U.S. Supreme Court's decision in *Harris v. Forklift Systems* (1993, p. 371), asserted that an "objectively hostile or abusive work environment" is created when "a reasonable person would find it hostile or abusive, and the victim subjectively perceives it as such." Considering the Justice O'Connor's definition, many of the 20 behaviors measured individually, and certainly in totality, would be considered hostile or abusive to any reasonable person. The 20 behaviors included jokes at individual's expense, sexist comments about either gender, demeaning comments, being excluded or ignored, being slapped or grabbed, silent treatment, lack of praise, being rude or disrespectful, hostile gestures or body language, contributions being ignored, being prevented from expressing oneself, condescension, being shoved or pushed, criticism and putdowns, being targeted for blame or scapegoated, sexual remarks or innuendo, and physical harm.

Studying gender harassment within the perioperative health care arena provided a rich organizational context in which to examine this behavior because health care has a lengthy patriarchal history and is predominantly male dominated by the physicians and health care administrators who work in tandem with primarily female nurses. Furthermore, the OR can be a stressful work environment, requiring keen team cohesion and close physician–nurse interaction (Brodin, 1999; Cook et al., 2001).

In addition, previous research has demonstrated that physicians are abusive to RNs (Cox, 1987, 1994; Diaz & McMillin, 1991; Rosenstein, 2002), particularly in the OR. In that setting, nurses often experience physicians yelling, swearing, and throwing instruments (Brodin, 1999; Cook et al., 2001; Rosenstein, 2002). Cox (1987) has stated, "Based on frequency percentage results, verbal abuse is so prevalent in nursing it is surprising that any of us stay in nursing" (p. 49), and many nurses accept this kind of abuse as part of the job of being a nurse (Diaz & McMillin, 1991). Such abusive behavior has been identified as one of the causes of the current nursing shortage in the United States (Rosenstein, 2002).

Surprisingly, male nurses *experienced* 3 of 20 abusive behaviors and *witnessed* 1 of the same 20 behaviors significantly more than their female colleagues (Strauss, 2007). However, 11 of the 20 behaviors experienced and 14 of the same 20 behaviors witnessed were perceived as more severe by the female RNs than the male RNs. The women also indicated that the behavior interfered with their work environment in 11 of the 14 behaviors; specifically, they noted that physician misconduct is a serious strain on daily work, reduces efficiency, is a serious problem, and decreases morale. In addition, female nurses indicated that an environment characterized by these behaviors leads to reduced job satisfaction, increases errors, and contributes to staff turnover, absenteeism, and a nursing shortage. Finally, the women indicated that the misconduct of physicians interferes with work relationships and diminishes teamwork, which in turn diminish the quality of patient care.

For all 20 abusive behaviors, female nurses identified the male physician as the perpetrator. Male nurses identified male physicians as the perpetrator for 15 of the 20 behaviors where they indicated that both genders equally were abusive.

Male nurses indicated they were treated better because of their gender and had job advantages that their female colleagues did not enjoy. In their responses to the open-ended questions posed on the survey, both female and male nurses discussed differences in the way each gender is treated by male physicians, with male nurses generally receiving friendlier treatment than their female colleagues, and not being treated with the same disdain that their female colleagues experience. Both male and female nurses reported that male nurses are treated with more respect and often have a male-to-male *buddy* relationship. Nurses also stated that physicians expected the male nurses to perform better than their female colleagues. They described both subtle and obvious sexisms, and both male and female nurses were aware of male nurses' preferential treatment. The nurses indicated that the gender harassment was the norm, that hospital management was absent or ineffective in intervening in cases involving misconduct, and that some nurses were told they would have to put up with the abuse because the surgeon brought in revenue.

Strauss (2007) concluded that the results of this study indicate that some female nurses may be experiencing gender harassment in their ORs. The criteria for this conclusion were based on the following legal parameters: nurses' acknowledgment of experiencing and witnessing only unwelcome behaviors; the assumption that any reasonable woman would experience the abuse as severe or pervasive (the men did not acknowledge severity); and gender differences in how the harassment interfered with the women's work as well as the preferential treatment of the men. Management's lack of prevention and intervention strategies added to the potential for Title VII liability of the sponsoring organization.

SUMMARY

To facilitate an understanding of gender harassment, and to address the apparent relationship between gender harassment and workplace abuse, there is a need to concentrate on theory building and testing and legal examination. Theoretical explanations of gender harassment and the relationship of gender harassment with workplace abuse will provide a framework for enhanced organizational interventions to prevent gender harassment from occurring. Also, a comprehensive understanding of the conditions that predispose the development of the behavior will help organizations equip themselves with knowledge that can lay a foundation in changing the organization's culture.

REFERENCES

Acker, J. (1990). Hierarchies, jobs, bodies: A theory of gendered organizations. *Gender & Society, 4*(2), 139–158.

Adams, A. (1997). Bullying at work. *Journal of Community & Applied Social Psychology, 7*(3), 177–180. Retrieved January 5, 2006, from EBSCO database.

Anderson, L. M., & Pearson, C. M. (1999). Tit for tat? The spiraling effect of incivility in the workplace. *Academy of Management Review, 24*(3), 452–471. Retrieved January 5, 2006, from ProQuest database.

Aquino, K., & Byron, K. (2002). Dominating interpersonal behavior and perceived victimization in groups: Evidence for curvilinear relationship. *Journal of Management, 28*(1), 69–87.

Ashforth, B. (1994). Petty tyranny in organizations. *Human Relations, 47*(7), 755–778.

Ayoko, O. B., Callan, V. J., & Hartel, C. E. J. (2003). Workplace conflict, bullying, and counterproductive behaviors. *International Journal of Organizational Analysis, 11*(4), 283–301. Retrieved January 5, 2006, from ProQuest database.

Bargh, J. A., & Raymond, P (1995). The naive misuse of power: Nonconscious sources of sexual harassment. *Journal of Social Issues, 51*(1), 85–96.

Baron, R. A., & Neuman, J. H. (1996). Workplace violence and workplace aggression: Evidence on their relative frequency and potential causes. *Aggressive Behavior, 22*(3), 161–173. Retrieved January 5, 2006, from EBSCO database.

Baron, R. A., Neuman, J. H., & Geddes, D. (1999). Social and personal determinants of workplace aggression: Evidence for the impact of perceived injustice and the Type A behavior pattern. *Aggressive Behavior, 25*(4), 281–296. Retrieved January 5, 2006, from EBSCO database.

Bassman, E. S. (1992). *Abuse in the workplace.* Westport, CT: Quorum Books.

Baumeister, R. F., Smart, L., & Boden, J. M. (1996). Relation of threatened egotism to violence and aggression: The dark side of high self-esteem. *Psychological Review, 103*(1), 5–33. Retrieved January 5, 2006, from PsychARTICLES database.

Berdahl, L., Magley, V., & Waldo, C. (1996). The sexual harassment of men? Exploring the concept with theory and data. *Psychology of Women Quarterly, 20*(4), 527–547.

Bjorkqvist, K., Osterman, K., & Hjelt-Back, M. (1994). Aggression among university employees. *Aggressive Behavior, 20*(3), 173–184. Retrieved January 15, 2006, from EBSCO database.

Bjorkqvist, K., Osterman, K., & Lagerspetz. K. M. J. (1994). Sex differences in covert aggression among adults. *Aggressive Behavior, 20*, 27–33. Retrieved January 29, 2006, from EBSCO database.

Braun, K., Christle, D., Walker, D., & Tiwanak, G. (1991). Verbal abuse of nurses and non-nurses. *Nursing Management, 22*(3), 72–76.

Brodin, B. (1999). *Disruptive verbal behavior in the operating room.* Unpublished master's thesis, St. Mary's University, Minneapolis, MN.

Brodsky, C. M. (1976). *The harassed worker.* Lexington, MA: Lexington Books.

Bullough, V. L. (1990). Nightingale, nursing and harassment. *Image: Journal of Nursing Scholarship, 22*(1), 4–7.

Burt, M. R. (1980). Cultural myths and supports for rape. *Journal of Personality and Social Psychology, 38*(2), 217–230.

Buss, A. H. (1961). *The psychology of aggression.* New York: John Wiley & Sons.

Byrne, M. M. (1997). Verbal abuse of staff nurses by physicians. *AORN Online, 66*(4), 738–739. Retrieved December 2, 2003, from Ovid database.

Cleveland, J. N., & Kerst, M. E. (1993). Sexual harassment and perceptions of power: An underarticulated relationship. *Journal of Vocational Behavior, 42*(1), 49–67.

Code of Federal Regulations. (2002). *Guidelines on discrimination because of sex* (Title 29, Volume 4.; 29CFR1604.11). Washington, DC: U.S. Government Printing Office.

Cook, J. K., Green, M., & Topp, R. (2001). Exploring the impact of physician verbal abuse on perioperative nurses. *AORN Online, 74*(3), 317–318, 320, 322–327, 329–331. Retrieved December 2, 2003, from Ovid database.

Cortina L. M., Magley, V. J., Williams, J. H., & Langhout, R. D. (2001). Incivility in the workplace: Incidence and impact. *Journal of Occupational Health Psychology, 6*(1), 64–80. Retrieved January 5, 2006, from PsychARTICLES database.

Cowie, H., Naylor, P., Rivers, I., Smith, P. K., & Pereira, B. (2002). Measuring workplace bullying. *Aggression and Violent Behavior, 7*(1), 33–51. Retrieved January 5, 2006, from ScienceDirect database.

Cox, H. C. (1987). Verbal abuse in nursing: Report of a study. *Nursing Management, 18*(11), 47–50.

Cox, H. C. (1994, January/February). Excising verbal abuse. *Today's OR Nurse,* 38–40.

Crawford, N. (1997). Bullying at work: A psychoanalytic perspective. *Journal of Community & Applied Social Psychology, 7*(3), 219–225. Retrieved January 5, 2006, from EBSCO database.

Crull, P. (1982). Stress effects of sexual harassment on the job: Implications for counseling. *American Journal of Orthopsychiatry, 52*(3), 539–544.

Culbertson, A. L., Rosenfeld, P., Booth-Kewley, S., & Magnusson, P. (1992). Assessment of sexual harassment in the Navy: Results of the 1989 Navy-wide survey, TR-92-11. San Diego, CA: Naval Personnel Research and Development Center.

Cusack, S. (2000). Workplace bullying: Icebergs in sight, soundings needed. *Lancet, 356*(9248). Retrieved January 15, 2006, from ProQuest database.

Dansky, B., & Kilpatrick, D. (1997). Effects of sexual harassment. In W. O'Donohue (Ed.), *Sexual harassment: Theory, research and treatment* (pp. 152–174). Boston: Allyn & Bacon.

Davenport, N., Schwartz, R. D., & Elliot, G. P. (2002). *Mobbing: Emotional abuse in the American workplace.* Ames, IA: Civil Society.

DeSouza, E. R., & Solberg, J. (2003). Incidence and dimensions of sexual harassment across cultures. In M. Paludi & C. A. Paludi (Eds.), *Academic and workplace sexual harassment* (pp. 3–45). Westport, CT: Praeger.

Diaz, A. L., & McMillin, D. J. (1991). A definition and description of nurse abuse. *Western Journal of Nursing Research, 13*(1), 97–109.

Donovan, M. S., & Drasgow, F. (1999). Do men's and women's experiences of sexual harassment differ: An examination of the differential test functioning of the Sexual Experiences questionnaire. *Military Psychology, 11*(3), 265–282.

Drobac, J. A. (2005). *Sexual harassment law: History, cases, and theory.* Durham, NC: Carolina Academic Press.

Dunn, H. (2003). Horizontal violence among nurses in the operating room. *Association of Operating Room Nursing, 78*(6), 977–988.

Einarsen, S. (1999). The nature and causes of bullying at work. *International Journal of Manpower, 20*(1/2), 16–27. Retrieved January 5, 2006, from EBSCO database.

Einarsen, S. (2000). Harassment and bulling at work: A review of the Scandinavian approach. *Aggression and Violent Behavior, 5*(4), 379–401. Retrieved January 5, 2006, from ScienceDirect database.

Einarsen, S., & Raknes, B. I. (1997). Harassment in the workplace and the victimization of men. *Violence and Victims, 12*(3), 247–263.

Einarsen, S., Raknes, B. I., & Matthiesen, S. B. (1994). Bullying and harassment at work and their relationships to work environment quality: An exploratory study. *European Work and Organizational Psychologist, 4*(4), 381–401. Retrieved January 5, 2006 from EBSCO database.

Einarsen, S., & Skogstad, A. (1996). Bullying at work: Epidemiological findings in public and private organizations. *European Journal of Work and Organizational Psychology, 5*(2), 185–201. Retrieved January 5, 2006 from EBSCO database.

Epstein, D. (1997). Keeping them in their place: Hetero/sexist harassment, gender and the enforcement of heterosexuality. In A. Thomas & C. Kitzinger (Eds.), *Sexual harassment* (pp. 154–171). Buckingham, UK: Open University Press.

Equal Employment Opportunity Commission (EEOC). (1990). *Policy guidance on current issues of sexual harassment.* Retrieved April 5, 2005, from www.eeoc.gov/policy/docs/currentissues.html.

Evans, J. (1997). Men in nursing: Issues of gender segregation and hidden advantage. *Journal of Advanced Nursing, 26*(2), 226–231.

Fain, T. D., & Anderton, K. L. (1987). Sexual harassment: Organizational context and diffuse status. *Sex Roles, 17*(5/6), 291–311.

Farley, L. (1978). *Sexual shakedown: The sexual harassment of women on the job.* New York: Warner Books.

Fitzgerald, L. F. (1993). Sexual harassment: Violence against women in the workplace. *American Psychologist, 48*(10), 1070–1075.

Fitzgerald, L. F., Drasgow, F., Hulin, C. L., Gelfand, M. J., & Magley, V. J. (1997). Antecedents and consequences of sexual harassment in organizations: A test of an integrated model. *Journal of Applied Psychology, 82*(5), 578–589. Retrieved April 14, 2004, from ProQuest database.

Fitzgerald, L. F., Gelfand, M. J., & Drasgow, F. (1995). Measuring sexual harassment: Theoretical and psychometric advances. *Basic and Applied Social Psychology, 7*(4), 425–445. Retrieved April 14, 2004, from ProQuest database.

Fitzgerald, L. F., & Hesson-McInnis, M. (1989). The dimensions of sexual harassment: A structural analysis. *Journal of Vocational Behavior, 35*(3), 309–326.

Fitzgerald, L. F., & Ormerod, A. J. (1993). Breaking the silence: The sexual harassment of women in academia and the workplace. In F. L. Denmark & M.A. Paludi (Eds.), *Psychology of women: A handbook of issues and theories* (pp. 553–581). Westport, CT: Greenwood Press.

Fitzgerald, L. F., Shullman, S. L., Bailey, N., Richards, M., Swecker, J., Gold, Y., et al. (1988). The dimensions and extent of sexual harassment in higher education and the workplace. *Journal of Vocational Behavior, 32*(2), 152–175.

Fitzgerald, L. F., Swan, S., & Fischer, K. (1995). Why didn't she just report him? The psychological and legal implications of women's responses to sexual harassment. *Journal of Social Issues, 51*(1), 117–138. Retrieved January 3, 2004, from ProQuest database.

Fitzgerald, L. F., Swan, S., & Magley, V. J. (1997). But was it really sexual harassment? Legal, behavioral, and psychological definitions of the workplace victimization of women. In W. O'Donohue (Ed.), *Sexual harassment: Theory, research, and treatment* (pp. 5–28). Boston: Allyn & Bacon.

Folger, R., & Baron, R. A. (1996). Violence and hostility at work: A model of reactions to perceived injustice. In G. R. Vandenbos & E. Q. Bulatao (Eds.), *Violence on the job* (pp. 51–85). Washington, DC: American Psychological Association.

Franke, K. M. (1997). What's wrong with sexual harassment? *Stanford Law Review, 49,* 691–772.

Glomb, T. M., Richman, W. L., Hulin, C. L., Drasgow, F., Schneider, K. T., & Fitzgerald, L. F. (1997). Ambient sexual harassment: An integrated model of antecedents and consequences. *Organizational Behavior and Human Decision Processes, 71*(3), 309–328. Retrieved March 17, 2004, from EBSCO database.

Grieco, A. (1987). Scope and nature of sexual harassment in nursing. *Journal of Sex Research, 23,* 261–266.

Griffin, R. W., O'Leary-Kelly, A., & Collins, J. M. (Eds.). (1998). *Dysfunctional behavior in organizations: Violent and deviant behavior.* Stamford, CT: JAI Press, pp. 119–141.

Gruber, J. (1992). A typology of personal and environmental sexual harassment: Research and policy implications for the 1990s. *Sex Roles, 26*(11/12), 447–464. Retrieved April, 24, 2004, from ProQuest database.

Gruber, J. (1997). An epidemiology of sexual harassment: Evidence from North America and Europe. In W. O'Donahue (Ed.), *Sexual harassment: Theory, research, and treatment* (pp. 84–98). Boston: Allyn & Bacon.

Gruber, J. (1998). The impact of male work environments and organizational policies on women's experiences of sexual harassment. *Gender & Society, 12*(3), 301–320.

Gruber, J., & Bjorn, L. (1986). Women's responses to sexual harassment: An analysis of sociocultural, organizational, and personal resource models. *Social Science Quarterly, 67*(4), 814–826.

Gruber, J., Smith, M., & Kauppinen-Toropainen, K. (1996). Sexual harassment types and severity: Linking research and policy. In M. S. Stockdale (Ed.), *Sexual harassment in the workplace: Perspectives, frontiers, and response strategies* (pp. 151–173). Thousand Oaks, CA: Sage.

Gutek, B. A. (1985). *Sex and the workplace.* San Francisco: Jossey-Bass.

Gutek, B. A., & Morasch, B. (1982). Sex-ratios, sex-role spillover, and sexual harassment of women at work. *Journal of Social Issues, 38*, 55–74.

Gutek, B. A., & Nakamura, C. (1980). Sexuality in the workplace. *Basic and Applied Social Psychology, 1*(3), 243–258.

Halford, S., & Leonard, P. (2001). *Gender, power, and organizations.* Basingstoke, UK: Palgrave Macmillan.

Hamilton, J. A., Alagna, S. W., King, L. S., & Lloyd, C. (1987). The emotional consequences of gender-based abuse in the workplace: New counseling programs for sex discrimination. *Women and Therapy, 6*, 155–182.

Harris, M. B., & Knight-Bohnhoff, K. (1996). Gender and aggression: Perceptions of aggression. *Sex Roles, 35*(1/2), 1–2. Retrieved November 7, 2003, from PsychINFO database.

Harvey, S., & Keashly, L. (2003). Predicting the risk for aggression in the workplace: Risk factors, self-esteem and time at work. *Social Behavior and Personality, 31*(8), 807–814. Retrieved January 5, 2006, from ProQuest database.

Hoel, H., Rayner, C., & Cooper, C. L. (1999). Workplace bullying. *International Review of Industrial and Organizational Psychology, 14*, 195–230.

Hofstede, G. (1980). *Culture's consequences: International differences in work related values.* Newbury Park, CA: Sage.

Infante, D. A., Riddle, B. L., Hovath, C. L., & Tumlin, S. A. (1992). Verbal aggressiveness: Messages and reasons. *Communication Quarterly, 40*(2), 116–126.

Jensen, I., & Gutek, B. (1985). Attributions and assignment of responsibility for sexual harassment. *Journal of Social Issues, 38*, 121–136.

Johnson, A. G. (1997). *The gender knot: Unraveling our patriarchal legacy.* Philadelphia: Temple University Press.

Kanter, R. M. (1977a). *Men and women of the corporation.* New York: Basic Books.

Kanter, R. M. (1977b). Some effects of proportions on group life: Skewed sex ratios and responses to token women. *American Journal of Sociology, 82*(5), 965–990.

Keashley, L. (1998). Emotional abuse in the workplace: Conceptual and empirical issues. *Journal of Emotional Abuse, 1*(1), 85–117.

Kivimaki, M., Elovainio, M., & Vahtera, J. (2000). Workplace bullying and sickness absence in hospital staff. *Occupational Environmental Medicine, 57*(10), 656–660.

Koss, M. P. (1990). Changed lives: The psychological impact of sexual harassment. In M. A. Paludi (Ed.), *Ivory power: Sexual harassment on campus* (pp. 365–393). Albany, NY: State University of New York Press.

Lee, D. (2000). An analysis of workplace bullying in the UK. *Personnel Review, 29*(5), 593–613. Retrieved January 14, 2006, from EBSCO database.

Lee, D. (2001). "He didn't sexually harass me, as in harassed for sex . . . he was just horrible": Women's definitions of unwanted male sexual conduct at work. *Women's Studies International Forum, 24*(1), 25–38. Retrieved June 26, 2005, from ProQuest database.

Lee, D. (2002). Gendered workplace bullying in the restructured UK civil service. *Personnel Review, 31*(1/2), 205–228. Retrieved June 26, 2005, from ProQuest.

Lengnick-Hall, M. L. (1995). Sexual harassment research: A methodological critique. *Personnel Psychology, 48*(4), 841–864.

Lenhart, S. (1996). Physical and mental health aspects of sexual harassment. In D. K. Shrier (Ed.), *Sexual harassment in the workplace and academia: Psychiatric issues* (pp. 21–38). Washington, DC: American Psychiatric Press.

Leymann, H. (1990). Mobbing and psychological terror at workplaces. *Violence and Victims, 5*(2), 119–126.

Liefooghe, A. P. D., & Olafsson, R. (1999). "Scientists" and "amateurs": Mapping the bullying domain. *International Journal of Manpower, 20*(1/2), 39–49. Retrieved January 5, 2006, from EBSCO database.

Livingston, J. A. (1982). Responses to sexual harassment on the job: Legal, organizational, and individual action. *Journal of Social Issues, 38*, 5–22.

Lundberg-Love, P., & Marmion, S. (2003). Sexual harassment in the private sector. In M. A. Paludi & C. A. Paludi, Jr. (Eds.), *Academic and workplace sexual harassment* (pp. 77–100). Westport, CT: Praeger.

MacKinnon, C. (1979). *The sexual harassment of working women.* New Haven, CT: Yale University Press.

Malamuth, N.M. (1981). Rape proclivity among males. *Journal of Social Issues, 37*, 138-157.

Malamuth, N. M., & Thornhill, N. W. (1994). Hostile masculinity, sexual aggression, and gender-biased domineeringness in conversations. *Aggressive Behavior, 20*(3), 185–193. Retrieved January 5, 2006, from EBSCO database.

Mansfield, P. K., Koch, P. B., Henderson, J., Vicary, J. R., Cohn, M., & Young, E. W. (1991). The job climate for women in traditionally male blue-collar occupations. *Sex Roles, 25*(1/2), 63–79.

McGuinness, S. (1992). Nurse abuse: Inhumanity tolerated. *AARN Newsletter, 48*(4), 17–19.

Miller, L. L. (1997). Not just weapons of the weak: Gender harassment as a form of protest for Army men. *Social Psychology Quarterly, 60*(1), 32–51. Retrieved March 8, 2006, from ProQuest database.

Mizrahi, R. (2004). "Hostility to the presence of women": Why women undermine each other in the workplace and the consequences for Title VII. *Yale Law Journal, 113*, 1579–1621.

Monson, M. (1997). Defining the situation. In C. Ronai, B. Zsembik, & J. Feagin (Eds.), *Everyday sexism in the third millennium* (pp. 137–151). London: Routledge.

Niebuhr, R. E., & Boyles, W. R. (1991). Sexual harassment of military personnel: An examination of power differentials. *International Journal of Intercultural Relations, 15*(4), 445–457.

Niedl, K. (1996). Mobbing and well-being: Economic and personnel development implications. *European Journal of Work and Organizational Psychology, 5*(2), 239–249. Retrieved January 29, 2006, from EBSCO database.

Northwestern National Life Insurance Company. (1993). *Fear and violence in the workplace*. Minneapolis, MN: Author.

O'Connell, C. E., & Korabik, K. (2000). Sexual harassment: The relationship of personal vulnerability, work context, perpetrator status, and type of harassment to outcomes. *Journal of Vocational Behavior, 56*(3), 299–329. Retrieved March 4, 2006, from ScienceDirect database.

O'Hare, E. A., & O'Donohue, W. (1998). Sexual harassment: Identifying risk factors. *Archives of Sexual Behavior, 27*(6), 561–580. Retrieved March 17, 2004, from ProQuest database.

O'Leary-Kelly, M., Paetzold, L. R., & Griffin, R. W. (2000). Sexual harassment as aggressive behavior: An actor-based perspective. *Academy of Management Review, 25*(2), 372–388. Retrieved April 3, 2003, from ProQuest database.

Olweus, D. (1978) *Aggression in the schools: Bullies and whipping boys*. London: John Wiley & Sons.

Paludi, M. A. (Ed.). (1990). *Ivory power: Sexual harassment on campus*. Albany, NY: SUNY Press.

Parker, S. K., & Griffin, M. A. (2002). What is so bad about a little name-calling? Negative consequences of gender harassment for overperformance demands and distress. *Journal of Occupational Health Psychology, 7*(3), 195–210.

Pearson, C. M., Anderson, L. M., & Porath, C. L. (2000). Assessing and attacking workplace incivility. *Organizational Dynamics, 29*(2), 123–137. Retrieved January 5, 2006, from EBSCO database.

Piotrkowski, C. S. (1998). Gender harassment, job satisfaction, and distress among employed White and minority women. *Journal of Occupational Health Psychology, 3*(1), 33–43. Retrieved April 25, 2004, from ProQuest database.

Pryor, B., & Whalen, N. J. (1997). A typology of sexual harassment: Characteristics of harassers and the social circumstances under which sexual harassment occurs. In W. O'Donohue (Ed.), *Sexual harassment: Theory, research, and treatment* (pp. 129–151). Boston: Allyn & Bacon.

Pryor, J. B. (1987). Sexual harassment proclivities in men. *Sex Roles, 17*(5/6), 269–290.

Quine, L. (1999). Workplace bullying in NHS community trust: Staff questionnaire survey. *British Medical Journal, 318*, 228–232.

Ragins, B. R., & Sundstrom, E. (1989). Gender and power in organizations: A longitudinal perspective. *Psychological Bulletin, 105*(1), 51–88.

Rayner, C. (1997). The incidence of workplace bullying. *Journal of Community and Applied Social Psychology, 7*(3), 199–208. Retrieved January 29, 2006, from EBSCO database.

Rayner, C. (1999). From research to implementation: Finding leverage for prevention. *International Journal of Manpower, 20*(1/2), 28–38. Retrieved January 5, 2006, from EBSCO database.

Rayner, C., & Cooper, C. L. (1997). Workplace bullying: Myth or reality—can we afford to ignore it? *Leadership and Organization Development Journal, 18*, 211–214.

Robinson, S. L., & O'Leary-Kelly, A. M. (1998). Monkey see, monkey do: The influence of work groups on the antisocial behavior of employees. *Academy of Management Journal, 41*(6), 658–672. Retrieved January 5, 2006, from PsychINFO database.

Rosenstein, A. H. (2002). Nurse–physician relationships: Impact on nurse satisfaction and retention. *American Journal of Nursing, 102*(6), 26–34. Retrieved December 2, 2003, from Ovid database.

Rospenda, K. M., Richman, J. A., & Nawyn, S. J. (1998). Doing power: The confluence of gender, race, and class in contrapower sexual harassment. *Gender & Society, 12*(1), 40–61.

Rubenstein, M. (1992). Combating sexual harassment at work. *Conditions of Work Digest, 11*, 285–290.

Russell, B. L., & Trigg, K. Y. (2004). Tolerance of sexual harassment: An examination of gender differences, ambivalent sexism, social dominance, and gender roles. *Sex Roles, 50*(7/8), 565–573. Retrieved January 4, 2004, from ProQuest database.

Schat, A. C. H., & Kelloway, E. K. (2003). Reducing the adverse consequences of workplace aggression and violence: The buffering effects of organizational support. *Journal of Occupational Health Psychology, 8*(2), 110–122. Retrieved March 17, 2004, from ProQuest database.

Schneider, K. T. (1996). *Bystander stress: The effect of organizational tolerance of sexual harassment on victims' co-workers.* Unpublished doctoral dissertation, University of Illinois at Urbana–Champaign.

Schneider, K. T., Swan, S., & Fitzgerald, L. F. (1997). Job-related and psychological effects of sexual harassment in the workplace: Empirical evidence from two organizations. *Journal of Applied Psychology, 82*(3), 401–415. Retrieved March 6, 2006, from ProQuest database.

Schultz, V. (1998). Reconceptualizing sexual harassment. *Yale Law Journal, 107*(6), 1683–1805.

Simpson, R., & Cohen, C. (2004). Dangerous work: The gendered nature of bullying in the context of higher education. *Gender, Work and Organization, 11*(2), 163–186.

Smith, P. K. (1997). Bulling in life-span perspective: What can studies of school bullying and workplace bullying learn from each other? *Journal of Community & Applied Social Psychology, 7*(3), 249–255. Retrieved January 5, 2006, from EBSCO database.

Spratlen, L. P. (1994). Workplace mistreatment: Its relationship to interpersonal violence. *Journal of Psychosocial Nursing, 32*(12), 5–6.

Spurgeon, A. (1997). Commentary I. *Journal of Community & Applied Social Psychology, 7*(3), 241–244. Retrieved January 15, 2006, from EBSCO database.

Stanko, E. (1988). Fear of crime and the myth of the safe home: A feminist critique of criminology. In J. Hanmer & M. Maynard (Eds.), *Women, violence and social control* (pp. 122-134). London: Macmillan.

Stockdale, M. S. (2005). The sexual harassment of men: Articulating the approach rejection theory of sexual harassment. In J. Gruber & P. Morgan (Eds.), *In the company of men: Male dominance and sexual harassment* (pp. 117–142). Boston: Northeastern University Press.

Stockdale, M., & Motoike, J. (2000, June). *The men's sexually harassing experiences scale: Development and validation study.* Paper presented at the Society for the Psychological Study of Social Issues, Minneapolis, MN.

Stockdale, M. S., Wood, M., & Batra, L. (1999). The sexual harassment of men: Evidence for a broader theory of sexual harassment and sex discrimination. *Psychology, Public Policy and Law, 5*(3), 630–664.

Strauss, S. (2007). *Quantitative and qualitative analysis of physician abuse as gender harassment to female and male registered nurses in the operating room.* Doctoral dissertation, St. Mary's University. Retrieved from ProQuest Digital Dissertations (DAI 3290679).

Strauss, S. (2008). Aggressive men and witchy women: The double standard. In M. A. Paludi (Ed.), *Women at work: Challenges and solutions for our female workforce* (Vol. 3, pp. 1–20), Westport, CT: Praeger.

Tangri, S. S., Burt, M. R., & Johnson, L. B. (1982). Sexual harassment at work: Three explanatory models. *Journal of Social Issues, 38*(4), 33–54.

Tangri, S. S., & Hayes, S. M. (1997). Theories of sexual harassment. In W. O'Donohue (Ed.), *Sexual harassment: Theory, research, and treatment* (pp. 112–128). Boston: Allyn & Bacon.

Terpstra, D. E., & Baker, D. D. (1986). A framework for the study of sexual harassment. *Basic and Applied Social Psychology, 7*(1), 17–34. Retrieved January 8, 2004, from EBSCO database.

Thacker, R. A., & Gohmann, S. F. (1996). Emotional and psychological consequences of sexual harassment: a descriptive study. *Journal of Psychology, 130*(4), 429–446. Retrieved March 5, 2006, from EBSCO database.

Till, F. (1980). *Sexual harassment: A report on the sexual harassment of students.* Washington, DC: National Advisory Council on Women's Educational Programs.

U.S. Merit Systems Protection Board (USMSPB). (1981). *Sexual harassment in the federal workplace: Is it a problem?* Washington, DC: U.S. Government Printing Office.

U.S. Merit Systems Protection Board (USMSPB). (1988). *Sexual harassment in the federal workplace: An update.* Washington, DC: U.S. Government Printing Office.

U. S. Merit Systems Protection Board (USMSPB). (1995). *Sexual harassment in the federal workplace: Trends, progress, and continuing challenges.* Washington, DC: U.S. Government Printing Office.

Vartia, M. (1996). The sources of bullying: Psychological work environment and organizational climate. *European Journal of Work and Organizational Psychology, 5*(2), 203–214.

Vaux, A. (1993). Paradigmatic assumptions in sexual harassment research: Being guided without being misled. *Journal of Vocational Education, 42*(1), 116–135.

Webb, S. (1994). *Shock waves: The global impact of sexual harassment.* New York: MasterMedia.

Welsh, S. (1999). Gender and sexual harassment. *Annual Review of Sociology, 25*(1), 169–190. Retrieved April 27, 2004, from ProQuest database.

Wiener, R. L., & Hurt, L. E. (1999). An interdisciplinary approach to understanding social sexual conduct at work. *Psychology, Public Policy, and Law, 5*(3), 556–595. Retrieved October 19, 2005, from PsychARTICLES database.

Wise, S., & Stanley, L. (1987). *Georgie Porgie: Sexual harassment in everyday life.* London: Pandora Press.

Yoder, J. D., & Aniakudo, P. (1996). When pranks become harassment: The case of African American women firefighters. *Sex Roles, 35*(5/6), 253–270. Retrieved March 8, 2006, from ProQuest database.

Young, A. M., Vance, C. M., & Ensher, E. A. (2003). Individual differences in sensitivity to disempowering acts: A comparison of gender and identify-based explanations for perceived offensiveness. *Sex Roles, 49*(3/4), 163–171. Retrieved January 4, 2006, from ProQuest database.

Zapf, D. (1999). Organisational, work group related and personal causes of mobbing/bullying at work. *International Journal of Manpower, 20*(1/2), 70–85. Retrieved January 5, 2006, from EBSCO database.

Chapter 14

Harder and Harder: The Content of Popular Pornographic Movies

Chyng Sun, Robert Wosnitzer, Ana J. Bridges,
Erica Scharrer, and Rachael Liberman

AGGRESSION AND SEXUAL ACTS IN POPULAR PORNOGRAPHIC MOVIES: AN UPDATE

Pornography is notoriously difficult to define. This term's Greek root means "the writing about prostitutes" (Easton, 1998, p. 605), but in current U.S. culture—where a stripper's pole dance is embraced by suburban, middle-aged married women (Kelley, 2007) and is routinely taught by gyms—the original definition of pornography no longer means much. In 1964 (in *Jacobellis v. Ohio*, 378 U.S. 184, 197), U.S. Supreme Court Justice Potter Stewart attempted to define "obscene" by saying, "I shall not today attempt further to define the kinds of material I understand to be embraced . . . [b]ut I know it when I see it." In other words, pornography was undefinable for Stewart. Boyle (2003), however, points out that when pornography encompasses such a wide range of meaning for different people—including *Playboy*'s centerfold, a pornographic novel, and a

The authors want to thank the three coders for their help, as well as Robert Jensen for his support, Gloria Cowan for her advice, and Patricia Malenfant for her excellent assistance.

movie documenting real rape—the term would miss the crucial differences among the diverse genres. Jensen (1998) argues that public debate about social issues has often been carried out without clear-cut definition, and he suspects that the demand for a stringent definition of pornography has been motivated by a desire to dodge the uncomfortable confrontation of the issue (p. 3).

The Attorney General's Commission on Pornography (1986) defined pornography as "material predominantly sexually explicit and intended for purposes of sexual arousal" (pp. 228–229). Barron and Kimmel (2000) defined pornography as "any sexually explicit material to which access was limited, either by signs or physical structure, to adults" (p. 162), but they avoided the sticky "intention" issue, which is always difficult to pin down. Instead, these authors stressed the access issue (18 years and older), which sets this genre apart from others. Investigating whether different types of pornography might yield different effects, the Attorney General's Commission further classified pornographic materials into four categories: nudity; nonviolent and nondegrading materials; nonviolent materials depicting degradation, domination, subordination, and humiliation; and sexually violent materials. Some scholars, who are particularly concerned about the violent depictions in sexually explicit materials but do not object to sexual depiction per se, define pornography in more negative terms, as does Russell (1993): "material that combines sex and/or the exposure of genitals with abuse or degradation in a manner that appears to endorse, condone, or encourage such behavior" (p. 3). Even though academics, researchers, and the Attorney General's Commission on Pornography used descriptions such as "degradation" or "violence," those terms are also challenging to define. (More on the definitions of the key terms later in this chapter.)

Jensen and Dines (1998) examined materials that were sold in porn shops, because those materials were readily defined by the industry as pornographic. Although Jensen and Dines and many other pornography researchers who used this approach (e.g., Cowan & Campbell, 1994; Prince, 1990; Yang & Linz, 1990) cut down on the number of semantic arguments surrounding pornography, they did not resolve the issue of how to objectively and systematically examine the overwhelming quantity of pornographic materials circulated in the market.

Coders

As part of the authors' study, we hired three coders to watch and record porn movies. Although we tried diligently to recruit male coders, none of them worked out, and we ended up with three female coders. Michelle Chang and Christine Larson were both New School graduate students, and Gabrielle Shaw was a New York University undergraduate. All three had previous experience in watching porn, but their exposure to this genre was limited, and they generally had open attitudes about pornography.

Robert Wosnitzer wrote the codebook and coding instructions and was the main trainer for the coders. Each coder worked on five movies for the pilot test, and intercoder reliability was calculated. After three rounds of testing using Scott's pi coefficient of reliability for all variables, it was determined that the overall composite level of agreement across all variables and all pairs of coder comparisons was 0.958 and had reached a satisfactory level. The coders then started coding the remainder of the sample films, using the operational definitions and coding schemes they had learned in the pilot. Each coder also kept a journal about her thoughts and feelings while working on the project.

Sample

While earlier content studies also attempted to examine popular pornography (Cowan & Campbell, 1994; Gossett & Byrne, 2002; Jensen & Dines, 1998; Malamuth & Spinner, 1980; McKee, 2005a, 2005b; Prince, 1990; Yang & Linz, 1990), they mostly relied on sample methods of convenience and lack a systematic approach—shortcomings that limit the generalizability of their findings. For example, Yang and Linz (1990) in Syracuse, Jensen and Dines (1998) in Boston, and Palys (1986) in Vancouver all based their sample selection on the recommendations of video store clerks, a method that may be tainted by individual idiosyncrasy and the socioeconomic bias of the neighborhood.

To avoid subjectivity, Cowan, Lee, Levy, and Snyder (1988) gathered lists of pornographic videos from seven video stores in Southern California and then selected the ones that appeared on at least four lists to determine their popularity, and Barron and Kimmel (2000) randomly selected pornographic videos from five stores in upstate New York. Both studies suffered from a lack of national representation. Prince's (1990) sample relied on a selection of ambiguous definitions of "classic" and "most popular" films that were produced between 1972 and 1985, but did not include a clear sampling method or a rationale of how the selections were made.

McKee (2005) merged two international mail-order catalogs in Australia and selected the 50 best-selling titles to analyze. Although he tried to capture popular pornography on a national level, it was unclear how the lists were compiled and how current the titles were. Furthermore, in Australia it is illegal to sell pornography but legal to purchase it, and it is difficult to determine how this regulatory difference might affect the methodological accuracy of duplicating the approach in the United States.

Overall, we did not find that previous studies, which were mostly done in the 1980s and early 1990s, used methods that could yield a sampling of popular, mainstream pornography in objective and systematic ways. Thus we decided to utilize a resource that was never tapped into by previous content studies. *Adult Video News* (AVN), a monthly magazine often described as "the *Variety* of the porn industry," is an influential and profitable trade journal with a circulation of 40,000 that reviews more than 500 new titles per issue. AVN also sponsors the yearly Adult Entertainment Expo and Oscars-like awards ceremony in Las Vegas (Rich, 2001; Wallace, 2006). When we began our study in the summer of 2005, the magazine was regularly surveying video stores across the United States and publishing a monthly list of the 250 top-selling and most-rented movies in the industry. We selected the top 30 videos from each list from the issues of December 2004 to June 2005 and, after deleting duplications, narrowed the list to 275 titles. From those items, we sampled 50 videos, yielding a total of 304 scenes.

Defining Key Terms

Violence and Aggression

Most content-analysis studies have been concerned with how "violence," "aggression," and "degradation" are depicted in pornographic films, and those terms are often used to set "good" porn apart from "bad" porn, or even to define "porn" and "not porn." As mentioned earlier, Russell (1993) limits pornography to sexual materials that depict "abuse or degradation"; others categorize nonviolent sexual materials as "erotica" (Laan, Everaerd, van Bellen, & Hanewald, 1994). However, defining specific terms is difficult and most often leads to additional terms to be defined or clarified.

Merriam-Webster Online Dictionary (2009) defines *violence* as "exertion of physical force so as to injure or abuse" and *aggression* as "a forceful action or procedure (as an unprovoked attack) especially when intended to dominate or master." Both definitions stress the power hierarchy within which one uses "force" to inflict harm upon another, but the difference between the two terms is fairly unclear. In content-analysis literature, the terms "violence" and "aggression" are used fairly interchangeably. Typically, physical acts are necessary for most content analysts to code something as violent, although verbal aggression is sometimes measured as a separate item in the analysis.

The definitions of violence or aggression used in different content-analysis studies are fairly consistent across the board. For example, Palys (1986) defined aggression as "occurring whenever one or more persons intentionally imposed or attempted to impose hurt, abuse, or force upon one or more other persons" (p. 26). He included self-inflicted aggression in this classification, but did not count aggression against inanimate objects or nonpersons. Duncan (1991) utilized Palys's definition in coding violent

scenes in randomly selected adult videos in a local store and found that
13.6 percent of video scenes depicted violence. Barron and Kimmel (2000)
defined pornography in similar terms, as "any sexually explicit material
to which access was limited, either by signs or physical structure, to
adults" (p. 162). These researchers coded different physical aggression
separately (such as pushing/shoving, pulling hair/biting, open-hand
punch-slap, spank, choke, closed-fist punch, kick, and confine/bondage)
but collapsed all types of verbal aggression into one category. They found
that 26.9 percent of the scenes analyzed contained some kind of violence,
either verbal or physical.

Cowan and Campbell (1994) did not include a clear definition of
aggression but used physical aggression indicators (hair-pulling, rape,
holding down, penis slapping, hitting, and pinching) and verbal aggression indicators (verbal orders, name-calling, coercion, and racial slurs) to
measure the degree of aggression. Prince (1990) also did not include a definition of violence but nonetheless coded coercion for sexual favor, verbal
threats and insults, and physically aggressive behaviors, such as striking
or slapping, and physical restraint (binding or tying someone down) and
found that 21 percent of the scenes depicted violence.

McKee (2005b) adopted Robert Baron's definition of violence as "any
form of behavior directed toward the goal of harm; or injuring another
living being who is motivated to avoid such treatment" (p. 282) and
argued that "consent" is ultimately important in determining whether a
sexual act is violent. Thus, if the actors all consent to the scene, even if
the target of aggression may show pain or discomfort or if the act may fit
most definitions of violence, it is actually not violent, as, for instance, in
sadomasochist, bondage, or domination/discipline acts. McKee did
emphasize that depictions of "rape myth," wherein a woman was forced
to have sex but eventually came to enjoy it, was not considered to be "consensual." Furthermore, the reactions of the targets of aggression often
determine whether certain actions are considered aggressive. For instance, pushing with force would normally be considered aggressive,
but McKee tried to differentiate "rough sex play" from violence, where
the former might mean pushing another person against the wall or onto
a bed, when in fact the person being pushed is laughing. Also, although
verbal aggression was defined as "language that would be insulting outside of the sexual context, e.g., 'you're a whore, what are you?' " (p. 283),
if the target was "pleased" (p. 283), it was not counted as violence. If the
target did not give verbal consent, but also did not respond to aggression
with avoidance or rejection and just passively allowed the violence to take
place or to continue, would it be considered violence?

McKee did not provide a list of behaviors that he would code as aggressive, as most researchers had done previously. It was also not firmly established whether, once the scene was deemed "consensual," then all

activities that others might consider aggressive—such as spanking and slapping—were not counted as aggression in McKee's coding scheme. McKee found only 1.9 percent of the scenes to be aggressive, a result that stands in stark contrast to the results of most previous studies.

Jensen (2004) states that one of the dominant themes in mainstream pornography is that "women enjoy all the sexual acts that men perform or demand" (p. 2). McKee's (2005a) study failed to identify a peculiar phenomenon in pornography that is rarely found either in real-life situations or in other media genres—namely, the targets of aggression (mostly women in heterosexual pornography) are frequently depicted as enjoying the aggression inflicted on them. Dines (2008) described this type of depiction in the following way: "When violence is sexualized, you render violence invisible."

Our team modified the definition of aggression that was introduced by Mustonen and Pulkkinen (1993) and conceptualized it as any action causing physical or psychological harm to oneself or another person, in which psychological harm is understood as assaulting another verbally or nonverbally. We did not code violence against objects or nonhumans, nor did we code violence that occurred accidentally. This definition remains unsatisfactory, because aggression is partly defined by harm, and harm by assault, and assault was left undefined. Nevertheless, this definition at least describes an action that may be considered to be aggressive in normal social situations, regardless of the intention of the perpetrator or the response of the target. We found a universal standard of aggression important precisely because we would like to identify actions that, although unacceptable or unwelcome in normal social settings (such as name-calling—"slut" or "whore"—or spanking and pulling hair), were not merely common in pornography but also depicted as inducing pleasure.

Degradation

Scholars disagree on whether violence and degradation are two separate concepts or are one unified concept. Palys (1986) treats violence and degradation separately, whereas Dines, Jensen, and Russo (1998) consider degradation to be a type of violence, and Cowan, Lee, Levy, and Snyder (1988) categorize violence as a type of degradation.

McKee (2005a) reviewed the ways in which degradation was categorized in different studies. He concluded that the term "degrading" often referred to sexual practices that were unusual or non-normative, with the assumption that participation in these acts is intrinsically degrading to some characters, and to sexual practices that imply differences in status between or among characters. To describe non-normative sexual acts as degrading could be problematic, because it may reflect the researcher's own biases; such value judgments may change over time as the culture becomes more open about sexuality. For instance, oral sex and casual sex were considered to be degrading by, respectively, Zillmann (1989) and Donnerstein, Linz, and Penrod (1987). Since the religious and cultural stigma has been lifted from oral sex, however, performing it is neither "non-normative" nor "degrading." In addition, in metropolitan areas such as New York City, where attitudes about sex are fairly relaxed, casual "hook-ups" between young people are accepted by many and may not be considered as degrading by either party.

Given these considerations, our coding strategy was not to determine if certain actions were degrading or not, but just to record them as they occurred (such as the frequency of ejaculating on a woman's face). We then examined the patterns that were revealed when we compared the data with previous studies.

Definitions of Concepts and Operationalization

We used two units of analysis in this study: each scene and each aggressive act. Almost every DVD we examined had "scene selections" in its menu, separating individual scenes. In the rare case that the DVD did not contain clear scene demarcations, a new scene was recorded if the primary characters changed, or if the setting changed, or if a temporal break occurred. The second unit of analysis was each aggressive act.

We coded the gender (male or female) and race (White, Black, Asian, Latino/a, other, or unknown) of the primary characters—that is, people who were engaged in explicit sexual interactions. We also coded common sexual acts in pornographic videos: male-to-female oral sex, female-to-male oral sex, female-to-female oral sex, male-to-male oral sex, vaginal penetration with penis, vaginal double penetration (simultaneous vaginal intercourse between one female and two males), simultaneous vaginal and anal penetration (one female being penetrated simultaneously, anally and vaginally, by two males), group sex (where numerous characters simultaneously engage in various sexual acts), anal penetration with penis, anal double penetration (one female being anally penetrated by two separate males, simultaneously), and ass-to-mouth sequence (where a penis or a sex toy is first inserted in a woman's anus, removed, and inserted in a woman's mouth).

Money shots—external ejaculations—are omnipresent in mainstream pornography. Where on a woman's body the ejaculation occurs may signify different meanings. For instance, some researchers consider ejaculations on the face as "degrading" (Cowan & Dunn, 1994). Thus the coders specifically recorded the money-shot locations, such as breast, mouth, or face.

Acts of aggression within each scene were recorded using the PAT technique as outlined in the National Television Violence Study (NTVS, 1998). The PAT technique tallies instances of aggression by counting as a unique act each time the perpetrator (P), target (T), or specific physical or verbal aggressive act (A) changes during the course of the scene. An individual instance of aggression is recorded only when one or more of these three components change, subsequent to initiation of the first aggressive act. In other words, in a scene where the perpetrator spanked a target 10 times in a row, the action would be counted as only one spank.

The aggressive acts we recorded were divided into physical and verbal types. Verbally aggressive acts included (1) name calling/insults and (2) threatening physical harm. Physically aggressive acts included (1) pushing/shoving; (2) biting; (3) pinching; (4) pulling hair; (5) spanking; (6) open-hand slapping; (7) choking; (8) threatening with weapon; (9) kicking; (10) closed-fist punching; (11) bondage/confining; (12) using weapons; (13) torturing, mutilating, or attempting murder; and (14) gagging. Gagging was an act of sexual aggression that, to our knowledge, had never been coded in previous content analyses. It is defined as when an object (e.g., a sex toy) or body part (e.g., penis or hand) is inserted into a character's mouth and induces a gag reflex.

We also coded the genders of both the perpetrators and targets of aggressive acts. Their responses to aggression were coded as one of four possibilities:

- *Target expresses pleasure or responds neutrally.* In this instance, the target expressed pleasure either verbally or physically, or did not appear affected in any manner by the aggressive act, and the scene continued.

- *Target expresses displeasure; perpetrator ignores.* The target expressed displeasure but the perpetrator ignored it.

- *Target expresses displeasure; perpetrator acknowledges with positive act.* The target expressed displeasure and the perpetrator either stopped the aggressive action or expressed remorse.

- *Target expresses displeasure; perpetrator acknowledges with negative act.* The target expressed displeasure but the perpetrator increased the aggressive action(s) in severity or frequency or continued with other aggressive acts.

In content analysis, one can find elements only when one sets out to find them. For this reason, we were concerned that if we focused only on aggression, we might overlook positive expressions. Researchers on sex and relationships (Denney, Field, & Quadagno, 1984; Guo, Ng, & Chan, 2004) have identified examples that indicate positive behaviors that we asked the coders to record—kissing, hugging, and/or giving one another compliments—and to describe qualitatively. Additionally, we cared about health issues, so the coders were instructed to take notice when the following occurred: the presence of condoms, discussions of sexually transmitted diseases, pregnancy, or safe sex.

Results

Generally speaking, the popular pornography that is marketed to heterosexual men was found to be inhabited mostly by White people (82.2% of the characters). Blacks had the most representation among racial minorities (8.8% of the characters). Latinos and Latinas were the most underrepresented (2.7% of the characters), given their status as the largest racial minority in the United States (12.5% of the whole population, according to the U.S. Census Bureau, 2000). Asians and Asian Americans accounted for the smallest number of characters among all minority groups (2.5% of the characters). There were slightly more men (53.1%) than women. Given that the setting depicted is a world in which sexual activity has no consequences, pregnancy and sexually transmitted diseases (STDs) were rarely discussed (only 0.3% of scenes discussed those issues), and condoms were seldom used (10.9% of scenes). Some of the positive behaviors within relationships, such as kissing, hugging, laughing, caressing, and verbal compliments, are rarely depicted (in 9.9% of scenes).

Sexual Acts

The sexual acts were generally geared toward pleasing men, an orientation particularly exemplified in scenes of oral sex. While female-to-male oral sex appeared in 90.1 percent ($n = 274$) of the scenes coded, male-to-female oral sex was found in only 53.9 percent ($n = 164$) of the scenes. Vaginal intercourse appeared in most of the scenes (86.2%; $n = 262$), and anal sex was also frequent (55.9%; $n = 356$). Same-sex activities appeared only between women, with female-to-female oral sex taking place in 22.7 percent ($n = 69$) of the scenes. Some extreme sexual acts that may cause pain or injury for the female performers if done without careful preparation were fairly common. For example, double penetrations were recorded in a total of 19.1 percent ($n = 58$) of scenes, most commonly simultaneous vaginal/anal penetrations (18.1% of scenes; $n = 55$); less common were double vaginal (1.6%; $n = 5$) and double anal penetration (2.0%; $n = 6$).

The ass-to-mouth (ATM) sequence, in which a man inserted his penis first in a woman's anus and then put it in a woman's mouth, is a relatively new phenomenon and was never recorded in any of the previous content analyses. This act was seen frequently in our study, occurring in 41.1 percent ($n = 125$) of scenes.

Money Shot

The "money shot," the male ejaculation, is omnipresent in pornographic movies. Almost all of the ejaculation scenes occurred outside of a woman's vagina (96.7%; $n = 295$), most frequently in her mouth (58.6%; $n = 178$). Less common locations included the anus (11.8%; $n = 36$), breasts

(6.9%; n = 21), and face (3.9%; n = 12). Multiple ejaculation sites were portrayed in 12.2 percent of scenes (n = 37).

Aggression

Overall, the popular pornographic movies depicted a world that mixed sexual excitement with aggression: only 10.2 percent (n = 31) of the scenes did not contain an aggressive act. Across all scenes, a total of 3,376 verbal and/or physically aggressive acts were observed. On average, scenes contained 11.52 acts of either verbal or physical aggression (standard deviation [SD] = 15.04) and ranged from zero to 128. Physical aggression (median [M] = 9.31; SD = 12.30) was much more common than verbal aggression (M = 2.13; SD = 4.01), occurring in 88.2 percent (n = 268) of the scenes. Verbal aggression occurred in 48 percent (n = 146) of the scenes; almost all the expressions (97.2% of verbally aggressive acts; n = 614) involved name calling (e.g., "bitch," "slut").

The most frequently observed physically aggressive act was spanking (35.7% of physically aggressive acts; n = 980). Data about spanking revealed drastic gender differences regarding the roles of spankers or spankees. Whereas women were spanked on 953 occasions, men were spanked merely 26 times, less than 3 percent of the total. Gagging, which was also unknown in previous content studies, appeared in 27.7 percent (n = 759) of the scenes. The data revealed other types of aggression, including open-hand slapping (12.1%; n = 408), hair pulling (8.2%; n = 276), and choking (5.5%; n = 184).

Women as Targets

In the popular pornographic movies analyzed in our study, women were overwhelmingly the targets of both physical and verbal aggression (94.4% of all aggressive acts, n = 3,191). Most of the perpetrators were men, who committed 70.3 percent (n = 2,373) of the aggressive acts, whereas female aggressors engaged in 29.4 percent (n = 991) of the offenses. Although the targets of male aggression were almost always of the opposite gender (98.4% of the aggressive acts), female aggressors mostly targeted other women (60.6% of their aggressive acts). Moreover, women were even more likely to be aggressive against themselves (24.4%) than against men (14.5%).

When aggression occurred, most of the targets (95.0%; n = 3,206) responded either with expressions of pleasure (encouragement, sexual moans, and so forth) or neutrally (e.g., no change in facial expression or interruption of action). However, there was a significant difference between female and male targets' responses to aggressive acts [χ^2 (1) = 51.31; p < .001]. Female targets were significantly more likely to express pleasure or neutrality (95.9%; n = 3,049) than male targets (84.0%; n = 147). In contrast, men were four times more likely to show displeasure when they were targets (16.0%; n = 28), compared to female targets (4.1%; n = 132).

Comparison with Previous Studies

Our content analysis of the best-selling and most-rented pornographic videos in 2005 suggested that those materials depicted high levels of both verbal aggression (48.7% of the scenes; n = 146) and physical aggression (81% of the scenes; n = 2,743). Only 10.2 percent of scenes did not contain aggression. Compared to our findings, previous content-analysis studies yielded much lower levels of overall aggression in scenes, ranging from 13.6 percent (Duncan, 1991) to 21 percent (Prince, 1990) and 26.9 percent (Barron & Kimmel, 2000). The vast difference between our study and the previous ones could be attributed to a few factors, such as operational definitions, sampling methods, or significant changes in the popular pornography analyzed across different eras.

In an attempt to explain this discrepancy, we first ruled out the possibility that our definition of aggression might have been too liberal—specifically, that it included acts that previous studies may not have considered aggressive. Upon reexamining the definitions used in previous studies—except McKee's (2005a, b), which was different from almost all the studies—we found that our definition was very consistent with others. Furthermore, our studies may have had the potential to underestimate the aggression level, because the PAT technique we employed does not distinguish between multiple instances and a single instance of the same act if the target(s) and the perpetrator(s) did not change. Thus our account might actually be considered as an underestimation of the amount of aggression present.

It is likely that our sampling methods helped us analyze popular pornographic videos on a national level, unlike most previous studies, which were confined to regional locations. Furthermore, researchers have argued that the trend in mainstream pornography in recent years is toward more extreme actions (Dines & Jensen, 2005), and our study may well capture this "up-the-ante" trend. Our study revealed a major increase in the incidence of sexual acts that were considered rare in earlier eras. For example, Palys (1986) found that 10.4 percent (n = 104) of the scenes in X-rated movies depicted anal intercourse, whereas our study found a 55.9 percent rate of these acts (n = 356). Double penetration was rarely reported in the previous literature, but that particular sexual act was fairly frequent in our study (19.1% of the scenes). Ass-to-mouth sequences were also prevalent (41% of the scenes), leading Gail Dines to report that some pornographers would joke about women eating their own shit (Sun & Picker, 2008).

Cowan and Campbell (1994), who considered male ejaculation on women's faces or mouths "degrading," found that 32 percent of the women characters received that treatment; in contrast, 62.5 percent (n = 190) of scenes in our study depicted that act. Although our unit of analysis was "scene" but not "character," even a conservative estimate that every scene depicted only one woman experiencing that act would have found double the amount of what Cowan and Campbell tallied. It is also notable that aggression appeared not only with much higher frequency, but it was qualitatively more intense. Gagging, which was never reported previously, occurred frequently (27.7% of scenes).

Numbers and patterns tell stories, but they are nonetheless incomplete. Qualitative descriptions helped us to visualize how sexual acts and aggression were actually depicted, and our coders' journals provided exactly that. Three coders coded the same five movies during the pilot test, and then they each coded additional movies on their own. Michelle Chang coded the most videos among the three, and she also provided the most detailed descriptions of the movies she watched. The following are the excerpts from Chang's journal.

Anal Sex and Gaping

Anal sex is very common now, and this is always accompanied by a fascination with the open asshole; the men in the scenes and the camera love to linger on the gaping openness of this hole as caused by anal sex.

What Chang describes here is an act that is neither violent nor sexual, but is frequently depicted: gaping. It happens during anal sex when a man abruptly pulls out his penis so that the woman's anus is left open, enlarged to the same diameter as the man's penis. The man then pulls apart the woman's buttocks, exposing the wide-open anus to the audience, while the camera quickly zooms in as close as possible. Christine Larsen, another coder, said that to watch gaping was like "looking at a wound."

Chang described how the act of ejaculation in a woman's mouth was usually carried out:

At the end of the scene, the girl would kneel down, open her mouth and look up at the standing man or men getting ready to ejaculate. And then the man/men would ejaculate into her mouth, over her face, sometimes hitting her in the eye. And the women always gulped it up like it was the best thing they ever tasted.

Among acts of aggression, Chang found gagging particularly hard on the women. She reflected on the reasons why she felt that way:

> When the gagging is occurring, the women clearly look like they're in a position of discomfort because they are gagging and because their eyes are watering and red but the men don't stop ... and it's often accompanied by saying, "Keep your eyes open. You got to keep your eyes open and look at me while it's happening" ... which makes it look extra painful because your instinct when you're gagging is to close your eyes. And they literally can't talk or protest while it's happening.

Chang's vivid descriptions of the sexual acts and aggression that frequently appear in pornographic movies place in context the sights and sounds that statistics and numbers could never express.

THE COMPARISON BETWEEN THE POPULAR PORNOGRAPHY MADE BY MALE OR FEMALE DIRECTORS: WHAT HAPPENS WHEN WOMEN ARE AT THE HELM?

Of the 50 videos we randomly selected for our sample, only two (4%) were made by women. Michelle Chang happened to code both of those movies, and she wrote detailed observations for both. Here are excerpts from Chang's journal on these two movies:

Cum Swappers, Directed by Kat Slater

> Her [Kat Slater's] penchant for talking dirty with the actresses and getting them to turn her on is remarkably similar in style to other male directors who have this sort of approach ... Their [female performers'] interactions with Slater are replete with words like "bitch," "whore," "sluts," "nasty," "filthy," etc. ... [There] was a lot of voluntary gagging on the part of the women, as well as one woman prying another woman's mouth open and holding it so she can be "throat fucked" [by the man] as well as a woman aggressively forcing another woman's head down onto the man's penis so she can be gagged repeatedly.

Belladonna's Fucking Girls, Directed by Belladonna

> Gagging yourself to the point of puking with a dildo ... The gagging is stronger here than in any film I've seen, and ... the women are doing it to themselves. ... The anus becomes a laboratory ... 2-foot-long thick ass bead got shoved up your rectum and colon ... now

this dildo, now ass beads, now 2 fingers, now 4 fingers, now your own fingers, now a butt plug . . . endless feats of anal endurance . . . Without the presence of men there, but knowing this is purely for the gratification of men.

In Chang's descriptions, the two female pornographers' movies were as aggressive—if not more so—than the average movies we analyzed, which were made predominantly by men (96%). This phenomenon raised our curiosity. Is there any difference between popular pornography made by men or by women? We found no previous research addressing this specific question, but there is related research that is informative—for example, studies on how women behave in male-dominated professions, or studies on whether the gender of media producers makes a difference in their portrayal of gender dynamics.

Research on women who enter traditionally male-dominated fields, such as mining, policing, and construction, indicate that these women, instead of changing the environment to be more women friendly, often adopt a working-class masculinity in an effort to be taken seriously and to fend off sexual harassment (Miller, Forest, & Jurik, 2002). A female police officer said in McElhinny's (1998) report, "When I'm in uniform, I'm not a woman/man—I'm a police officer" (p. 321). She also reported that female officers often stop exhibiting female traits such as "smiling" to be accepted among colleagues. This was consistent with Yoder's (2002) findings, which argue that one way women can effectively overcome their lower status is to heighten it in other ways, such as by adopting more "masculine" qualities (Timmons, 1992). When women display qualities that are conventionally classified as "masculine," they have greater opportunities for career advancement (Wong, Kettlewell, & Sproule, 1985). In the field of media, some research also suggests that women may be able to change not only the physical environment but also the symbolic environment under which they operate.

Some researchers assert that women may try to produce more powerful images of women once they become the creators of media content (Seger, 1996). For example, Steenland (1995) describes how female mid-level managers in television production, despite their lack of decision-making power, consciously create better representations of women by reducing violence, verbal abuse, and offensive camera angles.

Conversely, Lauzen and Dozier (1999) failed to find a consistent pattern of stronger female characters in their analysis of the top 65 prime-time series in the first 14 weeks of the 1995–1996 television season. In comparing speech patterns of female characters portrayed in television series that had either male or female workers behind the scenes, these researchers employed two possible theories to investigate the issue: (1) the auteur approach, favored by film scholars, which emphasizes the role of the directors and the way in which their personal vision may affect the content, and (2) the structural approach, utilized mostly by sociologists, which stresses the influence of business imperatives and market forces, which ultimately decide the content of a media product despite the intention of the creators. Lauzen and Dozier's findings suggested that the structural approach receives greater support and that, despite high numbers of female writers, creators, and producers of television shows, representations of gender inequities abound.

Lauzen and Dozier's (1999) research helps contextualize the experience of Tristan Taormino, the self-described feminist director and star of *The Ultimate Guide to Anal Sex for Women*, featuring a 10-person "anal orgy." This film was financed by John Stagliano, a director and producer who is credited with popularizing a type of pornography that contains nonstop explicit sex with minimal plot and set ("gonzo porn"). Even though Taormino did not want to include male actors' external ejaculations, she deferred to John Stagliano and to market forces: "John's loyal audience is primarily straight men," Taormino stated. In other words, despite her own wish to avoid filming visible external ejaculation, she adhered to what "sells tapes" (Taormino, 2005, p. 91). Taormino's example illustrates how a female director's vision may be compromised if she is required to follow a formula that has proven profitable.

The pornography industry is dominated by male producers and directors, and the major consumer base for heterosexual porn is men who are already accustomed to certain long-established pornographic tropes and conventions. If a female pornographer wanted to profit from this industry (and thus from these audiences), would she follow the same formula, or would she diverge and present an alternative version? Stated differently, how might male or female directors of popular pornographic videos differ? Does gender really make a difference in the work that directors create? Which other forces may be more or less significant than gender?

Based on the methodology and sampling methods we established in our first study on aggression and sexual acts in popular pornographic movies, we conducted a study that specifically examines the differences between pornography made by men and women.

Population and Sample

As detailed in the first section of this chapter, the videos for our research were drawn from a compilation of monthly lists published by *Adult Video News*. We selected the top 30 videos from each list from December 2004 to June 2005. After deleting duplications, 275 titles remained.

The sample process required two steps. First, we selected a total of 44 videos: all 11 female-directed films (61 scenes in total) from the original list (4%, or 11 videos out of 275) and an additional 33 randomly selected male-directed films (193 scenes in total). Second, from the 33 male-directed films, with a total of 193 scenes, we randomly selected 61 scenes, the same number as the female directors' scenes. Thus the final sample consisted of 122 scenes from 44 of the most-rented adult videos for 2004 and 2005.

Results

Generally speaking, the scenes directed by female pornographers or male pornographers yield few significant differences. The detailed results of this study (Sun, Bridges, Scharrer, Wosnitzer, & Liberman, 2008) may seem repetitive of the first part of this chapter, which reported on the aggression and sexual acts in popular pornographic movies that were made primarily by men (96%). This section highlights some of the findings that can help present the content of female-made pornographic movies as different from their male-made counterparts.

Characters

Female directors had significantly fewer male characters ($M = 0.87$; $SD = 0.70$) than did male directors ($M = 1.64$; $SD = 1.34$). On average, male directors tended to include approximately equal numbers of male and female characters; in contrast, female directors used more female performers, with the female-to-male ratio being approximately 2:1, suggesting many more "girl-on-girl" scenes than occur in male-directed pornography. Indeed, although male directors portrayed only 6.6 percent women-only scenes (4 of 61 total scenes), female directors depicted 29.5 percent (18 of 61 scenes); χ^2 (1) = 10.87, $p = .001$.

Positive Behaviors

Positive behaviors occurred in 24 of the 122 scenes (19.7% of all scenes; Table 14.1). Notably, female directors were significantly more likely to depict positive behaviors (31.1% of female-directed scenes) than male directors (8.2% of male-directed scenes); χ^2 (1) = 10.17, $p = .001$.

Comparisons of Aggression

Overall, the pornographic output of female directors examined in this study was laden with aggression. In fact, it was equally as aggressive—if not more so—than the work created by male directors. Female-directed scenes contained slightly more aggressive acts per scene (for female directors: $M = 13.44$, $SD = 15.10$; for male directors: $M = 10.92$, $SD = 14.16$). Specifically, there were more physically aggressive acts in the female directors' average scenes ($M = 10.03$; $SD = 11.45$) than in male directors'

Table 14.1

Comparisons of Male and Female Directors on Scene Categorical Variables

	Male directors (n = 61)		Female directors (n = 61)		
	n	%	n	%	Chi-square results
Condoms present	4	6.6	3	4.9	χ^2 (1) = 0.15, p = .697
Sex toy used*	10	16.4	27	44.3	χ^2(1) = 11.21, p = .001
Nonsexual object	0	0.0	3	4.9	χ^2(1) = 3.08, p = .079
Discuss safe sex	0	0.0	0	0.0	
Weapon present	1	1.6	2	3.3	χ^2 (1) = 0.34, p = .559
Ejaculation position					
Mouth	38	62.3	29	47.5	χ^2 (1) = 2.68, p = .102
Face	3	4.9	0	0.0	χ^2 (1) = 3.08, p = .079
Breasts	5	8.2	0	0.0	χ^2 (1) = 5.21, p = .022
Stomach	1	1.6	0	0.0	χ^2 (1) = 1.01, p = .315
Buttocks	2	3.3	0	0.0	χ^2 (1) = 2.03, p = .154
Internal	1	1.6	0	0.0	χ^2 (1) = 1.01, p = .315
Vagina (external)	1	1.6	1	1.6	χ^2 (1) = 0.00, p = 1.00
Other (e.g., anus)*	6	9.8	22	36.1	χ^2 (1) = 11.87, p = .001
Multiple locations	3	4.9	8	13.1	χ^2 (1) = 2.50, p = .114
Sex acts					
Male-to-female oral	34	55.7	26	42.6	χ^2 (1) = 2.10, p = .147
Female-to-male oral*	57	93.4	41	67.2	χ^2 (1) = 13.28, p < .001
Female-to-female oral*	9	14.8	25	41.0	χ^2 (1) = 10.44, p = .001
Male-to-male oral	0	0.0	1	1.6	χ^2 (1) = 1.01, p = .315
Vaginal penetration with penis	49	80.3	40	65.6	χ^2 (1) = 3.37, p = .067
Vaginal double penetration	2	3.3	0	0.0	χ^2 (1) = 2.03, p = .154
Simultaneous vaginal/anal penetration	12	19.7	6	9.8	χ^2 (1) = 2.35, p = .126
Group sex	9	14.8	0	0.0	χ^2 (1) = 9.72, p = .002
Anal penetration with penis	33	54.1	28	45.9	χ^2 (1) = 0.82, p = .365
Anal double penetration	2	3.3	0	0.0	χ^2 (1) = 2.03, p = .154
Ass-to-mouth sequence	27	44.3	25	41.0	χ^2 (1) = 0.13, p = .714
Presence of positive behaviors*	5	8.2	19	31.1	χ^2 (1) = 10.17, p = .001

*p ≤ .001.

scenes ($M = 8.93$; $SD = 11.71$). In addition, there were more verbally aggressive instances in female directors' average scenes ($M = 3.43$; $SD = 4.84$) than in male directors' scenes ($M = 1.97$; $SD = 2.97$). Female and male directors portrayed a similar amount of physically aggressive acts, including (1) pushing/shoving; (2) biting; (3) pinching; (4) hair pulling; (5) spanking; (6) open-hand slapping; (7) gagging; (8) choking; (9) kicking; (10) confining; and (11) using a weapon. Although rare, severely aggressive acts such as smothering or whipping someone with an object were found significantly more frequently in women-directed scenes (18.0%) than in scenes directed by their male counterparts (0 scenes).

Male directors were twice as likely to show men perpetrating aggression: 77.5 percent of all aggressive acts in male-directed scenes were perpetrated by men versus 38.8 percent of all aggressive acts in female-directed scenes. By comparison, female directors portrayed more female perpetrators than male perpetrators: 60.6 percent of all aggressive acts in female-directed scenes were perpetrated by women versus 21.3 percent of all aggressive acts in male-directed scenes.

The targets of aggression were almost always women. In male-directed scenes, 91.1 percent of the aggressive acts depicted female targets (607 out of 666 aggressive acts); in female-directed scenes, 96.1 percent of the aggressive acts were against women (788 out of 820). Female directors not only portrayed more female victims, but also included significantly more female perpetrators in their films (Table 14.2): 60.6 percent of all aggressive acts in female-directed scenes were perpetrated by women versus 21.3 percent of all such aggressive acts in male-directed scenes. Furthermore, while 32.4 percent of male-directed aggressive acts depicted woman-to-woman violence, female directors produced nearly three times the number of scenes depicting such dynamics (81.1% of female-directed scenes). Interestingly, although no male self-harm acts were present in the films included in this study, male directors depicted 6.3 percent of all aggressive acts that involved female self-harm, and female directors depicted even more of these incidents (8.2% of all aggressive acts), although the difference was not significant.

Comparisons of Target Responses

In both male- and female-directed aggressive acts, the targets of aggression overwhelmingly displayed pleasure or responded neutrally to the aggression (Table 14.2). Only 2.7 percent of male-directed acts of aggression and 1.1 percent of female-directed acts of aggression resulted in targets responding with displeasure.

Table 14.2

Comparisons of Male and Female Directors on Aggressive Act Variables, Controlling for Main Character Gender Composition

	Male-directed scenes ($n = 32$)		Female-directed scenes ($n = 32$)		Chi-square results
	n	%	n	%	
Aggression present in scene	27	84.4	24	75.0	χ^2 (1) = 0.87, p = .351
Verbal aggression present in scene	17	53.1	12	37.5	χ^2 (1) = 1.58, p = .209
Physical aggression present in scene	26	81.3	23	71.9	χ^2 (1) = 0.78, p = .376
Type of verbal aggression					
Name calling/insults	17	53.1	12	37.5	χ^2 (1) = 1.58, p = .209
Threat of physical harm	0	0.0	2	6.3	χ^2 (1) = 2.07, p = .151
Coercive language	0	0.0	0	0.0	
Type of physical aggression					
Push/shove	1	3.1	1	3.1	χ^2 (1) = 0.00, p = 1.00
Bite	2	6.3	2	6.3	χ^2 (1) = 0.00, p = 1.00
Pinch	0	0.0	3	9.4	χ^2 (1) = 3.15, p = .076
Pull hair	10	31.3	8	25.0	χ^2 (1) = 0.31, p = .578
Spank	21	65.6	21	65.6	χ^2 (1) = 0.00, p = 1.00
Open hand slap	14	43.8	8	25.0	χ^2 (1) = 2.49, p = .114
Gag	15	46.9	17	53.1	χ^2 (1) = 0.25, p = .617
Choke	7	21.9	6	18.8	χ^2 (1) = 0.10, p = .756
Kick	1	3.1	0	0.0	χ^2 (1) = 1.02, p = .313
Bondage/confine	1	3.1	8	25.0	χ^2 (1) = 6.34, p = .012
Use of weapon	1	3.1	2	6.3	χ^2 (1) = 0.35, p = .554
Other (e.g., smothering, whipping)	0	0.0	3	9.4	χ^2 (1) = 3.15, p = .076
Overall consequences of aggression					χ^2 (1) = 6.37, p = .012
Rewarded/paid off	22	68.8	23	95.8	
Punished	0	0.0	0	0.0	

(continued)

Table 14.2 (continued)

	($n = 261$) Total aggressive acts		($n = 319$) Total aggressive acts		Chi-square results
	n	%	n	%	
Male perpetrator					
Any target	171	65.8	182	57.2	χ^2 (1) = 4.39, p = .036
Female target	170	65.1	182	57.2	χ^2 (1) = 1.07, p = .302
Male target	0	0.0	0	0.0	
Self target	0	0.0	0	0.0	
Female perpetrator					
Any target	89	34.2	136	42.8	χ^2 (1) = 4.39, p = .036
Female target*	33	12.6	89	27.9	χ^2 (1) = 17.43, p < .001
Male target	27	10.3	24	7.5	χ^2 (1) = 1.43, p = .233
Self target	26	10.0	23	7.2	χ^2 (1) = 4.78, p = .029
Victim response to aggression					χ^2 (1) = 0.02, p = .889
Expresses pleasure/ neutral	253	96.9	311	97.5	
Expresses displeasure	7	2.7	8	2.5	

*$p \le .001$.

Controlling for Disparities due to Character Gender

Because female directors included many more female performers in an average scene than their male counterparts, it is important to rule out the possibility that the differences noted previously were not due to the gender predominance of characters in male- or female-directed pornography. Accordingly, data were reanalyzed for a subset of the sample, matching male- and female-directed scenes on main characters' gender composition. The resulting sample comprised 32 female-directed and 32 male-directed scenes. Comparisons for both scene-and aggressive-act-level variables were conducted. To control for the number of comparisons, a Bonferroni correction was used such that p values of .001 or less were considered to be significant.

All but one of the comparisons was nonsignificant. Even when controlling for gender composition of main characters, female-directed scenes continued to show significantly more women-to-women aggression

(27.9% of female-directed scenes) than male-directed scenes (12.6% of male-directed scenes); χ^2 (1) = 17.43, $p < .001$.

Discussion

The pornographic world constructed by popular mainstream female directors is not made up of "candles, lace, sunsets" (West & West, 2002, p. 11), nor does it portray egalitarian gender relationships, as some have advocated (West & West, 2002). Instead, it is a world infused with aggression—and not much different from the world portrayed by male directors, in terms of sexual acts and the types and frequencies of physical or verbal aggression. In a typical scene, the female directors depicted a variety of male and female oral sex, female vaginal penetrations (65.6% of the scenes), and anal penetrations (45.9% of the scenes). Compared to male directors, female directors depicted similar ratios of different types of aggression such as spanking, hair pulling, and slapping, although the incidence of "gagging" was noticeably higher (59.0% of female-directed scenes versus 54.1% of male-directed scenes). Some non-normative sexual acts were prevalent, such as "ass-to-mouth" acts (41% of the scenes) and ejaculation in the mouth (47.5% of the scenes), although depictions of these acts in female-directed scenes appeared to be less frequent than, but not significantly different from, those in the male directors' scenes.

Female directors portrayed significantly more positive behavior (31.1% of female-directed scenes versus 8.2% of male-directed scenes), but they also depicted significantly more female perpetrators, more female-to-female aggression, and a higher percentage of extreme sexual aggression. Female directors also depicted more aggressive acts per scene, although by a margin not statistically significant. In their portrayals, women enjoyed having aggression inflicted on them; they even—with higher frequency than in male directors' scenes—inflicted self-harm without anyone forcing it on them.

In other words, the world produced by female directors portrayed sex as intertwined with violence: frequently, sexual pleasure was contingent upon and derived from aggression. For both the perpetrators and the targets, aggression was intrinsic and integral for sexual excitement. In this regard, female-directed films did not offer an alternative construction of sexuality and gender roles relative to the films produced by their male counterparts.

Evidently, the ideals of such female pornographers as Candida Royalle, who are celebrated by pro-pornography scholars and are lauded for making "feminist" pornography (Agrell, 2006), have not been effective in changing popular mainstream pornography to be less misogynist. In fact, Royalle's movies were nowhere to be found in the 275 best-selling and most-rented video titles that we compiled. Furthermore, female-directed films accounted for only 4.4 percent of all best-selling, most-rented porn movies in the population of study. Such a weak showing indicates that only a very small percentage of women have "made it" in this male-dominated profession. Female pornographer Belladonna appears to have learned the conventions of commercially successful adult films from male pornographers. Perhaps confined by the industry's formulas and market pressures, these female directors have created a pornographic world that is remarkably similar to that of their male counterparts. This finding is consistent with the results of prior studies, which have supported the structural approach to media development (Lauzen & Dozier, 1999): money, rather than gender, dictates content.

Female directors' depictions of frequent and sometimes extreme aggression against women are consistent with studies of women who find success in male-dominated fields. While working in such jobs, some women display hypermasculine traits to earn respect and to gain favor from their male supervisors and peers (Wong et al., 1985). But why would female directors portray more female-to-female violence? Could it be that female directors have learned that to sell tapes, they need to portray aggression against women, and the female targets need to show pleasure? In other words, these those directors were not ignorant of the epidemic male violence against women in the real world, but they did not want to portray it. Thus they portrayed women-on-women or women's self-inflicted violence instead. Could it be that the significantly higher frequency of women-on-women violence in female-directed films than in their male counterparts' portrayals actually represented a compromise between the female directors' desire to make profits and their instinct not to perpetuate male violence? As this issue is beyond the scope of our study, these speculations cannot be verified.

Limitations

The findings from our study shed light on the research question of how male- or female-made popular pornography would differ, but nonetheless have limitations. We used a systematic method for investigating the content of popular pornographic movies. Because we selected only best-selling, most-rented videos, however, our research may not adequately describe the general patterns of female directors' work, particularly if those materials were targeted at a women-centered, niche market. In fact, the variety exhibited in female-directed films, even in this best-selling, most-rented sample, was greater than that of male-directed films. That is, women directors appeared to follow a less rigid formula by displaying both more positive behaviors and more aggression among women.

If combining sex and violence is the formula for market success, then depictions that are free of domination and degradation are unlikely to have made the best-selling lists we drew from and, therefore, would not have been analyzed by us. In other words, our research may have identified only those female directors who can appeal to the male-dominated consumer base but does not offer insights into the content of female-directed films that aim to appeal to alternative audiences. What this study has done, nonetheless, is to support the contention that in a capitalist economy where pornography is primarily consumed by men who are accustomed to certain sexual scripts and representations, if one wants to maximize profits, the gender of the pornography director may be irrelevant.

OVERALL LIMITATIONS

The two content-analysis studies our team conducted share the same methodology, coding schemes, and coders. Thus they also share similar limitations and contributions. Even though conflicting opinions exist regarding whether gender affects how people interpret pornographic images (Cowan & Dunn, 1994; Glascock, 2005), the use of exclusively female coders, although rigorously trained by a male researcher, may present a potential limitation to our study. Therefore, future studies may consider using both male and female coders. Additionally, intercoder reliability was calculated only at the beginning of the analysis. It would have been beneficial to check reliability again as the analysis progressed.

There are limitations as to how much a quantitative analysis that decontextualizes sexual and aggressive acts can help us understand images and decode meaning (Hall, 1989). As the entries from our coder's journal demonstrate, qualitative descriptions and analyses can provide far more vivid and descriptive accounts of pornography than simple numbers can convey. Therefore, future studies may seek to examine best-selling and most-rented pornography using qualitative analyses as a complement to quantitative findings. Similarly, understanding how pornography directors create their scripts, prompt sexual acts, and ascribe meaning to them, and how market forces and trends may have helped shape their decisions are all potentially valuable for enhancing the understanding of the construction of popular pornographic movies from multiple perspectives.

MAJOR CONTRIBUTIONS

Despite their limitations, these studies provide numerous important contributions to furthering our understanding of popular pornographic films. Three in particular are described here.

First, by exploring the content of popular pornography, we take seriously the socioeconomic forces that shape pornography's production.

While much attention has been paid to the patriarchal ideology manifested in pornography's production and consumption (e.g., Jensen & Dines, 1998), economic forces have less frequently been explored to examine how they shape the nature of the product. This study brings an important multidisciplinary, sociopolitical perspective to the discussion of the content of pornography directed by men and women.

Second, the pornography industry has gone through tremendous growth in the past two decades. However, while the output of pornographic products has increased significantly—in large part due to technological advances in the Internet, direct television, and home digital video equipment (Cooper, Putnam, Planchon, & Boies, 1999)—scholarly work charting its content has declined. Indeed, most recorded content analyses were conducted in the 1980s and early 1990s. As a consequence, new themes and genres (such as "gonzo porn") are not described in current academic texts. Our use of the industry's leading journal, *Adult Video News*, to sample movie titles provides a simple model that allows for relatively more systematic and objective sample selection, compared to the samples of convenience that were used by most of the previous studies aimed at capturing national and current trends. If our sampling method were to be followed by future researchers, study results could then be tracked and compared, and patterns of change and development of pornographic content could be revealed.

Third, our studies charted certain acts of aggression (such as gagging) and sexual acts (such as ass-to-mouth and double penetration) that were not tallied in earlier investigations, and that provide evidence that current pornography content may be not only quantitatively but also qualitatively different from that considered in previous studies. We also demonstrated that popular pornographic videos portrayed both a high level of aggression and a low frequency of positive behavior. In contrast with previous studies, we did not detect many depictions that perpetuated the "rape myth," in which the target first expresses pain or resistance to male dominance but eventually expresses enjoyment (Cowan et al., 1988; Duncan, 1991). In fact, while most of the targets of aggression were women, they overwhelmingly expressed enjoyment or did not respond while being subjected to aggression. It might be argued that in current popular pornography, the "education" of women accepting aggression has been completed. In these depictions, women do not exhibit resistance to aggression; instead, they welcome, invite, or just passively accept aggression. They also self-inflict harm, even without men on the scene to enforce the violence. Although such scenes may be directed by men or even women, they are still aimed at mostly heterosexual male customers.

These portrayals of women expressing pleasure while experiencing aggression have significant implications for the effects of pornography on consumers. Social cognitive theory (Bandura, 1994, 2001) suggests that whether an individual will model aggression learned from viewing a media text depends in large part on whether the act they observed was rewarded or punished. By extension, viewers of pornography learn that aggression against women during a sexual encounter is pleasure enhancing for both men and women. This "lesson" raises two questions: What might be the social implication for this type of learning? And would the social learning effect become even stronger if the message of women being masochists who enjoyed being hurt were actually produced by women themselves?

REFERENCES

Agrell, S. (2006, June 10). X-rated films for red-blooded feminists: New porn caters to female pleasure fantasies. *National Post (Toronto Edition)*, p. wp3.

Attorney General's Commission on Pornography. (1986). *Final report, Department of Justice*. Washington, DC: U.S. Government Printing Office.

AVN. (2006, January). State of the U.S. adult industry. *Adult Video News, 22*, 30–31.

AVN. (2006). Top 250 VHS & DVD rentals. Retrieved July 17, 2005, from http://www.avn.com/index.php_PrimaryNavigations=Charts.

Bandura, A. (1994). Social cognitive theory of mass communication. In J. Bryant & D. Zillmann (Eds.), *Media effects: Advances in theory and research* (pp. 121–154). Hillsdale, NJ: Erlbaum.

Bandura, A. (2001). Social cognitive theory of mass communication. *Media Psychology, 3*, 265–299.

Barron, M., & Kimmel, M. (2000). Sexual violence in three pornographic media: Toward a sociological explanation. *Journal of Sex Research, 37*(2), 161–168.

Boyle, K. (2000). The pornography debates: Beyond cost and effect. *Women's Studies International Forum, 23*(2), 187–195.

Cooper, A., Putnam, D. E., Planchon, L. A., & Boies, S. C. (1999). Online sexual compulsivity: Getting tangled in the net. *Sexual Addiction and Compulsivity, 6*, 79–104.

Cowan, G., & Campbell, R.R. (1994). Racism and sexism in interracial pornography: A content analysis. *Psychology of Women Quarterly, 18*(3), 323–338.

Cowan, G., & Dunn, K. F. (1994). What themes in pornography lead to perceptions of the degradation of women? *Journal of Sex Research, 31*(1), 11–21.

Cowan, G., Lee, C., Levy, D., & Snyder, D. (1988). Dominance and inequality in X-rated videocassettes. *Psychology of Women Quarterly, 12*, 299–311.

Denney, N. W., Field, J. K., & Quadagno, D. (1984). Sex differences in sexual needs and desires. *Archives of Sexual Behavior, 13*, 233–245.

Dines, G. (2008). Penn, porn and me. CounterPunch. Retrieved on 4/21/10 from http://www.counterpunch.org/dines06232008.html.

Dines, G., & Jensen, R. (2005, December 6). Pornography is a left issue. *Znet*.

Dines, G., Jensen, R., & Russo, A. (1998). *Pornography: The production and consumption of inequality*. New York: Routledge.

Donnerstein, E., Linz, D. G., & Penrod, S. (1987). *The question of pornography*. New York: Free Press.

Duncan, D. F. (1991). Violence and degradation as themes in "adult" videos. *Psychological Reports, 69*, 239–240.

Easton, S. (1998). Pornography. In *Encyclopedia of applied ethics*. Toronto: Academic Press.

Glascock, J. (2005). Degrading content and character sex: Accounting for men and women's differential reactions to pornography. *Communication Reports, 18*(1), 43–53.

Gossett, J. L., & Byrne, S. (2002). "Click here": A content analysis of Internet rape sites. *Gender and Society, 16*(5), 689–709.

Guo, Y. N., Ng, E. M. L., & Chan, K. (2004). Foreplay, orgasm and after-play among Shanghai couples and its integrative relation with their marital satisfaction. *Sexual and Relationship Therapy, 19,* 65–78.

Hall, S. (1989). Ideology and communication theory. In B. Dervin, L. Grossberg, B. J. O'Keefe, & E. Wartella (Eds.), *Rethinking communication: Volume 1, paradigm issues* (pp. 40–52). Newbury Park, CA: Sage.

Jensen, R. (1998). *Getting off: Pornography and the end of masculinity.* Cambridge, MA: South End Press.

Jensen, R. (2004, January/February). Cruel to be hard: Men and pornography. *Sexual Assault Report,* 33–48.

Jensen, R., & Dines, G. (1998). The content of mass-marketed pornography. In G. Dines, R. Jensen, & A. Russo (Eds.), *Pornography: The production and consumption of inequality* (pp. 65–100). New York: Routledge.

Kelley, T. (2007, February 24). Pole dancing parties catch on in book club country. *New York Times.*

Laan, E., Everaerd, W., van Bellen, G., & Hanewald, G. (1994). Women's sexual and emotional responses to male- and female-produced erotica. *Archives of Sexual Behavior, 23,* 153–169.

Lauzen, M. M., & Dozier, D. M. (1999). Making a difference in prime time: Women on screen and behind the scenes in the 1995–96 television season. *Journal of Broadcasting & Electronic Media, 43*(1), 1–19.

Malamuth, N., & Spinner, B. (1980). A longitudinal content analysis of sexual violence in the best-selling erotic magazines. *Journal of Sex Research, 16*(3), 226–237.

McElhinny, B. (1998). "I don't smile much anymore": Affect, gender and the discourse of Pittsburgh Police Officers. In J. Coates (Ed.), *Language and gender: A reader* (pp. 309–327). Oxford Blackwell.

McKee, A. (2005a). The need to bring the voices of pornography consumers into public debates about the genre and its effects. *Australian Journal of Communication, 32*(2), 71–94.

McKee, A. (2005b). The objectification of women in mainstream pornographic videos in Australia. *Journal of Sex Research, 42*(4), 277–290.

Merriam-Webster online dictionary. (2009). Retrieved October 17, 2009, from http:// www.merriam-webster.com/dictionary/amazon.

Miller, S., Forest, K. B., & Jurik, N. C. (2002). Diversity in blue: Lesbian and gay police officers in a masculine occupation. *Men and Masculinities, 5*(4), 355–385.

Mustonen, A., & Pulkkinen, L. (1993). Aggression in television programs in Finland. *Aggressive Behavior, 19*(3), 175–183.

National Television Violence Study (NTVS). (1998). *Executive summary,* pp. 3, 54.

Palys, T. S. (1986). Testing the common wisdom: The social content of video pornography. *Canadian Psychology, 27*(1), 22–35.

Prince, S. (1990). Power and pain: Content analysis and the ideology of pornography. *Journal of Film and Video, 42*(2), 31–41.

Rich, F. (2001, May 20). Naked capitalism. *New York Times Magazine.*

Russell, D. (1993). *Making violence sexy: Feminist views on pornography.* New York: Teachers College Press.

Seger, L. (1996). *When women call the shots.* New York: Henry Holt.

Steenland, S. (1995). Content analysis of the image of women on television. In C. M. Lont (Ed.), *Women and media: Content, careers, and criticism* (pp. 197–189). San Francisco: Wadsworth.

Sun, C., Bridges, A., Scharrer, E., Wosnitzer, R., & Liberman, R. (2008). A comparison of male and female directors in pornography: What happens when women are at the helm? *Psychology of Women Quarterly, 32*(3), 312–325.

Sun, C., & Picker, M. (Co-producers & co-directors). (2008). *The price of pleasure: Pornography, sexuality and relationships.* North Hampton, MA: Media Education Foundation.

Taormino, T. (2005). On crossing the line to create feminist porn. In C. Milne (Ed.), *Naked ambition* (pp. 87–98). New York: Carroli & Graf.

Timmons, T. (1992). "We're looking for a few good men": The impact of gender stereotypes on women in the military. *Minerva, 10*(2), 20.

Wallace, D. F. (2006). *Consider the lobster.* New York: Little, Brown.

West, D., & West, J. M. (2002). Women making porno: Feminism's final frontier? An interview with Marielle Nitoslawska. *Cineaste, 27*(3), 9–13.

Wong, P. T. P., Kettlewell, G., & Sproule, C. F. (1985). On the importance of being masculine: Sex role, attribution, and women's career achievement. *Sex Roles, 12*(7/8), 757–769.

Yang, N., & Linz, D. (1990). Movie ratings and the content of adult videos: The sex–violence ratio. *Journal of Communication, 40*(2), 28–42.

Yoder, J. D. (2002). Context matters: Understanding tokenism processes and their impact on women's work. *Psychology of Women Quarterly, 26,* 1–8.

Zillmann, D. (1989). Effects of prolonged consumption of pornography. In D. Zillmann & J. Bryant (Eds.), *Pornography: Research advances and policy considerations* (pp. 127–158). Hillsdale, NJ: Lawrence Erlbaum.

Appendix: Organizations Dealing with Sexual Assault and Abuse Worldwide

Abusive Men Exploring New Directions: www.amendinc.org

American Bar Association Commission on Domestic Violence: www.abanet.org/domviol/home.html

American Psychological Association: www.apa.org

Antistalking Website: www.antistalking.com

A Safe Passage: www.asafepassage.info

Asian Task Force Against Domestic Violence: www.atask.org

Asian and Pacific Islander Institute on Domestic Violence: www.apiahf.org/apidvinstitute

AYUDA Inc.: www.ayuda.com

Battered Women's Justice Project: www.bwjp.org

Battered Women's Support Services: www.bwss.org

Break the Cycle: www.breakthecycle.org

British Columbia Institute Against Family Violence: www.brokenspirits.com

California Family and Domestic Violence Referral Directory: www.safenetwork.net/AgencyList.aspx

Clearinghouse on Abuse and Neglect of the Elderly: http://db.rdms.udel.edu:8080/CANE/index.jsp

Coalition Against Trafficking of Women: www.catwinternational.org

College Violence: http://youthviolence.edschool.virginia.edu/violence-in-schools/collegecamput.html

Commission on Domestic Violence—American Bar Association: www.abanet.org/domviol

Communities Against Violence Network: www.cavnet2.org

Domestic Violence Clearinghouse and Legal Hotline: www.stoptheviolence.org

Domestic Violence Help Resources: www.ovw.usdoj.gov/hotnum.htm

Family Violence Prevention Fund: www.endabuse.org

Feminist Majority Foundation: http://feminist.org

HPP Earth: International Domestic Violence Information: www.hotpeachpages.net

Institute on Domestic Violence in the African American Community: www.dvinstitute.org

International Society for Research on Aggression: www.israsociety.com

Manavi: South Asian Women's Organization Against Violence: www.manavi.org

Men Can Stop Rape: www.mencanstoprape.org

Muslim Women's League: www.mwlusa.org

National Center on Domestic and Sexual Violence: www.ncdsv.org

National Center on Elder Abuse: www.ncea.aoa.gov

National Center for Missing and Exploited Children: www.missingkids.com

National Center for Victims of Crime: www.ncvc.org/ncvc/Main.aspx

National Coalition Against Domestic Violence: www.ncadv.org

National Domestic Violence Hotline: www.ndvh.org

National Latino Alliance for the Elimination of Domestic Violence: www.dvalianza.org

National Network to End Domestic Violence: www.nnedv.org

National Organization for Men Against Sexism: www.nomas.org

National Organization for Women: www.now.org/index.html

National Resource Center on Domestic Violence: www.nrcdv.org

National Sexual Violence Resource Center: www.nsvrc.org

National Tribal Justice Resource Center: www.tribalresourcecenter.org

New Mexico Coalition Against Domestic Violence: www.nmcadv.org

New York Model for Batterer Programs: www.nymbp.org

Nursing Network on Violence Against Women International: www.nnvawi.org

Pennsylvania Coalition Against Domestic Violence: www.pcadv.org

Rape, Abuse, and Incest National Network: www.rainn.org

Reclaim the Night Australia: www.isis.aust.com/rtn

Resource Center on Domestic Violence: Child Protection and Custody, National Council of Juvenile and Family Court Judges: www.ncjfcj.org

Security on Campus: www.securityoncampus.org

S.E.S.A.M.E (Stop Educator Sexual Abuse, Misconduct, and Exploitation): www.sesamenet.org

Stalking Resource Center: www.ncvc.org/src/Main.aspx

StopFamily Violence: www.stopfamilyviolence.org

Tibet Justice Center: www.tibetjustice.org

U.S. Department of Health and Human Services: www.4women.gov/violence/index.cfm

Vancouver Rape Relief and Women's Shelter: www.rapereliefshelter.bc.ca

Violence Against Women: www.vaw.umn.edu

Violence Against Women in American Indian/Native American and Alaska Native Communities: www.vawnet.org

Womenslaw: www.womenslaw.org

Index

About the Editors and Contributors

EDITORS

MICHELE A. PALUDI, Ph.D., is the Series Editor for Praeger's *Women's Psychology and Women and Careers in Management*. She is the author/editor of 33 college textbooks, and more than 170 scholarly articles and conference presentations on sexual harassment, campus violence, psychology of women, gender, and sexual harassment and victimization. Her book, *Ivory Power: Sexual Harassment on Campus* (1990, SUNY Press), received the 1992 Myers Center Award for Outstanding Book on Human Rights in the United States. Dr. Paludi served as Chair of the U.S. Department of Education's Subpanel on the Prevention of Violence, Sexual Harassment, and Alcohol and Other Drug Problems in Higher Education; she was one of six scholars in the United States to be selected for this Subpanel. She also was a consultant to and a member of former New York Governor Mario Cuomo's Task Force on Sexual Harassment. Dr. Paludi serves as an expert witness for court proceedings and administrative hearings on sexual harassment. She has had extensive experience in conducting training programs and investigations of sexual harassment and other equal employment opportunity (EEO) issues for businesses and educational institutions.

Dr. Paludi has held faculty positions at Franklin & Marshall College, Kent State University, Hunter College, Union College, and Union Graduate College, where she directs the human resources management certificate program. She teaches in the School of Management.

FLORENCE L. DENMARK, Ph.D., is an internationally recognized scholar, researcher, and policymaker. She received her Ph.D. from the University of Pennsylvania in social psychology and has five honorary degrees. Dr. Denmark is the Robert Scott Pace Distinguished Research Professor of Psychology at Pace University in New York. A past president of the American Psychological Association (APA) and the International Council of Psychologists (ICP), she holds fellowship status in the APA and the Association for Psychological Science. She is also a member of the Society for Experimental Social Psychology (SESP) and a Fellow of the New York Academy of Sciences.

Dr. Denmark has received numerous national and international awards for her contributions to psychology. She received the 2004 American Psychological Foundation Gold Medal for Lifetime Achievement for Psychology in the Public Interest. In 2005, she received the Ernest R. Hilgard Award for her Career Contribution to General Psychology. In 2007, she was the recipient of the Raymond Fowler Award for Outstanding Service to APA. Also in 2007, Dr. Denmark was elected to the National Academies of Practice as a distinguished scholar member. She received the Elder Award at the APA National Multicultural Conference in 2009.

Dr. Denmark's most significant research and extensive publications have emphasized women's leadership and leadership styles, the interaction of status and gender, aging women in cross-cultural perspective, and the history of women in psychology. She is the main nongovernment organization (NGO) representative to the United Nations for the APA and is also the main NGO representative for the International Council of Psychologists. She is currently Chair of the New York NGO Committee on Ageing and serves on the Executive Committee of the NGO Committee on Mental Health.

CONTRIBUTORS

HORTENSIA AMARO, Ph.D., is Associate Dean of the Bouvé College of Health Sciences at Northeastern University, Distinguished Professor of Health Sciences and of Counseling Psychology in the Bouvé College of Health Sciences, and Director of the Institute on Urban Health Research. She received her doctoral degree in psychology from the University of California at Los Angeles in 1982 and was awarded an Honorary Doctoral Degree in Humane Letters by Simmons College in 1994.

Over the past 27 years, Dr. Amaro's work has focused on improving the connections between public health research and public health practice. Her research has resulted in more than 120 scientific publications. Her work has focused on studies of alcohol and drug use and addiction among adolescents and adults; the development and testing of behavioral interventions for HIV/AIDS prevention; substance abuse and mental health treatment for Latina and African American women and incarcerated men; alcohol and drug use among college populations; and behavioral interventions for HIV medications adherence. She has served on the editorial board of prominent scientific journals such as the *American Journal of Public Health* and on review and advisory committees to the Institute of Medicine, the National Institutes of Health, the U.S. Department of Health and Human Services, the Substance Abuse and Mental Health Services Administration, and the Centers for Disease Control and Prevention. Dr. Amaro's "Love, Sex and Power," published in *American Psychologist*, had a wide-ranging impact on the field of HIV prevention among women; she received the 1996 Scientific Publication Award for her authorship of this work from the National Association of Women in Psychology.

Dr. Amaro's own journey as a Cuban refugee and immigrant to the United States has significantly influenced her life and informed her scholarly and community work in public health. In her free time, she enjoys long-distance cycling, kayaking, practicing and teaching yoga, Latin dancing, and summer gardening in her Cape Cod home.

ANA J. BRIDGES, Ph.D., is an assistant professor of clinical psychology at the University of Arkansas, Fayetteville. Since 1999, Dr. Bridges has been investigating the effects of explicit sexual media on women and couples. Her research has been featured in both academic and popular press, including *Psychology Today*.

NICOLE T. BUCHANAN, Ph.D., is an Associate Professor in the Department of Psychology at Michigan State University (MSU) and a core faculty affiliate in MSU's Center for Multicultural Psychology Research, Center for Gender in Global Context, and the Violence Against Women Research & Outreach Initiative. Her research examines the intersection of race and gender in harassment, racialized sexual harassment, health, coping, and resilience among women of color. Dr. Buchanan received the 2008 International Coalition Against Sexual Harassment Researcher Award; the 2008 Carolyn Payton Early Career Award for research making "a significant contribution to the understanding of the role of gender in the lives of Black women"; the Association of Women in Psychology's 2007 Women of Color Award for empirical research contributions; Michigan State University's 2007 Excellence in Diversity Award in the category of "Individual Emerging Progress" for outstanding research and teaching accomplishments in the areas of diversity, pluralism, and social justice and two Clinical Faculty Awards from the National Institutes of Health. Representative publications include "The Effects of Racial and Sexual Harassment on Work and the Psychological Well-Being of African American Women," *Journal of Occupational Health Psychology*; "Comparing Sexual Harassment Subtypes for Black and White Women: Double Jeopardy, the Jezebel, and the Cult of True Womanhood," *Psychology of Women*

Quarterly; "Sexual Harassment Across the Color Line: Experiences and Outcomes of Cross- vs. Intra-racial Sexual Harassment Among Black Women," *Cultural Diversity and Ethnic Minority Psychology*; and "Racialized Sexual Harassment in the Lives of African American Women," *Women & Therapy.*

JUNE F. CHISHOLM, Ph.D., is Professor of Psychology at Pace University. She is a clinical psychologist who worked for many years as a senior psychologist in the Outpatient Psychiatric Department at Harlem Hospital Center, providing psychological services to an ethnically diverse, primarily poor, urban population. Dr. Chisholm is in private practice in Manhattan and is a psychological consultant to the Metropolitan New York Synod of the Evangelical Lutheran Church of America. She is in her second term as Vice Chair of the State Board for Psychology. Her clinical and research interests include issues in the psychological treatment of women of color, psychological assessment of children and adults, parenting, community violence, school violence, and cyberbullying.

DONNA CASTAÑEDA, Ph.D., is a professor in the Psychology Department at San Diego State University–Imperial Valley. She completed her B.A. in psychology at the University of Washington and her M.A. and Ph.D. in social psychology at the University of California, Davis. Dr. Castañeda has investigated the impact of close relationship factors in HIV sexual risk behavior, particularly among Latinos, the HIV/AIDS prevention needs of women factory workers in Mexico, the close relationship context and how it affects intimate-partner violence, and the relationship between mental health and marital satisfaction. A second area of interest is the role of structural factors, or aspects of service delivery systems, in the provision of health and mental health services to Latina/o communities.

BRIAN K. COLAR is a senior at Argosy University working toward a bachelor of arts degree in psychology. His area of specialization is gender bullying, resiliency, masculinity, and the transition to manhood in African American men. He is the founder of the nonprofit organization Reflection Eternal, based in Chicago, which aims to increase opportunities for young men of color.

AJITHA CYRIAC is a Ph.D. candidate at the University of Toronto, pursuing a degree in public health. Her research focuses on the intersections of intimate-partner violence and HIV. In 2006, she was awarded a Canadian Doctoral Research Award from the Canadian Institutes for Health Research. Ms. Cyriac received her master of science degree from Columbia University, New York. She presently works at the Centre for Research on Inner City

Health at St. Michael's Hospital in Toronto, Canada, on various studies related to intimate-partner violence. She is also actively involved in health education among South Asian communities on issues of HIV and violence in Toronto and is a current member of the Board of Directors for the YWCA Toronto. She has been involved in women's health research for several years and plans to continue her research in this field.

EROS R. DESOUZA, Ph.D., is a Professor of Psychology at Illinois State University. He earned his Ph.D. in community psychology from the University of Missouri at Kansas City. Dr. DeSouza has carried out qualitative and quantitative research on sexuality and gender issues, including sexual orientation and sexual harassment from a cross-cultural perspective. As of August 2009, he had written nine book chapters and more than 40 scholarly articles; he has also co-authored 115 papers presented at conferences.

AUDREY HOKODA, Ph.D., is an Associate Professor in the Child and Family Development Department at San Diego State University. She received her B.S. in psychobiology from the University of California, Los Angeles, and her doctorate in clinical psychology at the University of Illinois, Urbana–Champaign. She has been the principal investigator for more than 15 studies and community projects focused on developing, implementing, and evaluating youth violence prevention programs. Her primary areas of research are peer abuse (bullying), teen relationship violence, and children's exposure to domestic violence.

BETTY A. HULSE is a Certified Physician Assistant and a member of the faculty for the South Dakota Physician Assistant Studies Program. Her interests include clinical education of physician assistant students, laboratory medicine applications in physician assistant education, and provision of primary care to underserved populations.

KATIE L. KELLY graduated from Union College in 2008 with a bachelor of science degree in psychology and a minor in classics. She will complete her HR Certificate at Union Graduate College in August 2009. Thereafter, she hopes to pursue a master's degree in industrial organizational psychology, using her skills in psychology and business in the human resources field.

RACHAEL LIBERMAN is a doctoral student in the Media Studies program at the University of Colorado at Boulder. While studying at The New School in New York City, she began researching issues surrounding the pornography industry, including violence and the presence of female directors. Her research in this area has continued into her doctoral study, leading to conference presentations and publications. Other research interests include sexual identity development in postmodernity, mediations of female competition, feminist methodology, and issues surrounding gender development and memory.

TRACY L. LORD, Psy.D., currently works at The Counseling Center at the College of William and Mary. She received her doctor of psychology degree from Indiana University of Pennsylvania in 2009. Her dissertation examined the relationship of gender-based public harassment to body image, self-esteem, and avoidance behavior. Dr. Lord received her bachelor's degree in psychology from Loyola University Maryland in 2004.

PAULA K. LUNDBERG-LOVE, Ph.D., is a professor of psychology at the University of Texas at Tyler (UTT) and the Ben R. Fisch Endowed Professor in Humanitarian Affairs for 2001–2004. Her undergraduate degree was in chemistry, and she worked as a chemist at a pharmaceutical company for five years prior to earning her doctorate in physiological psychology with an emphasis in psychopharmacology. After a three-year postdoctoral fellowship in nutrition and behavior in the Department of Preventive Medicine at Washington University School of Medicine in St. Louis, Dr. Lundberg-Love assumed her academic position at UTT, where she teaches classes in psychopharmacology, behavioral neuroscience, physiological psychology, sexual victimization, and family violence.

Subsequent to her academic appointment, Dr. Lundberg-Love pursued postgraduate training and is a licensed professional counselor. She is a member of Tyler Counseling and Assessment Center, where she provides therapeutic services for victims of sexual assault, child sexual abuse, and domestic violence. She has conducted a long-term research study on women who were victims of childhood incestuous abuse, constructed a therapeutic program for their recovery, and documented its effectiveness upon their recovery.

Dr. Lundberg-Love is the author of nearly 100 publications and presentations and is co-editor of *Violence and Sexual Abuse at Home: Current Issues in Spousal Battering and Child Maltreatment* as well as *Intimate Violence against Women: When Spouses, Partners, or Lovers Attack.* As a result of her training in psychopharmacology and child maltreatment, her expertise has been sought as a consultant on various death penalty appellate cases in the state of Texas.

JENNIFER L. MARTIN is the head of the English department at a public alternative high school for at-risk students in Michigan. She is also a lecturer at Oakland University, where she teaches graduate research methods in the department of Educational Leadership, as well as feminist methods and the "Introduction to WGS" course in the department of Women and Gender Studies. She is not only a feminist teacher, but a feminist activist. Ms. Martin has volunteered as an assault responder and engaged in political action for feminist causes. Currently she is the Title IX Education Task Force Chair for the Michigan National Organization for Women, where she advocates for Title IX compliance in Michigan's schools. She has conducted research and written articles on the topics of peer sexual harassment, teaching for social justice, service learning, and the at-risk student.

MAUREEN C. MCHUGH, Ph.D., is a social psychologist and gender specialist. A Professor of Psychology at Indiana University of Pennsylvania, she has introduced more than 2,500 students to the psychology of women. In addition to journal articles, Dr. McHugh has published 20 chapters, many in edited texts for the psychology of women, including the first *Handbook on the Psychology of Women*. Her work focuses on gender differences, feminist methods, and violence against women. She is currently researching intimate-partner violence, street harassment, and "slut bashing." She and Irene Frieze received the Distinguished Publication Award from the Association for Women in Psychology (AWP) for their co-edited special issue of *Psychology of Women Quarterly* on measures of gender role attitudes. With Irene Frieze, Dr. McHugh co-edited two additional special issues in 2005, of *Psychology of Women Quarterly* and *Sex Roles*, on gender and violence in intimate relationships. Dr. McHugh served as the President Equivalent of the Association for Women in Psychology (AWP) and received the Christine Ladd Franklin Award for service to AWP and feminist psychology. For her work with both graduate and undergraduate women, she was honored with the Florence Denmark Distinguished Mentoring Award.

JENNIFER A. PIAZZA is a graduate student in the M.S. Clinical Neuropsychology program at the University of Texas at Tyler (UTT), where she anticipates graduating in May 2010. She has participated in a variety of research projects while at UTT. Her academic goals include earning a doctorate in psychology and continuing research in childhood trauma. Ms. Piazza is a 2006 graduate of Texas Christian University in Fort Worth, Texas, were she earned a B.S. in psychology. While an undergraduate, she was accepted as a member of Psi Chi, the national honor society in psychology, and worked with several professors in a social psychology lab and a neuropsychology lab.

ERICA SCHARRER, Ph.D., is an Associate Professor in the Department of Communication at University of Massachusetts–Amherst. She received her doctoral degree from Syracuse University in 1998. She now studies opinions of media, media content, media effects, and media literacy, with an emphasis on gender and violence. She has co-authored three books (first author, George Comstock), including *Television: What's On, Who's Watching, and What it Means* and *Media and the American Child*. She is also the author of numerous journal articles and is currently editing a book for Blackwell Publishers, tentatively titled *Media Effects/Media Psychology*.

WILLIAM E. SCHWEINLE, Ph.D., received his doctoral degree in 2002 from the University of Texas at Arlington in experimental (social and quantitative) psychology. His research has focused on the social psychology of men's wife-directed aggression and men's sexual harassment of women, among other areas. He is currently an Assistant Professor in the University of South Dakota Physician Assistant Program and Chair of the South Dakota Medical Institutional Review Board.

ISIS H. SETTLES, Ph.D., is an Associate Professor in the Department of Psychology at Michigan State University (MSU) in the social–personality area. She is a core faculty affiliate of MSU's Center for Multicultural Psychology Research and MSU's Center for Gender in Global Context. Dr. Settles received her Ph.D. in personality psychology from the University of Michigan. Her research examines processes and outcomes associated with social group membership (e.g., race, gender) and social group identification. In particular, she is interested in how individuals negotiate multiple identities, and how members of devalued social groups (especially women and people of color) perceive and cope with unfair treatment. Dr. Settles was the 2006 recipient of the Carolyn Payton Early Career Award for research making "a significant contribution to the understanding of the role of gender in the lives of Black women." Her research has been funded by grants from MSU's Office of Inclusion and Intercultural Initiatives and the National Institute of Mental Health.

BRENT D. SHOWALTER earned his B.A. from the University of Missouri at Columbia and his M.S. in 2008 from Illinois State University. He has conducted and presented research on social disclosure of sexual orientation and psychological well- being at the Association for Psychological Science. He has also presented his research on sexual harassment of sexual minority college students at the American Psychological Association and Association for Psychological Science conventions.

SUSAN STRAUSS, RN, Ed.D., is a national and international speaker, trainer, and consultant. Her specialty areas include harassment and workplace bullying, organization development, and management/leadership development. Her clients are from business, education, health care, law, and government organizations from both the public and private sectors.

Dr. Strauss has authored book chapters and articles in professional journals, written curriculum and training manuals, and authored the book *Sexual Harassment and Teens: A Program for Positive Change*. She has been featured on *The Donahue Show, CBS Evening News*, and other television and radio programs; she has also been interviewed for newspaper and journal articles, including those appearing in *The Times of London, Lawyers Weekly*, and *Harvard Education Newsletter*. Dr. Strauss has presented at international conferences in Botswana, Egypt, Thailand, Israel, and the United States, and conducted sex discrimination research in Poland. She has also consulted with professionals from other countries, such as England, Australia, Canada, and St. Martin.

HARMONY B. SULLIVAN is a doctoral candidate at Indiana University of Pennsylvania (IUP). She is currently completing her dissertation, which focuses on the emotional and cognitive effects of gender-based street harassment on women. Ms. Sullivan has presented nationally on street harassment and on "slut bashing" and the sexual double standard. She currently provides services at the counseling center at IUP; previously, she worked at a sexual assault center and with a community action theater group.

LEKEISHA A. SUMNER, Ph.D., is a licensed clinical psychologist and an Assistant Research Psychologist in the Department of Psychiatry and Biobehavioral Sciences at the David Geffen School of Medicine at University of California–Los Angeles (UCLA). In this capacity, her research examines the role of psychosocial processes on the health and well-being of women, with a particular focus on trauma and chronic stress at the NIMH-funded UCLA Center for Culture, Trauma and Mental Health Disparities. Prior to this position, Dr. Sumner completed both her clinical psychology internship and two-year NIMH-funded psychobiology fellowship at the UCLA Semel Institute for Neuroscience and Human Behavior. She has presented research findings at some of the premier scientific conferences in the United States and has lectured widely on health and well-being.

CHYNG SUN, Ph.D., is a Clinical Assistant Professor of Media Studies at McGhee Liberal Arts, School of Continuing and Professional Studies, New York University. In addition to her teaching and scholarly research on audience, and the representations of gender, sexuality, and race in the media, Dr. Sun is the creator of the documentaries *Mickey Mouse Monopoly: Disney, Childhood and Corporate Power* and *Beyond Good and Evil: Children, Media and Violent Times*. Her research on pornography includes a large-scale content analysis on popular pornographic movies and the documentary film *The Price of Pleasure: Pornography, Sexuality, and Relationships*. She is currently working on an audience research on pornography.

JOSEPHINE C. H. TAN, Ph.D., is a Clinical Psychology faculty member at Lakehead University, Thunder Bay, Ontario, Canada. She is also a faculty member in the graduate collaborative Women's Studies program. Her research interests lie in women's clinical health, particularly depression and multicultural issues in clinical psychology. She is an integral part of the multi-institutional research Centre for Biological Timing and Cognition and is presently pursuing research in depression and suicide in northern and Aboriginal communities in Canada. Dr. Tan is also active in service to the profession, having been elected and served on the regulatory board of the College of Psychologists of Ontario (2004–2007); she is currently the President of the Canadian Council of Professional Psychology Programs (2009–2010). She was recently elected to Fellow Status within APA Division 35.

Dr. Tan's roots are in Asia. She came to Canada after finishing high school to pursue her undergraduate and graduate education. Her interests in multiculturalism and women's issues started at an early age, having been raised in an Asian family and societal environment that was multiracial, multilingual, and multireligious, and that featured a mix of contemporary and traditional beliefs. Her education and training in North America offered her the opportunity to appreciate the cross- and intra-comparisons of Western and Eastern views on a number of topics.

MONICA D. ULIBARRI is originally from Santa Fe, New Mexico. She received her B.A. in psychology from Claremont McKenna College, and her M.A. and Ph.D. in clinical psychology from Arizona State University. She is currently a postdoctoral fellow at the University of California, San Diego (UCSD), and a clinical supervisor in the Joint Doctoral Program in Clinical Psychology supported by UCSD and San Diego State University (SDSU). Her research focuses on HIV prevention in Latino communities, with an emphasis on how individual- and relationship-level factors such as mental health, substance use, history of childhood abuse, intimate-partner violence, and sexual relationship power intersect with HIV risk behaviors.

EMILIO ULLOA, Ph.D., is the director of undergraduate advising and programs in the Psychology Department at San Diego State University. He completed his B.A. in psychology at San Diego State University and his M.A. and Ph.D. in social psychology at the Arizona State University. Dr. Ulloa has published research investigating dating or relationship violence among teens and college students, the association between violence and HIV/AIDS risk, and the association between childhood sexual abuse and relationship violence.

KRYSTLE C. WOODS is a clinical doctoral candidate in the Department of Psychology at Michigan State University. She is the recipient of several research awards, including the 2009 Outstanding Multicultural Student Research Award from Michigan State University's Center for Multicultural Psychology Research, the 2008 American Psychological Association's (Division 12) Dalmas A. Taylor Award for Outstanding Student Research, and the 2005–2010 Michigan State University's Enrichment Fellowship "recognizing academic achievement, research goals, contribution to a diverse educational community, and a record of overcoming obstacles." Her research to date has examined the influence of African American cultural factors on (1) racial and sexual harassment, (2) the initiation/expression of psychological symptoms, and (3) approaches to mental health help seeking. Her work has appeared in scholarly journals such as *Cultural Diversity and Ethnic Minority Psychology, Psychology of Women Quarterly,* and *Basic and Applied Social Psychology.* She has also contributed a chapter on sexual harassment in the workplace in *The Psychology of Women at Work,* edited by Michele A. Paludi.

ROBERT WOSNITZER is a doctoral student at New York University's (NYU's) Department of Media, Culture and Communication, and an adjunct instructor at NYU's Stern School of Business. He teaches courses in media, business, politics, and globalization. In his current research, Mr. Wosnitzer draws on critical theory to engage the dynamics of cultural and economic globalization. He is doing research on the cultural implications and patterns in relation to microfinance as a circuit of global capital, and its structuring of identity formations.